+G 179. IS1
INN.

QM Library

KU-261-538

23 1351417 7

WITHDRAWN
FROM STOCK
QMUL LIBRARY

Innovations in Retirement Financing

Pension Research Council Publications

A list of current PRC publications appears at the back of this volume.

Innovations in Retirement Financing

Edited by Olivia S. Mitchell, Zvi Bodie, P. Brett Hammond, and Stephen Zeldes

Pension Research Council
The Wharton School of the University of Pennsylvania

PENN

University of Pennsylvania Press

Philadelphia

Copyright © 2002 The Pension Research Council of The Wharton School of the University of Pennsylvania
All rights reserved
Printed in the United States of America on acid-free paper

10 9 8 7 6 5 4 3 2 1

Published by
University of Pennsylvania Press
Philadelphia, Pennsylvania 19104-4011

Library of Congress Cataloging-in-Publication Data
  Innovations in retirement financing / edited by Olivia S. Mitchell . . . [et al.].
    p. cm.
  Includes bibliographical references (p.) and index.
  "Pension Research Council publications"
  ISBN 0-8122-3641-6 (alk. paper)
  1. Retirement income — planning. 2. Finance, personal. I. Mitchell, Olivia S. II. Wharton
School. Pension Research Council.
HG179.I4866   2002
332.024'01 — dc21   2001053386

QM LIBRARY
(MILE END)

Contents

Part III. Innovations for Managing Retirement Wealth

Preface

What can be done to help employees, their employers, and the public sector, perform more efficiently to enhance old-age security? We distill answers to this question in this volume from a wide range of economists, housing and benefits specialists, lawyers, and financial advisers. The consensus is that a strong retirement income system requires attention not only to assets conventionally "dedicated" to retirement purposes, such as pensions, but also to the broader components of wealth such as housing, longevity, health, and intellectual capital. Experts from financial institutions, government, and academia offer important lessons for stakeholders to better structure the environment for retirement asset accumulation and decumulation. This book should be required reading for all those seeking to improve retirement provision and retirement decision making for generations to come.

Sponsorship for the work leading to this volume was generously provided by the Wharton Financial Institutions Center and two other institutions at the University of Pennsylvania, the Boettner Center for Financial Gerontology and the Penn Aging Research Center. We also acknowledge research support from the Pension and Welfare Benefits Administration at the United States Department of Labor. The Pension Research Council continues to benefit from the invaluable input from our Senior Partners and Institutional Members, and the support of Victoria Jo. On behalf of the Pension Research Council at The Wharton School, I thank all of them along with the many contributors and editors who helped make this volume feasible.

Part I
Sources of Financial Retirement Risk

Chapter 1
Analyzing and Managing Retirement Risks

Zvi Bodie, P. Brett Hammond, and
Olivia S. Mitchell

This book offers new perspectives on financial innovations to improve risk management in retirement. This is important because in many parts of the world, advances in medicine and rising living standards have succeeded in producing longer life expectancies than anyone who is old today could reasonably have anticipated. Looking ahead, it is quite likely that many more of us will live beyond what was once considered the "normal" retirement age, surviving to celebrate our hundredth birthdays and beyond. Maintaining a decent standard of living during such a long period without relying on earned income presents a formidable challenge. Planning ahead for our retirement years requires confronting and managing a host of risks that threaten to undermine our prospect of retirement wellbeing.

These risks manifest themselves in two areas: those due to unexpectedly *low income* and those due to unanticipated *health shocks*. When asked to assess their prospects for old age, people everywhere are quick to think of financial insecurity and medical incapacity before almost all other considerations. New institutions and new financial products are required to help people at all ages better prepare for this increasingly long and uncertain period of life.

Poor income and health may mean different things to different people and groups, but in any case their manifestation in old age is the culmination of risk processes to which people are exposed over their lifetimes. The risk-management literature outlines two key types of risks, namely *individual* risk and *systematic* risk. Individual (or as sometimes called, idiosyncratic) risk includes individual-specific experiences that differentiate people from their larger group, cohort, or society. Individual risk tends to be the result of life-style choices that are to some extent under people's control, or at least are affected by behavior. For instance, it could arise from the shock of premature death, the sudden onset of chronic illness or disability, the result of poor investment choices, the outcome of consumption and saving choices, and/or unemployment. Factors influencing individual risk to which people are exposed are thought to include education including knowledge of personal finance, family social and economic circumstances, and other personality and preference factors.

By contrast, systematic risk stems from processes outside the reach of individual action, generally affected only at the political or institutional levels, if at all. This second class of risk focuses on shocks to life expectancies of groups or cohorts, unexpected developments in the overall economy, changes in aggregate economic and market dynamics (influencing overall asset markets), and/or unanticipated changes in government programs (e.g. taxes, social security benefits, inflation, etc.). Many older people are at least aware of the possibility of adverse movements in inflation or asset prices and the possibility of cutbacks in old-age benefits promised by governments, employers, and other institutions. Layered atop these concerns are important macrodemographic forces including sweeping financial sector reform and massive population aging, all of which will be likely to reshape global retirement income provision.

Sources of Old-Age Economic Insecurity

A schematic list of the main sources of economic insecurity in retirement is provided in Table 1. Developments in both areas—individual and systematic risks—are prompting policymakers and workers as well as retirees to seek new ways to assess the risks of retirement. At the same time, they are spurring innovations in financial instruments that might help people and institutions manage and protect against the financial ravages of old age.

People confront diverse risks when they are young, as they seek to save for retirement, and also when old, when they try to figure out how to draw down their assets during the retirement period. The conventional life-cycle economic recommends that workers build up assets during their work lives, and gradually draw them down during the retirement phase. In practice, however, this pattern is often difficult to implement. Some people find it unpleasant if not impossible to defer consumption, perhaps because they implicitly must face the fact of their own aging when doing so. Another explanation for undersaving when young and overconsuming when old is that people may expect that, in the future, the government will do what is necessary to cover old-age income and medical care needs. Unfortunately, social security systems in most developed nations face insolvency and will not easily be able to pay tomorrow's elderly benefits equal to those of today's retirees (Mitchell, Myers, and Young 1999). Furthermore, private undersaving is a major problem: U.S. data indicate that older workers' wealth accumulations are substantially below retirement saving targets, and many

TABLE 1. Understanding Old-Age Economic Insecurity

Old-age insecurity attributable to
- Low income
- Poor health

Sources of old-age retirement risk
- Idiosyncratic risk. Old-age income and healthcare concerns influenced by:
  Labor market history: earning and benefit coverage patterns, employment and un-employment outcomes, retirement behavior.
  Saving and consumption patterns, asset allocation strategies: ignorance regarding retire-ment goals and financial illiteracy; lack of access to assets of various types; risk preferences and discount rates.
  Individual morbidity/mortality: genetic makeup, personal health habits and hobbies, worklife exposure, healthcare in youth and old age.
- Systematic risk. Old-age income and healthcare concerns influenced by:
  Cohort changes: unanticipated rise in life expectancies; unexpected increases in medical care and long-term care costs.
  Portfolio developments: unexpected changes in values of housing, pension, other assets.
  Macroeconomic performance: economic booms or busts; increases in global volatility.
  Institutional innovations: unanticipated changes in tax and/or transfer policy (e.g., social security program insolvency); unexpected legal or regulatory changes (e.g., imposition of asset tests for receipt of government transfers).

retirees will be unable to maintain consumption levels in old age (Moore and Mitchell, 2000). Despite these observations, only half of all working Americans say they have thought about saving for retirement, with the avoiders motivated by fear of finding out how insecure they might be and by concern that they might have to make sacrifices (Selnow 2000). These prob-lems are global, with baby boomers in Europe and increasingly in Asia reporting that they have serious concerns about a comfortable retirement.

Another possible explanation for why people are poorly prepared for re-tirement is the sheer difficulty of obtaining and processing information about the underlying risks that they face. For example, human life expec-tancy has increased well above projections just a hundred years ago, and dra-matic improvements are potentially plausible in the developed world in the future. Nevertheless, reasonable experts have erred in the past about mor-tality improvements and looking ahead, the magnitudes of future changes are again in dispute.[1] Consequently, it is understandable that the public remains uncertain regarding what to assume about future life expectancy trends. To take another example, most workers and even their retired coun-terparts are unaware of the need for long-term (nursing home) care in retirement, and as a result they fail to make adequate provision for their own coverage. In the U.S., for instance, one-quarter of the elderly eventually

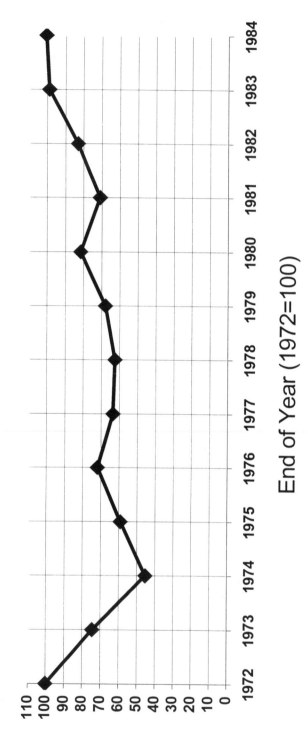

Figure 1. The U.S. stock market has not always tracked inflation well. Source: Bodie and Crane (1999).

require long-term care, yet many believe, wrongly, that nursing home coverage is provided by the government free of charge (Warshawsky et al., this volume). In fact, in the U.S. only the indigent can rely on long-term nursing home coverage, requiring the elderly to exhaust almost all of their own assets before becoming eligible. Lacking correct information on such provisions, people may make serious mistakes by not saving for their own needs and not making provision for long-term care coverage.

Other important risks facing workers and retirees are also poorly understood by the average citizen, and often by the experts. As yet little is known about the variability of and correlations in returns to human capital, financial capital, and benefits promised by pension and other old-age programs. But as we show in this volume, there are rather close links between earnings and pension benefits that can be paid by public and private pension systems. These linkages merit much more exploration to determine their impacts on old-age economic security. For example, the study by Levine et al. (this volume) indicates that differences in people's retirement incomes can be directly tied to their lifetime pay levels, and linked more strongly than to differences in the length of time employed or to other sociodemographic factors. A related analysis by Davis and Willen (this volume) also highlights correlations between earnings and asset returns, and also evaluates how aging changes how these correlations should influence investors' portfolio mixes.

One of the largest sources of idiosyncratic risk is inadequate knowledge about financial market processes. That is, ordinary people (and their advisers) often appear poorly informed regarding volatility in asset returns and inflation rates. For example, the U.S. has for some time experienced a relatively low rate of inflation and rising stock prices, both of which have contributed to a widespread belief that equities serve as a good hedge for inflation. But the evidence is not supportive of this surmise: during the 1970s, inflation rates reached double digits and stock prices fell by more than half in just two years (1974–75). This is illustrated in Figure 1, which shows that the inflation-adjusted NYSE stock index fluctuated substantially over the period 1/1968 to 12/1984. Similarly, Brown et al. (2000) report that stocks are not a good inflation hedge, at least in the short to medium term. As a result, retirees seeking to protect against the corrosive effect of inflation over a 25-year retirement period would probably benefit from investing a portion of their financial assets in inflation-protected assets (Brown et al., this volume).

Approaches to Old-Age Risk Management

In the personal finance literature the risks and rewards of retirement financial decision making are often cast in a *risk management* context. Traditionally, the term has referred mainly to the purchase of insurance and is distinguished from *investment management.*[2] From an analytical viewpoint, however, risk and investment management should be thought of in an integrated manner. This is because the purchase of insurance is an integral part of the decision making process in which risk and reward are traded off, when the unit of analysis is an individual or a family. For example, one could decrease one's exposure to the risk of income loss by buying disability insurance; alternatively one could insure against a decline in stock prices by buying put options.

In taking this broader perspective on risk management in the retirement context, we find it useful to distinguish three methods of managing risk: *hedging, insuring,* and *diversifying.* Table 2 illustrates the key focus of these three approaches.[3]

Hedging against risk means eliminating the risk of a loss by sacrificing the potential for gain. For example, as a worker grows older, it is often argued that he should reduce the fraction of his wealth held in stocks by boosting the fraction in risk-free bonds or annuities.[4] In so doing, he is perceived to hedge against stock market risk. Hedging can take other forms, of course, including the use of derivatives such as futures and swap contracts. Thus if someone held a portfolio of stocks and sought to hedge it without selling the stocks, he could do so by selling short a futures contract on a stock index.

Insuring against risk means paying a known sum of money (the insurance premium) to eliminate the risk of losing a much larger sum. In this case, the insured party protects against loss but retains the potential for gain. To continue our example, if the investor bought put options on stocks instead of selling them, he would be insuring against stock market risk. If stock prices went up by more than enough to offset the cost of the puts, he would come out ahead.

Diversification, the third risk management tool, means investing in many different risky assets instead of putting all of one's money in a single asset. Diversification is useful when it reduces one's total exposure to risk without lowering one's expected rate of return. In practice, however, the power of diversification to reduce risk is limited by positive correlations across one's portfolio of risky assets. Thus a stockbroker whose human capital returns depend solely on equity markets will be undiversified if his financial assets consist only of stocks.

In contrast to this integrated view of retirement risk management, many in the investment industry have taken a much narrower view of retirement preparedness. Their strategy has been mainly to advocate diversification in one's financial personal portfolio to the virtual exclusion of hedging and insuring. This is to some extent driven by the relatively strong average performance of publicly traded U.S. equities in the past two decades. Nevertheless there appears to be little public awareness of how risky stocks are, even in the long run. This leads to the observation that in some cases, hedging and insuring may be at least as effective as diversification. For instance, this

TABLE 2. Approaches to Old-Age Risk Management

Conventional risk management tools
- *Hedging.* Seeks to eliminate a risk of loss by sacrificing possibility of gain. Example: reduce expected risk by giving up return, buy bonds
- *Insuring.* Seeks to exchange a known premium for protection against possibility of larger loss. Example: buy life annuity or long-term care insurance; invest in inflation-indexed bond
- *Diversifying.* Seeks to minimize total risk exposure while maximizing expected return. Example: invest pension fund in globally diversified asset portfolio

Institutions for managing old-age risk
- Individual and family. Examples: self insure via saving and continued work; family care and offsetting work effort
- Employers and/or unions. Examples: group employment-based life, disability, health, pension and related benefits
- Community organizations. Examples: welfare and charity support
- Governments. Examples: old-age and healthcare programs; tax/ transfer policies
- International agencies. Examples: bail-outs for bankrupt pension systems; low-cost loans for pension reform programs.

could be true in the case of longevity risk, the risk of wage and real interest rate shocks, inflation, and the shocks to the stock market as a whole.

In addition to hedging, insurance, and diversification, education and investment in financial literacy is a separate element that can improve the chances for success of any approach to risk management. Knowing which approach to take in what circumstances and, even more importantly, knowing when to ask for additional information, analysis, and other forms of assistance, is often key to retirement security. To illustrate these points, we turn next to a discussion of recent developments in individual financial planning for retirement.

Developments in Retirement Planning Models

Institutional change and the process of financial disintermediation may have brought a "new era of individual responsibility for retirement security" (Leibowitz et al., this volume). For example, the advent of participant-directed defined contribution pension plans has given workers the ability to decide how much to save for retirement (if any), how much stock to hold in the retirement portfolio (if any), when (or if) one should alter asset allocations, and how much of the money to annuitize at retirement (if any). One advantage of this type of retirement plan is that it makes pension saving more popular than previously, but a cost is that it forces important financial decisions on the relatively financially unsophisticated (see Mitchell and Schieber, 1998).

In this environment, in appears that workers and retirees require additional help if they are to confront retirement risks and seek ways to manage them effectively. Good retirement planning models can be useful in this regard, though, as we show in this volume, designing them to make sense to average people is a challenge. It is worth pointing out that retirement planning models differ from behavioral economic models in that the former are *prescriptive*, while the latter are *descriptive*. That is, planning models embed objectives that the planner then tries to attain: for instance, one might want to smooth consumption before and after retirement, protect a widow's consumption after the death of a spouse, avoid running out of money in old age, or have a fund to leave to the children (among other possible targets). By contrast, an economic model of behavior instead tries to explain observed behavior and predict how outcomes might change if initial conditions were changed (Bernheim et al., this volume).

In the prescriptive context, a retirement planning model will typically offer the worker or retiree advice on how much to save, where to place one's investments, and how much to consume, depending on the targets specified and the instruments available. Of course, such models can yield very different prescriptions about saving and investment, depending on how they are structured and the assumptions they use as inputs. The approach proposed by Leibowitz et al. (this volume) formulates a user-friendly tool called the Asset/Salary Ratio. In this framework, a model user first specifies his target replacement ratio, or the ratio of postretirement to preretirement income. This income flow target can then be converted to a present discounted value and compared to actual assets in hand. From this calculation, asset shortfalls can be converted into increased saving objectives. This approach serves as a useful check on one's overall position, and it can offer the opportunity for sensitivity analysis as investment portfolios are changed.

More complex approaches are also available. For example, the approach taken by Bernheim et al. (this volume) builds in a great deal of detail about state and federal tax rules crucial for determining net-of-tax income streams. This model, however, does not currently incorporate uncertainty when modeling asset portfolio returns. By contrast, modeling uncertainty is a primary objective of the Financial Engines structure described by Scott (this volume). Of course, model structure matters: for instance, using one approach a worker might conclude he is "well protected" under a particular saving and investment path, but with another approach the same individual might be told that his retirement plan is a failure (Bernheim et al., this volume; Warshawsky and Ameriks 2000; Moore and Mitchell 2000). Perhaps it is no wonder that workers face retirement planning with trepidation.

Looking ahead, there remain several key challenges in the retirement planning field. One is that it is essential to help workers and retirees understand how to incorporate uncertainty into thinking about retirement needs and retirement assets. Another is that modelers need to better understand users' risk tolerance toward uncertainty and their willingness to change behaviors, given model prescriptions. But doing a better job in this arena will require new research to ascertain correlations across risky assets including human wealth, housing equity, and pension wealth from both public and private sources, and measuring risk tolerances.

Other research is also needed, gathering data on how people process information and how they act on it. A confounding influence is that as retirement planning models grow more elaborate, they also tend to become far too complex for ordinary people to use, particularly if they are not financially sophisticated. Learning more about human limitations will be key to making these models more useful. As Steven Utkus (2000) noted, experts should focus more on learning about how system participants think "about the educational barriers and limits, and . . . capturing the systemic effects of emotional behavior. There has to be some way of incorporating this understanding in our models of how participants might use retirement products." The first step may be to improve education that enables people to choose appropriate tools and techniques for assessing and ameliorating the financial risks of retirement.

Developments in Products to Increase Retirement Wellbeing

Several financial products appear to offer innovative opportunities for people to diversify, hedge, and insure their old-age economic security. Here we review some of the attributes of these products, including a form of hybrid pension plan as a means to structure pension wealth; the reverse annuity mortgage as a means to access illiquid housing wealth; and the role of international asset diversification as a means to protect investors against certain kinds of risk in old-age income streams.

Turning first to the pension case, pundits and policymakers have both praised and excoriated the variety of employer-provided pension known as the "cash balance" plan. This is sometimes called a hybrid pension, since it has elements of both a defined benefit and a defined contribution plan. It is not a particularly novel approach, in fact, since it was first developed in 1985 for employers seeking to move away from conventional defined benefit pensions.

More recently, the cash balance model attracted public scrutiny when the IBM Corporation announced it was transitioning away from its traditional defined benefit toward a cash balance format. The old IBM plan rewarded early retirement with a relatively backloaded benefit formula, whereas the new plan incorporates smoother benefit accruals across years of service with the firm, with no special reward for working up to the age of eligibility for early retirement. The trend toward eliminating early retirement subsidies is found to be widespread in survey results for 77 pension conversions examined by Clark and Schieber (this volume). The companies adopting these cash balance plans offered larger and more portable benefits to younger and more mobile employees, and virtually eliminated the spikes in accruals that had previously been offered to high levels of seniority. In this sense, the new plans are more age-neutral than those they replaced, and as such they will tend to encourage workers to extend their employment careers. Of course, working longer is one way to help finance a longer anticipated retirement period, so these pensions may well be consistent with greater retirement security.

Turning from pensions to housing, we note that most older Americans have home equity, and their homes represent a key source of personal wealth. That is, Moore and Mitchell (2000) report that housing wealth amounted to about $150,000 for the median household on the verge of retirement, and half the population had little financial assets of any kind. This finding gives rise to two questions. First, do older Americans actually use their housing wealth to finance retirement consumption? Second, if they do not, are there financial products that could facilitate the conversion of this wealth stock into an income flow, and if so, how costly would it be?

The first question is explored empirically by Venti and Wise (this volume), who rely on longitudinal datasets to examine how housing wealth appears to change with age. One way that older persons might extract income from their housing wealth would be to "trade down" to less expensive dwellings. But Venti and Wise find little evidence that people who remain homeowners through time draw down their housing wealth smoothly as they age. This is a difficult hypothesis to test, of course, since homes may depreciate due to poor upkeep and/or neighborhood decline, but respondents might not report de facto drops in housing values. In any event, there are sharp changes in housing wealth when life events intervene, such as the death of a spouse or entering a nursing home. In other words housing wealth appears to be used by the elderly as a type of self-insurance rather than as a liquid asset. This wealth discontinuity result may be due to high transaction costs imposed on home sellers plus moving costs that may be quite substantial, particularly for the elderly.

In view of the difficulty people seem to have converting their housing wealth to income, economists have suggested the need for a product known as a "reverse annuity mortgage" (RAM). This instrument permits the homeowner to sell a portion of his net home equity to a financial institution, which in turn pays that individual a fixed monthly income flow in the form of a life annuity. The annuity is supposed to be structured so that the homeowners receives a cash flow equal in present value to the fraction of his equity secured, but he never must sell the house to access the equity value of the asset. At the homeowner's death, the financial institution sells the home and recovers remaining equity. RAMs are currently available in the U.S.

market, but as described by Caplin (this volume), only some 50,000 of these products have been sold to date. It appears that the product's theoretical appeal is offset in practice by several problems, including limits on the total amount of homeowner equity that is accessible, upfront costs totaling 14 percent of capital, the risk of foreclosure, and continuing uncertainty about the tax status of the product. There realities mean that this sort of financial innovation will have to be reconfigured to be simpler and more transparent, less costly, and better regulated, if it is to meet retirees' needs in the next several decades.

Next we turn to the role of international diversification in retirement portfolios, a topic of growing interest to investors in Europe, Asia, and Latin America. In his analysis, P. S. Srinivas (this volume) shows that many countries explicitly limit retirement portfolio investments in nondomestic assets, with the restrictions motivated by diverse policy considerations. What is critical, of course, is that these investment caps and restrictions impose an implicit tax on investors by restricting them to a less favorable risk-return tradeoff than they might have had from a globally diversified portfolio. Whether they might have preferred to invest globally is not observed in many cases, because of currency controls prohibiting registering of this demand. In the specific cases examined here, restrictions imposed by government regulatory constraints on key Latin American pension fund portfolios are shown to have exposed plan participants to lower returns with inferior risk exposure, as compared to the next best alternative. This analysis therefore highlights the fact that political factors often influence retirement wellbeing by undermining what markets can do to help protect against retirement risk. Once again, institutional rigidities and barriers erected by governments at times preclude implementing the risk management strategies which appear most sensible from an economic and finance perspective.

Developments in Annuities and Bundled Insurance Products

From an individual's perspective, a fundamental reason for investing in bonds and fixed annuities is to transfer resources safely over time. Three features of bonds and annuities are essential in achieving this objective: they must be free of default risk; they must match the maturity and time pattern of the spending target; and they must match the unit of account of the spending target. Hence if someone plans an expenditure 20 years from now, the only way to hedge it precisely is with a default-free, 20-year, pure discount bond or its functional equivalent. Investing in a bond of any other maturity would expose the person to interest-rate risk. Shorter maturity bonds would expose the investor to "reinvestment" risk when the bonds have to be "rolled over," and longer maturity bonds would expose her to "price" risk because the bonds would have to be liquidated before maturity.

Unfortunately in the real world, nominal bonds and annuities have not always done a good job in carrying out their fundamental economic function of transferring resources safely over time. In some cases, the issuers (including some governments) have defaulted on their promise to pay, or have confiscated the payment through taxation. In other cases, bondholders have lost value because the currency used as unit of account suffers from inflation. The problem of inflation risk may be dealt with by denominating bonds in units of constant purchasing power: that is, by tying payments to an index of the cost of living. In many countries, however, private sector borrowers have been reluctant historically to issue bonds indexed to the cost of living. In consequence, financial economists have urged governments to issue inflation-indexed bonds to provide households with the much needed long-run hedge for retirement saving.

For many years no major industrialized country government proved willing to do so, but things began to change in the 1980s. In 1981, the British government began issuing inflation-indexed gilts (i.e., bonds) with the stated goal of providing a means for pension funds to hedge retirement benefits that were indexed to the cost of living. The government of Canada followed the UK lead in 1994, and the U.S. Treasury followed suit in 1997. Today, U.S. Treasury-issued inflation-indexed bonds can be stripped by qualified financial institutions to provide a complete array of pure discount bonds with maturities up to 30 years. As a result, it is now possible for investors to hedge real spending targets completely as far as 30 years into the future using these bonds.

A further development occurred in 1998 when the U.S. Treasury also began issuing inflation-indexed savings bonds, known as Series I (I-bonds). Although the interest rate on I-bonds is lower than on the Treasury's marketable inflation-protected bonds (TIPS), I-bonds have features that make them especially attractive to individual investors.[5] Among these are the fact that I-bonds are accrual-type bonds, so the holder receives all the interest and principal at redemption. Income tax is paid on I-bonds only at redemption; by contrast, on TIPS, income tax must be paid each year and the tax is levied on both coupons received and the increase in the nominal value of principal due to inflation. (Both types of bonds are exempt from state and local income tax.) Furthermore, the U.S. Treasury guarantees a fixed schedule of inflation-adjusted redemption values on I-bonds, so the holder always receives principal plus accrued interest no matter when they are cashed in. By contrast, Treasury guarantees TIPS inflation-adjusted value only at the maturity date; selling them before maturity requires engaging a broker-dealer in the secondary market. Consequently, if real interest rates have risen since the TIPS were issued, the holder will sell at a loss. Finally, the purchaser pays no fees when buying or redeeming I-bonds at the local bank at any time, whereas if TIPS are purchased after issue (or sold before maturity), the broker-dealer must play a role and bid-ask spreads can be large.

If these products are as beneficial as they seem to be, one might well ask why the market seems so thin for them. One explanation is that they are not particularly well known in much of the developed world. In the U.S., for instance, the Treasury has not marketed I-bonds or TIPS particularly aggressively, and inflation-linked annuities have been slow to get started. Inflation-linked annuities are better known in the U.K., Israel, and Australia, among other countries. Another explanation may be that financial advisors have yet to recommend them to their clients, probably in large part due to low commissions and some illiquidity (at least for TIPS). A different argument has been that anticipated inflation and inflation rate volatility have been low for some time, so the real returns on these products seem relatively unattractive (Brown et al., this volume). Also investors may be attracted by higher expected returns on stocks, believing that stocks are not risky in the long run; if so, stocks might appear to offer a higher risk-adjusted expected return than I-bonds.[6]

These questions become of key importance with the rapid growth of individually managed retirement accounts, resulting both from changes in the corporate pension world and from the growth in individual retirement accounts. Currently the individual annuity market is small in the U.S., but as Brown et al. (this volume) point out, the fraction of the retiree population having self-directed accounts will burgeon in the next two decades. In many analysts' view, this asset growth will spur demand for annuities of many types. Supportive of this conclusion is the finding that administrative expense loadings on life annuities have fallen substantially. For instance in both the U.S. and the UK, many years ago as much as 25–30 percent of the asset value was devoted to administrative costs in a single-premium immediate nominal annuity, but this figure is down to 5 percent today. The costs associated with adverse selection also appear to be lower than previously. Finally, the advent of TIPS and I-bonds means that insurers now have the potential to offer inflation-indexed annuities which would do a great deal to protect old-age retirement consumption. The U.S. market for such products is still nascent; it is better developed in the U.K., Australia, and other nations.

A different approach to annuities is taken by Blake et al. (this volume). Here the risk of special concern is cross-cohort mortality risk, which is different from the within-cohort mortality normally the purview of life insurers. However, it is natural to ask if there is any way to protect an entire cohort against sudden mortality changes for the group as a whole, and if so how this risk might be spread and financed. Private insurers may be able to pool cross-cohort mortality if they can invest in assets that permit hedging, but Blake and his coauthors surmise that enforcing cross-generational contracts of this sort might require support from a government. Of course this in turn requires measuring and pricing appropriately for this insurance.

One reason that older people might not annuitize much of their wealth is that they feel they need to hold on to assets in case they have to finance nursing home care. The problem is that annuities, once bought, tend to be illiquid, so that buyers cannot readily access the needed funds to pay for nursing home bills. In point of fact, longer life expectancies have coincided with increased health care costs near the end of people's lives, and the specter of needing two to three years of long-term care (LTC) figures prominently in many discussions of retirement planning. Warshawsky et al. (this volume) discuss how an integrated instrument could help resolve this problem by combining a life annuity with long-term care insurance. They argue that combining the coverage mitigates the adverse selection that would occur in the demand for each of the two products on a stand-alone basis.

Global and Local Institutions: Changing Delivery Systems

As products and services for addressing the financial risks of retirement are changing, so too are the varieties of institutions available to provide support to the elderly. Today, many diverse retirement-income systems coexist around the world, each relying in varying proportions on one or more of the following institutional forms:

- Support from family or community;
- Pension plans sponsored by employers and/or labor unions;
- Social insurance programs run by governments;
- Personal savings in the form of real and financial assets — equity in one's home or business, savings accounts, insurance contracts, mutual funds, etc.

Many experts agree, however, that the mix of these institutional forms will change significantly in the next few years. This is particularly true for industrialized countries such as the United States, the UK, Australia, Western Europe, and Japan, where people are both living longer and having many fewer children. In these nations, people will find they can rely less on family and government support than in the past, instead turning to financial markets and related institutions by saving and investing for their own retirement. Even in emerging markets, new demographic and economic realities have prompted the beginning of widespread retirement system reforms, as seen in the pension reform movements of Latin America and Eastern Europe, and more recently, in Asia.[7]

In response to global population aging and financial deregulation trends, governments and financial firms are seeking to create new institutions and services that might afford better protection against the financial consequences of old-age illness, disability, and longevity, and to insulate people against both inflation and asset price fluctuations. New opportunities will become available for older persons to continue employment, perhaps on a part-time basis, and to convert their assets, particularly housing wealth, into spendable income. For better or for worse, these financial marketplace developments are paired with widespread financial disintermediation, meaning that people are being given more individual choice over their own asset accumulation and decumulation processes. As these new financial instruments transfer more responsibility and choice to workers and retirees, it will be a challenge to frame risk-reward tradeoffs and cast financial decision making in a format that ordinary people can understand and implement.

Conclusions

Several common themes emerge in our overview of retirement needs and innovative financial products to help people meet their old-age security goals. First, that there is a profound need for better data on and understanding of retirement risks. Additional research must explore the entire range of retirement assets, both private and public, and include both financial and human wealth. Second, retirement planning models must incorporate these findings regarding retirement risks (including cross-asset correlations). Retirement planning modelers must also develop better tools to help users make more informed retirement planning decisions. Third, retirement planning analysts should use all the tools of risk management — hedging, insurance, and diversification — to guide those making retirement plans. Fourth, users, modelers, and policymakers all require broader perspectives on the retirement accumulation and decumulation process, and more financial education.

Despite these reasons for caution, we also have identified several innovative financial products that offer interesting new opportunities for people to diversify, hedge, and insure their old-age security. Some of these products are currently marketed around the world, while others have yet to be brought to market; they include inflation-linked annuities, survivor bonds, and reverse annuity mortgages. Some of the innovations arise from bundling existing insurance products: for example, long-term care insurance with life annuities, or possibly reverse mortgage annuities linked to market-risk insurance. New products are also needed to protect retirement income, but sometimes their development has been slowed by market failures and institutional rigidities as well as information barriers. There remains a profoundly important role for additional economic and financial research to better inform all stakeholders on the costs and benefits of developing innovative products for retirement security.

Notes

We are grateful to Pension Research Council members for research support and comments. Views expressed are solely those of the authors.

1. See the 1994–96 Technical Panel Report to the Social Security Advisory Council (SSAC) on alternative mortality projections.

2. See for example Hughes and LeClair (1996).

3. Bodie and Merton (2000) elaborate on this discussion.

4. For examples of financial planners offering advice to this effect see Canner et al. (1997).

5. Features of these bonds are detailed at ⟨www.savingsbonds.gov/sav/sbifaq.htm⟩.

6. Principal-protected investment contracts linked to stock market indexes have been available to individual investors since the 1970s, and recently they have become popular in Europe. In the U.S., however, they have not yet taken off. Although they lack standardization, these contracts guarantee that at the maturity date the investor will receive at least some part of his original principal back. In addition, if the underlying market index has risen over the life of the contract, the investor receives some "participation rate" times the proportional increase in the index. For more on these securities see McDowell (2000); an in-depth treatment appears in Bodie and Crane (1999).

7. See Bodie and Mitchell (1996), for instance.

References

Bernheim, B. Douglas, Lorenzo Forni, Jagadeesh Gokhale, and Laurence J. Kotli-koff. This volume. "An Economic Approach to Setting Retirement Saving Goals."

Blake, David, William Burrows, and J. Michael Orszag. This volume. "Survivor Bonds and Compulsory Annuitization: Reducing the Cost of Pension Provision."

Bodie, Zvi and Dwight B. Crane. 1999. "The Design and Production of New Retirement Savings Products." *Journal of Portfolio Management* 25, 2 (January/February): 77–82.

Bodie, Zvi and Robert C. Merton. 2000. *Finance.* Upper Saddle River, N.J.: Prentice-Hall.

Bodie, Zvi, Olivia S. Mitchell, and John A. Turner, eds. 1996. *Securing Employer-Provided Pensions: An International Perspective.* Pension Research Council. Philadelphia: University of Pennsylvania Press.

Brown, Jeffrey R., Olivia S. Mitchell, and James M. Poterba. This volume. "Mortality Risk, Inflation Risk, and Annuity Products."

Canner, Niko, N. Gregory Mankiw, and David N. Weil. 1997. "An Asset Allocation Puzzle." *American Economic Review* 87, 1 (March): 181–91.

Caplin, Andrew. This volume. "Turning Assets into Cash: Problems and Prospects in the Reverse Mortgage Market."

Clark, Robert L. and Sylvester J. Schieber. This volume. "Taking the Subsidy Out of Early Retirement: Converting to Hybrid Pensions."

Davis, Steven J. and Paul Willen. This volume. "Income Shocks, Asset Returns, and Portfolio Choice."

Hughes, Charles and Robert T. LeClair. 1996. "Financial Planning as an Employee Benefit." In *The Handbook of Employee Benefits: Design, Funding, and Administration,* ed. Jerry S. Rosenbloom. 4th ed. Chicago: Irwin. 455–70.

Levine, Philip B., Olivia S. Mitchell, and John W. R. Phillips. This volume. "Worklife Determinants of Retirement Income: Differences Across Men and Women."

Leibowitz, Martin L., J. Benson Durham, P. Brett Hammond, and Michael Heller. This volume. "Retirement Planning and the Asset/Salary Ratio."

McDowell, Dagen. 2000. "Alternative Downside Protection on Your Investment." ⟨www.thestreet.com/funds/deardagen/924234.html⟩

Mitchell, Olivia S., Robert J. Myers, and Howard Young, eds. 1999. *Prospects for Social Security Reform.* Pension Research Council. Philadelphia: University of Pennsylvania Press.

Mitchell, Olivia S. and Sylvester J. Schieber, eds. 1998. *Living with Defined Contribution Pensions.* Pension Research Council. Philadelphia: University of Pennsylvania Press.

Moore, James F. and Olivia S. Mitchell. 2000. "Projected Retirement Wealth and Saving Adequacy." In *Forecasting Retirement Needs and Retirement Wealth,* ed. Olivia S. Mitchell, P. Brett Hammond, and Anna M. Rappaport. Pension Research Council. Philadelphia: University of Pennsylvania Press. 68–94.

Selnow, Gary. 2000. Discussion at the Pension Research Council Conference on Financial Innovations for Retirement Income, Wharton School.

Scott, Jason. This volume. "Outcomes-Based Investing with Efficient Monte Carlo Simulation."

Social Security Advisory Council (SSAC) Technical Panel. 1994–96. *Final Report and Appendices.* ⟨www.ssa.gov⟩

Srinivas, P. S. and Juan Yermo. This volume. "Risk Management Through International Diversification: The Case of Latin American Pension Funds."

Utkus, Steven. 2000. Discussion at the Pension Research Council Conference on Financial Innovations for Retirement Income, Wharton School.

Venti, Steven F. and David A. Wise. This volume. "Aging and Housing Equity."

Warshawsky, Mark J. and John Ameriks. 2000. "How Prepared Are Americans for Retirement?" In *Forecasting Retirement Needs and Retirement Income,* ed. Olivia S. Mitchell, P. Brett Hammond, and Anna M. Rappaport. Pension Research Council. Philadelphia: University of Pennsylvania Press. 33–67.

Warshawsky, Mark J., Brenda C. Spillman, and Christopher M. Murtaugh. This volume. "Integrating Life Annuities and Long-Term Care Insurance: Theory, Evidence, Practice, and Policy."

Chapter 2
Income Shocks, Asset Returns, and Portfolio Choice

Steven J. Davis and Paul Willen

Other chapters in this book stress the importance of portfolio allocation decisions in managing the financial risks associated with asset accumulation and decumulation for retirement purposes (Leibowitz et al., this volume; Bernheim et al., this volume). In this chapter, we develop and apply a simple graphical approach to portfolio selection that accounts for correlation between asset returns and an investor's labor income.[1] Our approach easily handles the realistic case in which income shocks are partly, but not fully, hedgeable.[2]

We first show how the properties of labor income shocks and their correlation with asset returns affect portfolio choice. Next, we estimate the properties of shocks to the occupation-level components of individual income and investigate their correlations with aggregate equity and bond returns, selected industry-level equity returns, and the returns on portfolios formed on firm size and book-to-market equity values. We then use the theoretical framework and empirical results to calculate optimal portfolio allocations over the life cycle for workers in selected occupations.

Our analysis captures several important factors that influence portfolio choice over the life cycle: the drawdown of human capital as a worker ages, the impact of labor income innovations on the present value of lifetime resources, the increase in an investor's effective risk aversion as income smoothing ability declines with age, and systematic life cycle variation in the correlation between labor income shocks and asset returns. Each of these factors affects an investor's optimal level of risky asset holdings, as we show below.

According to the two-fund separation principle of traditional mean-variance portfolio analysis, all investors should hold risky financial assets in the same proportions, with only the level of holdings differing across people. We show why and how this simple prescription breaks down when an investor has a risky income stream (from work or business ownership) that is correlated with asset returns. We quantify this breakdown and several contributory factors, and we show that even moderate correlations between income shocks and asset returns can drive large differences between optimal portfolio shares and the shares implied by a more traditional approach that ignores risky labor income.

Portfolio Choice with Risky Labor Income

If an investor can only borrow and lend but cannot invest in risky assets, her consumption is limited by the sum of her initial risk-free asset holdings (e.g., government bonds) and the present discounted value of her current plus future labor income. Now suppose she can also invest in a risky asset that offers an expected rate of return greater than the risk-free interest rate. If she borrows a dollar and invests it in the risky asset, then her expected future income increases by the difference between the expected return on the risky asset and the amount she has to pay back on the loan — in other words, by the excess return on the risky asset. The same point holds if she finances the investment in the risky asset by drawing down her initial position in the risk-free asset. Either way, this increase in expected income comes at a cost, because the riskiness of future consumption also rises.

This tradeoff between higher risk and higher return is well known in finance and economics. Based on various characteristics such as age, wealth, and risk aversion, investors may be more or less willing to take on risk in order to increase their expected level of consumption.

Age, Wealth, Risk Aversion, and Portfolio Choice

Let PVLR stand for the expected present value of lifetime earnings from working plus the present value of lifetime excess returns on risky assets. Investing in risky assets increases PVLR and thus the expected amount an investor can consume over her life cycle. In this sense, investing in risky assets increases wealth. The solid line in Figure 1 shows this wealth measure as a function of investment in a risky asset with an excess return of 8 percentage points.

But every dollar of investment in risky assets also increases the risk of her consumption, as mentioned above. The dashed line in the top panel of Figure 1 shows the cost of increased consumption variability as a function of investment in a risky asset with a standard deviation of 15 percent. We measure the cost as the amount of wealth that the investor would forgo to eliminate the consumption variability caused by the additional risky asset holdings. Suppose, for example, that you invest $10,000 in risky assets, and this increases the variability of your future consumption by 10 percent. To measure the cost of the added risk, we ask how much additional income you would require to compensate for the 10 percent increase in consumption variability. Note that the slope of the cost curve increases with investment —

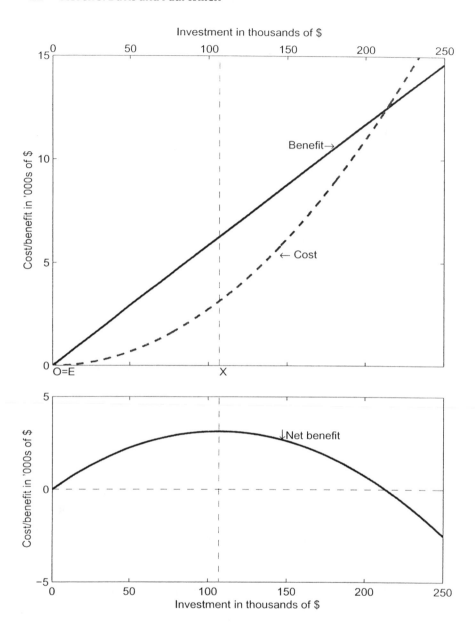

Figure 1. Portfolio choice.

in contrast to the slope of the benefit curve, which is constant. The more of a particular risk an investor takes on, the less willing she becomes to take on yet more of that same risk.[3]

Given this tradeoff between risk and return, how should an investor choose the optimal level of the risky asset? To answer this question, observe that the net benefit of the risky asset equals the difference between the solid and dotted lines — that is, between the benefit of higher expected consumption and the cost of higher risk. The bottom panel of Figure 1 shows the net difference between cost and benefit as a function of the amount invested. To maximize utility, an investor chooses the amount that maximizes the net benefit, point X in Figure 1. We call the distance from point O to point X an investor's "desired exposure" to the risky asset.

Investors differ by age, wealth level, risk aversion, occupation, region, and many other characteristics. How do these things affect portfolio choice? They do not affect the benefit of risky asset investment — a dollar investment in a risky asset increases PVLR by the same amount for all people who face the same risk-free interest rate. They typically do affect the cost to an investor of taking on the type of risk implied by investments in the risky asset. To develop this point, we first discuss how age, wealth, and risk aversion affect the cost of risky asset holdings. We then consider the role of labor income uncertainty, especially as it relates to an investor's occupation.

Risk aversion. Some people find risk highly unpleasant, so that they are willing to forego a relatively large amount of wealth to eliminate a given amount of risk. Hence, the cost curve is higher and steeper for investors with greater risk aversion (see Figure 2). As a consequence, desired exposure is lower, other things equal.

Age. Younger investors have more time to smooth income or wealth shocks, so the cost of income variability is lower for younger persons. For example, a dollar shock to wealth for an investor who only expects to live for another year results in a dollar shock to consumption. By contrast, a dollar shock to wealth for an investor who expects to live for another forty years results in a very small shock to consumption. Thus for old people the cost curve (the dashed line) is higher and "desired exposure" is lower. A shorter planning horizon, because of more advanced age or other reasons, affects portfolio choice in much the same way as greater risk aversion.

Wealth. The more wealth you have, the less overall effect a dollar shock to your wealth has on your consumption. If you lose $50,000 on the stock market and you have a net worth of $100 million, that is not so bad. But if you lose $50,000 on the stock market and you have a net worth of $50,000, that is a disaster. Thus the less wealth you have, the higher and more steeply sloped is the cost curve and the lower your desired exposure. Increased wealth affects portfolio choice in a similar way to decreased risk aversion.

Figure 2 shows portfolio choice for two investors, one with high risk

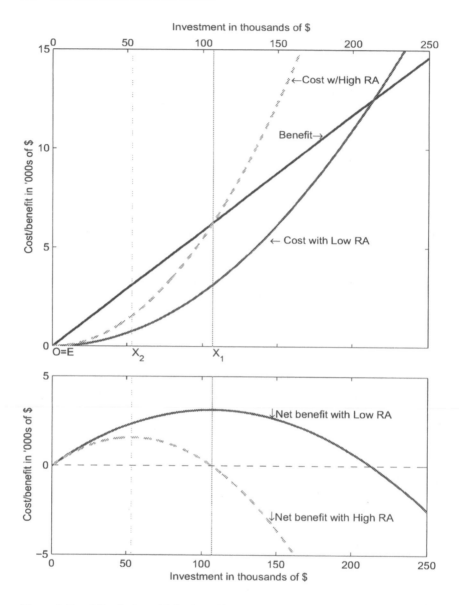

Figure 2. Portfolio choice with high and low risk aversion (RA).

aversion and the other with low risk aversion. The picture would look the same if we compared high age and low age or low wealth and high wealth.

Risky Labor Income

The focus of this chapter is on risky labor income, particularly labor income risk tied to a worker's occupation. How does the presence of risky labor income affect portfolio choice? Unlike risk aversion, age, and wealth, risky labor income does not change the shape of the cost curve. Rather, risky labor income changes its location.

Consider the following example. Suppose an investor works for Ford. Suppose she knows that the price of Honda stock is negatively correlated with her labor income. When things go well for Honda—sales of Odyssey minivans increase, for example—Ford sales drop and bonuses shrink. When things go poorly for Honda—the original Odyssey minivan was something of a dud—Ford sales increase and bonuses increase. Suppose she invests some money in Honda. When things go poorly at Ford (and well at Honda), her wealth and consumption fall by less than they would without the investment in Honda. When things go well at Ford (and badly at Honda), her wealth and consumption increase by less than they would without the investment in Honda. What has happened here? For the Ford employee, an investment in the risky Honda asset actually *reduces* the variability of her consumption! Figure 3 illustrates this graphically. The benefit of investing in a risky asset is still the same as before, but now the cost curve initially slopes down as she invests.

In the preceding example, our investor can increase her wealth and lower her risk at the same time. This seems like a free lunch, and it is, but only up to a point. Since her exposure to Ford risk is fixed (determined by her employment situation) the effects of added exposure to Honda risk eventually swamp the reduction in Ford risk as she adopts larger positions in the risky Honda asset. Her net benefit is maximized at point X. To sum up, negative correlation between returns and labor income shifts the cost curve down and to the right.

One can make a related argument for an investor who has labor income that is positively correlated with the returns on a risky asset. For example, a Honda employee may find that, by taking a short position in Honda stock, she can reduce the variability of her total income. But for any long position the cost is higher than it would be if she had no risky labor income at all, or risky labor income that was uncorrelated with the returns on Honda stock. Figure 4 illustrates this situation graphically. By taking a short position—that is, moving to the left of point O,—our investor sees her risk fall. But in contrast to the case of negative correlation in Figure 3, now her benefit falls as well. And for any positive investment the cost curve will be higher than it would be in the absence of labor income risk.

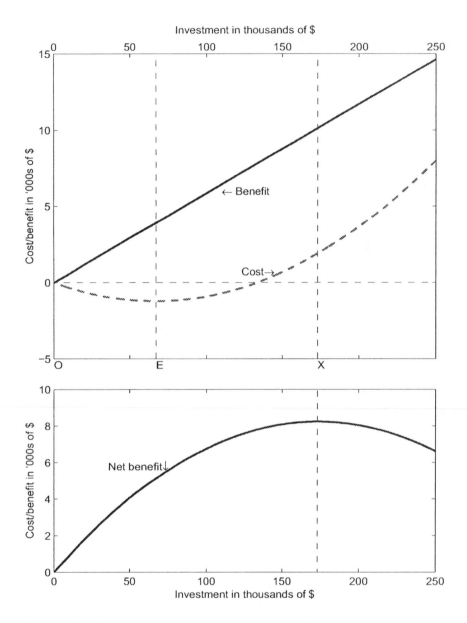

Figure 3. Portfolio choice with negative correlation between asset returns and labor income.

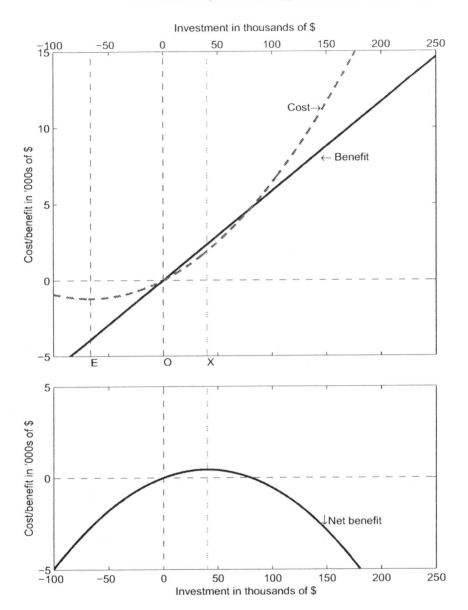

Figure 4. Portfolio choice with positive correlation between asset returns and labor income.

TABLE 1. Summary of Portfolio Choice Decision

Distance			
From	*To*	*Name*	*Description*
E	*X*	Desired exposure	Quantity invested in the risky asset in the absence of any labor income risk
O	*E*	Endowed exposure	Quantity invested to minimize variability of consumption
O	*X*	Optimal portfolio choice	Desired Exposure minus Endowed Exposure

Why is this so? Labor income for a Honda employee is (by assumption) positively correlated with returns on Honda stock, so our investor already has exposure to the stock, even if she owns none of it. Hence, she reaches the point of maximum net benefit from Honda stock much sooner than she would if she had no risky labor income or worked for Ford. To sum up, positive correlation between returns and labor income shifts the cost curve down and to the left.

How can we relate this to our earlier discussion of age, wealth, and so forth? The key point here is that age, wealth, and risk aversion affect the shape of the cost curve. In contrast, the risk characteristics of labor income move the whole curve while preserving its shape. The invariance of the shape of the cost curve to the risk characteristics of labor income provides a convenient decomposition for portfolio choice analysis. Since the shape of the cost curve doesn't change with occupation, the distance from the optimal portfolio choice point X to the minimum cost point E is also unaffected. We call this distance the desired exposure. It is equivalent to the optimal investment level for an investor whose minimum cost point coincides with zero investment in the risky asset. We call the distance from zero investment O to the minimum variance point E "endowed exposure." Endowed exposure reflects the risk characteristics of the investor's labor income, and it also measures the level of disinvestment required to minimize risk.

The optimal portfolio choice is simply desired exposure minus endowed exposure (the distance from O to X in the figures). The decomposition makes it possible to capture all the effects of occupation in one number, "endowed exposure," and to capture the effects of age, risk aversion, and wealth in another number, "desired exposure."[4] Table 1 summarizes the relationship between desired exposure, endowed exposure, and optimal portfolio choice.

Previous research on portfolio choice has focused on the determinants of desired exposure. We focus on endowed exposure, which is ignored in most analyses of portfolio choice.

Measuring Endowed Exposure

The magnitude of an investor's endowed exposure to a risky asset depends on three things:

Correlation. As we have discussed already, the higher the correlation, the higher is endowed exposure.

Variability of income. The higher the variability of income, all else equal, the higher is endowed exposure. Why? Return to our example. If you work for Ford and your compensation is well insulated from the ups and downs of Ford's fortunes, then the effect of a shock to Ford on your income will be very small. Even if the correlation between Ford stock returns and your income is high, the potential for risk reduction is low, because you simply don't have very much risk to begin with.

Persistence. An investor's lifetime consumption possibilities, as we already noted, depend on the present value of her lifetime resources. A shock to labor income obviously affects current labor income, but current labor income is typically only a small part of the present value of lifetime resources. In general, a shock to labor income today also conveys information about future labor income, and thus may have a large impact on lifetime resources. Consider a Ford employee who gets a reduced bonus because of poor sales one year. From a life cycle perspective, the reduced income this year is not so important. And if she expects the company to rebound quickly, this shock will have little impact on her PVLR or her consumption. We call this a shock of *low persistence*. But if the reduced bonus presages major long-term cutbacks at the company, her lifetime resources may decline sharply—we call this a shock of *high persistence*. The more persistent the shock, the more the shock affects PVLR and consumption, and the higher the endowed exposure to a given shock.

Persistence also depends on the retirement horizon. If a worker is only one year from retirement, a shock to income can only affect current income—so all shocks are of low persistence. Because of this horizon effect, labor income shocks effectively become less persistent as an investor ages.

When we actually go to the data below we measure persistence as the shock to the present value of lifetime resources of a dollar shock to labor income this year. If a shock to labor income is highly persistent, then future labor income will be significantly affected and PVLR will change considerably—often by as much 20 times the shock to current income. By contrast, if a shock to labor income is of low persistence, then future labor income won't be greatly affected and PVLR will change by only a small amount.

To measure endowed exposure, therefore, we need to measure three things: the variability of income shocks, the persistence of those shocks, and the correlation of labor income shocks with stock returns or other risky assets under consideration.

Multiple Risky Assets

So far, we have considered an investor investing in only one risky financial asset. In reality, investors have tens of thousands of risky financial assets to choose from, from stocks in tiny start-up companies to mutual funds that try to mimic the entire universe of stocks in the U.S. How can we analyze these financial decisions? In the absence of labor income risk, this decision is actually remarkably simple. Consider two investors who have different levels of risk aversion and no labor income risk. Using methods described above, we can calculate their optimal portfolios for each asset separately. For each asset, the cost of risk curve will be higher for the more risk averse investor. Conveniently, the difference in costs across agents will be the same for each asset—which means that the relative investment in any two stocks will be the same—the ratio of shares held of Ford and Honda stock will be the same for all investors. This means that all investors will hold portfolios with identical weights on individual stocks and mutual funds. This drastic simplification of the portfolio problem is known as the principle of *two-fund separation*, because it says that a single mutual fund with the correct weights will enable all investors to implement optimal financial plans using just the mutual fund and a riskless bond.

When we add occupational or other sources of labor income risk, the principle of two-fund separation breaks down. Why? The key to two-fund separation is that risk aversion, age, and wealth affect demand for all assets by the same amount—they change the shape of the cost curve for every asset in the same way. But labor income risk changes the *location* of the cost curve for each investor in a potentially different way. To return to our example, for a Ford employee, labor income risk moves her Ford cost curve to the left and her Honda cost curve to the right—whereas for a Honda employee, labor income risk moves her Ford cost curve to the right and her Honda cost curve to the left. The ratio of holdings of Honda and Ford stock will no longer, in general, be the same for different investors.

Limitations of Our Approach

Our approach makes many assumptions about life cycle portfolio choice. It allows for unlimited borrowing of the riskless asset and unlimited short-sales of the risky asset. Short-sale restrictions on risky assets can be treated without great difficulty, but a proper treatment of borrowing constraints for the riskless asset complicates the analysis greatly in a many-period setting. Our approach also requires certain assumptions about the utility function and the time series processes for labor income and asset returns, which allow us to consider each period separately. In other words, investors do not need to worry about the effects of their current choices on their choice sets in future periods. (A mathematical treatment of these issues appears in Davis and Willen 2000b.)

Occuaption-Level Earnings Innovations

The chief empirical requirements of our approach are measures of (1) correlation between labor income shocks and asset returns, (2) variability of income shocks, and (3) persistence of income shocks. It is interesting that asset returns have received substantial attention from financial researchers, but only a handful of scholars have investigated their correlation with labor or proprietary business income. One such study, by Campbell et al. (1999), considers the correlation between aggregate equity returns and the permanent component of household income for three education groups. A second, by Davis and Willen (2000a), uses a synthetic panel to create demographic groups defined by sex, educational attainment, and birth cohort. Although they use rather different empirical designs, both of these studies find that the correlation between labor income shocks and equity returns rises with education. Heaton and Lucas (2000) emphasize a positive correlation between equity returns and the income of self-employed persons.[5]

Whereas prior studies have relied on panel data sets or synthetic panels constructed from repeated cross sections as the basis for analysis, here we pursue a somewhat different empirical approach. In particular, we rely on the repeated cross-section structure of the Current Population Survey to extract mean occupation-level income shocks, while controlling for a host of observable worker characteristics. We then focus our empirical investigation on the properties of the occupation-level shocks and their correlation with asset returns.

Data Sources and Definitions

The Current Population Survey (CPS) randomly samples about 60,000 U.S. households every month. Among other items, the survey inquires about labor earnings, employment status, hours worked, educational attainment, occupation, and demographic characteristics for each household member. The Annual Demographic Files in the March CPS contain individual data on these items for the previous calendar year. Using the CPS March files, we estimate occupation-level components of individual annual earnings from 1967 to 1994.

To compute annual earnings, we use CPS data on wage and salary workers in the private and public sectors who were 23 to 59 years old in the earnings year. Excluded from the earnings calculations are unincorporated self-employed persons, though we do include self-employment and farm income for persons who were mainly wage and salary workers. The sample is

TABLE 2. Occupational Classifications and Summary Statistics

Occupational Description	1980 Standard Occupational Classification	Sample Period	Mean Cell Count	Minimum Cell Count	Average Earnings in 1982$
Accountants and Auditors	23	1967–94	542	327	24,881
Electrical Engineers	55	1967–94	246	150	33,923
Registered Nurses	95	1967–94	704	392	17,823
Teachers, Elementary	156	1967–94	842	679	18,325
Teachers, Secondary	157	1967–94	733	487	20,886
Janitors and Cleaners	453	1967–94	805	336	11,846
Auto Mechanics	505	1967–94	389	306	17,675
Electricians	575	1967–94	325	267	23,646
Plumbers	585	1967–94	220	168	22,437
Truck Drivers	804, 805	1967–94	1079	744	18,665

Source: Authors' tabulations from the Annual Demographic Files of the March CPS; see text.
Note: Average earnings is the simple mean from 1967 to 1994 of the unweighted mean annual earnings among persons who satisfy the selection criteria.

limited to those persons who worked at least 500 hours during the year, and people who were not students and not in the military.[6] In addition to these individual-level selection criteria, we also limit attention to 57 detailed occupational classifications that can be tracked from 1967 (or 1970) to 1994. We further restrict our analysis to 10 detailed occupations with large numbers of individual-level observations in each year. These ten occupations differ widely in terms of educational requirements and annual labor income.[7] These occupations and associated summary statistics on cell counts and average annual earnings in 1982 dollars appear in Table 2.[8]

The Occupation-Level Component of Earnings Innovations

To extract the occupation-level component of individual earnings shocks, we first fit ordinary least squares earnings regressions to the individual-level data. Separate models are fitted for each occupation after pooling the data over all available years. Explanatory variables include sex, educational attainment, age interacted with sex, and a full set of occupation-specific year effects. We estimate regressions using annual earnings as the dependent variable.[9] The specification allows the age-earnings profile to vary freely across occupations (and sex), but not to shift over time. Effectively, we treat the occupation's average age-earnings profile over the 1967–94 period, adjusted for sex and education, as predictable variation in a worker's earnings. As implied by the occupation-level earnings specifications described below, we also treat the average occupational earnings growth from 1967 to 1994 (conditional on worker characteristics) as part of expected earnings growth.

To characterize the stochastic properties of the occupation-level component of individual earnings shocks, we fit autoregressive moving average (ARMA) models to the first-differenced values of the occupation-year effects. We denote the occupation-year effects estimated in the first-stage earnings regressions as ϵ_t, $t = 1967, 1968, \ldots, 1994$. Then we fit second-order moving average processes, following MaCurdy (1982), who uses panel data on individuals, and Davis and Willen (2000a), who use synthetic panel data for demographic groups:

(1)
$$\Delta\epsilon_t = \alpha + \eta_t + \psi_1\,\eta_{t-1} + \psi_2\,\eta_{t-2} \ .$$

Here η_t denotes the time-t innovation to the occupation-level component of individual earnings shocks. These innovations and their correlation with asset returns are the main focus of the empirical investigation and the applied portfolio analysis below.[10]

Magnitude and Persistence of Earnings Innovations

The standard deviation of η_t in equation (1) quantifies the magnitude of innovations to the occupation-level component of individual earnings. As described earlier, we measure persistence as the shock to PVLR of a dollar shock to income. We refer to this persistence measure as the present value multiplier (PVM). The magnitude of the PVM depends on the persistence of η (a function of ψ_1 and ψ_2), the risk-free rate of interest, and the number of years remaining until retirement. By combining these elements, we can easily calculate the magnitude of a typical shock to PVLR at a given age. The magnitude of this shock declines with age, because fewer years remain until retirement.

Table 3 reports the present value multipliers on the occupation-level earnings shocks at ages 30 and 50, assuming a real discount rate of 2.5 percent per year and retirement after age 59. To illustrate the calculation of the shock to PVLR implied by an occupation-level income innovation, consider the example of the accountants and auditors occupation at age 30. According to Table 3, the standard deviation of innovations to the occupation-level component of earnings is $1,080, or 4.3 percent of annual earnings. At age 30, the present value multiplier on this innovation is 20.0, so that the implied impact on PVLR amounts to 1080 (20.0) = $21,600. This figure is 87 percent of the average annual earnings for accountants and auditors reported in Table 2. These calculations show that occupation-level earnings innovations are of modest size, but the implied effects on the present value of lifetime earnings are not.

Occupations differ in terms of magnitude and persistence of occupation-level earnings innovations. The standard deviation of the occupation-level innovations ranges from 2.9 to 6.9 percent of annual earnings. Plumbers have the most volatile occupation-level earnings component in both dollar

TABLE 3. Selected Statistics for the Occupational Component of Individual Earnings, 1968–1994

Occupational Description	Standard Deviation of Labor Income Shocks	Standard Deviation as % of Income	Present Value Multiplier at:	
			Age 30	Age 50
Accountants and Auditors	1080	4.34	20.0	8.3
Electrical Engineers	1283	3.78	6.8	3.4
Registered Nurses	446	2.50	40.2	15.9
Elementary School Teachers	525	2.86	27.2	11.0
Secondary School Teachers	637	3.05	22.5	9.4
Janitors and Cleaners	583	4.92	13.3	5.8
Auto Mechanics	714	4.04	18.9	8.0
Electricians	951	4.02	13.2	6.1
Plumbers	1453	6.48	12.8	5.7
Truck Drivers	790	4.23	18.5	8.0

Source: Authors' calculations, CPS data.

Notes: For each occupation, a second-order moving average process is fit to the occupational component of individual annual earnings in 1982 dollars. The moving average process is estimated by (conditional) nonlinear least squares. See Davis and Willen (2000b) for an explanation of how the occupational component of individual earnings is identified. Present value multipliers computed using a real discount rate of 2.5 percent per year and assuming retirement after age 59.

and percentage terms, while registered nurses and elementary school teachers have the least volatile. Likewise, the present value multiplier at age 30 is 6.8 for plumbers and 40.2 for registered nurses. These two occupations are outliers in terms of persistence. For the other occupations, the present value multipliers at age 30 range from 13 to 27. The last two columns in Table 3 show how the present value multiplier declines between ages 30 and 50, given the assumptions about discounting and retirement. The age-50 multipliers are fairly sensitive to alternative assumptions about retirement age, but the basic point is not. As workers near retirement, earnings innovations have smaller and smaller effects on lifetime resources.

Correlation Between Occupation-Level Income Innovations and Asset Returns

To investigate the correlation between occupation-level earnings innovations and aggregate equity returns, we next regress η_t from equation (1) on the realized market rate of return during period t. Recall that we can use the slope coefficient in an ordinary least squares (OLS) regression of y on x to generate an estimate of the correlation of x with y. Hence, we can use standard regression methods to quantify the correlation between income shocks and equity returns and to test whether the relationship is statistically significant.

Correlation with Aggregate Equity Returns

We find little evidence that occupation-level income innovations and aggregate equity returns are linearly related in annual data over the period 1968 to 1994. None of the ten occupations considered evinces a statistically significant relationship between income innovations and returns on the value-weighted market portfolio (in regressions not detailed here).[11] As a check, we also considered the returns on several other broad-based equity indexes: the S&P 500, the New York Stock Exchange, the Wilshire 5000, and a value-weighted composite of the New York Stock Exchange, American Stock Exchange and NASDAQ. For each measure, we see the same pattern of little or no evidence for a relationship between occupation-level income innovations and contemporaneous aggregate equity returns.

This result is puzzling from the vantage point of standard economic theories of growth, fluctuations, and asset pricing. Equilibrium models that obey standard asset-pricing relationships and embed a conventional specification of the aggregate production technology imply a high positive correlation between aggregate equity returns and shocks to labor income.[12] While we note this puzzle here, it is not necessary to resolve it to pursue the remainder of our agenda.

Other Asset Return Measures

We also investigate the correlation between occupation-level income innovations and the returns on long-term government bonds and other assets.
Bond returns are significantly correlated with income innovations for a
few occupations. In most cases, bonds account for a greater fraction of
occupation-level income innovations when the returns are measured in
nominal terms.

We examine two additional types of assets which might be highly correlated with labor income shocks. First, we sought to construct industry equity
portfolios that respond sensitively to labor income shocks in particular occupations. For example, demand shocks in the construction sector induce
a positive correlation between equity returns in Construction industries
(SICs 15, 16, 17) and occupation-level income innovations for Electrical
Engineers, Electricians, and Plumbers. More generally, industry-level demand shocks and factor-neutral technology shocks impart a positive correlation between returns on industry equity and occupation-level income
innovations.

However, prior reasoning alone cannot determine the sign, let alone the
magnitude, of the correlation between industry equity returns and labor
income innovations for industry workers. For example, labor-saving technological improvements in construction activity might be good for shareholders but bad for the earnings of Electricians and Plumbers. As another
example, the deregulation of the trucking industry during the 1970s and
early 1980s was bad news for many truck drivers (Rose, 1987) but good news
for many trucking firms (Keeler, 1989). The basic point is that factor-biased
technology shifts (construction example) and rent shifting between owners
and workers (trucking example) impart a negative correlation between
industry-level equity returns and occupation-level income innovations.

Clearly the relationship between industry-level equity portfolios and labor income shocks is very much an empirical issue. Furthermore, if the mix
of underlying shocks and economic response mechanisms changes over
time, the correlation between industry-level equity returns and occupation-
level income innovations is likely to change. The weight of this concern is
also largely an empirical issue. No single study can definitively settle these
empirical issues, so our results in this regard are best viewed as one install-
ment in a broader empirical inquiry.

We construct industry portfolios using firm-level equity returns and market values in the Center for Research in Security Prices (CRSP) database.
For each occupation (except Janitors and Cleaners) we identify one or more
industries that account for a large fraction of the occupation's employment.
In some cases, we had to omit natural SIC counterparts for particular occupations, because CRSP contains no firm-level observations during part of
the sample period.[13] In the end, the SIC industry groups listed in Table 4 are

TABLE 4. Asset Return Measures, Definitions, and Summary Statistics

Variable Name	Description	Mean Annual Return (%), 1968–94	Standard Deviation of Annual Return	Occupation Match
SMB	Fama-French Size Portfolio, Small-Big	0.2	15.5	All
HML	Fama-French Book-to-Market Portfolio, Value — Growth Stocks	5.9	12.9	All
Bonds	Nominal Return on 10-Year Constant Maturity U.S. Government Bonds	8.5	10.1	All
Autos	Real Return on SIC 371 (Auto Mfg.)	6.4	25.0	Auto Mechanics
Elmach	Real Return on SIC 36 (Electrical Machinery Manufacturing)	5.8	21.4	Electrical Engineers
Build	Real Return on SICs 15, 16, 17 (Construction)	3.2	27.8	Elec. Engs., Electricians, Plumbers
Freight	Real Return on SIC 42 and 472, ex. 4725 (Freight Transport by Road)	6.4	27.8	Truck Drivers
Technical	Real Return on SICs 871 and 7336 (Engineering, Architectural and Technical Services)	8.1	31.9	Electrical Engineers
Education	Real Return on SICs 82, ex. 823, and 833 (Education Services)	6.4	37.1	Elementary and Secondary Teachers
Health	Real Return on SIC 80 (Medical, Dental and Health Services)	12.8	37.1	Registered Nurses
Utility	Real Return on SICs 46 and 49, ex. 495 (Electricity, Gas, Steam, Water Works)	5.4	15.8	Electrical Engineers, Electricians, Plumbers
Finance	Real Return on SICs 62, 67 (Investment Banking, Securities Markets, Exchanges)	7.9	19.8	Accountants and Auditors

Sources: Returns data for the SMB and HML portfolios taken from (web.mit.edu/kfrench/www/data.library.html); see also Fama and French (1993) for construction of these portfolios. Returns data on Bonds from Center for Research in Security Prices; all industry-level return series constructed from value-weighted portfolios of firm-level equity returns in the Center for Research in Security Prices database; see Davis and Willen (2000a).

Notes: Nominal returns for the industry-level measures converted to real returns using the GDP deflator for personal consumption expenditures. Data points missing for Health in 1968 and for Technical in 1987 and 1988. Last column lists the occupation for which the returns measure is used as a regressor.

targeted for further analysis. We construct value-weighted industry returns using firms in the CRSP data and update the firm-level weights annually. The rightmost column in Table 4 shows the occupations to which we match each industry-level return measure.

In a different approach, we consider the correlation between occupation-level income innovations and returns on equity portfolios formed on firm size (market equity value) and the ratio of book-to-market equity value (Fama and French 1993).[14] The Fama-French SMB portfolio pays off the return on a portfolio of firms with small market values minus the return on a portfolio of firms with large market values. The Fama-French HML portfolio pays off the return on a portfolio of "value" stocks with a high ratio of book-to-market equity minus the return on a portfolio of "growth" stocks with a low ratio of book-to-market equity. The Fama-French portfolios are reblanced quarterly and adjusted for transactions costs when firms are bought and sold. Prior research shows that size and book-to-market factors account for much of the cross-sectional variation in returns on common stocks (Fama and French 1992, 1993, 1996). Many other asset-pricing studies confirm an important role for these two factors.[15]

A question naturally arises as to what types of risk are being priced by size and book-to-market value. In other words, why do small cap stocks earn a higher average return than large cap stocks? And, why do value stocks earn a higher average return than growth stocks? One possibility is that shocks to labor income covary positively with the size and book-to-market factors. If so, then investors who are exposed to labor income risk will demand a return premium to hold small cap and value stocks. This asset-pricing logic suggests that labor income innovations might be correlated with the returns on the size or book-to-market portfolios. Following this logic, we investigate the correlation between occupation-level income innovations and returns on the SMB and HML portfolios.

Correlation with Other Asset Returns

We examine bivariate and multivariate regressions of occupation-level income innovations on returns for bonds, SMB and HML. For several occupations, the regression results show a fairly large negative correlation between income innovations and the SMB return.

The results in Table 5 suggest there is some scope for hedging occupation-level income risk, as suggested by the asset-pricing logic outlined above. However, the pattern of results runs directly counter to our original motivation for investigating the SMB portfolio. Most of the correlations in Table 5 and all the statistically significant ones imply that the relative return on small cap stocks covaries negatively with occupation-level income innovations. Thus investors who are exposed to labor income risk should be willing to hold small cap equities at a return discount relative to large cap equities. In

TABLE 5. Determinants of Endowed Exposure for SMB Portfolio, 1968–94

Occupational Description	Correlation	Variability (std. dev.)	PVM at Age 30
Accountants and Auditors	−0.37	1080	20.0
Electrical Engineers	−0.33	1283	6.8
Registered Nurses	−0.14	446	40.2
Teachers, Elementary	−0.36	525	27.2
Teachers, Secondary	−0.39	637	22.5
Janitors and Cleaners	−0.32	583	13.3
Auto Mechanics	−0.10	714	18.9
Electricians	0.22	951	13.2
Plumbers	−0.28	1453	12.8
Truck Drivers	0.03	790	18.5

Source: Authors' calculations; see text.
Notes: All regressions estimated by ordinary least squares. For regression results, see Davis and Willen (2000b).

fact, the average return on small cap stocks is higher.[16] So, while the findings can be useful for portfolio design purposes, they serve to *heighten* rather than resolve asset-pricing puzzles related to the return premium on small cap stocks.

Life Cycle Portfolio Choice with Risky Labor Income: Some Examples

We now solve the life cycle portfolio problem with risky labor income, drawing on the just presented empirical evidence to characterize the magnitude, persistence, and correlation properties of labor income shocks.

Preliminaries and Two-Fund Separation

Optimal portfolio allocations when asset returns and labor income are uncorrelated appear in Table 6. The table considers three risky assets—market, size, and value portfolios—and uses a real risk-free return of 3.5 percent per year. We do not impose short-sale constraints on risky asset holdings or restrictions on borrowing at the risk-free rate. Since two-fund separation holds under these conditions, every investor has the same risky asset portfolio shares, as shown in the top row. These shares depend on the joint return distribution for the three assets, which we fit to the first two sample moments in the data. The table also displays optimal risky asset holdings at ages 40 and 60 for two occupations under various assumptions about relative risk aversion and expected returns.

We measure risk aversion using the Arrow-Pratt coefficient of relative risk aversion (RRA). To understand RRAs, consider the following experiment.

TABLE 6. Investment in Risky Assets with Zero Correlation between Earnings and Returns: Two-fund Separation

	RRA	Age	Reduction in Returns (%)	SMB	HML	Market	Total
Portfolio Shares				−25	88	37	100
Asset Levels	3	40	0	−257	903	381	1027
Electrical Engineers	5	40	0	−154	542	229	616
	3	60	0	−148	520	220	592
	3	40	50	−129	451	191	514
Secondary School Teachers	3	40	0	−158	556	235	632
	5	40	0	−95	334	141	379
	3	60	0	−91	320	135	364
	3	40	50	−79	278	117	316

Source: Authors' calculations.
Notes: Portfolio shares are percentage of total investment in risky assets. Asset levels in thousands of 1982 dollars. RRA stands for relative risk aversion level.

An investor is given a choice of a fixed sum of money next period or a lottery that pays $800 with probability 0.5 and $1200 with probability 0.5. A risk-neutral investor would be indifferent between the actuarial value of the lottery ($1000) and the lottery. An investor with a RRA of 3 is indifferent between $940 and the lottery, and an investor with a RRA of 5 is indifferent between $900 and the lottery.

The results show that an electrical engineer with relative risk aversion of 3 should, according to the theory, hold a $1.03 million portfolio of risky assets. This consists of a $257,000 short position in SMB and long positions in HML and the market portfolio. The optimal risky positions are smaller if we consider an otherwise identical investor who is sixty years old, or one who has relative risk aversion of 5. Optimal holdings are also about 40 percent smaller for a secondary school teacher, because her permanent income is about 40 percent smaller. In line with the two-fund separation principle, none of these changes alter the optimal portfolio shares.

In each of these cases, optimal holdings are quite large relative to casual and systematic evidence regarding actual holdings (40-year-old electrical engineers with million dollar equity portfolios are not the norm!). One possible explanation for this gap between theory and evidence is the high returns on U.S. equities over the last century. Some analysts believe that these high returns are unlikely to hold in the future, so the last row in each panel of Table 6 shows optimal allocations for expected returns on risky assets that are only half as large as the corresponding sample means. Investment positions drop by half as well, but the optimal allocations remain quite large compared to observed holdings for the typical person. This portfolio puzzle has received little attention in previous research because of the strong proclivity to focus on portfolio shares and to disregard theoretical implications for the level of risky asset holdings.[17]

We believe that the resolution of this puzzle rests at least partly on the opportunity cost of investor funds. In computing the portfolio allocations in Table 6, investors are allowed to borrow unlimited amounts at the risk-free interest rate. If, instead, investors must borrow at an interest rate that approximates the expected return on risky assets, then the optimal risky asset position is approximately *zero* when asset returns and labor income are uncorrelated. Many (potential) investors face an opportunity cost of funds at least as great as the expected return on equities, so it is not surprising that half or more of all households have little or no holdings of risky financial assets.

Endowed Exposure and the Breakdown of Two-Fund Separation

Nonzero correlations between asset returns and labor income cause two-fund separation to break down in a particular way. To illustrate this point, Table 7 shows optimal allocations for seven occupations when we account for correlation with labor income shocks. Recall from above that optimal holdings in the zero-correlation case, "desired exposure," depend only on risk aversion, age, wealth, and asset returns. "Endowed exposure" gives the risky asset position implicit in the correlation between asset returns and the worker-investor's labor income.

The results in Table 5 above demonstrated that most occupational groups have a negative endowed exposure to the SMB portfolio. As we explained above, the endowed exposure reflects the size and persistence of labor income innovations and their correlation with asset returns. Consequently, although income shocks for janitors and cleaners and electrical engineers have almost the same correlation with SMB, the endowed exposure of electrical engineers is much lower because their income shocks are more variable and more persistent.

To calculate an investor's optimal portfolio, we simply subtract endowed exposure from desired exposure. Since endowed exposure is not proportional to desired exposure, two-fund separation fails. Other things equal, the bigger the endowed exposure the bigger the departure from the two-fund separation principle. Table 8 illustrates this breakdown by showing optimal portfolio shares under different assumptions about risk aversion and excess returns for each occupation that has a non-zero correlation with one or more of the assets. The base case uses sample average excess returns and a relative risk aversion of 3. Given these assumptions, the departures from two-fund separation are modest. For example, the optimal shares for

TABLE 7. Endowed exposure, desired exposure and portfolio holdings

		SBM	HML	Market	Total
Accountants and Auditors	Endowed Exposure	−36	0	0	−36
	Desired Exposure	−189	662	280	753
	Portfolio position	−153	662	280	789
Electrical Engineers	Endowed Exposure	−28	0	0	−28
	Desired Exposure	−257	903	381	1027
	Portfolio position	−229	903	381	1055
Elementary School Teachers	Endowed Exposure	−42	0	0	−42
	Desired Exposure	−139	488	206	555
	Portfolio position	−97	488	206	597
Secondary School Teachers	Endowed Exposure	−52	0	0	−52
	Desired Exposure	−158	556	235	632
	Portfolio position	−106	556	235	684
Janitors and Cleaners	Endowed Exposure	−13	0	0	−13
	Desired Exposure	−90	315	133	359
	Portfolio position	−76	315	133	372
Plumbers	Endowed Exposure	−46	0	0	−46
	Desired Exposure	−170	597	252	679
	Portfolio position	−124	597	252	725
Truck Drivers	Endowed Exposure	−0	16	−0	16
	Desired Exposure	−141	497	210	565
	Portfolio position	−141	481	210	550

Source: Authors' calculations.
Notes: Entries show endowed exposure, desired exposure and optimal portfolio position for indicated risky assets in thousands of 1982$. Calculations assume a 40-year-old investor who has a relative risk aversion of 3.

electrical engineers never differ from the zero-correlation optimum by more than three percentage points. For secondary school teachers, the traditional zero-correlation portfolio understates SMB holdings by nine percentage points.

Because these effects are small, a portfolio manager might be forgiven for ignoring them. However, if one believes that high equity returns in recent decades are an aberration, or that expected returns have declined in recent years, then the effects of correlation on optimal portfolio shares become more important. As an example, the second line for each occupation in Table 8 shows optimal portfolio shares when we set excess returns to one-half their sample averages. Recall that this change has no impact on the optimal shares when two-fund separation holds. In particular, the optimal SMB share is −25 percent under two-fund separation, regardless whether we scale down excess returns. This invariance result fails when we take correlation into account. As an example, the optimal SMB portfolio share for secondary school teachers is +2 percent when excess returns are half their sample values and relative risk aversion is 5. To understand this result,

TABLE 8. Risk Aversion, Excess Returns, and Optimal Portfolio Shares in the Case of Three Risky Assets

	Reduction in Excess Returns (%)	RRA	SMB	HML	Market
Accountants and Auditors	0	3	−19	84	35
	50	5	−8	76	32
	75	5	5	67	28
Electrical Engineers	0	3	−22	86	36
	50	5	−15	81	34
	75	5	−6	75	31
Elementary School Teachers	0	3	−16	82	35
	50	5	0	70	30
	75	5	17	58	25
Secondary School Teachers	0	3	−16	81	34
	50	5	2	69	29
	75	5	19	57	24
Janitors and Cleaners	0	3	−21	85	36
	50	5	−11	85	33
	75	5	−0	70	30
Plumbers	0	3	−17	82	35
	50	5	−2	72	30
	75	5	14	61	26
Truck Drivers	0	3	−26	88	38
	50	5	−28	87	41
	75	5	−31	85	46

Source: Authors' calculations.
Notes: "Percent Reduction In Excess Returns" of 0 means that expected returns on risky assets are set to realized sample values.
A 50 percent reduction means that the excess return (sample mean return minus a risk-free rate of 3.5%) is set to half its sample value, and similarly for a 75 percent reduction. RRA stands for relative risk aversion level. Entries in the last three columns show the percentage of risky financial asset holdings in the indicated asset. All calculations assume an investor 40 years old.

recall that the level of excess returns has no effect on "endowed exposure." So, as we reduce excess returns and hence desired exposure, the relative size of endowed exposure goes up.

Higher risk aversion has the same effect, and for much the same reason. Greater risk aversion lowers desired exposure but does not affect endowed exposure. The last line in each panel of Table 8 shows optimal portfolio shares for the case of high risk aversion and low excess returns. In this case, the optimal portfolio shares sometimes differ substantially from the two-fund separation case. Based on traditional mean-variance analysis, a portfolio advisor would recommend a 25 percent short position in SMB. In contrast, the optimal position for secondary school teachers is a 17 percent long position in a plausible case that accounts for correlation between asset returns and labor income.

Life Cycle Variation in Endowed Exposure

Endowed exposure to occupation-specific assets varies over the life cycle, as illustrated in Table 9. Given an age-invariant correlation between labor income innovations and asset returns, the endowed exposure declines monotonically with age as the worker-investor draws down the present value of future labor income. This result follows immediately when the correlation between labor income innovations and asset returns is age invariant.[18]

A final issue involves life cycle variation in the extent of departures from two-fund separation. Other things equal, a declining path of endowed exposure leads to ever smaller departures from two-fund separation as an investor ages. However, income smoothing capacity also declines with age, which creates a countervailing force. In particular, age intensifies the effect of correlation on optimal portfolio shares, as we discussed above. So, for any given level of endowed exposure, the departure from two-fund separation is bigger for an older investor.

Conclusion and Discussion

When labor income and asset returns are correlated, investors are implicitly endowed with certain exposures to risky financial assets. These endowed exposures have important effects on optimal portfolio allocation. The two-fund separation principle that governs optimal portfolio choice in a traditional mean-variance setting breaks down when investors have endowed exposures to risky assets. In simple terms, an investor's optimal portfolio can be calculated as the difference between her desired exposure to risky assets and her endowed exposure. Because investors typically differ in their endowed exposures, they also differ in their optimal portfolio allocations (levels and shares), even when they have the same tolerance for risk and the same beliefs about asset returns.

Our graphical approach to portfolio choice over the life cycle accounts for an investor's endowed and desired exposures. The approach easily handles risky labor income, multiple risky assets, many periods, and several determinants of portfolio choice over the life cycle. As an added virtue, the chief empirical inputs into the framework are easily estimated using simple statistical procedures.

The empirical model relies on repeated cross sections to extract occupation-level components of individual income innovations. Annual data from 1968 to 1994 yield little evidence that occupation-level income innovations are correlated with aggregate equity returns. This finding, along with similar findings in other work, presents something of a puzzle for standard equilibrium models of economic fluctuations, growth, and asset pricing. Given rational asset pricing behavior, frictionless financial markets, and standard specifications of the production technology, dynamic equi-

TABLE 9. Endowed Exposure to Occupation-Specific Assets

	Age						
	30	*35*	*40*	*45*	*50*	*55*	*Asset*
Electrical Engineers	9.5	8.9	8.2	7.4	6.4	5.2	Build
Registered Nurses	−6.7	−6.0	−5.1	−4.1	−2.9	−1.4	Health
Elementary School Teachers	12.2	10.9	9.4	7.7	5.5	3.0	Educ
Secondary School Teachers	17.2	15.5	13.5	11.1	8.3	4.9	Educ
Electricians	14.5	13.3	11.9	10.2	8.2	5.8	Build
Plumbers	21.2	19.5	17.3	14.8	11.8	8.2	Build

Source: Authors' calculations.
Notes: Table entries report the endowed exposure to the indicated asset based on the best-fitting specification in regressions of occupation-level income innovations on SMB, HML, Bonds and the indicated industry-level return measure. See Table 7 in Davis and Willen (2000b) for the underlying regression results.

librium models imply a high correlation between aggregate equity returns and shocks to the present value of labor income. That implication finds little support in our empirical results.

We do find that several other asset return measures are correlated with occupation-level income innovations. The returns on portfolios formed on firm size (market capitalization) are significantly correlated with occupation-level income innovations for about half the occupations we consider. In a few occupations, income innovations are correlated with returns on long-term bonds. In several instances, industry-level equity returns are correlated with the occupation-level income innovations of the workers in those industries. Both a priori reasoning and our empirical results suggest that industry-level equity returns can covary negatively or positively with labor income innovations for industry workers. It follows that the optimal hedge portfolio for occupation-specific and industry-specific components of risky labor income cannot be discerned without intensive empirical study.

Applying the estimated correlations to our portfolio choice framework, we find sizable departures from the two-fund separation principle for plausible assumptions about expected asset returns and investor risk aversion. To the extent that future research more fully uncovers the correlation structure between labor income shocks and asset returns, the gap between optimal portfolio allocations and the uniform portfolio shares implied by the two-fund separation principle will be larger than the ones shown in our examples.

Notes

The authors thank Deborah Lucas, Olivia Mitchell, and Stephen Zeldes for helpful comments. Jeremy Nalewaik provided valuable research assistance. Davis gratefully acknowledges research support from the University of Chicago Graduate School of Business.

1. This paper draws heavily on Davis and Willen (2000b). We direct the interested reader to that paper for a more thorough mathematical treatment of the issues and the approach developed herein.

2. Bodie, Merton, and Samuelson (1992) derive analytical solutions for portfolio choice in a continuous time finite horizon setting with fully hedgeable labor income risks. Much other work adopts computationally-intensive approaches to the portfolio implications of unhedgeable or partly hedgeable labor income risks. (For example, see Cocco, Gomes, and Maenhout 1999 for analysis in a finite horizon setting, and Heaton and Lucas 1997, Viceira 1998 and Haliassos and Michaelides 1999 in infinite horizon settings.)

3. For the utility specification that underlies our analysis, absolute risk aversion is unaffected by wealth shocks, and an investor's cost of a particular risk is unaffected by uncorrelated risks. However, an increase in the particular risk under consideration reduces the investor's willingness to take on more of that same risk. If the investor has constant relative risk aversion, then an increase in uncorrelated risks also reduces the investor's willingness to take on more of any particular risk.

4. Endowed exposure depends on the number of years to retirement, as we discuss more fully below, but this horizon effect on endowed exposure is distinct from the age effect on desired exposure.

5. Other studies investigate the issue at a more aggregated level in an international setting. Botazzi, Pesenti, and van Wincoop (1996) consider the covariance of national labor income shocks with financial asset returns, and Baxter and Jermann (1997) consider their covariance with the returns on hypothetical claims to a country's capital stock. Davis, Nalewaik, and Willen (2000) consider the covariance between national output shocks and a variety of domestic and foreign asset returns for 18 industrialized countries.

6. We also exclude persons who report an hourly wage less than 75 percent of the federal minimum. We handle top-coded earnings observations in the same manner as Katz and Murphy (1992).

7. The detailed occupational classification schemes in the CPS underwent major changes over time. Where possible, we constructed a uniform classification scheme from 1967 or 1970 to 1994 based on the occupational descriptions in the CPS documentation and an examination of changes over time in occupational cell counts and mean occupational earnings. We omitted individual-level observations that met any of the following occupation-level selection criteria: (1) the occupational group could not be extended back to 1970 or earlier in a consistent manner; (2) self-employed persons account for a large fraction of occupational employment (examples include physicians, dentists, lawyers, and farmers); (3) the occupational category was vague (examples include "General Office Supervisors" and "Financial Managers"); and (4) the number of individual-level observations in the occupation had a mean annual cell count less than 100 or a minimum annual cell count less than 50. These selection criteria reduced the number of individual-level observations by about one-half. From these 57 occupations, we selected for further analysis 10 occupations with large cell counts and a consistent definition back to 1967.

8. All earnings are expressed in 1982 dollars using the GDP deflator for personal consumption expenditures.

9. A log earnings specification is more commonly used by empirical researchers, but the specification in natural units fits more closely with our underlying theoretical model. In Davis and Willen (2000b), we show that log specifications yield results that are highly similar to specifications in natural units.

10. The empirical approach abstracts from potential selection issues associated with worker mobility across occupational groups, as well as mobility between the employment and not working. As a consequence, our estimates of the stochastic process for the occupation-level component of individual earnings may be incorrect even for infra marginal workers who do not move. A more complicated treatment of these issues requires long panel data sets. Davis and Willen (2000a) construct long times series for synthetic persons defined in terms of sex, birth cohort, and educational attainment; alternatively, one could use a true panel such as the Panel Survey of Income Dynamics. In practice, the true panel approach has serious limitations imposed by the nature and limited size of available surveys.

11. The data were taken from Professor French's web site ⟨web.mit.edu/kfrench/www/data.library.html⟩.

12. By "conventional" we mean a production technology that is approximately Cobb-Douglas over capital and labor. Given a stable Cobb-Douglas technology and a competitive economy, factor income shares are constant over time. Hence, if the same discount rates apply to future capital and labor income, and asset prices reflect fundamentals, the unobserved value of aggregate human capital fluctuates in a manner that is perfectly correlated with the observed value of claims to the aggregate capital stock. Models with these ingredients are standard, but they are hard to reconcile with the emerging body of work that finds how correlations between aggregate equity returns and labor income innovations.

13. For example, SIC 872 (Accounting and Auditing) is a natural industry counterpart for the Accounting and Auditing occupation, but CRSP contains no firm-level observations for SIC 872 during much of the sample.

14. These data are obtained from Professor French's web site ⟨web.mit.edu/kfrench/www/data.library.html⟩.

15. For references to related work see Fama and French (1992, 1993, 1996). Cochrane (2000) reviews the asset-pricing evidence related to size and book-to-market factors and provides references to more recent work.

16. Table 4 shows a very modest return premium on small cap stocks during our sample period. As others have observed, the realized premium on small cap stocks has declined in recent decades. The average annual value of the Fama-French SMB portfolio return was about 8 percentage points from 1964 to 1980 and -4 percentage points from 1981 to 1994.

17. Davis, Nalewaik, and Willen (2000) discuss this portfolio puzzle in connection with the gains to international trade in risky financial assets.

18. This covariance is allowed to vary smoothly with age in Davis and Willen (2000a), but they find only modest life cycle variation for demographic groups defined in terms of sex, education and birth cohort. Given their findings, and since their empirical design is better suited for uncovering age effects of this sort, we imposed an age-invariant covariance structure in this paper.

References

Ameriks, John and Stephen P. Zeldes. 2000. "How Do Household Portfolio Shares Vary with Age?" Columbia University Working Paper, Columbia University. May 22.

Baxter, Marianne and Urban J. Jermann. 1997. "The International Diversification Puzzle Is Worse Than You Think." *American Economic Review* 87, 1 (March): 170–80.

Bernheim, B. Douglas, Lorenzo Forni, Jagadeesh Gokhale, and Laurence J. Kotlikoff. This volume. "An Economic Approach to Setting Retirement Saving Goals."

Bodie, Zvi, Robert C. Merton, and William F. Samuelson. 1992. "Labor Supply Flexibility and Portfolio Choice in a Life Cycle Model." *Journal of Economic Dynamics and Control*, 16: 427–449.

Botazzi, Laura, Paolo Pesenti, and Eric van Wincoop. 1996. "Wages, Profits, and the International Portfolio Puzzle." *European Economic Review* 40, 2: 219–54.

Campbell, John Y., João F. Gomes, Francisco J. Gomes, and Pascal J. Maenhout. 1999. "Investing Retirement Wealth: A Life-Cycle Model." NBER Working Paper 7029.

Canner, Niko, N. Gregory Mankiw, and David N. Weil. 1998. "An Asset Allocation Puzzle." *American Economic Review* 87, 1 (March): 181–91.

Cocco, Joao, Francisco J. Gomes, and Pascal Maenhout. 1999. "Consumption and Portfolio Choice over the Life-Cycle." Harvard University Working Paper.

Cochrane, John H. 2000. "New Facts in Finance." In *Economic Perspectives*. Chicago: Federal Reserve Bank of Chicago.

Davis, Steven J. and Paul Willen. 2000a. "Using Financial Assets to Hedge Labor Income Risks: Estimating the Benefits." University of Chicago and Princeton Working Paper.

——. 2000b. "Occupation-Level Income Shocks and Asset Returns: Their Covariance and Implications for Portfolio Choice." NBER Working Paper 7905.

Davis, Steven, Jeremy Nalewaik, and Paul Willen. 2000. "On the Gains to International Trade in Risky Financial Assets." NBER Working Paper 7796.

Davis, Steven J., Wendy Edelberg, Jeremy Nalewaik, and Paul Willen. 2000. "The Opportunity Cost of Funds and Cross-Sectional Variation in Risky Asset Holdings." In progress, University of Chicago Graduate School of Business.

Dréze, Jacques H. and Franco Modigliani. 1972. "Consumption Decisions Under Uncertainty," *Journal of Economic Theory* 5: 308–35.

Fama, Eugene F. and Kenneth F. French. 1992. "The Cross-Section of Expected Stock Returns." *Journal of Finance* 47, 2 (June): 427–65.

——. 1993. "Common Risk Factors in the Returns on Stocks and Bonds." *Journal of Financial Economics* 33: 3–56.

——. 1996. "Multifactor Explanations of Asset-Pricing Anomalies." *Journal of Finance* 51, 1 (March): 55–84.

Fama, Eugene F. and William Schwert. 1977. "Human Capital and Capital Market Equilibrium." *Journal of Financial Economic* 4, 1 (January): 95–125.

Haliassos, Michael and Alexander Michaelides. 1999. "Portfolio Choice and Liquidity Constraints." Working Paper, University of Cyprus.

Heaton, John and Deborah Lucas. 1997. "Market frictions, Savings Behavior and Portfolio Choice." *Macroeconomic Dynamics* 1, 1: 76–101.

——. 2000. "Portfolio Choice and Asset Prices: The Importance of Entrepreneurial Risk," *Journal of Finance* (June).

Ingersoll, Jonathan E., Jr. 1987. *Theory of Financial Decision Making*. Totowa, N.J.: Rowman & Littlefield.

Jagannathan, R. and Narayana R. Kocherlakota. 1996. "Why Should Older People Invest Less in Stocks Than Younger People?" *Federal Reserve Bank of Minneapolis Quarterly Review* 20, 3: 11–23.

Katz, Lawrence F. and Kevin M. Murphy. 1992. "Changes in Relative Wages, 1963–87: Supply and Demand Factors." *Quarterly Journal of Economics* 107: 35–78.

Keeler, Theodore E. 1989. "Deregulation and Scale Economies in the U.S. Trucking Industry." *Journal of Law and Economics* 32: 229–55.

Leibowitz, Martin L., J. Benson Durham, P. Brett Hammond, and Michael Heller. This volume. "Retirement Planning and the Asset/Salary Ratio."

MaCurdy, Thomas E. 1982. "The Use of Time Series Processes to Model the Error Structure of Earnings in a Longitudinal Data Analysis," *Journal of Econometrics* 18: 83–114.

Rose, Nancy L. 1987. "Labor Rent Sharing and Regulation: Evidence from the Trucking Industry." *Journal of Political Economy* 95: 1146–78.

Samuelson, Paul A. 1969. "Lifetime Portfolio Selection by Dynamic Stochastic Programming." *Review of Economics and Statistics* 51: 239–43.

Viceira, Luis. 1998. "Optimal Portfolio Choice for Long-Horizon Investors with Nontradable Labor Income." Harvard University Working Paper, Cambridge, Mass.

Willen, Paul. 1999. "Welfare, Financial Innovation and Self Insurance in Dynamic Incomplete Market Models," Princeton University Working Paper, Princeton, N.J. May.

Chapter 3
Worklife Determinants of Retirement Income: Differences Across Men and Women

Philip B. Levine, Olivia S. Mitchell, and
John W. R. Phillips

Persons age 65 and over were once among the poorest members of the U.S. population, but today the rate of poverty for the elderly is at least as low as that of younger people and may be even lower. Nonetheless, there remain pockets of elderly poverty. Specifically, women over the age of 65 are about twice as likely to live in poverty as are similarly aged men.[1] Prior research has emphasized the loss of a spouse as a key factor causing retirement income shortfalls for women (Weir and Willis 1999; Burkhauser et al. 1991; Boskin and Shoven 1988). In this chapter, we extend the analysis to examine how variations in people's labor market experiences translate into differential pension and social security benefits later in life. We use the Health and Retirement Study (HRS) to evaluate the role that differences in labor market attachment and pay may play in explaining why older women face relatively poor retirement income prospects.

Our analysis first presents a series of descriptive analyses regarding the levels of retirement income by sex, race, marital status, and source of income. We find that the median wealth of a married couple on the verge of retirement today exceeds half a million dollars, with substantial accumulations in social security, pensions, housing, and other holdings. By contrast, nonmarried people approaching retirement have considerably less wealth. More than half of the nonmarried population have less than $200,000, counting all forms of retirement wealth. Few can look forward to future pension benefits, and even social security wealth is not large. Within the nonmarried group, women are particularly disadvantaged, having a level of wealth about one-quarter lower than that of nonmarried men. This difference is concentrated among the white population, since blacks and His-

,panics have very low and relatively similar levels of retirement wealth. Next we report on a statistical analysis of the determinants of these differences in anticipated retirement income that shows how lifetime labor market experiences translate into women's retirement income that is low relative to men's. Our estimates indicate that 85 percent of the retirement income gap between nonmarried men and women can be attributed to differences in these factors. We conclude with a look to the future.

Labor Market Effects on Retirement Income: Previous Research

Previous studies examining the impact of labor market rewards on men and women typically focus on the wages of *currently employed* workers. A commonly used methodology asks whether observed wage gaps can be "explained," or accounted for in a statistical sense, by differences in characteristics likely to be related to worker productivity such as age, education, and labor market experience. To the extent that a wage differential exists after controlling for these factors, it is typically attributed to labor market discrimination. This literature consistently finds evidence of discrimination, by this definition.[2]

Though the literature on younger workers is large, only very few researchers have sought to follow workers into retirement, to determine whether labor market differences continue to have an impact at older ages. One exception is the study by Levine, Mitchell, and Moore (1999) that asked whether differences in lifetime labor market attachment accounted for differences by sex in projected retirement income. Results from that work indicated that employment patterns played a large role, while health and family responsibilities had only tiny measured impacts on projected retirement incomes. One drawback of that study was that only *self-reported* labor market data could be used, rather than *actual* employment records taken from administrative records on labor market experience. In addition, that analysis focused on *total* retirement income and did not consider its components separately.

Determinants of Retirement Income in the Health and Retirement Study

In the recent analysis, by contrast, we use better data than heretofore available on pension and Social Security wealth, and we also explore how labor market and other factors influence anticipated retirement income by source.

Empirical Data Sources

Our analysis uses the Health and Retirement Study (HRS), a nationally representative sample of U.S. households drawn from a cohort on the verge of retirement (age 51–61 in 1992).[3] This survey provides extensive and very detailed demographic, health, wealth, income, and family structure data for both age-eligible respondents and their spouses. Linked to this under special restrictive conditions are two additional files containing invaluable information on respondents' pension and social security benefits. One file, known as the Earnings and Benefits File (EBF), provides measures of expected retirement income derived from Social Security benefits as well as labor market history data. A second file, the Pension Provider File (PPF), contains estimates of anticipated pension benefits. These merged files have been obtained for a majority of HRS respondents who gave permission to link their survey data with administrative records supplied by the Social Security Administration, and also with pension plan descriptions provided by respondents' employers.[4] Together, the HRS, EBF, and PPF data represent one of the richest data resources available to analyze retirement. There is no other current data source with equivalently detailed linked administrative records for this cohort.[5]

Using these three files, we compute anticipated retirement wealth for each household.[6] This wealth value is allocated or spread over the household's retirement period using conventional annuity factors.[7] In other words, we take each household's assets and divide them up to reflect the annual payments that a given level of wealth would yield if it were drawn down to zero over the household's remaining life expectancy. Annuity factors used to convert wealth to annual income flows reflect the different life expectancies of men and women at different ages: consequently, annuity factors for older respondents and men are smaller than those for younger respondents and women, since older respondents and men have shorter life expectancies than younger respondents and women. Turning a stock of wealth into an annual income flow makes it easier to interpret and understand exactly what retirement resources older Americans can expect to command.

Evaluating HRS respondents' access to anticipated retirement income requires us to distinguish between an individual's own resources and those available to other household members.[8] In the present analysis, we assess projected retiree wealth available within each household, without seeking to divide assets across individual members of a married couple. In other words, the model assumes that retirement income generated by different assets is equally available to a husband and a wife in a married couple; in this way, we presume that household resources are consumed jointly as long as both spouses are living.[9] As a result, sex differences in retirement wellbeing will result only from measured differences in the wellbeing of nonmarried men and women.[10]

We develop and use two indicators to capture patterns in respondent employment and earnings over their working lives. One is "prime-age" earnings, defined as average annual earnings between the respondent's 20th and 50th birthday, based on pay up to the social security earnings ceiling. It spans the period from the age when most respondents would have completed their schooling to the age that labor market activity would probably be influenced by early retirement preparations. In general, we anticipate that people with higher prime-age earnings will anticipate higher retirement wealth and hence more annual income in retirement. This is a reflection of the way pension formulas work, and also the way earnings are translated into social security benefits. Empirically, of course, it is of interest to estimate the specific way in which higher earnings result in higher retirement income. Our second indicator of labor market attachment is described as "years of work to age 50," or the count of years of covered social security employment to the respondent's 50th birthday. This is helpful in assessing how another year of work is converted into additional retirement income via pension, social security, and saving mechanisms.[11]

The remaining information on respondent characteristics is available directly from the HRS. Thus, for instance, survey respondents supplied extensive information on the economic, social, demographic, and other attributes of household members. The survey delved into household members' incomes, assets, debt, and health for respondents, age 51–61 in 1992, and their spouses of any age.

Two main criteria were used to generate the sample for empirical analysis. We restricted the respondent sample to include only those "age-eligible," namely the 9,714 respondents who were age 51–61 in 1992. It should be noted that people in this age bracket were interviewed as well as their spouses (irrespective of the spouse's age).[12] In addition, the sample included only those respondents and spouses who furnished a consent form, for whom the Social Security Administration could locate a matched file, and who were not receiving disability benefits at the time of the 1992 interview. These restrictions were required in order to obtain anticipated social security benefits. The analysis sample consists of 5,906 individuals.[13]

Methodological Approach

Our methodological approach is informed by prior studies that have sought to explain differences in pay for *active* workers. In this analysis, by contrast, we focus on the influence of labor market history on *retirement income differences* by sex. Along with measures of years in the labor market and average prime-age pay, we also include socioeconomic factors (e.g. education, marital history, and number of children) and race/ethnic indicators. In the case of married respondents, we also include the same measures for the respondent's spouse, since his/her characteristics may also contribute to differences in family resources available in retirement.

In the empirical analysis we estimate multivariate models of annual retirement income for men and women. These regression models are estimated separately by sex and marital status so that results can be compared across groups. Identical model specifications are estimated for three dependent variables of most interest, namely income flows from social security, pensions, and financial wealth including housing. More formally, the multivariate model uses the natural log of retiment income RY_{ig}, where i refers to the individual; g refers to the respondent's sex (f for female, m for male); WH is lifetime pay and work experience ("work history"); X is a vector of age, ethnicity, previous marital status, number of children, and education; and u refers to a disturbance term that captures otherwise unmeasured characteristics:

$$\ln(RY)_{ig} = b_{0g} + (WHI_{ig})b_{1g} + X_{ig}b_{2g} + u_{ig}.$$

For married respondents, analogous variables are included for spouse's characteristics.[14]

Having in hand estimates of the effects of each factor on projected retirement income, we then evaluate how much of anticipated retirement income differences by sex could be attributed to differences in the workers' characteristics.[15] With regard to differences in labor market characteristics , we ask the hypothetical question: how much would the gap in projected retirement income decrease if lifetime labor market characteristics of men and women were identical? In other words, based on estimated returns to these characteristics, we predict what women's retirement income would be if they had characteristics that were equal in value to those of men, on average. Since men tend to have had stronger labor force attachment during their working years, one would expect the gap between men and women's projected retirement income to be smaller, or potentially even zero, when it is based upon this prediction. Finally, we estimate and report the dollar reduction in the gender gap in projected retirement income between the predicted and observed level.

We conduct this decomposition for nonmarried men and women exclusively. As indicated previously, we assign household resources equally to husbands and wives, so that married men and women are defined to have equal retirement wealth. Using the HRS, we can identify differences in retirement wealth among married men and women because both members of the couple need not be age-eligible, which is a requirement for inclusion in our sample, and the characteristics of the age-ineligible men and women may differ. Without such cases, retirement wealth would be identical and there would be no gender gap to explain. Therefore, we restrict this part of the analysis to nonmarried men and women only.

Empirical Findings

Turning to the evidence, we first describe HRS respondents' wealth levels along with the anticipated annual income flows these represent. Next, we present results from the multivariate estimation, and finally report the decomposition results linking worklife patterns and retirement income differentials.

Descriptive Statistics

Median retirement wealth for HRS respondents appears in Table 1 by sex, marital status, and race/ethnic group.[16] Retirement wealth levels are quite substantial for married couples, exceeding half a million dollars when pensions, social security, and other financial assets are counted. Married men and women have similar levels of retirement wealth because retirement wealth is pooled at the household level. Projected retirement wealth for nonmarried people appears much lower, totaling only about one-third as much as for married couples ($157,000–$198,000).[17] There are striking sex differences disfavoring women: nonmarried men are projected to have 20 percent more retirement wealth than nonmarried women.

These overall differences become even sharper when we examine the sub-components of wealth. For example, married couples' social security wealth totals about $180,000, a figure not too different from their $155,000 in housing and net financial assets. Their employer-provided pension wealth amounts to approximately $100,000–$116,000. By contrast, social security wealth represents a much more dominant component of total wealth for the nonmarrieds, housing is less important, and — particularly striking — employer pension wealth is very tiny indeed. The median nonmarried woman, for instance, has no pension wealth at all, comparing poorly with her nonmarried male counterpart at $23,000, and her married female counterpart with about $100,000 in household pension assets.

Patterns of retirement wealth by race/ethnic status in Table 1 indicate that the relative disadvantage faced by nonmarried women versus men is most concentrated among the white population. This is because the wealth gap for black and Hispanic nonmarried men versus women is very small or even nonexistent. Thus nonmarried black women actually have higher levels of total wealth ($84,000) than their nonmarried black male counterparts ($77,000); for Hispanics total wealth is $91,000 for nonmarried men and $62,000 for nonmarried women. Pension wealth is effectively nil for black and Hispanic nonmarried people, and other wealth is similarly minuscule. In sum, differences in retirement wealth between whites and minorities are considerably larger than those between men and women.

How these wealth figures would translate into annual retirement income flows by sex, marital status, and race/ethnicity is evident in Table 2. The retirement assets shown previously will produce annual income equivalents for married men and women that are similar to each other, on the order of about $28,000–29,000 per year. Over one-third of the anticipated retirement income is attributable to social security benefits totaling about

TABLE 1. Median Total Projected Household Retirement Wealth by Race / Ethnicity, Sex, and Current Marital Status ($)

	White		Black		Hispanic		All	
	Nonmarried	*Married*	*Nonmarried*	*Married*	*Nonmarried*	*Married*	*Nonmarried*	*Married*
Men								
Total Wealth	261,702	560,900	76,964	340,407	91,345	242,398	198,108	533,742
Social Security Wealth	87,450	178,836	53,683	147,048	60,968	125,851	80,763	175,903
Pension Wealth	32,078	127,627	0	94,179	0	27,542	23,073	116,156
Other Wealth (Housing + Net Fin)	61,204	166,142	1,902	60,866	2,003	47,113	45,206	154,202
Women								
Total Wealth	194,093	555,868	84,362	340,054	61,594	239,966	157,023	528,823
Social Security Wealth	64,714	187,046	54,324	153,745	19,407	133,363	61,099	185,012
Pension Wealth	8,283	104,839	0	101,924	0	717	0	100,371
Other Wealth (Housing + Net Fin)	55,993	175,13	8,000	60,866	609	58,551	42,927	157,379

Source: Authors' calculations, Health and Retirement Study W1 ($1992)
Note: All data weighted by HRS sample weights.

TABLE 2. Median Projected Annual Household Retirement Income by Race/Ethnicity, Sex, and Current Marital Status ($)

	White		Black		Hispanic		All	
	Nonmarried	*Married*	*Nonmarried*	*Married*	*Nonmarried*	*Married*	*Nonmarried*	*Married*
Men								
Total Income	17,300	29,818	5,212	18,678	6,080	12,198	13,125	27,987
Social Security Income	5,851	9,399	3,582	7,859	4,079	6,659	5,379	9,260
Pension Income	2,141	6,742	0	5,178	0	1,440	1,556	6,104
Other Income	4,084	8,829	127	3,325	136	2,551	3,009	8,152
(Housing + Net Fin)								
Women								
Total Income	11,066	30,799	4,826	19,536	3,538	13,724	9,016	29,480
Social Security Income	3,727	10,286	3,120	8,665	1,107	7,261	3,507	10,178
Pension Income	476	5,901	0	5,924	0	41	0	5,568
Other Income	3,198	9,526	460	3,337	35	3,221	2,460	8,865
(Housing + Net Fin)								

Source: Authors' calculations, Health and Retirement Study W1 ($1992)
Note: All data weighted by HRS sample weights.

$10,000 per year for the median married household, exceeding the annuitized value of housing and financial wealth that totals about $8,000–9,000 annually. Median pension income for married couples is somewhat lower, at about $5,500–6,000 per year.[18]

Projected annual retirement income for nonmarried people is expected to be only about one-half to one-third the size of married couples' income, at $13,000 for nonmarried men and $9,000 for nonmarried women. The relative disadvantage of nonmarried women stems partly from the fact that they are anticipated to live longer than men on average, which makes the gap in annual retirement income flows larger than the wealth gap. Furthermore, nonmarried people probably require more than half a married couple's income to maintain a comparable living standard. Hence the finding that nonmarried respondents expect so much less income in retirement than do married couples does not bode well for their prospective retirement wellbeing.

Looking further at the components of retirement income flows, it appears that the redistributive nature of social security benefits somewhat narrows the retirement gap between nonmarried men and women. However, median expected annual benefit levels are low, on the order of $5,400 for men and $3,600 for women. A problem confronting the median nonmarried woman approaching retirement is that she has no pension wealth at all, whereas nonmarried men have small accumulations, and the median married couple can expect $5,500–6,000 of pension income annually. Nonmarried men and women have similar levels of net financial and housing wealth, but it is worth pointing out that more nonmarried men have very high levels of other wealth, since the medians are similar but the means are higher for the men.

Finally, focusing on the differences in anticipated annual retirement income by race/ethnicity, we find that the median married black couple would anticipate $19,000 annually, and the married Hispanic couple $12,000–14,000 annually. This compares to much lower levels expected by nonmarried persons, with black and Hispanic women expecting $3,500–5,000 per year in total income, and black as well as Hispanic men anticipating slightly higher income. Table 2 clearly shows minority groups' heavy reliance on social security since they can expect relatively little income from sources other than social security. These very low income levels do not differ much by sex for minorities.

Regression Results

Moving beyond simple tabulations of the data, we next evaluate how changes in respondent characteristics might improve retirement wellbeing. Specifically, we are interested in the "returns" that people anticipate receiving in the form of higher retirement income, for a given increase in earnings and

TABLE 3. Predicted Changes in Total Projected Annual Household Retirement Income Associated with Key Explanatory Variables (standard errors in parentheses)

Change in Explanatory Variable	Nonmarried Women	Nonmarried Men	Married Women	Married Men
+1 Year of Work				
Total Retirement Income	$879	$486	−$52	$62
	(177)	(430)	(86)	(209)
Social Security Income	$645	$914	$167	$642
	(52)	(150)	(32)	(117)
Pension Income	−$65	−$825	−$89	−$486
	(88)	(275)	(65)	(93)
Other Income	$115	$259	−$130	$95
	(109)	(532)	(86)	(160)
+$1,000 Average Prime-Age Earnings				
Total Retirement Income	$374	$1,147	$215	$391
	(111)	(260)	(56)	(137)
Social Security Income	$145	$151	$23	$155
	(19)	(63)	(15)	(60)
Pension Income	$88	$355	$83	$89
	(56)	(148)	(34)	(27)
Other Income	$156	$700	$95	$207
	(54)	(248)	(40)	(72)

Source: Authors' calculations, Health and Retirement Study W1 ($1992)

work experience. To facilitate interpretation of these findings, we focus on the results reported in Table 3, which shows how a change in one of the labor market history variables of reasonable magnitude might be expected to influence the average person's annual retirement income.[19] (A full set of results from our multivariate statistical analysis is reported in Appendix Table 2.)

Simulations of this type are carried out for total retirement income and also for the three components of wealth. For example, the first panel of Table 3 shows how working an extra year between the ages of 20 and 50 influences overall retirement income as well as the three components of wealth. For nonmarried women, an additional year of work is found to have a large positive effect ($879) on annual retirement income, holding other things constant. Nonmarried men also receive a sizeable increase in retirement income of almost $500 per year, for an extra year of work.

By contrast, an additional year worked has no statistically significant effect on retirement income for married men and women. This result is due to the offsetting effects on the three main components of retirement income. Specifically, the results indicate that additional years of work translate into higher social security benefits for both groups (also true for nonmarried women). But an additional work year is associated with lower lifetime pension payments, particularly for married men. One explanation for this finding may be potential endogeneity bias in which those with greater anticipated retirement income may work fewer years, even prior to the age of 50. Having higher lifetime earnings translates into higher anticipated retirement income levels for all groups, holding other factors constant. Thus an additional $1,000 in average annual pay earned during the prime-age period (age 20–50) is associated with an additional $200–$400 per year in retirement income for women, and $400–$1,100 per year for men. This positive effect is robust across all retirement income components: that is, higher average prime-age earnings are consistently associated with higher social security income, pension income, and other income (although two of the estimated effects are not significantly different from zero).

It is also interesting that, at the margin, social security benefit formulas reward nonmarried men and women, and married men, more for higher earnings than they do married women. This is because many married women in this cohort are entitled to receive a social security benefit based on the earnings history of their husbands rather than their own work histories. As a result, increases in average pay influence the benefits of the relatively few women who will receive benefits based on their own earnings history. Further, married couple benefits are heavily influenced by social security survivor payments that pay off in the event of the death of one spouse, and this valuable benefit stream is influenced only modestly by additional earnings during the prime-age period. By contrast, a nonmarried person's social security benefit is payable only as long as the retiree is alive; lacking the death benefit, retirement income streams become more closely earnings-linked than is true for married persons. Also as a result, higher earnings translate directly into higher pension income, with higher effects for nonmarried men ($355) than for women ($88); this may be because men are covered by more generous pension benefit formulas than women. The fact that other income rises more for additional pay may suggest that personal saving is more feasible for those earning higher salaries.

Decomposition Results

Having described how anticipated retirement income patterns vary across the population, we next decompose projected retirement income gaps into their component parts. This exercise asks the question: how would women fare in terms of retirement income if their labor market and other characteristics were to become equivalent to those of men? Specifically, we evaluate the difference in annual retirement income by sex that can be attributed to differences in labor market experience and other factors. We conduct this exercise for nonmarried respondents only since we have assumed that re-

TABLE 4. Decomposing Differences in Retirement Income by Type: Fraction Attributable to Differences in Respondent Characteristics

Nonmarried Men vs. Women	Total*	Social Security*	Pension**	Other*
Av. Total Retirement Income Gap	$11,286	$1,487	$5,192	$6,906
Percentage of gap attributable to:				
All Labor Market Differences	85%	151%	10%	82%
Years of Work to Age 50	51%	112%	−6%	26%
Average Prime-Age Earnings	34%	39%	16%	56%

Source: Authors' calculations, Health and Retirement Study W1 ($1992), weighted data.
* Nonnegative wealthholders only.
** Positive wealthholders only.
Note: Decompositions use regression coefficients reported in Appendix Table A2 and means reported in Appendix Table A1.

sources are split evenly among married couples, eliminating the possibility of sex differentials in their retirement wealth.

The results of this analysis appear in Table 4, where we show that nonmarried men anticipate receiving about $11,000 more per year in retirement on average than nonmarried women. Using the decomposition framework, this gap favoring men is accounted for mainly by lifetime work history differences. Roughly one-third of the gap appears to be due to differences in average prime-age earnings, and half to different lengths of labor market attachment. The potent role of the labor market variables for the nonmarried groups is reiterated for each of the three income types, though by far the most powerful influence is for income from social security. Indeed, labor market differences account for more than the entire gap in social security income, indicating that if women had men's labor market experience and pay, the retirement income gap would be expected to be more than fully closed.

Taken as a whole, the decomposition results confirm the central role of labor market variables in accounting for projected retirement gaps by sex. A nonmarried woman with lifetime labor force attachment and pay similar to those of her male counterpart would reasonably expect retirement income quite similar to his.[20]

Conclusions and Discussions

The continuing problem of poverty among older people has prompted analysts and policymakers to ask why some groups have a high likelihood of being poor in old age. Prior studies find that marital status changes (widowhood in particular) influence older women's incomes. In this chapter we take a different tack, asking instead how labor market events influence eventual retirement income. We used the Health and Retirement Study to explore how earnings patterns and years of labor market experience affect retirement income flows, while controlling for differences in other socio-economic factors.

We find that the typical older married couple on the verge of retirement today commands around half a million dollars in retirement assets, while the median nonmarried man has about $200,000 and the median nonmarried woman about $160,000. When these asset levels are converted into annual retirement income flows, women's longer life expectancies in retirement exacerbate the gender gap. But the main reason older nonmarried women on the verge of retirement expect lower levels of retirement income than their male counterparts is that they have much lower retirement assets than do other demographic groups. This gap is most prominent for whites, since blacks and Hispanics have fewer assets so differences between men and women are consequently smaller. The median nonmarried minority in the sample expects no employer pension income and only modest income from other financial assets. Our decomposition analysis asks to what extent differences in these factors can explain why women arrive on the doorstep of retirement with fewer resources and lower projected income as compared to men. The results indicate that an additional year of labor market work between the ages of 20 and 50 has a sizeable impact on the retirement income of nonmarried men and women, but only a tiny one for those who are married. An additional $1,000 in average annual earnings raises women's eventual retirement income, but by much less than it improves men's retirement income. Overall, the model indicates that closing the sex gap in years of work and average pay could help shrink quite substantially the retirement income gap for nonmarried people. That is, 85 percent of the overall retirement income gap would be eliminated if, over their lifetimes, women and men had similar lifetime earnings and labor market attachment.

Looking ahead, what might be projected regarding the future? If women's pay levels continue to climb over time as they have in the last decade or so, and retirement income vehicles maintain their same form and structure, it could be anticipated that future cohorts of women will do better. Those approaching retirement will have worked more, and earned more, over their lifetimes, enchancing their wellbeing both absolutely and relative to men.

Appendix

In this study we use age 62 as the common age at which retirement assets are computed. This is the modal age for Social Security benefit filing purposes and is the earliest age at which one can currently file for Social Security benefits. While it is straightforward to specify an assumed retirement age for a nonmarried individual, it is more complex for a married couple since the retirement date for spouses of differing ages may differ. Here we follow HRS practice where the survey interviewer designated as the "primary respondent" that household member having the greatest knowledge of the household's financial matters. Usually this respondent was age-eligible for the HRS survey, in which case we assume the retirement assumption is triggered on this person's attainment of age 62. If the primary respondent was not HRS age-eligible, this guarantees that the secondary respondent is age-eligible. In this instance, we assume that the age eligible household member keys off retirement at the attainment of age 62.

Values for each of the main retirement asset classes are projected to retirement using a range of projection technologies and assumptions (the approach is described in Moore and Mitchell, 1999). In brief, net financial wealth is projected forward using averages of market returns based on historical rates; housing wealth is projected forward using survey data on the purchase price of the respondent's house, year of purchase, outstanding debt owed on homes, and mortgage payment amount and frequency. We assume that the market value of the house grows in line with the general inflation rate, so there is no real appreciation in housing values, though mortgage payments decrease the remaining principal on the mortgage. Respondents' pension and social security wealth values are projected assuming workers remain employed to their retirement age (see Gustman et al. 1999). Pension benefits are derived based on the plan provisions of employer provided pensions and respondents' answers to salary and years of service (where appropriate). Social security projected amounts are computed as described in Mitchell, Olson, and Steinmeier (1999) for those respondents agreeing to supply a data link; for them we also have available work history and average pay variables for each respondent. This includes average lifetime salary and total labor market experience up to age 50. Present values of benefits are calculated using mortality, interest rate, inflation, and wage growth assumptions as described in Moore and Mitchell (1999). All dollar values are given in $1992. After the death of one spouse, we assume that remaining housing and net financial assets transfer to the survivor; social security benefits are available to the widow(er) according to program rules; and pension rules now require survivor benefits unless a spouse agrees to the contrary in writing. Other research studies using some of these data include Dwyer and Mitchell (1999), Mitchell and Moore (1998), and Mitchell et al. (1999).

We eliminate from the analysis any sample respondents with negative projected total wealth at age 62 (37 individuals), and to produce viable log values, we impute one dollar of wealth to respondents reporting zero total wealth. Similar issues arise with the components of total wealth, namely Social Security, employer pensions, and housing/financial wealth. The last category, which we term "other wealth" here, is the aggregate of financial and housing wealth. It too can take on negative and zero values. The

APPENDIX TABLE 1. Mean Values of Explanatory Variables by Sex and Marital Status

	Nonmarried Women		Nonmarried Men		Married Women		Married Men	
	Mean	Standard Deviation	Mean	Standard Deviation	Mean	Standard Deviation	Mean	Standard Deviation
Projected Household Wealth ($)								
Total	244,574	283,270	378,844	624,910	715,375	772,985	733,717	823,544
Social Security	61,219	38,623	74,672	32,723	173,205	50,967	163,382	47,051
Pension	71,519	138,616	113,907	171,782	203,305	288,692	226,169	314,348
Other Wealth	111,836	223,686	190,265	581,513	338,866	699,758	344,166	755,091
Projected Annual HH Income ($)								
Total	14,007	16,229	25,294	41,510	39,761	42,716	39,018	44,084
Social Security	3,507	2,214	4,993	2,193	9,668	2,990	8,705	2,671
Pension	4,093	7,932	7,602	11,456	11,274	16,043	12,004	16,622
Other Income	6,429	12,809	12,716	38,611	18,845	38,577	18,339	40,315
Labor Market Variables								
Years of Work to Age 50	18.7	8.78	25.1	6.69	15.3	8.64	26.3	6.13
Average Earnings ($)	11,762	7,768	19,745	8,784	9,934	6,613	23,484	7,968
Socioeconomic Factors								
Age	55.6	3.27	55.4	3.16	55.5	3.22	55.8	3.22
Black (%)	19	39	17	38	05	21	06	23
Hispanic (%)	07	26	07	25	04	20	05	21
No High School (%)	28	45	25	43	19	39	20	40
College (%)	12	33	14	35	12	33	17	38
Graduate School (%)	09	29	08	28	06	23	10	31
Ever Divorced (%)	59	49	61	49	21	40	27	44
Ever Widowed (%)	30	46	10	31	04	20	03	15
Number of Children	2.64	1.99	2.14	1.98	3.46	1.98	3.33	1.84

Labor Market Variables

Years of Work to Age 50	—	—	26.5	5.79	17.0	8.60
Average Earnings	—	—	22,207	7,921	10,503	7,064

Socioeconomic Factors

Age	—	—	58.6	5.61	52.1	5.69
No High School (%)	—	—	22	42	16	37
College (%)	—	—	16	36	14	35
Graduate School (%)	—	—	10	30	06	24
Ever Divorced (%)	—	—	20	40	23	42
Ever Widowed (%)	—	—	05	21	03	18

Source: Authors' calculations, Health and Retirement Study W1 ($1992), weighted data.
Note: Earnings reported in 1992 dollars (not in natural logs)

APPENDIX TABLE 2. Regression Results for Projected Retirement Income by Type: Coefficients (Standard Errors)

	Total	Social Security	Pension	Other
Nonmarried Women				
Labor Market Variables				
Years of Work to Age 50	0.06**	0.18**	−0.01	0.02
	(0.01)	(0.02)	(0.01)	(0.02)
Average Prime-age Earnings	0.31**	0.49**	0.16	0.27**
	(0.09)	(0.06)	(0.10)	(0.09)
Socioeconomic Factors				
Age	0.02	0.04	−0.05**	0.02
	(0.02)	(0.02)	(0.02)	(0.03)
Black	−0.71**	−0.61**	0.43**	−1.60**
	(0.16)	(0.16)	(0.11)	(0.29)
Hispanic	−1.52**	−1.06**	−0.51	−1.81**
	(0.40)	(0.33)	(0.32)	(0.44)
No High School	−0.92**	0.01	−0.36*	−1.78**
	(0.17)	(0.18)	(0.16)	(0.26)
College	0.62**	0.41*	0.54**	0.68*
	(0.15)	(0.21)	(0.15)	(0.32)
Graduate School	1.08**	−0.26	0.93**	1.22**
	(0.18)	(0.29)	(0.16)	(0.36)
Ever Divorced	−0.01	0.16	−0.11	−0.31
	(0.13)	(0.15)	(0.13)	(0.23)
Ever Widowed	0.44**	0.14	−0.09	0.82**
	(0.14)	(0.17)	(0.15)	(0.28)
Number of Children	−0.02	0.09*	−0.12**	−0.01
	(0.04)	(0.04)	(0.04)	(0.06)
R-Squared Sample Size	0.41	0.58	0.26	0.28
	939	939	438	882
Nonmarried Men				
Labor Market Variables				
Years of Work to Age 50	0.02	0.18**	−0.06**	0.02
	(0.02)	(0.03)	(0.02)	(0.04)
Average Prime-age Earnings	0.90**	0.60*	0.60*	1.02**
	(0.20)	(0.25)	(0.25)	(0.36)
Socioeconomic Factors				
Age	0.03	0.07**	−0.07*	0.07
	(0.02)	(0.02)	(0.03)	(0.06)
Black	−0.54**	0.18	0.06	−2.32**
	(0.15)	(0.19)	(0.23)	(0.42)
Hispanic	−0.54	0.53	−0.01	−1.88*
	(0.30)	(0.32)	(0.25)	(0.92)
No High School	−0.28*	−0.03	−0.03	−0.94**
	(0.13)	(0.14)	(0.20)	(0.38)

APPENDIX TABLE 2. *Continued*

	Total	Social Security	Pension	Other
College	0.65**	−0.56	0.33	0.54
	(0.20)	(0.28)	(0.30)	(0.42)
Graduate School	0.87**	0.18	0.58*	1.31**
	(0.22)	(0.20)	(0.25)	(0.45)
Ever Divorced	−0.04	−0.08	0.42*	−0.14
	(0.13)	(0.16)	(0.20)	(0.32)
Ever Widowed	−0.02	−0.39	0.40	0.21
	(0.18)	(0.34)	(0.30)	(0.54)
Number of Children	−0.03	0.13**	−0.06	−0.09
	(0.03)	(0.04)	(0.05)	(0.08)
R-Squared Sample Size	0.43	0.59	0.15	0.32
	452	452	238	419

Married Women
Labor Market Variables

	Total	Social Security	Pension	Other
Years of Work to Age 50	−0.001	0.02**	−0.01	−0.01
	(0.00)	(0.00)	(0.00)	(0.01)
Average Prime-age Earnings	0.05**	0.02	0.06*	0.05*
	(0.01)	(0.02)	(0.02)	(0.02)

Socioeconomic Factors

	Total	Social Security	Pension	Other
Age	0.00	0.02	0.00	0.02
	(0.01)	(0.01)	(0.01)	(0.02)
Black	−0.20**	−0.05	0.16	−0.70**
	(0.07)	(0.08)	(0.10)	(0.15)
Hispanic	−0.32**	0.26*	−0.41	−0.77**
	(0.08)	(0.13)	(0.23)	(0.21)
No High School	−0.22**	−0.03	−0.18*	−0.48**
	(0.04)	(0.05)	(0.09)	(0.11)
College	0.14**	0.03	0.28**	0.18
	(0.06)	(0.08)	(0.09)	(0.10)
Graduate School	0.32**	−0.15	0.56**	0.45**
	(0.09)	(0.17)	(0.11)	(0.12)
Ever Divorced	−0.19**	−0.03	−0.20	−0.43**
	(0.05)	(0.06)	(0.11)	(0.12)
Ever Widowed	−0.26**	−0.03	−0.27	−0.50*
	(0.10)	(0.10)	(0.22)	(0.22)
Number of Children	−0.02	0.01	−0.01	−0.03
	(0.01)	(0.01)	(0.02)	(0.02)
R-Squared Sample Size	0.34	0.39	0.15	0.22
	2,163	2,163	1,612	2,121

Married Men
Labor Market Variables

	Total	Social Security	Pension	Other
Years of Work to Age 50	−0.002	0.07**	−0.03**	0.01
	(0.01)	(0.01)	(0.01)	(0.01)

APPENDIX TABLE 2. *Continued*

	Total	Social Security	Pension	Other
Average Prime-age Earnings	0.24**	0.42**	0.14**	0.26**
	(0.08)	(0.16)	(0.04)	(0.09)
Socioeconomic Factors				
Age	0.00	0.03**	−0.03**	0.01
	(0.01)	(0.01)	(0.01)	(0.01)
Black	−0.28**	0.05	−0.02	−0.75**
	(0.08)	(0.09)	(0.09)	(0.13)
Hispanic	−0.33**	0.51**	−0.45**	−0.76**
	(0.09)	(0.17)	(0.14)	(0.22)
No High School	−0.29**	−0.01	−0.43**	−0.54**
	(0.04)	(0.04)	(0.08)	(0.10)
College	0.25**	0.07	0.17	0.40**
	(0.05)	(0.06)	(0.10)	(0.09)
Graduate School	0.43**	0.07	0.45**	0.57**
	(0.06)	(0.09)	(0.10)	(0.10)
Ever Divorced	0.05	−0.03	0.02	0.17
	(0.06)	(0.09)	(0.10)	(0.10)
Ever Widowed	0.16	−0.07	0.36*	0.43*
	(0.12)	(0.08)	(0.18)	(0.21)
Number of Children	−0.03**	0.01	−0.05**	−0.06**
	(0.01)	(0.01)	(0.02)	(0.02)
R-Squared Sample Size	0.30	0.43	0.14	0.22
	2,315	2,315	1,766	2,261

Source: Authors' calculations, Health and Retirement Study W1 ($1992).
* Coefficient statistically significant at the 5% level.
** Coefficient statistically significant at the 1% level.
Notes: Retirement income and average earnings expressed in natural logs. Estimates exclude respondents with negative total wealth. Pension income estimates conditional on positive pension wealth. Other income estimates exclude respondents with negative other wealth. Our estimates also include variables that controls for spousal characteristics where appropriate.

empirical analysis of these other wealth values proceeds in the same fashion as the total wealth analysis: persons reporting negative values are dropped from the sample, and cases with zero wealth are assigned one dollar. There are no negative reports of employer pension wealth in the sample, but 31 percent of the respondents report they anticipate no employer pension. Persons without pensions are excluded from the analysis of employer pension wealth. We have separately estimated, but do not describe here, additional Probit models to explore factors associated with having positive values of each type of wealth. Controlling for sample selection does not change the qualitative conclusions reported here.

The explanatory variables in the multivariate analysis control for various socioeconomic characteristics of survey households (descriptive statistics appear in Appendix Table 1). We also include controls for spouse variables for married couples, which must be included because retirement wealth measures relate to households rather than individuals.

While most explanatory variables (age, race, and education) do not require description, the marital history variables require a brief description. We estimate separate equations for currently married and nonmarried men and women, but each set of estimates controls for respondents' marital history. Qualitative variables identifying previous divorce and widowhood appear in each equation, where the omitted category varies depending on the sample group. (For example, in the case of single women, the omitted category is never married; for married women it is married.) In separate analyses we also focus on the never-married, divorced, and widowed among the nonmarried population; however, sample sizes are small.

Notes

The authors acknowledge research support from the AARP and the Pension Research Council at the University of Pennsylvania, and computer support from the National Institute on Aging via a grant to the Population Aging Research Center at the University of Pennsylvania. Opinions remain solely those of the authors.

1. For references on this topic see Levine, Mitchell, and Moore (1999).

2. See Blau and Kahn (1997); Gunderson (1989); and Blau and Ferber (1987).

3. Additional information on the HRS dataset is available at ⟨www.umich.edu/~hrswww⟩; the Data Appendix describes variable creation for the present study; see also Mitchell, Olson, and Steinmeier (1999).

4. Because of the confidential nature of these data, researchers may access the files under restricted conditions; see ⟨www.umich.edu/~hrswww⟩ for details.

5. The availability of the Social Security and pension match data makes the HRS uniquely valuable among all datasets covering retiring Americans. Though Social Security benefits were calculated for most of the age-eligible HRS respondents in the sample, in a few cases this information could not be computed and the respondent had to be omitted from the sample analyzed in this paper (more detail on sample sizes is given below). One reason for missing Social Security benefits was that respondents gave permission for the University of Michigan to request their Social Security records, but no match was obtained because their records did not match SSA identification information. Another reason is that the Social Security Administration excluded from the match file any respondents receiving Social Security Disability Insurance benefits. Also some age-eligible respondents declined to sign the release form permitting their social security data to be matched with the HRS. In this study we rely on social security wealth estimates as well as earnings histories provided in the EBF, so respondents lacking these data are excluded from our analysis. This selection might bias results if those with an EBF file differ from those without a match; we have no evidence that results are biased and indeed respondents lacking consents for a social security match are quite diverse. Thus some of the very wealthy (having high levels of financial assets) did not sign the special release, while some blacks and Hispanics also did not provide consent. Inasmuch as missing EBF matched records appear among people at both ends of the wealth distribution, we believe the direc-

tion of potential bias is ambiguous. More formally, an econometric solution to this sample issue would require finding an instrumental variable correlated with the probability of having an EBF match but uncorrelated with social security wealth. Such a variable does not exist in our sample.

6. Dollar figures throughout this chapter are given in constant 1992 dollars.

7. Levine, Mitchell, and Moore (1999) discuss several ways to model well-being; here we simply focus on levels of retirement income, since these are more readily understood. Burkhauser et al. (1985), Moon (1977), and Hurd (1989) employ similar measures.

8. All values are computed assuming retirement will occur at age 62. See Appendix for more discussion of this point.

9. After one party dies, the surviving spouse is assumed to keep half the pension in a joint-and-survivor arrangement; social security benefits continue for eligible widow(er)s. Housing and other wealth is bequeathable to the surviving spouse in its entirety. While the HRS dataset does not report ownership of assets within couples, other research has acknowledged the potential for intrahousehold bargaining for married couples (McElroy 1990). Incorporating the possibility of spousal behavior of this sort may be feasible with other data sources.

10. Nonmarried persons in the HRS are those who are not currently married; this population includes the never married, the divorced, and the widowed, based on self-reported marital status. Married persons are likewise self reported. Practically speaking, there are slight differences in married men's and women's measured resources in the HRS because the age-eligible women in HRS couples have husbands who are slightly older than do women in couples with HRS age-eligible men.

11. The analysis acknowledges the possibility that there may be dual causality in the regression models between retirement income, on the one hand, and earnings as well as work years, on the other. That is, more work at higher pay could raise retirement income, but conversely, having higher retirement assets might discourage people from working more years or seeking out higher pay. In order to diminish the possibility of variable endogeneity, the labor market measures used are strictly retrospective measures: that is, a worker's years of labor market experience are measured up to age 50 but not thereafter, and average pay is likewise computed based on the worker's social security earnings reported between age 20 and 50. Of course, there is still a chance that retirement wealth considerations could influence the labor market behavior of individuals before age 50. Similar issues of endogeneity may be present regarding decisions made over the lifecourse, including educational attainment, marital history, and childbearing. To assess the influence of this potential problem, we have also estimated reduced form models that include only the labor market history measures with no other covariates and obtained qualitatively similar results to those reported below.

12. In any event, spouse's wealth is included in the analysis irrespective of the spouse's age.

13. To arrive at the final sample, two minor sample restrictions were made as well. Some households were dropped because they lacked a "financial respondent" responsible for providing financial data to the interviewers. We also omit respondents whose race/ethnic status was not white, black, or Hispanic.

14. Levine, Mitchell, and Moore (1999) and Blau and Graham (1990) estimate similar specifications.

15. Oaxaca (1973) devised the statistical technique used here to show how differences in outcomes might be allocated to different sources. In the present context, we have adapted this approach to decompose the difference in projected log annual retirement income between older women and men into two parts: the portion due

to differences in characteristics that differ by sex, and the portion due to differences in returns to those characteristics between the sexes. These analyses are conducted separately by marital status groups. We use women's returns to characteristics to determine how much of the gap in log retirement income would be closed if women's characteristics became like those of men. Specifically, we compute:

$$\overline{R}\overline{Y}^m - \overline{R}\overline{Y}^f = \sum_{i=1}^{k} \beta_i^f \cdot (\overline{X}_i^m - \overline{X}_i^f) + \sum_{i=1}^{k} \overline{X}_i^m \cdot (\beta_i^m - \beta_i^f) \ ,$$

where RY represents a particular measure of economic well-being, β represents the vector of regression coefficients estimated using the multivariate model described above, the X-values represent a vector of mean characteristics, f and m represent women and men respectively, and k indexes characteristics. The first expression on the right-hand side of this equation is said to represent the "explained" part of the differential in retirement income because it is attributed to the different characteristics of men and women. The second expression is said to represent the "unexplained" part of the differential because it would result in differences in income even if men and women had the same characteristics. Our simulation computes the percentage reduction in the retirement income gap between men and women that would occur if both had identical characteristics. Formally, this involves estimating:

$$\% \ \text{gap} = \frac{\sum_{i}^{k} \beta_i^f \cdot (\overline{X}_i^m - \overline{X}_i^f)}{\overline{R}\overline{Y}^m - \overline{R}\overline{Y}^f} \cdot 100$$

This expression represents the gap in log retirement income that can be "explained" by differences in characteristics as a percentage of the size of the gap. Below we also compute the *dollar* contribution to the gap in retirement income by applying the percentages to the dollar gap in projected annual retirement income.

16. We focus on medians since differences in averages may be driven by a relatively small number of individuals with very large levels of wealth. Mean levels used in the decomposition analysis appear in Appendix Table 1.

17. The difference in wealth levels by marital status goes well beyond differences in household size since a simple division by two of a married household's wealth still surpasses that of nonmarried individuals. Moreover, equivalence scales typically assign a value of less than two to adequately correct for differences in household size (cf. Ruggles 1990; Nelson 1993).

18. Tables 1 and 2 include respondents with zero values for all these wealth sources, but in the multivariate analysis we exclude those with zero, or negative, wealth values. While some may anticipate retirement income from other sources, we expect this to be true for a very small number of respondents. For example, less than 2 percent of HRS households report receiving financial support from friends or relatives over the course of the previous year.

19. Values are computed at the sample mean unless otherwise noted (see Appendix Table 1). We have also examined predicted changes in retirement income associated with changes in the labor market histories of spouses of married respondents; these prove to be similar to those for male and female married respondents themselves.

20. Another multivariate approach (not reported in detail here) indicates that anticipated retirement income does not vary much as a function of prior marital history among nonmarried men, but it does for women. That is, the median never-married woman expects about 60 percent more retirement income than nonmar-

ried divorced or widowed women. The main source of this difference is pension income: the median never-married woman expects over $2,000 in annual pension benefits, while the median widowed and divorced woman expects none. The values may in fact actually be closer than they appear in our data. This is because divorced and widowed respondents have claims to the social security benefits of their former spouses if they had been married for at least 10 years prior to the marital breakup (the 10-year requirement does not pertain to a spouse who becomes widowed while still married). On the other hand, our estimate of Social Security wealth for divorced and widowed women will be somewhat understated for those who had been married at least a decade, since the EBF file does not report social security earnings and benefits for previous spouses because of confidentiality restrictions; see Mitchell, Olson, and Steinmeier (1999).

References

Blau, Francine D. and Marianne A. Ferber. 1987. "Discrimination: Empirical Evidence from the United States." *American Economic Review* 77, 2: 316–20.

Blau, Francine D. and J. W. Graham. 1990. "Black-White Differences in Wealth and Asset Composition." *Quarterly Journal of Economics* (May): 321–39.

Blau, Francine D. and Lawrence M. Kahn. 1997. "Swimming Upstream: Trends in the Gender Wage Differential in the 1980s." *Journal of Labor Economics* 15, 1: 1–42.

Boskin, Michael J. and John B. Shoven. 1988. "Poverty Among the Elderly: Where Are the Holes in the Safety Net?" In *Pensions in the U.S. Economy*, ed. Zvi Bodie, John B. Shoven, and David A. Wise. Chicago: University of Chicago Press. 115–138.

Burkhauser, Richard V., J. S. Butler, and Karen C. Holden. 1991. "How the Death of a Spouse Affects Economic Well-Being After Retirement: A Hazard Model Approach." *Social Science Quarterly* (September): 504–19.

Burkhauser, Richard V., J. S. Butler, and J. T. Wilkinson. 1985. "Estimating Changes in Well-Being Across Life: A Realized vs. Comprehensive Income Approach." In *Horizontal Equity, Uncertainty, and Economic Well-Being*, ed. Martin David and Timothy Smeeting. Chicago: University of Chicago Press: 69–90.

Dwyer, Debra and Olivia S. Mitchell. 1999. "Health Problems as Determinants of Retirement: Are Self-Rated Measures Endogenous?" *Journal of Health Economics* 18: 173–93.

Filer, Randall K. 1989. "Occupational Segregation, Compensating Differentials, and Comparable Worth." In *Pay Equity: Empirical Inquiries*, ed. Robert Michael, Heidi I. Hartmann, and Brigid O'Farrell. Washington, D.C.: National Academy Press.

Gunderson, Morley. 1989. "Male-Female Wage differentials and Policy Responses." *Journal of Economic Literature* 27, 1: 46–72.

Gustman, Alan, Olivia S. Mitchell, Andrew A. Samwick, and Thomas L. Steinmeier. 1999. "Pension and Social Security Wealth in the Health and Retirement Study." In *Wealth, Work, and Health: Innovations in Survey Measurement in the Social Sciences*, ed. James P. Smith and Robert J. Willis. 150–208.

Hurd, Michael D. 1989. "The Poverty of Widows: Future Prospects," in *The Economics of Aging*, ed. David A. Wise. Chicago: University of Chicago Press. 201–30.

Levine, Phillip B., Olivia S. Mitchell, and James F. Moore. 1999. "Women on the Verge of Retirement: Predictors of Retiree Well-Being." In *Forecasting Retirement Needs and Retirement Wealth*, ed. Olivia S. Mitchell, P. Brett Hammond, and Anna M. Rappaport. Pension Research Council. Philadelphia: University of Pennsylvania Press. 167–207.

McElroy, Marjorie R. 1990. "The Empirical Content of Nash-Bargained Household Behavior." *Journal of Human Resources* 25, 4: 559–83.

Mitchell, Olivia S. and James F. Moore. 1998. "Can Americans Afford to Retire? New Evidence on Retirement Saving Adequacy." *Journal of Risk and Insurance* 65, 3: 371–400.

Mitchell, Olivia S., James F. Moore, and John W. Phillips. 1999. "Explaining Retirement Saving Shortfalls." In *Forecasting Retirement Needs and Retirement Wealth,* ed. Olivia S. Mitchell, P. Brett Hammond, and Anna M. Rappaport. Pension Research Council. Philadelphia: University of Pennsylvania Press. 139–63.

Mitchell, Olivia S., Robert J. Myers, and Howard Young, eds. 1999. *Prospects for Social Security Reform.* Pension Research Council. Philadelphia: University of Pennsylvania Press.

Mitchell, Olivia S., Jan Olson, and Thomas L. Steinmeier. 1999. "Social Security Earnings and Projected Benefits." In *Forecasting Retirement Needs and Retirement Wealth,* ed. Olivia S. Mitchell, P. Brett Hammond, and Anna M. Rappaport. Pension Research Council. Philadelphia: University of Pennsylvania Press. 327–59.

Moon, Marilyn. 1977. *The Measurement of Economic Welfare.* New York: Academic Press.

Moore, James F. and Olivia S. Mitchell. 1999. "Projected Retirement Wealth and Saving Adequacy in the Health & Retirement Study." In *Forecasting Retirement Needs and Retirement Wealth,* ed. Olivia S. Mitchell, P. Brett Hammond, and Anna M. Rappaport. Pension Research Council. Philadelphia: University of Pennsylvania Press. 68–94.

Nelson, J. A. 1993. "Household Equivalence Scales: Theory Versus Policy?" *Journal of Labor Economics* (July): 471–93.

Oaxaca, Ronald L. 1973. "Male-Female Wage Differentials in Urban Labor Markets." *International Economic Review:* 693–709.

Porter, Kathryn H., Kathy Larin, and Wendell Primus. 1999. "Social Security and Poverty Among the Elderly." Working Paper, Center on Budget and Policy Priorities, Washington, D.C. April.

Ruggles, Patricia. 1990. *Drawing the Line: Alternative Poverty Measures and the Implications for Public Policy.* Washington, D.C.: Urban Institute Press.

Weir, David R. and Robert Willis. 1999. "Prospects for Widow Poverty." In *Forecasting Retirement Needs and Retirement Wealth,* ed. Olivia S. Mitchell, P. Brett Hammond, and Anna M. Rappaport. Pension Research Council. Philadelphia: University of Pennsylvania Press. 208–34.

Part II
Developments in Retirement Planning Models

Chapter 4
An Economic Approach to Setting Retirement Saving Goals

B. Douglas Bernheim, Lorenzo Forni, Jagadeesh Gokhale, and Laurence J. Kotlikoff

Effective retirement planning begins with the establishment of appropriate goals for saving. If these goals are set too high, households may sacrifice present wellbeing excessively to sustain future high living standards. If these goals are set too low, households may indulge immediate desires at the expense of future living standards. Thus having inappropriate retirement saving goals may produce undesired and perhaps abrupt changes in living standards. By contrast, with appropriate saving goals, households will tend to "smooth" consumption, thereby avoiding undesirable changes.

Consumption smoothing is a fundamental prediction and prescription of modern economic theory. This theory rests on a *life cycle model* of behavior which posits that each household is motivated by a sense of wellbeing that depends both on current satisfaction and on expectations of future satisfaction. The principle of consumption smoothing follows directly from the law of diminishing returns: individuals are well advised to reallocate dollars from time periods in which they are consuming a great deal (and in which incremental dollars therefore add relatively little to wellbeing), to periods in which they are consuming relatively little (and in which incremental dollars are therefore particularly valuable). To economists, consumption smoothing is the central purpose of saving.

Traditional financial planning methods are inconsistent with, and in some instances antithetical to, standard economic doctrine. The hallmark of these methods is the establishment of an asset target derived from either income or spending objectives. Unfortunately, such objectives are not typically derived from the principles of consumption smoothing. As a result, traditional financial plans frequently guarantee dramatic swings in spending as households age.

Despite this fundamental shortcoming, virtually every financial planning software package available today embodies the traditional targeted-saving approach. In some instances, users are asked to specify future spending or income targets with reference to current spending or income, but this is a far cry from consumption smoothing. To illustrate, imagine a household attempting to set a spending target. If it selects its target with reference to current spending, and if its current spending is not sustainable over its planning horizon, then it will be told to reduce its current consumption and save more than is required for consumption smoothing. Were the household to follow this prescription, it would experience an undesired surge in spending at retirement. To put it differently, the household would sacrifice too much when young so as to benefit from a higher living standard after retirement. Conversely, if the household's spending is currently less than it can sustain over its planning horizon, it will be told to increase its current consumption and save less than is required for consumption smoothing. Were the household to follow this prescription, it could experience a sudden and undesired drop in living standard at retirement. In other words, the household would deprive itself of a more satisfactory retirement by consuming excessively in earlier years. Setting future income targets with reference to current income is even less likely to generate a sensible path for consumption. A household's current income may fluctuate because of one-time bonuses, temporary unemployment, enrollment in higher education, childcare, and a variety of other factors.

By assuming a spending or income target, traditional financial planning techniques implicitly require households to perform the most complex and important planning tasks by themselves. This is because setting a target consistent with consumption smoothing requires a household to consider a wide range of factors including current and future household composition, the age and likely lifespan of each spouse, current and future labor earnings, special expenditures and receipts, social security benefits, current net worth, income from taxable and nontaxable assets, current and future contributions to retirement accounts, current and future federal and state taxes, asset returns, current housing and future housing plans, and borrowing constraints. Each of these factors interacts with others, and none can be evaluated appropriately in isolation. Consider, for example, future housing plans. Downsizing or upsizing a home alters the future path of housing expenses, mortgage and property tax deductions, saving, capital income, and federal and state taxes. To determine the impact of housing choices on sustainable living standards, one must solve a complex dynamic programming problem. Many individuals will not know how to see this problem when selecting a target for future spending or income.

Mindful of these overwhelming complexities, traditional financial planners often advise households to set their targets using simple rules of thumb, such as 70 percent income replacement. Unfortunately these seemingly straightforward recommendations are often highly inappropriate, and many households tend to adopt them uncritically, deferring to a planner's expertise. In following such advice, a household smoothes its saving, rather than its consumption, so its living standard could potentially fluctuate wildly from year to year.

The shortcomings of existing financial planning techniques have prompted the development of an economics-inspired financial planning software package known as Economic Security Planner, or ESPlanner.[1] Its underlying algorithm determines a household's maximum sustainable living standard as well as the rate of saving and level of life insurance holdings required to preserve that living standard through time. In order to elucidate how the model works, we first describe its logic and compare our economic approach to financial planning, as embodied in ESPlanner, with a conventional approach as embodied in Quicken Financial Planner. Finally, we expand on Bernheim et al. (2000) by using the software to determine appropriate saving goals for typical Americans approaching retirement.

An Economic Approach to Financial Planning

It is important to realize that the principle of consumption smoothing applies to the individual, rather than to a household. That is, while individuals may smooth consumption, household expenditures will shift with the arrival and departure of family members. Since larger households benefit from economies of scale with respect to shared expenses, consumption smoothing on the part of each individual does not require household expenditures to increase proportionately with household size. Accordingly, our software smoothes a measure of the household's living standard, which depends on consumption per adult-equivalent (based on children's ages), accounting for the economies of scale that are associated with family size.

It is also important to realize that the principle of consumption smoothing does not apply to all household expenditures. Exceptions occur when particular expenditures are either nonrecurring or difficult to modify. Examples might include college tuition and housing expenses (down payments, mortgages, and property taxes). ESPlanner deducts these special expenditures directly from income "off the top," and smoothes the living standard derived from all remaining expenditures. Application of the consumption-smoothing dictum may also be limited by institutional constraints. For example, lenders are often reluctant to extend unsecured credit. To smooth consumption, households with rapidly growing income must borrow against future receipts. If they cannot, then their consumption may rise (and even fluctuate) with income. Accordingly, our model smoothes consumption to the greatest extent possible, subject to the limitations on each household's ability to borrow.

The principle of consumption smoothing applies to decisions about life insurance, as well as to decisions about saving. Households use life insurance to moderate the impact of a family member's death on the survivors' living standards. Moreover, decisions about life insurance and saving are inextricably linked. Current budgeted expenses must include an adequate allotment for life insurance premiums, and saving must be sufficient to cover future premiums. Accordingly, in deriving a financial plan, our model solves simultaneously for the ideal levels of saving and life insurance. It thereby ensures that survivors can sustain the same living standard as the intact family, irrespective of which family members die or when they die.

Naturally, many things can change following the death of a spouse. The survivor may move to a new house, change jobs, or return to work. He or she may incur additional child care expenses, or revisit plans to send the child to an expensive private university. To accommodate these important possibilities, ESPlanner encourages *contingent planning*. In particular, each spouse may specify different levels of earnings, special expenditures, and tax-favored retirement contributions in the event that he or she is widowed. Changes in contingent plans often have substantial effects on appropriate life insurance holdings.

Required Information

To apply the principle of consumption smoothing while accounting for the various considerations mentioned above, our software requires several types of inputs:

Demographics. ESPlanner solicits the birth dates of the household head and spouse as well as the birth years of children under age 19. Children are assumed ordinarily to remain in the household through age 18. Each spouse must also specify a maximum length of life, which refers to the limit of the individual's planning horizon (note that this differs from life expectancy). The program smoothes consumption over this horizon, thereby protecting household members from the possibility that they might outlive their resources. Users also identify their state of residence, which is used to determine applicable tax rates.

Standard of living index. Economic theory allows for the possibility that a household might prefer either a rising or falling standard of living, over one that is constant over time. A household might also prefer to change its level of consumption upon retirement because it anticipates increased spending on activities that are complementary with leisure, and/or reduced spending on activities that are substitutes for leisure. Our model accommodates these possibilities by permitting users to specify how they would like their living standard to change through time. By adjusting a living standard index from its default value of 100 in any year or collection of years, a user can customize the *shape* of his living standard profile (for example, one can specify that the living standard is to grow at the rate of one percent per year or should decline by 10 percent at retirement). The model then determines the highest current living standard, as well as the associated financial plan, consistent with the characteristics specified by the user.

Labor earnings. For each spouse, software solicits current labor earnings as well as the amount that he or she would expect to earn if widowed (contingent earnings). Separate information is collected on employee wages and self-employment income. It is necessary to distinguish between these forms of income because they are treated differently under the payroll tax. Each spouse also specifies a retirement date and a growth path for labor earnings up to retirement, as well as a (potentially different) retirement date and earnings growth path that would apply in the event he or she were widowed.[2]

Special expenditures and receipts. Our model also provides users with the ability to specify nonrecurring (or briefly recurring) expenditures and receipts. Each special expenditure must be designated as either deductible or nondeductible and each special receipt is described as either taxable or nontaxable. For each briefly recurring item (such as college tuition), the user provides a start and an end date. Each spouse specifies special expenditures and receipts that would apply in the event that he or she were widowed.[3]

Estate plans. In many instances, people may wish to leave a bequest in excess of the amount required to sustain the surviving spouse's living standard through his or her maximum lifespan, and to sustain the living standard of children through age 18. Accordingly, our model permits users to specify special (incremental) bequests, including resources to defray death-related expenses such as funerals.

Net worth. Information on net worth is essential for accurate financial planning, and accordingly, our software separately solicits data on non-tax-favored and tax-favored assets. In the case of tax-favored accounts, each spouse's holdings are detailed, as well as a) the last year he or she will contribute to the account, b) the first year he or she will start withdrawing from the account, and c) the year he or she will stop withdrawing from the account. Users may select one of two options for withdrawing tax-favored balances: uniform withdrawals, or the smallest legally permissable withdrawals.

Saving. An individual who attaches a high value to liquidity may be reluctant to tie up too much of net worth in tax-favored accounts. Conversely, someone less concerned about liquidity may wish to maximize tax-favored holdings. Accordingly, the model permits the user to determine the composition of saving by indicating current non-tax-favored saving, as well as current and intended future employee and employer contributions to tax-favored accounts (for both joint-survivor and widowed contingencies).

Housing. For most Americans, housing represents both a major expense and an important store of wealth. Accordingly, the softward solicits information on both primary and secondary (vacation) homes. Homeowners estimate current market value, provide information on loans, and detail current expenses, while renters list housing-related expenses. Users also describe future plans concerning refinancing and moves (including upsizing, downsizing, liquidation of second homes, shifts between homeowner and renter status, and so forth).

Pensions. Accurate financial planning requires detailed information on work-related retirement benefits. The model treats defined contribution (DC) accounts as tax-favored assets. Each spouse separately supplies information on defined benefit (DB) pensions, including the year or years in which benefits will be received, projected amounts (either lump-sum, annual, or both), whether the benefits are indexed to inflation, and the level of benefits received by a survivor.

Social security. Social security remains an important source of retirement and disability income for many Americans. Our software uses past and future earnings in covered employment to estimate benefits for those who are not yet collecting benefits. Its benefit calculator takes into account eligibility rules, early retirement reductions, delayed retirement credits, benefit recomputations, the phased increase in the normal retirement age, the earnings test between ages 62 and 65, family benefit maximums, the wage indexation of Average Indexed Monthly Earnings, and the price indexation of benefits once they are received. All these elements are needed to determine anticipated retirement, spousal, mother, father, child, and widow(er) benefits.

Economic assumptions. Meaningful financial planning requires a variety of assumptions about the economic environment. Our model supplies default values for all critical economic parameters including the inflation rate, nominal rates of return on tax-favored and non-tax-favored assets, the degree of economies in shared living, child-adult equivalency factors, the maximum amount the household can borrow (apart from mortgages), future rules governing payroll taxes and social security benefits, and the share of total non-tax-favored capital income accruing in the form of long-term capital gains. Users are permitted to substitute alternative values for these parameters.

Taxes. Meaningful financial planning requires proper recognition of tax liabilities. Accordingly, ESPlanner calculates federal and state income and payroll taxes for each future year, for each survival state (both spouses alive and husband deceased, husband deceased and wife alive). The model also computes estimated federal income taxes reflecting deductions and exemptions, the partial taxation of social security benefits, the earned income tax credit, the child tax credit, the phase-out of deductions and exemptions at higher income levels, the indexation of tax brackets to the consumer price index, and the preferential taxation of long-term capital gains. In computing deductions, the household is assumed to itemize if eligible expenses exceed the standard deduction (principally mortgage payments, property taxes, state income taxes, spousal support payments, charitable contributions, and other designated special expenses). Estimated state income tax liabilities (for each year and for each survival state) reflect state of residence, as well as the specific exemptions, deductions, and rate structure appropriate for that state. In computing both federal and state taxable income, the program deducts, as appropriate, contributions to tax-favored accounts and includes, as appropriate, withdrawals from these accounts. Finally, the determination of social security payroll taxes accounts for the ceiling on covered earnings, which applies to the portions of the tax that finance retirement and disability benefits, but not to the portion that finances Medicare.

Model Recommendations

ESPlanner's principal outputs are recommended time paths for consumption expenditure, non-tax-favored saving, and term-life insurance holdings (for each spouse individually, in the case of married couples). All outputs are displayed in current-year (i.e., real) dollars, and recommendations for saving and life insurance are compared with current choices. Although the derivation of the recommended financial plan involves a complex dynamic programming algorithm, reports and recommendations are easily interpreted. Moreover, from an inspection of the reports, it is readily evident that the program achieves the objective of consumption smoothing, thereby identifying the highest sustainable living standard for the household.

In this context, "consumption" refers to all spending over and above "off-the-top" items, including housing expenses, special expenditures, life insurance premiums, taxes, and net contributions to tax-favored accounts. Recommended consumption expenditures vary from year to year when the household's composition changes, and when the household moves into or out of a liquidity-constrained period. Naturally, recommended household consumption may also change over time when the user has expressed a preference for a rising or declining living standard (as discussed above). Recommended taxable saving in any year equals the household's total income (non-asset plus asset income) minus the sum of (a) recommended spending on consumption and insurance premiums, (b) specified spending on housing and special expenditures, (c) taxes, and (d) net contributions to tax-favored accounts (contributions less withdrawals).

Recommended levels for term life insurance are either positive or zero.[4] If recommended term insurance in a particular year is positive for a particular potential decedent (the household head or, if married, the spouse), and if the decedent dies at the end of that year, the surviving household will have precisely the same living standard as the household would have had absent the decedent's premature death. If the potential decedent's recommended insurance in a particular year is zero, the surviving household will have the same or higher living standard if the decedent dies in that year. These statements are, of course, conditional on complete execution of the recommended financial plan, as well as on the correctness of underlying economic assumptions and information concerning future income, current asset holdings, and special expenditures.

Illustrating the ESPlanner Results

To indicate how the model works we introduce Al and Peg, a married couple, who decide to formulate a detailed financial plan. In the year 2000, Al is 50 years old and Peg is 45, and they reside in the state of New York with two children, Kelly, age 15, and Bud, age 13. Al and Peg each plan to work through age 65, earning respectively $25,000 and $100,000 each year (these figures all all others mentioned in this illustration refer to year-2000 dollars). If Al were to die, Peg would still earn $100,000, but if Peg were to die, Al would switch jobs and expect to earn $40,000. The couple plan to send each child to college for four years, and to spend $30,000 per child per year on tuition. Al and Peg wish to allocate $5,000 each for their funerals. Anticipating a desire to pursue costly leisure activities during retirement, they decide to specify a 10 percent increase in living standard upon Al's retirement. They currently own and live in their home. The house has a market value of $300,000. Annual property taxes are $5,000, annual homeowners' insurance is $750, and annual maintenance averages $1,500. Al and Peg have 25 years remaining on a 30-year mortgage; their current mortgage balance stands at $200,000, and they pay $2,200 each month. They plan to sell their home when Al is 70 years old and rent an apartment for $2,000 per month (in today's dollars). Each spouse works in social security-covered employment and the past covered earnings of each spouse grew smoothly to their current values. The couple wants to set aside $100,000 by 2020 (when Al is age 70 and Peg is age 65) as an emergency fund for medical expenses. If only one spouse is alive in 2020, they plant to put only $50,000 aside.

Table 1 shows our model's annual non-tax-favored saving, consumption, and life insurance recommendations. The couple's future spending, including consumption, housing expenses, special expenditures, life insurance premiums, and funeral expenses is tracked in Table 2, while Table 3 is a balance sheet—it tracks the household's non-tax-favored assets. Al and Peg's income over time is depicted in Table 4, where non-asset income refers to labor income, pension income, and social security benefits. These first four tables all assume that both spouses live to their assumed maximum life expectancy.[5]

Consider first the consumption recommendations in Table 1. Recommended discretionary expenditures equal $58,018 through 2004, the year Kelly goes to college, at which point consumption falls to $49,622. It drops again to $40,486 in 2006 when Bud goes to college. Consumption remains at this level until 2015 when Al reaches age 65. At this point, consumption rises

TABLE 1. Annual Recommendations for Saving, Consumption, and Life Insurance

Year	Al's Age	Peg's Age	Non-Tax-Favored Saving ($)	Consumption ($)	Al's Life Insurance ($)	Peg's Life Insurance ($)
2000	50	45	1,751	58,018	0	468,868
2001	51	46	2,395	58,018	0	452,345
2002	52	47	2,591	58,018	0	431,413
2003	53	48	3,208	58,018	0	408,272
2004	54	49	(18,153)	49,622	0	377,605
2005	55	50	(17,775)	49,622	0	347,278
2010	60	55	21,981	40,486	0	148,952
2015	65	60	23,138	44,534	0	0
2020	70	65	(107,898)	44,534	0	0
2025	75	70	(11,297)	44,534	0	0
2030	80	75	(11,804)	44,534	0	0
2035	85	80	(12,334)	44,534	0	0
2040	90	85	(12,863)	44,534	0	0
2045	95	90	(18,441)	44,534	0	0
2050		95	(20,162)	27,834	0	0

Source: Authors' calculations, based on hypothetical family characteristics for Al and Peg; see text.

by 10 percent to $44,534 in accordance with Al's and Peg's desire to have a 10 percent higher living standard in retirement. Finally, in 2046, when Al is deceased, consumption falls to $27,834, since then only Peg remains in the household. Note that the ratio of consumption when Al and Peg are both alive ($44,534) to the value when only Peg ($27,834) is alive is 1.6. This reflects our assumption that, with the addition of a second adult, spending must increase by a factor of 1.6 (i.e. by 60 percent) to preserve the same living standard.

In contrast to the relatively smooth trajectory for the household's living standard, non-tax-favored saving patterns fluctuate widely. Saving is positive until the children go to college, negative when they are in college, positive after they leave college, and negative once Al and Peg are retired. Note that Al's and Peg's non-tax-favored saving is largest immediately prior to Peg's retirement. This is what one would expect, since in their younger years Al and Peg must pay for a mortgage and college tuition. After these obligations are met, Al and Peg can concentrate on saving for retirement. The largest increment to their liquid assets occurs when they sell their home. Their highest rate of dissaving occurs when they make special expenditures. Likewise, as indicated in Table 2, total spending also fluctuates more than discretionary spending due to changes in special expenditures, housing costs, life insurance premiums, and funeral expenses.

Our model recommends that the couple initially obtain $468,868 in insurance on Peg's life. Over time, Peg's recommended life insurance declines and reaches zero at age 64. For Al, recommended life insurance is zero,

TABLE 2. Annual Decomposition of Spending Patterns

Year	Al's Age	Peg's Age	Consumption ($)	Special Expenditures ($)	Housing Expenditures ($)	Al's Life Insurance Premium ($)	Peg's Life Insurance Premium ($)	Excess Funerals & Bequests ($)	Total Spending ($)
2000	50	45	58,018	0	32,881	0	1,052	0	91,951
2001	51	46	58,018	0	32,135	0	1,080	0	91,233
2002	52	47	58,018	0	31,410	0	1,123	0	90,551
2003	53	48	58,018	0	30,706	0	1,130	0	89,854
2004	54	49	49,622	30,000	30,023	0	1,123	0	110,768
2005	55	50	49,622	30,000	29,360	0	1,115	0	110,097
2010	60	55	40,486	0	26,322	0	760	0	67,568
2015	65	60	44,534	0	23,702	0	0	0	68,236
2020	70	65	44,534	100,000	24,000	0	0	0	168,534
2025	75	70	44,534	0	24,000	0	0	0	68,534
2030	80	75	44,534	0	24,000	0	0	0	68,534
2035	85	80	44,534	0	24,000	0	0	0	68,534
2040	90	85	44,534	0	24,000	0	0	0	68,534
2045	95	90	44,534	0	24,000	0	0	5,000	73,534
2050	—	95	27,834	0	24,000	0	0	5,000	56,834

Source: Authors' calculations, based on hypothetical family characteristics for Al and Peg; see text.

TABLE 3. Balance Sheet for Non-Tax-Favored Assets

Year	Al's Age	Peg's Age	Total Income	Net Tax-Favored Payments	Total Spending	Total Taxes	Non-Tax-Favored Saving	Non-Tax-Favored Net Worth
2000	50	45	129,500	3,000	91,951	32,798	1,751	156,251
2001	51	46	129,551	3,000	91,233	32,923	2,395	158,647
2002	52	47	129,621	3,000	90,551	33,479	2,591	161,238
2003	53	48	129,696	3,000	89,854	33,634	3,208	164,445
2004	54	49	129,790	3,000	110,768	34,175	(18,153)	146,292
2005	55	50	129,261	3,000	110,097	33,939	(17,775)	128,516
2010	60	55	125,965	3,000	67,568	33,416	21,981	55,117
2015	65	60	119,113	(4,786)	68,236	32,525	23,138	173,520
2020	70	65	51,777	(24,293)	168,534	15,434	(107,898)	391,369
2025	75	70	47,418	(24,293)	68,534	14,474	(11,297)	338,329
2030	80	75	45,744	(24,293)	68,534	13,307	(11,804)	280,332
2035	85	80	43,994	(24,293)	68,534	12,087	(12,334)	219,729
2040	90	85	42,166	(24,293)	68,534	10,788	(12,863)	156,430
2045	95	90	40,259	(24,293)	73,534	9,459	(18,441)	85,390
2050		95	23,089	(17,507)	56,834	3,924	(20,162)	0

Source: Authors' calculations, based on hypothetical family characteristics for Al and Peg; see text.

TABLE 4. Components of Income

Year	Al's Age	Peg's Age	Al's Non-Asset Income ($)	Peg's Non-Asset Income ($)	Special Reces ($)	Non-Tax-Favored Asset Income ($)	Total Income ($)
2000	50	45	25,000	100,000	0	4,500	129,500
2001	51	46	25,000	100,000	0	4,551	129,551
2002	52	47	25,000	100,000	0	4,621	129,621
2003	53	48	25,000	100,000	0	4,696	129,696
2004	54	49	25,000	100,000	0	4,790	129,790
2005	55	50	25,000	100,000	0	4,261	129,261
2010	60	55	25,000	100,000	0	965	125,965
2015	65	60	14,733	100,000	0	4,380	119,113
2020	70	65	14,733	22,501	0	14,542	51,777
2025	75	70	14,733	22,501	0	10,183	47,418
2030	80	75	14,733	22,501	0	8,509	45,744
2035	85	80	14,733	22,501	0	6,759	43,994
2040	90	85	14,733	22,501	0	4,931	42,166
2045	95	90	14,733	22,501	0	3,024	40,259
2050		95	0	22,501	0	587	23,089

Source: Authors' calculations, based on hypothetical family characteristics for Al and Peg; see text.

since even without life insurance, Peg and the children would enjoy a higher material living standard were Al to die than were he to live.

The balance sheet in Table 3 proves one can readily see that our model's consumption recommendations are affordable. This balance sheet tracks the evolution of the couple's non-tax-favored net worth, which in turn translates into recommended non-tax-favored saving. This flow then equals the difference between the household's income, detailed in Table 4, and the sum of its net contribution to retirement (non-tax-favored) accounts, total spending, and taxes. Note that household net worth is never negative. This implies that the plan is feasible. Note also that net worth is zero when Peg reaches her maximum lifespan, indicating that there are no unused resources. Since it is infeasible to increase consumption in any year without reducing it in another year, the program has identified the highest consumption profile with the characteristics that the couple desires (an unchanging living standard, except for a 10 percent rise at retirement).

One can also verify that a surviving spouse could maintain his or her accustomed living standard in the event of widowhood. For instance, Table 5 details Al's recommended spending assuming that Peg dies at age 46, one year after adopting the plan. Recommended consumption for Al declines when the children leave the household and then rises by 10 percent when Al reaches age 65. Note that when Al is living by himself, the ratio of his consumption in any year to the corresponding value in Table 2 is 1 divided by 1.6. Given our assumption concerning the magnitude of household scale economies, this implies that Al is enjoying the same living standard as a survivor that he would have enjoyed had Peg not died. Similarly the balance sheet in Table 6 shows that consumption recommendations are affordable for Al if Peg dies. This follows from the fact that Al never goes into debt. Note also that net worth is zero when Al reaches his maximum lifespan, implying that there are no unused resources. It is therefore infeasible to increase consumption in any year without reducing it in another year. Upon Peg's death, Al's non tax-favored wealth is $605,992. This amount equals the couple's $158,647 in non tax-favored assets at the end of 2001 plus the $452,345 in term insurance recommended for Peg in 2001, less the $5000 payment for Peg's funeral. Were the couple to purchase less insurance on Peg's life, Al would not be able to finance the same living standard as a survivor.

Limitations of This Approach

Although our model considers many key factors that enter into saving and insurance decisions, it is important to acknowledge that some relevant factors are omitted. Two specific omissions merit discussion. First, the software does not take into account the uncertainty of future income or expenditures on necessities such as noninsured health care costs. Users are required to perform sensitivity analysis to understand the implications of uncertainty,

TABLE 5. Al's Spending, Assuming That Peg Dies

Year	Al's Age	Consumption ($)	Special Expenditures ($)	Housing Expenditures ($)	Al's Life Insurance Premium ($)	Excess Funerals & Bequests ($)	Total Spending ($)
2002	52	45,813	0	31,410	0	0	77,223
2003	53	45,813	0	30,706	0	0	76,519
2004	54	36,261	30,000	30,023	0	0	96,284
2005	55	36,261	30,000	29,360	0	0	95,621
2010	60	25,304	0	26,322	0	0	51,626
2015	65	27,834	0	23,702	0	0	51,536
2020	70	27,834	50,000	24,000	0	0	101,834
2025	75	27,834	0	24,000	0	0	51,834
2030	80	27,834	0	24,000	0	0	51,834
2035	85	27,834	0	24,000	0	0	51,834
2040	90	27,834	0	24,000	0	0	51,834
2045	95	27,834	0	24,000	0	5,000	56,834

Source: Authors' calculations, based on hypothetical family characteristics.

TABLE 6. Balance Sheet for Al's Non-Tax-Favored Assets, Assuming That Peg Dies

Year	Al's Age	Total Income ($)	Net Tax-Favored Contributions ($)	Total Spending ($)	Total Taxes ($)	Non-Tax-Favored Saving ($)	Non-Tax-Favored Net Worth ($)
2001	51	605,992	0	0	0	605,992	605,992
2002	52	79,304	1,000	77,223	11,984	(10,903)	595,089
2003	53	79,020	1,000	76,519	11,686	(10,185)	584,902
2004	54	72,526	1,000	96,284	12,801	(37,559)	547,343
2005	55	71,433	1,000	95,621	12,158	(37,346)	509,997
2010	60	48,114	1,000	51,626	8,775	(13,287)	265,283
2015	65	26,897	(18,968)	51,536	3,619	(9,290)	205,066
2020	70	32,303	(23,501)	101,834	8,526	(54,556)	340,862
2025	75	29,648	(25,848)	51,834	10,439	(6,777)	299,850
2030	80	28,303	(25,176)	51,834	8,642	(6,997)	252,835
2035	85	26,767	(19,375)	51,834	6,167	(11,859)	198,010
2040	90	24,592	(12,425)	51,834	2,623	(17,440)	115,284
2045	95	21,474	(8,239)	56,834	1,048	(28,169)	0

Source: Authors' calculations, based on hypothetical family characteristics.

examining a variety of alternative scenarios to assess their exposures and vulnerabilities. Second, the software does not account for possible changes in marital status, such as remarriage after a spouse's death. To some extent, the remarriage option may mitigate financial vulnerabilities associated with the risk of a spouse's death. There are, nevertheless, legitimate reasons to ignore this possibility. Arguably, the choice of whether to remarry should not be dictated by financial necessity. In addition, the economic wellbeing of a remarried individual may be determined by his or her financial status prior to remarriage, insofar as this affects bargaining power within the new marriage (cf. Lundberg 1999). Finally, remarriage after a spouse's death is less common among older individuals.

Comparing the Economic Approach and the Traditional Approach to Financial Planning

In prior research Gokhale et al. (1999) compared the economic approach, embodied in the ESPlanner, with a more traditional approach, as embodied in Quicken Financial Planner (QFP). Table 7 reports consumption, saving, and life insurance recommendations for three households—a low-income, young married couple with no children; a upper-income, middle-aged married couple with two children; and a high-income, older married couple with adult children.

In deriving financial plans with the Quicken Financial Planner software, Gokhale et al. (1999) attempted to emulate the manner in which a somewhat sophisticated household might use the program. After soliciting current spending levels, QFP asks the user whether he or she wishes to spend the same amount in the future. We assume that most households would, at least initially, answer this question in the affirmative. Using information on income and net worth, the program then determines whether desired expenditures are feasible. If planned spending is not feasible, the user must adjust planned expenditures downward. If planned spending is feasible, the user can choose to adjust planned expenditures upward. A sophisticated household could follow this procedure iteratively until it determined the highest feasible level of consumption, though this manual process of "trial and error" is time consuming. Consequently, it is unlikely that even sophisticated households would further fine tune their expenditure plans to accommodate changes in household composition (such as the arrival and departure of children from the household), borrowing constraints, or other factors that our model handles automatically.

Case A: A Young, Low Income Couple

For this case we assume that both spouses are 35 years old in 1999 and both retire at age 65. They plan to have two children, one in 2001 and one in

TABLE 7. Comparing Recommendations From ESPlanner (ESP) and Quicken Financial Planner (QFP)

A. A Young, Low Income Couple

Age of Husband	Age of Wife	Consumption (Living Expenses)		Taxable Saving		Taxes		Taxable Assets		Wife's Tax-Deferred Assets		Husband's Life Insurance		Wife's Life Insurance	
		QFP	ESP	QFP	ESP	QFP	ESP	QFP	ESP	QFP	ESP	QFP	ESP	QFP	ESP
35	35	26,920	26,866	7,863	5,424	19,901	20,355	21,683	19,845	4,419	4,380	340,000	242,122	340,000	236,396
45	45	26,920	38,500	16,947	3,447	19,222	16,812	132,998	46,839	18,400	17,984	N.C.	169,566	N.C.	197,139
65	65	26,920	26,866	21,667	(797)	16,439	312	374,766	43,794	64,356	59,321	N.C.	25,735	N.C.	31,197
85	85	26,920	26,866	(16,730)	(2,414)	3,083	96	266,097	11,375	35,592	15,489	N.C.	9,477	N.C.	10,813
90	90	13,460	26,866	0	(1,030)	3,316	7	0	0	3,013	0	N.C.	0	N.C.	0

B. A Middle-Aged, Upper Income Couple

Age of Husband	Age of Wife	Consumption (Living Expenses)		Taxable Saving		Taxes		Taxable Assets		Couple's Tax-Deferred Assets		Husband's Life Insurance		Wife's Life Insurance	
		QFP	ESP	QFP	ESP	QFP	ESP	QFP	ESP	QFP	ESP	QFP	ESP	QFP	ESP
39	40	39,390	48,909	102,508	57,063	48,366	70,217	324,909	289,328	262,661	262,162	960,000	474,795	0	0
45	46	39,390	48,909	21,883	4,526	30,154	28,969	494,700	366,871	411,295	411,486	N.C.	184,907	N.C.	0
65	66	39,390	35,925	0	0	11,804	7,364	0	0	843,756	675,978	N.C.	0	N.C.	0
85	86	39,390	41,823	(623)	194	10,191	7,468	1,489	3,130	343,461	288,373	N.C.	0	N.C.	0
95	Deceased	21,008	28,683	0	0	5,781	6,710	0	0	1,325	0	N.C.	0	N.C.	0

C. An Older, Very High Income Couple

Age of Husband	Age of Wife	Consumption (Living Expenses)		Taxable Saving		Taxes		Taxable Assets		Couple's Tax-Deferred Assets		Husband's Life Insurance		Wife's Life Insurance	
		QFP	ESP	QFP	ESP	QFP	ESP	QFP	ESP	QFP	ESP	QFP	ESP	QFP	ESP
64	57	186,880	204,510	(138,380)	(317,615)	237,681	182,449	2,608,876	2,566,384	835,135	835,135	0	0	0	0
75	68	186,880	204,510	64,289	(64,357)	110,389	131,659	2,474,844	1,815,234	1,005,179	1,086,296	N.C.	0	N.C.	0
85	78	186,880	204,510	(37,627)	(133,145)	74,006	55,720	1,958,129	799,840	748,607	980,869	N.C.	0	N.C.	0
Deceased	90	24,917	127,819	0	(118,883)	8,961	46	0	0	7,131	0	0	0	0	0

Source: Gokhale, Kotlikoff, and Warshawski (1999).

Notes: N.C. – not computed. QFP does not allow employer's matching contribution to a tax-deferred account to reflect inflation-induced pay increases.

2003. The husband earns $43,000 initially, declining by 2001 to $35,000 and staying constant in real terms thereafter. The wife earns $37,000 in 1999, zero in 2000, $35,000 in 2001, $36,000 in 2002, $37,000 in 2003, and $38,000 thereafter. The husband receives a gift from his father of $10,000 in 1999 and 2000 (in current dollars). Special expenditures include truck loan payments of $4,500 in 1999 and 2000. The couple also plan to spend $20,000 on college tuition for each child between the ages 19 and 22. The couple allocate $5,000 for each spouse's funeral, but do not wish to leave incremental bequests over and above the level necessary to assure survivors of an undiminished living standard. The couple's current assets include $14,000 in taxable accounts as well as $3,000 in an IRA under the wife's name. The wife intends to contribute $1,200 to her IRA annually until she retires. She will begin withdrawing funds from her IRA at age 65 in equal annual installments. The couple purchases a house in 1999 for $150,000, making a down payment of $15,000 and taking out a $135,000, 30-year mortgage. Monthly mortgage payments total $990 including principal and interest. Annual housing expenses include $2,500 in property taxes, $400 in homeowner's insurance payments, and $2,000 in maintenance. Both spouses will begin collecting social security retirement benefits at age 65. All calculations presented incorporate ESPlanner's default assumptions concerning economic parameters, including a 6 percent nominal interest rate on taxable and nontaxable assets, a 3 percent inflation rate, and a nonnegativity constraint on nonhousing wealth (equivalently, no unsecured borrowing).

If the couple follows ESPlanner's recommendations, Table 7 shows it will never encounter liquidity constraints nor will it ever accumulate a significant stock of taxable assets. The couple is advised to consume $26,866 initially, and $38,500 when both children are present. QFP, on the other hand, recommends constant consumption of $26,920 as long as both spouses are living, irrespective of whether children are present. We would propose that our model's recommendation is more reasonable since spending and saving decisions account for the costs of childrearing. Both programs indicate that husband and wife should have similar life insurance holdings, reflecting their similar economic contributions to the household. Nevertheless ESP recommends significantly less life insurance than QFP.

Case B: A Middle-Aged, Upper Income Couple

For this case, we assume that the wife is 40 years old and the husband 39, in 1999. The couple reside in Massachusetts with two children, one born in 1991 and the other 1993. The wife does not work, while the husband earns $200,000 in 1999 and 2000. Starting in 2001 and continuing until his retirement at age 55, the husband expects to earn $100,000. They plan to send each of their children to college for four years at a cost of $30,000 per child per year. They allocate $5,000 for each spouse's funeral, but they do not wish to leave incremental bequests above the level necessary to assure survivors of an undiminished living standard. The couple's taxable assets are $225,500. The wife has an IRA with a 1999 balance of $84,700, and the husband has a 401(k) with a 1999 balance of $148,000. Both plan to withdraw their nontaxable assets (thereby making them subsequently taxable) at age 59. The couple currently saves $11,765 per year in taxable forms. The husband plans to contribute $9,500 to his 401(k) plan each year and expects his employer to contribute $6,000. The wife does not intend to make additional IRA contributions. The couple owns a $475,000 house with annual property taxes of $5,200, annual maintenance of $1,500, and annual homeowner's insurance of $500. They have 29 years remaining on a 30-year mortgage; their current mortgage balance stands at $170,000 and they pay $1,131 per month. Each spouse intends to begin receiving his/her social security retirement benefits at age 62.

QFP's and ESPlanner's recommendations for consumption, taxable saving, and life insurance differ dramatically, as is clear from Table 7. For example, QFP recommends more than twice as much insurance on the husband's life, and this is traceable to several factors. First, ESPlanner recomments that spending should decline sharplyw hen the children leave the household, so initial consumption (with children present) exceeds that recommended by QFP. Second, ESPlanner's estimate of the couple's short-term tax liabilities is significantly higher than QFP's, due to our treatment of Massachusetts income taxes, which impose high rates on capital income. Third, QFP does not allow the employer's matching 401(k) contribution to rise with inflation-induced increases in pay, while our model does. Finally, QFP's social security benefit estimates are lower than ours.

Case C: An Older, High Income Couple

In this case, the husband is 64 years old, the wife is 57, and the husband intends to work for two more years, earning close to $400,000 over this period. The couple have a variety of large special expenses in the short run, including an expensive home renovation. The husband has two pensions providing almost $200,000 (nominal) annually; he expects to begin receiving this income as soon as he retires. The couple each allocates $5,000 in funeral expenses, and the couple also wants to provide gifts or bequests for the children totaling $2 million as of 2025. The couple's taxable net worth is close to $3 million. The wife has a small IRA account, and the husband has a 401(k) account worth close to three-quarters of a million dollars. Each spouse elects to withdraw the smallest amount of funds permitted by law from these tax-favored accounts. The couple own a house with a market value of $1.2 million; annual property taxes, maintenance, and homeowner's insurance total $6,000, $13,000, and $1,000, respectively. They have 25 years remaining on a 30-year mortgage; their current mortage balance is

$525,000, and they pay $3,318 per month. The couple plans to sell its home in 2025 and thereafter rent a home for $4,000 per month.

Neither model prescribes life insurance for either spouse in this case, but recommendations for consumption and saving diverge considerably. According to our software, the household can spend $204,510 in 1999 (on items other than housing, taxes, life insurance premiums, and special expenditures), whereas QFP indicates that it should spend no more than $186,880. This discrepancy is mainly attributable to the treatment of taxes: ESPlanner's estimate of the couple's 1999 tax liabilities is $182,449, whereas QFP's estimate is $237,681. This 30 percent difference is apparently attributable to the deductibility of certain special expenditures which ESPlanner recognizes, while QFP does not. ESPlanner's estimate of the couple's tax liabilities actually exceeds QFP's by the time the husband reaches age 75, but then it falls below QFP's. Due in part to the presence of very large, short-term special expenditures on home remodeling not captured by QFP, ES-Planner recommends that the couple dissave $317,615 in 1999. In contrast, QFP recommends that the couple dissave only $138,380.

Implications

As these results demonstrate, it is extremely difficult to achieve consumption smoothing with traditional financial planning tools, even when one uses these tools in a relatively sophisticated way. Households that rely on these tools could easily experience significant, predictable, unintended, and avoidable changes in living standards over the course of their lives. We must also underscore the importance of accurate financial planning. Economic research indicates that people are able to change their financial decision making in response to information and guidance, particularly when provided through employers.[6]

How Much Should Americans Save as They Approach Retirement?[7]

Over the next two decades, a significant fraction of Americans belonging to the 75-million-member baby boom generation will reach retirement age. Impending retirement magnifies the importance of saving, particularly for those who are currently over age 50. Moreover, in planning for retirement, boomers must recognize the possibility that fiscal pressures may eventually force cuts in social security benefits. Short-term surpluses notwithstanding, the social security system is seriously underfunded. That is, benefits may have to be cut to ensure system solvency within baby boomers' lifetimes.

To understand how this may influence baby boomer needs for retirement saving, Bernheim et al. (2000) apply the ESPlanner model to a sample of individuals drawn from the Health and Retirement Study. Recommended levels of saving are contrasted under two alternative policies. In the first, a "base case" scenario Congress avoids reductions in social security benefits. In the second, "fiscal distress" scenario, Congress is forced to reduce benefits by 30 percent in 2015.

The Health and Retirement Study (HRS) Sample

The 1992 wave of the Health and Retirement Study (HRS) collected information on a nationally representative sample of Americans age 51–61 and their spouses of any age. The survey contains a great deal of economic and demographic data, and additional information required by ESPlanner is imputed following Bernheim et al. (1999). The analysis is restricted to households satisfying the following criteria: (1) the head's age was between 51 and 61 in 1992; (2) information on social security earnings in past covered employment is available for both the head and the spouse (if any); and (3) the respondent answered all critical survey questions. We excluded an additional 141 because their economic resources were insufficient to cover their housing costs and other off-the-top expenditures. Our analysis consists of 1,714 married couples and 1,145 single individuals.

Recommended Saving Rates

Our median recommended saving patterns for HRS households appear in Table 8. The saving rate is defined as non-tax-favored saving divided by income; we note that this measure of saving excludes contributions to, or withdrawals from, retirement accounts. Our measure of income also excludes net contributions to tax-favored accounts. We sort heads into two age groups — 50–55 and 56–61 — and then further stratify the sample based on household income, marital status, race, and education. We present results for both social security policy scenarios. Our calculations assume a 6 percent nominal interest rate and a 3 percent inflation rate.

Consider first the base case policy scenario which involves no social security benefit cuts. If we focus for the moment on Panel A, for the 50 to 55 year-old age group, we note that the median recommended saving rate for those with incomes below $15,000 is very small — only one percent. For those with incomes over $100,000, the median recommended saving rate is fairly high, 17 percent. For middle income households, those with incomes between $15,000 and $45,000, and those with incomes between $45,000 and $100,000, the median recommended saving rates are 13 and 14 percent respectively. The strong positive relation between recommended saving rates and income is, in large part, attributable to the progressive structure of the social security benefit formula, which provides lower income individuals with significantly higher rates of earnings replacement. In the older subsample (ages 56–61), we find again that median recommended saving rates

TABLE 8. Median Recommended Non-Tax-Favored Saving Rates in the HRS (ratio of non tax-favored saving to income by income and demographic group)

	$0 to $15,000			$15,000 to $45,000			$45,000 to $100,000			Over $100,000		
	Full Benefits	Benefit Cut	N	Full Benefits	Benefit Cut	s	Full Benefits	Benefit Cut	N	Full Benefits	Benefit Cut	N
A. Age 50–55												
Total Sample	.01	.06	243	.13	.20	533	.14	.19	502	.17	.20	116
Married	.00	.10	37	.09	.17	272	.14	.19	429	.17	.20	111
Single	.01	.05	206	.17	.24	261	.20	.24	73	.28	.29	5
Non-White	.02	.06	126	.19	.25	169	.18	.22	61	.21	.23	17
Non-College	.01	.05	226	.13	.20	445	.16	.21	317	.18	.21	52
B. Age 56–61												
Total Sample	.00	.03	320	.17	.23	582	.20	.25	454	.23	.25	109
Married	−.11	.01	48	.14	.21	310	.20	.25	408	.23	.25	99
Single	.02	.03	272	.23	.28	272	.23	.26	46	.19	.20	10
Non-White	.01	.02	153	.23	.29	153	.24	.30	56	.06	.08	8
Non-College	.00	.03	303	.18	.24	474	.22	.27	290	.23	.26	50

Source: Bernheim et al. (2000) using HRS 1992 data.

increase sharply with income. With the exception of the lowest income group, these rates also rise steeply with age; they range from 17 percent for older households with incomes of $15,000–$45,000, to 23 percent for older households with incomes over $100,000.

To some extent, households can achieve these saving rate targets by reinvesting income earned from previously accumulated assets. It is therefore natural to wonder whether reinvested capital income is sufficient to reach the targets, or whether households must also put away significant fractions of take-home pay. To examine this issue, we calculate recommended rates of saving for non-asset income. Specifically, we adjusted the recommended saving rates by subtracting non-tax-favored capital income from both the numerator and the denominator of the ratio. For the lowest and second lowest income segments of both age groups, median recommended saving rates are essentially unchanged. For households with incomes from $45,000–$100,000, the adjustment reduces the median recommended saving rate among younger households from 13 percent to 12 percent, and leaves the median recommended saving rate among older households unchanged at 17 percent. Hence, our model indicates that most older households do need to save significant fractions of non-asset income.

Rcommended saving rates tend to be higher for single individuals, nonwhites, and those without college education. For example, among nonwhite households aged 56–61 with incomes of $15,000–$45,000, the median recommended saving rate is 23 percent. This is six percentage points higher than the corresponding rate for whites and nonwhites combined. Likewise, in the same age and income group, the median recommended saving rate is 23 for single households, compared with 14 percent for married couples. Though these systematic differences are important, we note that they also mask considerable variation within groups.

The impact of potential social security benefit cuts. We have also completed recommended saving rates for the second "fiscal distress" policy scenario, in which social security benefits are cut by 30 percent as of 2015. The results in Table 8 differ dramatically from those of the base case scenario. Consider, for example, married households in the lowest income category. The median recommended rate of saving rises by 10 percentage points for the younger age group, and by 12 points for the older group. In the second lowest income group, recommended saving rates rise by eight and seven percentage points, respectively, for the younger and older age groups. Among high income households, the increases are smaller but still important. Recommended rates of saving out of non-asset income also rise sharply; for the middle income groups, these rates range from 16 to 22 percent.

Alternative assumptions: lifespan, market performance, retirement, and nursing home care. Table 9 explores the sensitivity of results to several alternative assumptions.[8] First, we recalculate recommended saving rates assuming a maximum lifespan (for both the respondent and the spouse) of 100, rather

TABLE 9. Median Recommended Non-Tax-Favored Saving Rates with Alternative
Assumptions (Ration of Non-Tax-Favored Saving to Income by Income
and Demographic Group)

		Annual Income		
	$0–$15,000	$15,000–$45,000	$45,000–$100,000	Over $100,000
Married Age 50–55				
Base Case	.00	.09	.14	.17
Fiscal Distress	.10	.17	.19	.20
Max. Age = 100	.01	.10	.15	.19
Assets Drop 30%	.01	.10	.15	.20
Ret. 2 Yrs Early	−.01	.14	.17	.19
Nursing Home	.20	.18	.18	.20
All of the Above	.39	.32	.29	.29
Married Age 56–61				
Base Case	−.11	.14	.20	.23
Fiscal Distress	.01	.21	.25	.25
Max. Age = 100	−.09	.16	.21	.24
Assets Drop 30%	−.09	.14	.22	.24
Ret. 2 Yrs Early	−.12	.15	.19	.23
Nursing Home	.19	.25	.25	.25
All of the above	.31	.35	.32	.32
Single Age 50–55				
Base Case	.01	.17	.20	.28
Fiscal Distress	.05	.24	.24	.29
Max. Age = 100	.03	.18	.21	.30
Assets Drop 30%	.01	.19	.21	.32
Ret. 2 Yrs Early	.03	.23	.24	.31
Nursing Home	.19	.23	.23	.29
All of the Above	.31	.36	.32	.39
Single Age 56–61				
Base Case	.02	.23	.23	.19
Fiscal Distress	.03	.28	.26	.20
Max. Age = 100	.07	.24	.24	.21
Assets Drop 30%	.02	.24	.27	.31
Ret. 2 Yrs Early	.00	.23	.23	.22
Nursing Home	.32	.29	.26	.20
All of the Above	.33	.37	.33	.39

Source: Authors' calculations based on HRS (1992).

than 95. Second, we assume that there is an immediate 30 percent decline in the market value of stocks and other financial assets, after which these assets earn the same return as in our base case. Third, for each household, we accelerate retirement by two years. Fourth, we assume that respondents and spouses must each accumulate a reserve fund sufficient to defray the costs of nursing home care at $15,000 per year for five years (in current dollars). We recognize that the cost of nursing home care may exceed $15,000 per year; however, other spending presumably declines when an individual is institutionalized, so the $15,000 figure is intended to represent the net increment to total expenditures. Finally, we consider the combined effects of all of these assumptions, along with the fiscal distress scenario examined previously.[9] For purposes of comparison, Table 9 also summarizes findings for the base case and fiscal distress scenarios, where the latter requires a social security benefit cut.

The evidence reveals that the fourth assumption, saving for nursing home care, has the largest impact on recommended saving rates. It is particularly important for those with the lowest levels of income, raising recommended median saving rates by 18 to 30 percentage points. These figures may be somewhat exaggerated, in that low income families are more inclined to rely on Medicaid, even though this tends to reduce the quality of care received. Nevertheless, our results suggest more generally that low income families may need to save at high rates if they wish to establish nontrivial emergency funds. Increasing the maximum lifespan from 95 to 100 years has a more modest effect on median recommended saving rates, which generally rise by 1 to 2 percentage points, with the exception of older, low income, single individuals, for whom the increase is 5 percentage points. A 30 percent decline in asset values also has a relatively small effect on recommended savings rates, except among high-income households. Finally, accelerating retirement by two years has a sizable impact on recommendations for particular subgroups. For example, the median recommended saving rate rises by five percentage points for married couples between the ages of 50 and 55, with incomes between $15,000 and $45,000. In some groups, recommended saving stays constant or declines. This occurs because the acceleration of retirement renders some households unable to cover housing expenses and other off-the-top commitments.

When we consider the combined effects of all four assumptions, along with the benefit cut scenario, recommended median saving rates rise dramatically for all subgroups, from 30 to 40 percent. For example, among the lowest income married couples, the median recommended saving rate increases from zero to 39 percent. Moreover, the numbr of households with infeasible planning problems (that is, those who can no longer cover off-the-top expenditures) rises from 141 to 346. This statistic sheds additional light on the degree of undersaving and financial vulnerability among HRS households.

Comparisons with Prior Studies

Previous studies have explored the adequacy of saving patterns using different data and/or alternative methodologies.[10]

Kotlikoff et al. (1983) compare the level of consumption that a household could have sustained over its entire lifetime given its total resources, with the level of consumption that it can sustain over its remaining lifetime given its remaining resources. Absent Social Security, they conclude that a significant fraction of the elderly will suffer a decline in living standard during old age. Actual asset profiles among baby boomers are compared with recommended asset profiles generated by a stylized life cycle model by Bernheim (1994), and there typical baby boomers are found to be saving only one-third of what is required to maintain living standards. Bernheim and Scholz (1993) compare changes in wealth and asset profiles with the predictions of a life cycle model, and they find evidence of inadequate saving among individuals without college education. Warshawsky and Ameriks (2000) use Quicken Financial Planner to assess saving adequacy, concluding that more than half of the households examined would run out of money prematurely if they tried to maintain the living standards that they enjoyed in 1992.

A paper closely related to the resent analysis Moore and Mitchell (2000), which calculates saving needed to maintain preretirement living standards for a sample of HRS households. Their methodology differs from ours in that they assume that people treat housing as a fungible store of wealth, whereas we assume that older individuals retain their homes until death. The available evidence is sparse but favors the latter assumption: thus Venti and Wise (this volume) conclude that "very little reduction in home equity . . . can be construed as converting home equity to liquid assets for purposes of supporting non-housing consumption." Likewise, Caplin (this volume) finds that few individuals use reverse mortgages to convert housing equity into income streams for the purpose of supporting consumption expenditure. Despite this difference (and others), Moore and Mitchell's principal finding — that the median HRS household needs to save 16 percent more of its income to preserve its living standard — is consistent with our results.

Conclusions and Discussion

Traditional financial planning models are based on targeted saving. This approach requires a household to choose future spending or income levels, and then to save to meet associated targets. Since setting an appropriate target is a highly complex problem, households are often encouraged to rely on rough rules of thumb, even though this may not produce a smooth and sustainable living standard. Our alternative method of financial planning is rooted in economic theory and does not require households to undertake complex aspects of planning by themselves. Instead, our software derives a saving target for each household by determining its highest sustainable living standard, as well as the levels of saving and life insurance needed to preserve that living standard.

It is interesting that this economic approach to financial planning, embodied in our ESPlanner package, generates different recommendations from the traditional approach (typified by Quicken Financial Planner). Although the differences in saving recommendations are large, they are not systematically high or low. For some households, the traditional model recommends far too little saving compared with our model; for others, it recommends far too much. Differences in life insurance recommendations are also typically large, but they tend to be more systematic, with the traditional approach generally overstating life insurance requirements. Applying our model to a sample of several thousand households, we find that most older Americans approaching retirement need to save at quite high rates — rates that are much higher than those commonly observed. Our conclusion is strengthened once we account for potential cuts in social security benefits, gains in longevity, stock market declines, and the costs of nursing home care.

Notes

We are grateful to the National Institute of Aging for research support and to Economic Security Planning, Inc. for permitting the use of Economic Security Planner (ESPlanner) in this study. Opinions expressed in this paper are solely those of the authors.

1. The developers of the ESPlanner software package are Douglas Bernheim, Jagadeesh Gokhale, Laurence Kotlikoff, and Lowell Williams and the product is available through Economic Security Planning, Inc. at MIT Press. For additional information see ⟨www.esplanner.com⟩. This paper draws on and extends Gokhale et al. (1999) and Bernheim et al. (2000).

2. To speed data entry, users may elect a default that sets the contingent earnings path equal to the joint-survivor path. Users may specify future income in either present-year (real) dollars, or future-year (nominal) dollars.

3. To speed data entry, users may elect a default that sets the contingent expenditures and receipts equal to the joint-survivor values. Users may specify future expenditures and receipts in either present-year (real) dollars, or future-year (nominal) dollars.

4. Negative life insurance is formally identical to the purchase of an inverted life annuity, that is, the receipt of annual payments for life purchased by the estate of the deceased in a predetermined lump sum amount.

5. ESPlanner produces several main reports including current recommendations, annual recommendations, non-tax-favored balance sheet, income, spending, non-asset income (for each spouse), housing, taxes, tax-favored balance sheets (for each spouse), estate reports (for each spouse and for couples if both spouses die in the same year), social security benefit reports (for the household and for each spouse). ESPlanner's survivor reports are essentially the same as the main reports.

6. See Bernheim and Garrett (1999); Bayer, Bernheim, and Scholz (1996); Bernheim (1998); and Clark and Schieber (1998).

7. This section draws and extends on Bernheim et al. (2000).

8. Qualitatively similar conclusions follow for plausible alternative values of the key economic parameters. For example, with an 8 percent nominal (5 percent real) rate of return, the median recommended saving rates for 50–55-year-olds are respectively 1, 11, 11, and 10 percent for the first through fourth income categories. The corresponding figures from Table 8 are 1, 13, 14, and 17 percent. For 56–61-year-olds, median recommended saving rates with the higher rate of return are respectively 1, 16, 17, and 20 percent for the first through fourth income categories. The comparable figures from Table 8 are 0, 17, 20, and 23 percent. Thus, recommended saving rates are lower with the higher interest rate. However, recommendations are still highly sensitive to assumptions about social security benefits. For our second policy scenario, median recommended saving rates among 56–61-year-olds are respectively 4, 17, 16, and 12 percent for the first through fourth income categories, assuming a nominal return of 8 percent. Among 50 to 55 year olds, the comparable figures are 3, 21, 21, and 22 percent. Each of these rates is significantly higher than the corresponding figure for the base case policy scenario.

9. Another important possibility is that tax rates may rise in the future, particularly if the social security system runs into fiscal problems. This consideration would magnify the need for saving, thereby reinforcing our conclusions.

10. Some research disputes the view that U.S. households tend to save too little. For instance, Manchester (1994) concluded that members of the baby boom generation accumulated wealth more rapidly than did their parents, while Hubbard et al. (1994) argue that low saving may be optimal for many low income households, in that saving may adversely affect eligibility for Medicaid and other income-support programs. Engen et al. (1999) point out that apparent instances of low saving sometimes result from transitory periods of low income. They also claim that the age trajectory of median net worth matches or exceeds the predictions of a stylized life cycle model.

References

Bayer, Patrick J., B. Douglas Bernheim, and John Karl Scholz. 1996. "The Effects of Financial Education in the Workplace: Evident from a Survey of Employers." Mimeo, Stanford University.

Bernheim, B. Douglas. 1994. "The Adequacy of Saving for Retirement and the Role of Economic Literacy." In *Retirement in the 21st Century . . . Ready Or Not . . .* Washington, D.C.: Employee Benefit Research Institute. 73–81.

———. 1998. "Financial Illiteracy, Education, and Retirement Saving." In *Living with Defined Contribution Pensions*, ed. Olivia S. Mitchell and Sylvester J. Schieber. Pension Research Council. Philadelphia: University of Pennsylvania Press. 38–68.

Bernheim, B. Douglas, Lorenzo Forni, Jagadeesh Gokhale, and Laurence J. Kotlikoff. 1999. "The Adequacy of Life Insurance: Evidence from the Health and Retirement Survey." NBER Working Paper 7372. October.

———. 2000. "How Much Should Americans Be Saving for Retirement?" *American Economic Review* 90, 2 (May): 288–92.

Bernheim, B. Douglas and Daniel Garrett. 1999. "The Determinants and Consequences of Financial Education in the Workplace: Evidence from a Survey of Households." Mimeo, Stanford University.

Bernheim, B. Douglas and John Karl Scholz. 1993. "Private Saving and Public Policy." *Tax Policy and the Economy* 7: 73–110.

Caplin, Andrew. This volume. "The Reverse Mortgage Market: Problems and Prospects."

Clark, Robert L. and Sylvester J. Scheiber. 1998. "Factors Affecting Participation Rates and Contribution Levels in 401(k) Plans." In *Living with Defined Contribution Pensions,* ed. Olivia S. Mitchell, and Sylvester J. Schieber. Pension Research Council. Philadelphia: University of Pennsylvania Press. 69–97.

Engen, Eric M., William G. Gale, and Cori E. Uccello. 1999. "The Adequacy of Household Saving." *Brookings Papers on Economic Activity* 2: 65–165.

Gokhale, Jagadeesh, Laurence J. Kotlikoff, and Mark J. Warshawsky. 1999. "Comparing the Conventional and Economic Approaches to Financial Planning." NBER Working Paper 7321. August.

Hubbard, Glen R., Jonathan Skinner, and Stephen P. Zeldes. 1994. "The Importance of Precautionary Motives in Explaining Individual and Aggregate Saving." *Carnegie-Rochester Conference Series on Public Policy* 40 (June): 59–125.

Kotlikoff, Laurence J., Avia Spivak, and Lawrence H. Summers. 1982. "The Adequacy of Savings." *American Economic Review* 72, 5 (December): 1056–69.

Lundberg, Shelly. 1999. "Family Bargaining and Retirement Behavior." In *Behavioral Economics and Retirement Policy,* ed. Henry Aaron. Washington, D.C.: Brookings Institution.

Manchester, Joyce. 1994. "Baby Boomers in Retirement: An Early Perspective." In *Retirement in the 21st Century . . . Ready Or Not . . .* Washington, D.C.: Employee Benefit Research Institute. 63–67.

Mitchell, Olivia S. and James F. Moore. 1998. "Retirement Wealth Accumulation and Decumulation: New Developments and Outstanding Opportunities." *Journal of Risk and Insurance* 65, 3 (December): 371–400.

Moore, James F. and Olivia S. Mitchell. 2000. "Projected Retirement Wealth and Saving Adequacy." In *Forecasting Retirement Needs and Retirement Wealth,* ed. Olivia S. Mitchell, P. Brett Hammond, and Anna M. Rappaport. Pension Research Council. Philadelphia: University of Pennsylvania Press. 68–94.

Venti, Steven F. and David A. Wise. This volume. "Patterns of Housing Equity Use Among the Elderly."

Warshawsky, Mark J. and John Ameriks. 2000. "How Prepared Are Americans for Retirement?" In *Forecasting Retirement Needs and Retirement Wealth,* ed. Olivia S. Mitchell, P. Brett Hammond, and Anna M. Rappaport. Pension Research Council. Philadelphia: University of Pennsylvania Press. 33–67.

Chapter 5
Retirement Planning and the Asset/Salary Ratio

Martin L. Leibowitz, J. Benson Durham, P. Brett Hammond, and Michael Heller

In this era of individual responsibility for retirement security, interest in retirement income adequacy is at an all-time high. Concern over low U.S. personal savings rates and the possibility of social security system insolvency prompt this interest, in concert with the growth of popular alternatives to traditional defined benefit plans, the introduction of retirement savings education programs, and the development of new individual retirement software products. Such interest has generated a wide array of research studies. A first group asks whether Americans in specific age cohorts, employment situations, pension plans, and income and wealth categories are saving enough for retirement (e.g., Moore and Mitchell 2000; Gale and Sabelhaus 1999; Samwick and Skinner 1998). The second type of research focuses on how retirement savers allocate contributions and accumulations among asset classes and investment vehicles, and the effects of such allocations on future retirement income (e.g., Ameriks and Zeldes 2000). Finally, a third set of studies asks how individual workers or families ascertain whether they are in the retirement savings "ballpark," especially when retirement may be years away (e.g., Bernheim et al., this volume).

This chapter seeks to extend thinking about asset adequacy by constructing and testing a simple measure of retirement savings adequacy that is analogous to (but not identical to) the *funding ratio* concept used in defined benefit pension plans. Our hope is that this measure, which compares required assets-in-hand to salary, will provide retirement savers with a rough indication of where they stand on the path to adequate retirement income.

We call our measure the *Asset/Salary Ratio*, a breakeven number similar to but simpler than tools such as an income replacement ratio, a life cycle consumption model, or a stochastic asset return model. It does not embody the sophistication of these other tools, but it does have the advantage of enabling individuals to determine at a glance whether they are on track for a faroff retirement. As such, it has the advantages of simplicity, and all attendant caveats associated with simplifying the complexities of nature and finance.

Funding Measures in the Defined Benefit Environment

The Asset/Salary Ratio reflects, but is not identical to, concepts and methods widely used to measure the overall funding status of a defined benefit (DB) pension plan. In the DB world, a plan manager is responsible for ensuring that future annual revenues cover future annual pension payments. In other words, the job of the pension manager is to match required assets to the present value of future liabilities for all covered employees, where the liabilities depend on all employees' eventual credited service, final or final average salary, and an accrual percentage (Leibowitz, Bader, and Kogelman 1996b). There are several ways to define a defined benefit plan's funding ratio (*FR*), but a common one is the current market or actuarial value of a pension fund's assets (i.e., a weighted average of book versus market value) divided by the discounted value of the plan's future liabilities (actuaries often call this the "actuarial accrued liability").[1] For example, a state government DB retirement system might use a variation of the following basic measure to determine funding progress and the overall financial status of the plan:

(1) $$\text{FR}_t = \frac{\text{Assets}_t}{\text{PV Future Liabilities}_t}.$$

If FR >1, this could indice that the plan currently enjoys a funding *surplus* (an excess of assets over liabilities). A plan with FR >1 should theoretically be well funded as long as the investment and actuarial assumptions that underlie it continue to be validated by subsequent experience. In contrast, when FR <1, there is a need for incremental funding to bring the required level of assets up to match the estimate of discounted future liabilities.

Over time a plan's funding ratio may change as it is affected by new experience, such as changes in inflation, mortality, retirement rates, salaries, and other actuarial gains and losses, all of which can affect future liabilities. Also, unexpected changes in investment returns could affect the future value of the assets. As a result, the funding ratio should be examined regularly to assess the probability of a shortfall due to investment or actuarial experience differing from the model's initial characterization (Leibowitz, Bader, and Kogelman 1996a). Even at its most basic, this concept can direct a plan manager's attention to a crucial issue associated with pension plan solvency, namely the ability of the plan to meet the obligations it has incurred. The DB funding ratio, as well as expected and unexpected changes in it, can provide signals for managers, such as the need to consider whether contribution rates and/or investment strategy should be adjusted.

Funding Measures in a Defined Contribution Case

In the defined contribution (DC) pension plan case, we would like to construct a simpler measure of an individual retirement saver's retirement funding adequacy. We suggest that a DC funding ratio can be conceived of, under normal circumstances, as the relationship between assets and a present-value liability measure. A key difference between DB and DC pensions, of course, is that different parties bear responsibility for achieving and maintaining the asset-liability match. Another difference between the plan types is how the liabilities are characterized. Usually, DB plans are characterized by the pooling of investment and actuarial risk, whereas DC plans do so in very limited ways or not at all. DC plans trade off pooling of retirement income certainty for a greater individual investment and actuarial control.

In the DC context, our interest focuses on the role of the individual saver rather than the employer or employer pension plan. This is because, even though DC plan rules apply to all covered employees, any given employee can be thought of as acting as his or her own plan sponsor and provider. As such, the individual takes on certain increased risks in a DC plan, making investment choices and facing market risks associated with those choices (within plan limits). On the other hand, DC participants do retain the choice of whether or not to join the mortality pool by annuitizing their accumulated assets at retirement. If they choose not to annuitize, they face greater mortality risk since the "pool" would then essentially represent a sample of one (Brown et al. 2001 and this volume).

Thus in a DC plan it is the individual rather than his or her employer who must be responsible for and concerned with retirement plan "solvency," i.e., the match between an individual's assets and liabilities at retirement. Therefore, we believe that an individual's DC pension income can be related to a kind of Asset/Salary Ratio. Taking the DB funding ratio relationship in (1) as a starting point, we translate the asset figure or numerator directly into the DC context: the individual's current marked-to-market pension accumulations or assets are equivalent to the DB plan assets. An analogous individual liability figure for the denominator in (1), however, is less transparent. Unlike a DB plan, there is no formula that tells an individual in a DC plan exactly how much income he will receive at retirement, based on service and salary. In the strict sense, the asset-liability ratio in a DC plan, unlike a DB plan, is always inherently equal to 1, since by definition the individual's liabilities are always equal to his or her accumulated assets in the plan. Nevertheless we seek to measure that would indicate whether the individual was "on track" for achieving an adequate retirement income, in the spirit of a DB funding ratio.

Despite the lack of a specific, contractual promise in the DC context, some well understood and often recommended targets are helpful in pro-jecting retirement income needs. A useful one is the income replacement ratio (RR), or the proportion of preretirement income that a retiree can replace with a payout annuity purchased at the time of retirement (Heller and King 1989, 1994). The replacement ratio is, of course, closely related to the notion of a funding ratio at the point of retirement, in that both are dependent on projections of salary growth, investment returns, annuity purchase costs, contribution rates, and lengths of covered employment. A precise mathematical relationship can be used to calculate the income re-placement ratio (see Appendix A). We note that the replacement ratio is particularly sensitive to the difference between investment earnings rate and salary growth rate. For example, with an annual contribution rate of 10 percent of salary and a retirement payout annuity based on a six percent interest rate, a person who spends 30 years in a DC plan where investment returns exceed salary growth by three percent per year will achieve an in-come replacement ratio of about 40 percent of final preretirement income. This compares to only a 20 percent replacement ratio if salary growth and investment returns were equal to each other.

In addition to its use in making projections, the replacement ratio can be used to set retirement saving and investment goals. For example, the Ameri-can Association of University Professors and the American Association of Colleges recommend that educational institutions design pension plans to enable employees to replace about two-thirds of their inflation-adjusted annual disposable salary (averaged over the last few full-time work years) through a combination of pension annuity income and social security bene-fits (American Association of University Professors 1990). This policy was reaffirmed by a National Academy of Sciences committee in 1991 (Ham-mond and Morgan 1991). This two-thirds clearly is a "one-size-fits-all" ap-proach that overlooks variations in life cycle circumstances, though it does provide a starting point for planning purposes. Slightly higher targets were recommended by Palmer (1993), using tax and social security benefit rules and consumer expenditure data. He proposed that required income re-placement ratios for individuals and married couples range from 70 to 80 percent of gross preretirement income.[2]

Building on this work, we take a conservative approach by selecting an overall retirement income target of 75 percent. If we further assume that social security benefits will pick up about 25 percent of the total, then an average individual or couple with a DC plan would need the pension to produce about 50 percent of annual preretirement income. Low income workers might need a lower ratio than the 50 percent target, and very high income workers might require a higher ratio to achieve an overall 75 per-cent replacement ratio, because social security benefits are progressive. Starting with 50 percent as a target pension replacement ratio, it is then possible to solve for any one of the other variables that go into it—the needed contribution rate, years of service, or difference between invest-ment earnings and salary growth rates.

Nevertheless, a key challenge facing a retirement planner is to evaluate how alternative circumstances and actions can influence future financial viability. For this reason we propose that the DB plan funding ratio ap-proach could help people develop a sense of whether they are on track for retirement. Accordingly, we recast the DB funding ratio for a participant in a DC plan as follows:

$$(2) \qquad\qquad ASR_t = \frac{A_t}{S_t} .$$

This says that the Asset/Salary Ratio (ASR) is the liability (assets) divided by an individual's annual salary S at t years before retirement.[3] This Asset/Salary Ratio can be thought of in two ways: as a person's *current* Asset/Salary Ratio or as the Asset/Salary Ratio *required* to achieve a target income re-placement ratio in the future.

What does the Asset/Salary Ratio mean? How can a ratio of assets to salary tell an individual anything about the adequacy of his or her retire-ment savings? It should be noted that, although the DB Funding Ratio may hover near 1, the required Asset/Salary Ratio (RASR) will increase over time, since the accumulated assets needed to fund future retirement in-come must grow faster than a person's salary. But a worker who knows his current ASR can roughly estimate the ratio that would be *required* to fund retirement income years into the future and then assess whether the current ratio is "on track" for retirement. Both current salary and current savings can be brought forward through working life to retirement with some as-sumptions (e.g., an asset growth rate and a salary growth rate). Hence, at any point t years prior to retirement, it can be determined whether current ASR equals the required ASR and thus whether current savings rates might eventually produce assets sufficient to fund an annuity that would provide an income equal to 50 percent of salary at retirement (or whatever target replacement ratio is desired).

The mathematical relationships between the elements making up the RASR include the desired replacement ratio (RR), pension contribution rate, investment rate of return on pension contributions, salary growth rate, investment rate of return on annuity assets, and the respective number of years remaining prior to and following retirement. Using these variables, someone with a current ASR equal to his or her RASR could be said to be "on track" for retirement, other things being equal (see Appendix B). A person whose current ASR is currently higher than the required ratio enjoys a cushion to protect against unforeseen trends or events (unexpected stock market declines, better-than-expected retiree life spans, etc.). And someone with a current ASR lower than required might need to take corrective action (e.g., increase plan contributions, start other kinds of retirement savings, change investment strategies, or delay retirement).

Implementing the Asset/Salary Ratio

We next illustrate how the RASR works with a few simple assumptions listed in Table 1, all of which will vary depending on an individual's circumstances and appetite for risk.

First, we assume an income replacement ratio target of 50 percent. Second, we use a DC pension plan contribution rate of 10 percent.[4] Third, although the formula for RASR does not require knowing the worker's current income, it does require projecting growth. We use a real rate of percent on top of a 2-percent inflation rate, since aggregate salaries in higher education have grown at about this rate over time (*Academe,* 1998). Fourth, we must project asset returns, and we begin by assuming that assets are invested in either government bonds, long-term inflation-indexed bonds, or a partially guaranteed, fixed income account such as the traditional TIAA account. Fifth, we assume that at retirement the individual purchases a 25-year certain annuity (a date-certain annuity was chosen instead of a life annuity for standardization and ease of replication). In this case, the payout annuity interest rate is similarly set at 6 percent.

The base-case RASR appears in Table 2 for calculations based on assumptions in Table 1. Reading across, it starts with a desired income replacement ratio. It then displays the future value of replacement income (i.e., for the 50 percent income replacement ratio target, half of the future salary of $1.80 or $.90 for every $1.00 of current income). The next column displays the corresponding future cost of an annuity sufficient to provide the replacement income and the following column shows the future value of all future pension contributions. The fifth column is the difference between the cost of the annuity and the future contributions, while the sixth column is the present value of that difference. The final column shows the RASR for the corresponding target replacement ratio.

For example, for an individual 15 years from retirement, the RASR is as follows:[5]

$$(3) \qquad RASR_{15} = \frac{(AC - FV_p) / (1 + r)^{15}}{S_{15}} \, ,$$

where

AC = the cost of a 25-year annuity at retirement assuming a 50 percent income replacement ratio,

FV_p = the future value of premium contributions until retirement,

r = investment rate of return, and

S = current salary.

TABLE 1. Baseline Asset/Salary Ratio Modeling Assumptions

Target income replacement ratio RR	50%
Plan contribution rate P	10%
Salary growth w	4%
Pre-retirement rate of return r	6%
Annuity length years K	25
Annuity rate of return r_{AN}	6%

Source: Authors' calculations.

Plugging in the numbers from Tables 1 and 2, we obtain

$$\text{RASR}_{15} = \frac{(\$11.51 - \$2.98) / (1 + .06)^{15}}{\$1.00} = 3.56 \ .$$

(For ease of calculation, salary is set at $1.00. Since we are using the required ASR, salary level does not affect this ratio.)

Figure 1 shows a set of required Asset/Salary Ratios calculated in a similar fashion for several points prior to retirement. For each year, the funding ratio shown is associated with a 50 percent retirement income replacement ratio. For example, a 65-year-old about to retire, who began saving at age 25 with a salary of $30,000, should by now have accumulated about $885,000 ($138,500 times the RASR of 6.39) in order to purchase an annuity with a 50 percent income replacement ratio.[6] Fifteen years prior to retirement, the same individual would have needed about $274,000 ($76,900 times the RASR of 3.56) to be on the pathway to retirement. With 25 years to go, he would have needed about $108,000 ($52,000 times the RASR of 2.08).

Surplus and Deficit Relative to the RASR Curve

The required Asset/Salary Ratio curve defines the Asset/Salary Ratios needed to be on track for meeting a relatively conservative retirement goal using a conservative low risk investment approach. Someone whose circumstances place him or her exactly on the line would deemed to be neither over nor underfunded for retirement. On the other hand, a current ASR that falls below the line implies a projected retirement income shortfall, or an income replacement ratio less than the standard 50 percent target. Note that this is meant to be a crude rather than a precise signal, since circumstances might vary considerably from the assumptions used in the base case. For example, participation in a DB plan and the presence of other personal savings would effectively raise the current ASR. Unusually high temporary income might depress the current ASR for a time, until future income dropped back into line with past income. A person's contribution rate might be over 10 percent, so assets would accumulate more quickly than in the

TABLE 2. Required Asset/Salary Ratios for Various Replacement Ratios 15 Years from Retirement

Target Income Replacement Ratio (%)	Future Value Replacement Income ($)	Annuity Cost ($)	Total Premium Payments ($)	Future Value Annuity Cost Less Future Value Premiums	Present Value Annuity Cost Less Future Value Premiums ($)	Required (par) Asset/Salary Ratio
30	0.54	6.91	3.10	3.81	1.59	1.59
40	0.72	9.21	3.10	6.11	2.55	2.55
50	0.90	11.51	3.10	8.41	3.51	3.51
55	0.99	12.66	3.10	9.56	3.99	3.99
60	1.08	13.81	3.10	10.72	4.47	4.47
70	1.26	16.12	3.10	13.02	5.43	5.43
80	1.44	18.42	3.10	15.32	6.39	6.39
100	1.80	23.02	3.10	19.92	8.31	8.31

Source: Authors' calculations.
Note: Calculations use assumptions in Table 1 and current salary = $1.

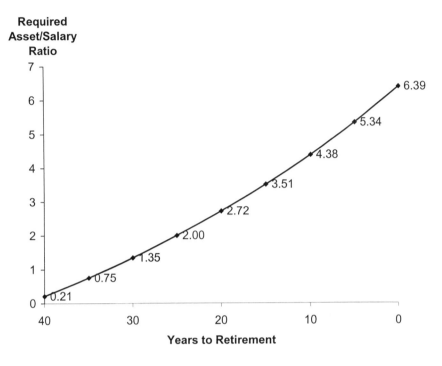

Figure 1. Required asset/salary ratio for 50 percent replacement ratio. Source: Authors' calculations.

base case, and the person's current funding curve would rise more steeply through time. Conversely, a current ASR below the line could provide warning of a future shortfall, a signal to expand the asset base through increased retirement plan contributions or other savings. Of course, having a longer time horizon offers opportunity and can avoid crises that demand precipitous action.

Developing a Risk Cushion

A worker with a current ratio substantially above the RASR curve could expect that assets are in excess of those needed to fund the desired retirement annuity. In essence, he or she would have a *risk cushion* for retirement. This is useful because the ASR as described here is deterministic, while risk will influence retirement planning over an extended period of time. Such uncertainty might be associated with employment (i.e., under- or unemployment risk), investment returns (e.g., allocation choices or market risk), pension contributions, and special needs such as expensive health conditions or unforeseen family expenditures. So a risk cushion could be a luxury or a necessity, depending on how well the assumptions behind the RASR match an individual's future circumstances.

If a risk cushion exists, it might be used in at least four ways. First, the "extra" assets could be used to project the target income replacement ratio. For example, a drop in future contributions below the 10 percent rate assumed here would cause the current ASR to fall relative to the RASR. The presence of a risk cushion would help to protect against a dip in the current ASR for whatever reason.[7] Second, a risk cushion could permit the replacement target to be raised. Figure 2 displays several families of retirement funding ratio curves that reflect the effect of boosting the target income replacement ratio. It shows that if an individual can sustain a position above the RASR curve over the years (e.g., through a consistently higher contribution rate), then he or she will achieve a higher retirement income replacement ratio.

The risk cushion could also be used to provide a safety net under a higher risk investment strategy. That is, some or all of the assets corresponding to the risk cushion could be invested in riskier assets that hold the possibility of higher returns. Alternatively, having a risk cushion through time might accumulate enough assets to retire earlier while still meeting the 50 percent income replacement goal. Finally, a risk cushion could be used to make gifts or leave legacies to charities or to children, depending on the individual's tax status and predilections.

Portfolio in Hand

Sometimes people stop making DC plan contributions well before retirement, and in this instance it is interesting to examine the future value of what they have already accumulated. Alternatively, we might wish to know the future value of future contributions as a proportion of total accumulations. To see the nonlinear nature of the relationship between required assets and salary, we turn to Table 3, which uses the same numbers as those behind the RASR curve in Figure 1 to show the proportion of final (total) retirement accumulations a person would have in hand for selected years prior to retirement. For example, a low risk RASR 35 years before retirement implies that the accumulated assets, as well as the future earnings on those assets, will represent only about 23 percent of total projected accumulations at retirement. This implies that over 75 percent of a person's final accumulation is associated with future contributions and the earnings on those contributions. This suggests that the young investor may consider the effect of taking on additional risk in his or her portfolio. For example, if current assets experienced a one-time 20 percent loss 35 years from retirement, this would reduce final accumulations by about 4 percent (.23 times .20). This is because most of the final accumulation is represented by *future* contributions.

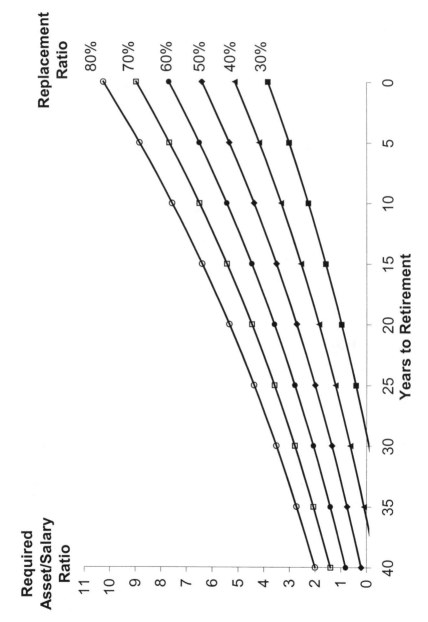

Figure 2. Required asset/salary ratio for alternative replacement rates. Source: Authors' calculations.

TABLE 3. Portfolio in Hand (% of Final Accumulation)

Returns	Years to Retirement								
	0	*5*	*10*	*15*	*20*	*25*	*30*	*35*	*40*
6 ("Par")	100	92	83	73	62	50	37	23	7
8	100	92	81	69	54	36	14		
10	100	91	80	64	44	17			

Source: Authors' calculations.

Conversely, someone nearing retirement might be less able to stomach a sharp reduction in assets. An individual 5 years from retirement who is at the RASR would have about 92 percent of his or her final portfolio in hand. If there were a significant market loss — say, the same 20 percent one-time reduction — he or she would end up with 18 percent less assets at retirement (.20 times .92). These numbers suggest that we may need to adjust the familiar admonition that the power of compounding over a long time period makes retirement saving early more valuable than similar contributions later. Although it is important to save early in one's career, it also appears easier to recover from market downturns and other events that cause asset losses. This may explain the finding that young people in recent years have placed a higher percentage of their retirement savings in higher risk equities than did older people (Ameriks and Zeldes, 2000).

Effect of Higher Expected Returns on the ASR

The RASR curve assumes a relatively low risk 6 percent rate of return, but few people in DC plans invest all their savings at or near a risk-free rate. We next explore how investing at higher returns affects the RASR as well as the portfolio in hand. Figure 3 shows that if retirement savings average 10 percent per year, then the RASR or ASR needed to achieve a 50 percent retirement income replacement ratio drops considerably in the early years, as compared to the base percent case. At 25 years from retirement, the RASR would be a little over two times salary, if investment returns average 6 percent. At 10 percent return, the ASR drops to less than 30 percent of current salary. At 15 years from retirement, the 6 percent return par ASR ratio would be 3.5 times salary, while the 10 percent return funding ratio would be only 1.8 times salary.

With higher asset returns, the portfolio in hand calculation shows a similar decline. As shown in Table 3, a 10 percent asset return would imply only about 17 percent of final accumulations in hand 25 years from retirement, compared to 50 percent in the 6 percent return case. This means that asset gains (or losses) on early career savings would have less influence on final accumulations, than in the more conservative case.

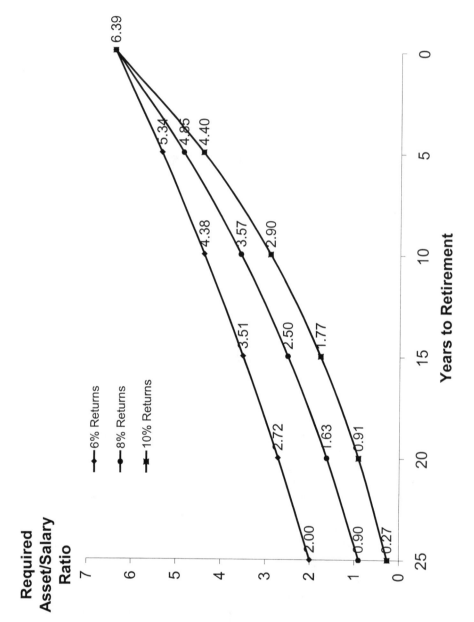

Figure 3. Required asset/salary ratio for alternative rates of return. Source: Authors' calculations.

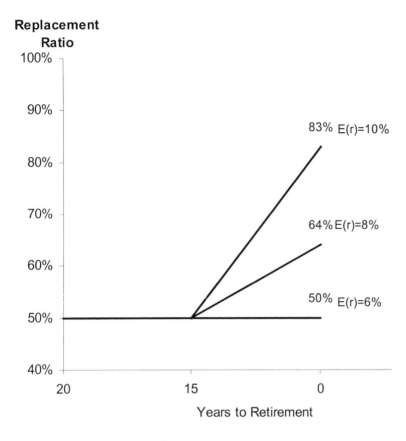

Figure 4. Projected replacement rates with alternative portfolio returns. Source: Authors' calculations. Note: $E(r)$ refers to the expected value of portfolio returns.

Higher asset returns could also be used to get to a higher retirement income replacement ratio. Figure 4 assumes that at 15 years prior to retirement, the individual has achieved a RASR of 3.5 (e.g., prior to that point, assests were invested at the RASR, low risk rate of 6 percent). Thenceforth all assets and future contributions are invested in assets whose expected returns average 10 percent. If assets did provide 10 percent returns, the individual could achieve much higher expected retirement income replacement ratios: over 80 percent in the case of the pure 10 percent return, and over 60 percent in the case of a portfolio that blended riskier and low-risk assets.

Investment Risk Implications of Higher Returns

There is, of course, additional investment risk that could lead to retirement income lower (or higher) than the "expected" result. For example, to boost expected returns from the six to the 10 percent range, an investor could purchase stocks that have enjoyed historically higher average rates of return than bonds or money market returns. An investor who had held the Ibbotson index of large capitalization U.S. stocks for all (overlapping) 15-year periods since 1926 would have experienced annual returns averaging 10.75 percent, well in excess of our low risk 6 percent rate. Yet about half the time, the Ibbotson large cap stock index return was lower than the 10.75 percent average. And about 15 percent of the time, the Ibbotson return was less than or equal to 6 percent per year, the same annual return as the low risk, fixed income investment used in the previous examples. (For 10 percent of the 15-year returns, the annual return was less than four percent.)

How would this variability of equity returns affect our Asset/Salary Ratio and the individual's chances of achieving his or her retirement income target? To examine this question, we simulated a case in which a worker 15 years from retirement had achieved the par Asset/Salary Ratio of 3.5. If he continued to save and invest at the six percent low risk rate, he or she would achieve the target 50 percent income replacement ratio at retirement in the certainty case. To see what the range of outcomes and probabilities might be if that person selected a riskier portfolio, we undertook Monte Carlo simulations using four different mixes of a low risk fixed-income asset and higher risk equities with a savings and investment period of 15 years.[8] For every individual iteration, each investment year's return was drawn independently from a normal distribution of equity returns with a expected nominal annual return of 10 percent (instead of the 10.75 percent historical return for a large-cap all-equity portfolio) and a standard deviation of 17 percent. Assets were rebalanced at the beginning of each year.

Figure 5 illustrates the resulting Asset/Salary Ratio and target replacement ratio, showing the probability of achieving a range of income replacement ratios using 100 percent equities with a 15-year retirement horizon. Recall that the original target replacement ratio was 50 percent, which was the "expected" outcome for an individual with a par Asset/Salary Ratio investing in assets using six percent. By investing 100 percent in equities, the individual could increase his or her expected replacement ratio from 50 to over 80 percent. Using stochastic simulation, Figure 5 shows that there is a 50 percent chance of attaining at least a 72 percent income replacement ratio at retirement, and a 20 percent chance of reaching nearly 120 percent of preretirement income.[9] However, the figure also shows that there is a 25 percent chance that the replacement income will fall short of the original 50 percent target, and a 10 percent chance that the individual will have to settle for an income replacement ratio of less than 36 percent.

What alternative blend of risky and low risk assets could balance those expected risks and rewards of equity investment? Answering this question depends on the individual's tolerance for shortfall risk, but several alternatives appear in Figure 6 using three mixed portfolios along with the original

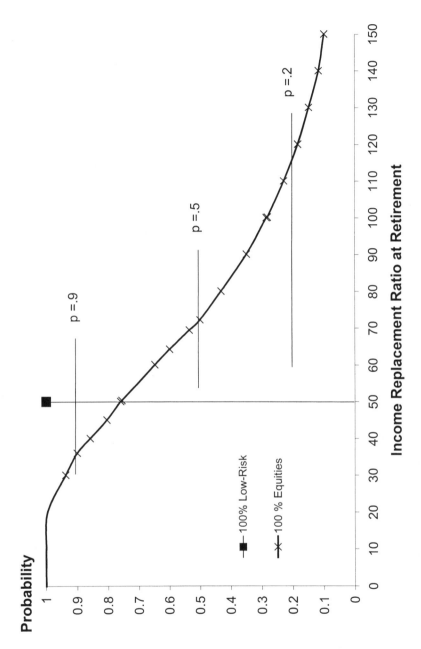

Figure 5. Probability of alternative asset/salary and replacement rate outcomes (stochastic simulation) with 100 percent in equities. Source: Authors' calculations.

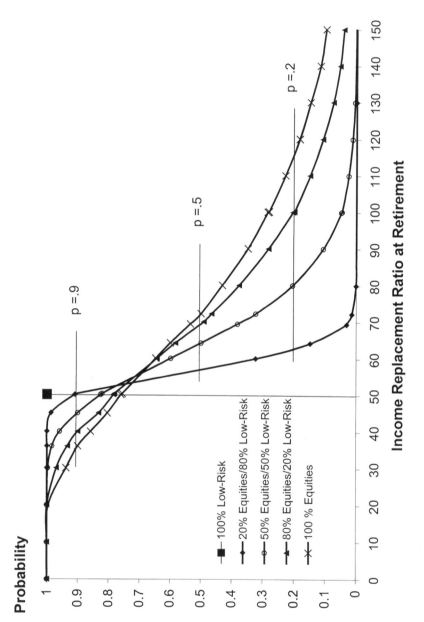

Figure 6. Probability of alternative asset/salary and replacement rate outcomes (stochastic simulation) with alternative investment portfolio. Source: Authors' calculations.

100 percent low risk and 100 percent higher risk portfolios. For example, a mix of 20 percent equities and 80 percent of the fixed-income asset falls short of the 50 percent replacement ratio 10 percent of the time. All the same, this portfolio has limited potential for doing better than the low risk alternative, in that about half the time it would achieve a replacement ratio of 58 percent or less (compared to 72 percent replacement ratio in the 100 percent equity case). A 50-50 mix of equities and the fixed income asset, one which returned 8 percent, would do better. On average, it would achieve a 64 percent replacement ratio and would reach the 45 percent replacement ratio or even better about 90 percent of the time.

Someone who could tolerate a little more risk might wish to adopt an allocation policy that would limit the income risk to a ten percent chance of falling 10 percent below the target income replacement ratio (RR = 40 percent). An 80-20 mix of equities and the low-risk asset would achieve this goal. Such a portfolio would also have a fifty percent chance of achieving at least a 70 percent income replacement ratio, and a 20 percent chance of matching 100 of preretirement income. Such an asset allocation strategy might be a good way of at least partially "immunizing" a portfolio against the chance of a retirement income shortfall, while still participating in the possibility of achieving a retirement income "cushion."

Implications of Other Risks

Of course investment volatility and asset allocation choice are not the only sources of risks facing a retirement saver: others include under or unemployment, health or family consumption needs, and inflation. Even modest inflation, for example, can seriously erode the real value of retirement savings and retirement income (Brown et al. 2001 and this volume). The Asset/Salary Ratio does recognize some inflation effects prior to retirement, in that it assumes a nominal salary growth of four percent, which in current circumstances implies an inflation rate of 2 to 2.5 percent (long-term wage growth for workers in the U.S. has been about one percent in real terms). Similarly, nominal investment returns of 6 percent for the low risk case and 10 percent for the higher risk case incorporate a comparable inflation rate.

Nevertheless the damaging effects of inflation are not built into the retirement payout annuity income, and the impact can be significant. As Figure 7 shows, if inflation remains steady at 2.5 percent, an individual whose first-year retirement income was $40,000 would after 10 years have an inflation-adjusted income of only about $31,000. After 25 years, a little more than the median unisex lifespan for a person age 65, real income would be only $21,500, which is more than a 45 percent decline. If inflation were higher, say 4 percent, then the same $40,000 would be worth only about $27,000 after 10 years and $15,000 after 25 years, a 62.5 percent decline.

To cope with inflation in retirement, the RASR calculation could be ad-

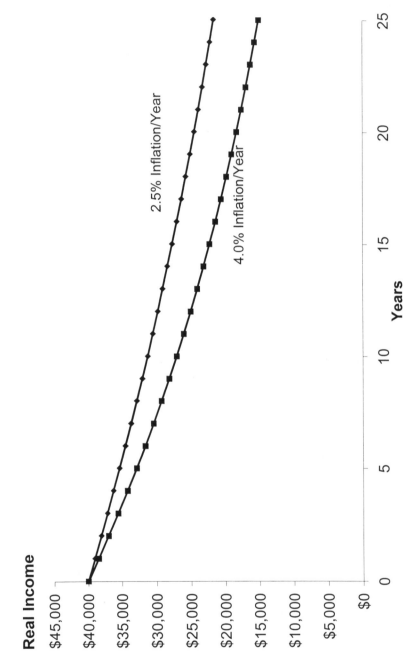

Figure 7. Effect of alternative inflation rates on retirement income. Source: Authors' calculations.

justed to assume a "real" payout annuity interest rate in retirement (for a discussion of the cost of real annuities, see Brown et al., 2000). For example, inflation-linked bonds currently carry a coupon of about four percent with a built-in inflation adjustment. Figure 8 shows the effect on the required Asset/Salary Ratio of purchasing an annuity based on a long-term inflation bond at four percent coupon. The required Asset/Salary Ratio 15 years prior to retirement increases by more than one (from 3.56 to 4.63) as compared to the nominal six percent annuity par ASR curve. In essence, this means that to purchase inflation protection, the saver would need to have 30 percent more assets at that time. Because the Asset/Salary Ratio curve is not linear, the required Asset/Salary Ratio would increase by nearly 50 percent at 25 years prior to retirement. With five years to go before retirement, the required Asset/Salary Ratio would increase by 24 percent. Taking future inflation into account requires more saving or a higher return, higher risk investment strategy that involves a greater probability of not achieving the target income replacement ratio.

Conclusions and Discussion

Knowing years in advance whether one is on track to achieving a retirement goal is one of the most fundamental and, at the same time, most challenging issues any individual or couple faces. Sophisticated efforts have been made to construct better tools for estimating the adequacy of retirement income strategies, some of which are reported elsewhere in this volume (Bernheim et al. this volume; Scott this volume). Our measure, the Asset/Salary Ratio, is less sophisticated than some of these, in that it uses a number of projections and does not attempt to estimate stochastic returns and risk levels from a portfolio of actual assets. Nevertheless, our approach has the advantage of clarity with respect to the assumptions that an individual makes or needs to make in setting goals and achieving an adequate retirement income.

No matter what the approach, assessing retirement income adequacy involves projecting how much annual income people need for retirement; what proportion of that income social security will provide; what other sources of retirement income — such as a spouse's defined benefit plan — they can expect; and what their tolerance is for retirement income shortfall risk. Having ascertained all that, the ultimate question is how much in the way of assets they need to accumulate to produce an adequate retirement. The more years away from retirement, the more uncertain the answers to all these questions can seem.

The Asset/Salary Ratio, when used in conjunction with a target income replacement goal, employs numbers that people commonly have at hand — current salary and assets — to arrive at a rough estimate of current savings adequacy that can be used as a snapshot view for further retirement income planning. An actual Asset/Salary Ratio that is substantially below the

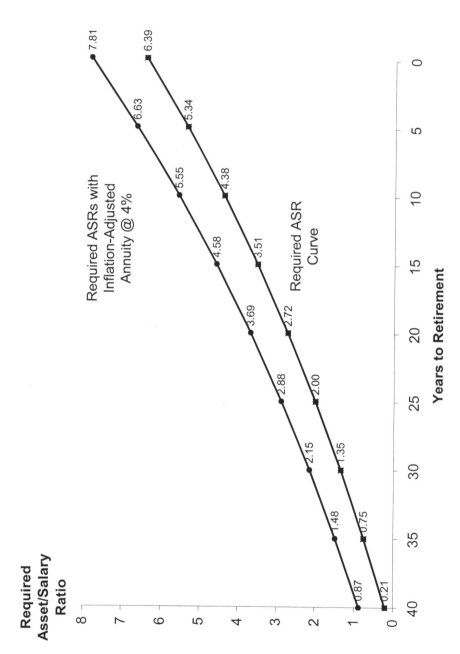

Figure 8. Asset/salary ratio required to purchase inflation protection. Source: Authors' calculations.

required par ASR curve could provide a signal that the individual or couple should start saving more, examine other sources of retirement income, work longer, or plan lower consumption in retirement. An actual Asset/Salary Ratio that is significantly above the par ASR curve could be a sign of a risk cushion or could permit riskier asset allocations. Finally, the Asset/Salary Ratio can inform investment strategies to reduce the risk of a retirement income shortfall. We could imagine, for example, an electronic Asset/Salary Ratio calculator that allowed people to customize assumptions about target replacement ratios, salary growth, and investment return and risk.

Appendix A: The Income Replacement Ratio

The replacement ratio can be summarized as follows (Heller and King 1989 and 1994):[10]

$$
\text{(A1)} \qquad \text{RR} = \frac{P}{\text{AC}} \sum_{n=1}^{N-1} \left[\frac{1+r}{1+w} \right]^n ,
$$

where P = plan contribution rate as a percentage of salary,
  r = annual preretirement investment earnings rate,
  w = annual salary increase rate,
  N = total number of years in the DC plan, and
  AC = annuity purchase cost, or the cost per \$1 of an income for life or for a specified period.
We can rewrite this formula as follows:

$$
\text{(A2)} \qquad \text{RR} = \left(\frac{\text{FV}_{\text{Assets}}}{\text{AC}} \right) \frac{1}{S(1+w)^{N-1}} ,
$$

where
  $\text{FV}_{\text{Assets}}$ = future value of all plan contributions, which depends on a contribution rate (percentage of salary) and an investment return rate,
  S = first-year annual salary, and $S(1+w)^{N-1}$ = salary in the final working year before retirement.

Appendix B: The Asset/Salary Ratio

We define the *Asset/Salary Ratio* as the ratio of current retirement assets to current salary at time t years before retirement.

$$
\text{(B1)} \qquad \text{ASR}_t = \frac{A_t}{S_t} ,
$$

where S is the salary earned over the previous year.

The Asset/Salary Ratio can be thought of in two ways: the existing Asset/Salary Ratio or the asset/salary that would be *required* to achieve a target income replacement ratio. Taking the latter meaning of the Asset/Salary Ratio, we can say that without any future contributions (i.e., pension premiums) beyond the current moment, the *required* current level of assets or initial principal would be equal to the discounted present value of the cost of an annuity at retirement divided by future salary growth.

(B2) $$A_t \text{ (no contributions)} = \frac{FV_A}{(1 + r)^t} \,,$$

where FV_A = the discounted present value of the cost of an annuity at retirement that would be sufficient to produce the desired replacement ratio and r = the rate of investment return on the existing assets.

If we add future pension contributions and any other incremental savings, then required current assets is reduced accordingly to:

(B3) $$A_t \text{ (with contributions)} = \frac{FV_A - FV_P}{(1 + r)^t} \,,$$

where FV_P is the accumulated value of annual premium payments (and any other retirement savings) at retirement. These in turn depend on initial salary, salary growth, and investment return on premiums such that:

(B4) $$FV_p = \sum_{n=1}^{t} PS_t (1 + w)^{n-1} (1 + r)^{t-n} \,,$$

and w = nominal salary increase rate, including a real salary increase and an inflation component.

Substituting equation (B4) into equation (B3), the required assets size becomes:

(B5) $$A_t = \frac{FV_A - \sum_{n=1}^{t} PS_t (1 + w)^{n-1} (1 + r)^{n-t}}{(1 + r)^t}$$

Now the future value of an annuity can be recast in terms of the replacement ratio (RR), salary, salary growth, and an annuity purchase cost:

(B6) $$FV_A = \left[S_t (1 + w)^t RR \right] AC,$$

where $$AC = \frac{1 - \left(1 / (1 + r_{AN})^K \right)}{r_{AN}} \,,$$

r_{AN} = investment rate of return on annuity assets, and K = total number of years in the annuity. Substituting (B6) into (B5) yields

(B7) $A_t = \dfrac{S_t}{(1 + r)^t} \left[[RR(1 + w)^t AC] - \sum\limits_{n=1}^{t} P(1 + w)^{n-1} (1 + r)^{t-n} \right].$

Simplifying further yields

(B8) $\dfrac{A_t}{S_t} = \dfrac{RR(1 + w)^t AC}{(1 + r)^t} - \dfrac{P(1 + w)\left[(1 + r)^t - (1 + w)^t\right]}{(r - w)(1 + r)^t},$

or

(B9) $ASR_t = \dfrac{A_t}{S_t} = RR * AC \left(\dfrac{1 + w}{1 + r}\right)^t - \dfrac{P(1 + w)}{r - w}\left[1 - \left(\dfrac{1 + w}{1 + r}\right)^t\right].$

There are at least two things to note about this characterization of the Asset/Salary Ratio. First, the annuity value is based on a date certain rather than a life annuity. If a life annuity is used then the annuity cost AC depends on the annuity's interest rate, i, the probability of a person age b at retirement of living to age $b + h$ (hPb), and on the last age in a mortality table, m, as follows:

(B10) $AC_b = \sum\limits_{h=0}^{m-b} \dfrac{hPb}{(1 + i)^h}.$

Second, the preretirement investment return, annuity investment return, and salary growth terms may all be different. If any of them are similar, the Asset/Salary Ratio equation collapses further. For example, if the preretirement investment rate of return and the salary growth rate are equal, then:

(B11) $ASR_t = \dfrac{A_t}{S_t} = RR * AC - P * t.$

Notes

We are grateful to Gary Selnow, John Ameriks, Mark Warshawsky, Harry Klaristenfeld, Deanne Shallcross, Yuewu Xu, and anonymous readers for helpful comments and suggestions.

1. FASB 87 requires private pension plan sponsors to report their surplus, or the excess of assets over present-value liabilities, on a marked-to-market basis. GASB 5, on the other hand, does not require public pension plans to measure liabilities with a discount rate that reflects current market conditions.

2. At that time, social security benefits at age 65 replaced about 20 percent of income in the upper income categories ($90,000 in 1990 dollars), about 50 percent of income for the middle income range ($35,000), and about 70 percent of income for those with lower incomes ($15,000).

3. To be precise, S_t is the individual's salary or income over the last year.

4. DC plan contribution rates vary considerably among employers. In higher edu-

cation, many college and university plans are designed so that the employer and employee together contribute 10 percent or more of annual salary.

5. This assumes that salary equals $1 or that the right-hand side of the equation is divided by S_t.

6. These examples assume 4 percent nominal (2 percent real) annual salary growth.

7. One of the limits of the Asset/Salary Ratio should be noted in connection with this first point. Other things being equal, a future salary *decrease* would in fact lead to an *increase* in the actual Asset/Salary Ratio. But in most cases individuals would not prefer to increase their own Asset/Salary Ratio in this manner.

8. Using the @Risk commercial software program, the Latin Hypercube sampling method was used along with expected value recalculation. In repeated simulations, the results converged consistently after about 1,500 iterations.

9. Note that the mean replacement ratio result was 83 percent, consistent with the non-stochastic expected value. However the $p=.50$ replacement ratio is 72 percent. Repeated simulations produced distributions of replacement ratios that exhibited skewness (1.8) and considerable kurtosis (9.8). Not surprisingly, these distributions resembled a log normal rather than a normal distribution.

10. The following formula follows the Heller and King convention, but it has been reduced to a simplified form that assumes contributions to the plan are made only once each year at year's end.

References

Academe. 1998. "The Annual Report on the Status of the Profession." (March/April).

American Association of University Professors (AAUP). 1990. *Policy Documents & Reports.* Washington, D.C.: AAUP.

Ameriks, John and Stephen P. Zeldes. 2000. "How Do Household Portfolio Shares Vary with Age?" Columbia University Working Paper. February.

Bernheim, B. Douglas, Lorenzo Forni, Jagadeesh Gokhale, and Laurence J. Kotlikoff. This volume. "An Economic Approach to Setting Retirement Saving Goals."

Brown, Jeffrey R., Olivia S. Mitchell, and James M. Poterba. This volume. "Mortality Risk, Inflation Risk, and Annuity Products."

———. 2001. "The Role of Real Annuities and Indexed Bonds in an Individual Accounts Retirement Program." In *Risk Aspects of Social Security Reform,* ed. John Campbell and Martin Feldstein. Chicago: University of Chicago Press.

Gale, William G. and John Sabelhaus. 1999. "Perspectives on the Household Saving Rate." Working Paper, Brookings Institution, March 26.

Hammond, P. Brett and Harriet Morgan. 1991. *Ending Mandatory Retirement for Tenured Faculty.* Committee on Mandatory Retirement in Higher Education, National Research Council. Washington D.C.: National Academy Press.

Heller, Michael and Francis P. King. 1989. "Estimating Real Income Replacement Ratios in Defined Contribution Retirement Plans." Research Dialogues 23. New York: TIAA-CREF. October.

———. 1994. "Replacement Ratio Projections in Defined Contribution Retirement Plans: Time, Salary Growth, Investment Return, and Real Income." Research Dialogues 41. New York: TIAA-CREF. September.

Leibowitz, Martin L., Lawrence N. Bader, and Stanley Kogelman. 1996a. "Return Targets, Shortfall Risks, and Market Realities." In Leibowitz, Bader, and Kogelman, *Return Targets and Shortfall Risks: Studies in Strategic Asset Allocation*. Chicago: Irwin. Chapter 7.

———. 1996b. "Funding Ratio Return: A More 'Universal' Measure for Asset/Liability Management." In Leibowitz, Bader, and Kogelman, *Return Targets and Shortfall Risks: Studies in Strategic Asset Allocation*. Chicago: Irwin. Chapter 10.

Moore, James F. and Olivia S. Mitchell. 2000. "Projected Retirement Wealth and Savings Adequacy." In *Forecasting Retirement needs and Retirement Wealth*, ed. Olivia S. Mitchell, P. Brett Hammond, and Anna M. Rappaport. Pension Research Council. Philadelphia: University of Pennsylvania Press. 68–94.

Palmer, Bruce A. 1993. "Planning for Retirement: Using Income Replacement Ratios in Setting Retirement Income Objectives." Research Dialogues 37. New York: TIAA-CREF. July.

Samwick, Andrew A. and Jonathan Skinner. 1998. "How Will Defined Contribution Pension Plans Affect Retirement Income?" NBER Working Paper 6645. April.

Scott, Jason. This volume. "Outcomes-Based Investing with Efficient Monte Carlo Simulation."

Chapter 6
Outcomes-Based Investing with Efficient Monte Carlo Simulation

Jason Scott

Defined contribution pension plans have become an increasingly important component of many people's retirement plans. More than 50 million Americans participated in these plans as of 1998 (PSCA 1999), and their assets exceed $2 trillion (EBRI 1999). A distinguishing characteristic of defined contribution plans is that participants have much greater responsibility for determining both the contribution level and the investment allocation, as compared to the norm in defined benefit plans. In view of this increase in the need for individual responsibility for retirement saving and investing, it is of interest to explore whether workers are financially literature enough, and sufficiently prepared, to be do an effective job of saving for retirement.

The news is not particularly encouraging. In a recent survey on retirement readiness, EBRI (1999) found that only 8 percent of workers were doing a "very good" job of retirement preparation. The same survey found that only about half of workers had ever even assessed their retirement needs. Other studies have uncovered similarly discouraging findings: Bernheim et al. (this volume) report that households need roughly to triple their retirement assets to secure a comfortable retirement; Moore and Mitchell (2000) conclude that the typical older household needs to save an additional 16 percent of income to maintain its preretirement standard of living; and Warshawsky and Ameriks (2000) estimate that more than half of U.S. households will fail to fund their retirement sufficiently.

Given this apparent lack of readiness, the question becomes: why are so many people underprepared for retirement? One answer may be that they are already saving as much as they possibly can. However, Moore and Mitchell (2000) concluded that this is unlikely for all but the poorest of households studied. A more likely answer may be that the difficulty and enormity of the computations simply overwhelm people, and certainly the problem is an extremely complex one to solve. For instance, simply assessing how much one might need in retirement is difficult, and if one then considers the complexity of projecting investment returns under uncertainty, many will feel that the problem becomes unmanageable. This chapter shows how Monte Carlo simulation techniques can be used in the context of outcomes-based investing to help people make retirement decisions. Three key questions are considered:

- What is outcomes-based investing, and how does it relate to Monte Carlo simulation?
- What are the potential benefits of outcomes-based investing?
- What difficulties arise when implementing an outcomes-based approach?

Special emphasis is placed on the third question because addressing the difficulties is crucial to implementing a workable solution.

Monte Carlo Simulation and Outcomes-Based Investing

Outcomes-based investing simply refers to the process of evaluating possible outcomes associated with different portfolio allocation decisions, to determine what investment path is most consistent with the decision-maker's goals. In fact, anyone seeking to evaluate possible outcomes prior to making a decision under uncertainty is employing a variant of "outcomes-based decision making." Typically this requires the development of simulation methods, and indeed simulations in the context of financial decision-making have been practiced in the financial community for decades. For instance, large pension funds have employed Monte Carlo-based simulation approaches to evaluate investment choices, asking which investment policy minimizes the probability of exhausting pension assets given a particular contribution schedule. In the context of a defined contribution pension, an individual participant might want to know which investment portfolio maximizes the chance of achieving a particular retirement goal.

Though the concept of outcomes-based investment is not new, the complexity and cost of creating reasonable simulation models to help make investment-decisions has limited the availability of this approach to a relatively limited segment of the financial services industry. In recent years, however, two technological developments have made it possible to extend Monte Carlo-based methods to the individual retirement decision-making problem. The first has been the huge fall in the cost of computation. Monte Carlo methods are inherently computationally intensive, and fast, cheap computers now make implementing them more cost effective than before. The second has been the rise of the Internet, which has dramatically decreased distribution costs for software-based investment services. Together, these innovations make it much more likely that simulation based methods will become accessible to individuals seeking help in the retirement decision-making process.

Consider the problem an individual faces when seeking to accumulate retirement assets. If the target amount of wealth needed is W^* by retirement, the saver may ask whether, given a current portfolio and planned saving level, he or she reach the goal. One way to answer this question is to turn to one of the widely available retirement calculators on the Internet. These calculators typically assume that the investor's portfolio grows at a prespecified annual rate of return, and that inflation erodes a constant fraction of the portfolio each year. They may then generate an expected shortfall or "grade" associated with the saver's plan, deeming it adequate or inadequate to meet the goal.

A difficulty with this type of simplified calculator model is that it can easily output wrong information regarding expected portfolio values at retirement. For example, if the user has extremely optimistic beliefs regarding likely future investment performance, and supplies the calculator with an expected annual return of 20 percent, he or she will likely leave the exercise confident in achieving the retirement objective. With a more reasonable return assumption the analysis would indicate that the worker was woefully unprepared for retirement. In practice, we find that people are often surprised that they have a relatively small chance of achieving the wealth implied even by average historical returns. Even if historical returns are predictive of future returns (possibly an over-optimistic assumption), the average return is difficult to achieve. One reason is that returns are reduced by administrative and other costs including management fees, taxes, and transaction costs. Another reason is that the volatility of market returns implies that average returns overestimate cumulative returns.[1] Since these calculator models do not address the issue of investment uncertainty directly, users will tend to construct retirement plans based on insufficient or faulty information. Even worse, people may believe and act as if they were on track for a "dream" retirement, when a much less happy outcome could reasonably occur.

The major drawback with a calculator approach to wealth projection is that portfolio returns are uncertain. Because of this complexity, the likely range of wealth outcomes at retirement cannot easily be derived analytically, even with relatively simple assumptions for portfolio returns. This is where Monte Carlo simulation is useful. Specifically, Monte Carlo simulation involves constructing an economic model capable of capturing many of the important characteristics of investment returns. Using this model, it becomes possible to simulate thousands of potential paths an asset portfolio may take over time, as people move toward retirement. The user can then examine numerous potential scenarios to determine what range of outcomes is most reasonable, what outcomes are unusually optimistic, and what the range of quite pessimistic outcomes might be. Instead of determining the distribution of retirement wealth analytically, Monte Carlo simulation generates an empirical estimate of the final wealth distribution. This step is helpful in producing informative statistics such as a saver's chances of reaching a target wealth level. As explained below, the number of simulations evaluated determines the quality of the approximation to the final retirement wealth distribution.

In short, outcomes-based investing means evaluating different investment plans based on the likely outcomes the plan can deliver. Monte Carlo simulation allows extremely complex stochastic distributions to be evaluated without knowledge of the actual analytic distribution of outcomes.

Potential Benefits of Outcomes-Based Investing

At its core, outcomes-based investing — or more generally, outcomes-based planning — helps one make better decisions through improved information. By providing individuals with better information about the likely impact of portfolio risk, savings level, investment horizon, and other factors, the expectation is that the saver can make decisions that ultimately lead to improved outcomes.

To assess the benefits of outcomes-based investing, it is helpful to examine a prominent alternative, namely the results of basing investment decisions on deterministic returns. This latter deserves scrutiny because of the potential for investors to ignore portfolio risk. With deterministic returns, a given portfolio generates an anticipated average return. As described above, this average return can be used to calculate a single value of projected retirement wealth. Typically this final wealth level is compared to the wealth target, and the resulting shortfall (or surplus) is reported.[2] A saving plan is deemed "successful" if a surplus is identified, while a projected shortfall indicates the need to adapt the saving path and investment decisions. A fundamental problem occurs, however, when an investor compares portfolios having different risk levels. If, as is typically the case, the higher risk portfolio generates a higher expected return, then the higher risk portfolio would appear to dominate the lower risk portfolio. In short, the saver would be encouraged to think that higher risk is better because higher risk generates a higher average return. This conundrum is termed by Sharpe (1997) as the "return/return trade-off." As he notes, the loss potential of the portfolio is usually described in the discussion of the decision process, but usually it does not influence the calculator's surplus/shortfall calculation. So the key measure of a saving plan's success depends only on the average return rather than the risk and return of the portfolio, which can lead to inappropriate investment decisions.

Avoiding the return/return tradeoff is a specific illustration of how outcomes-based investing can improve decision-making. The more general point is that simulation models do a better job at helping people understand risk. Outcomes-based investing allows users to determine their risk tolerance in the context of the impact of risk on their own particular outcomes. For example, someone who is sensitive to losses over the short term, absent any context, might be slotted into a conservative portfolio by a risk questionnaire. On the other hand, minimizing short-term risk might mean that this individual has little chance of achieving his long-term objective. This might indeed turn out to be the appropriate portfolio, but the individual might arrive at a different portfolio if the full range of risk/return trade-offs were illustrated. Casting the decision as a choice between low short-term risk with minimal chance of reaching long-term objectives, versus moderate short-term risk and a better long-term chance of hitting the target, would allow this user to make a more informed decision.

Outcomes-based investing also has the potential to allow investors to view their overall consumption/saving/investment process in the context of their own long-term objectives. For example, analyzing the myriad financial products on the market becomes easier when the answer to the question "Is this financial product right for me?" turns into an evaluation of whether the product improves the individual's likely outcomes. Other questions also become more manageable in an outcomes-based framework. For example, this framework can answer the following question: "The DOW dropped 500 points, what does this mean to me?" Ultimately, having a single framework to analyze financial uncertainty and make financial decisions could result in improved decision-making.

Challenges in Implementing an Outcomes-Based Approach

Some problems arise in the process of implementing an outcomes-based approach, many of which we have solved in the process of devising a new simulation model offered by Financial Engines.[3] In developing the program, the most significant challenges were (a) to summarize vast amount of information generated by the simulation, and (b) to create a Monte Carlo simulation with sufficient precision to facilitate decision making summarizing all the information generated is challenging because at each point in time, the situation model generates a full wealth distribution. Determining which characteristics of the simulation are most relevant to making decisions ultimately depends on the preferences of the person making the decisions. It is possible, although unlikely, that someone thinking of retiring in thirty years worries most about the 75th percentile of the wealth distribution ten years prior to retirement. Likewise, some other individual might care deeply about a different point on the outcomes distribution, at some other point in time. Implementing an outcomes-based system requires determining which pieces of information are relevant to individual decision making.

To help determine which pieces of information to display, Financial Engines relies on behavioral finance research. This literature is summarized by Shefrin (2000), who describes some of the key elements to investor decision-making as follows:

According to folklore, greed and fear drive financial markets. But this is only partly correct. While fear does play a role, most investors react less to greed and more to *hope*. Fear induces an investor to focus on events that are especially unfavorable, while hope induces him or her to focus on events that are favorable. In addition to hope and fear, that apply *generally*, investors have *specific* goals to which they aspire. (120)

This research, along with user testing, leads us to summarize the Monte Carlo information generated using five summary statistics. The most important one relates to the chances of achieving a specific goal. In particular, the user is shown the probability that he will have enough wealth to achieve the retirement income objective. Given that many people are unaccustomed to seeing and interpreting probabilities, Financial Engines uses a weather analogy to help communicate the financial forecast (sunny, cloudy, stormy, etc.). The second highest priority statistic deals with investor fear regarding the short-term loss potential, defined as the 5th percentile of portfolio wealth distribution over the next year. Highlighting these two pieces of information allows the user to trade off hope and fear. A higher risk portfolio may improve one's chance of long-term success, but it also implies larger short-term volatility.[4] In addition to measures focused on hope and fear, Financial Engines models also report other key information regarding the user's retirement prospects. In particular, the program generates estimates of upside, median, and downside wealth outcomes at the specified investment horizon, where upside, median, and downside are defined as the 95th, 50th, and 5th wealth percentiles respectively.

While determining which statistics to show can be a difficult task, presenting these statistics is also challenging, since many people do not handle probabilities comfortably. To address this concern, each of the five statistics is reported in an accessible way. For example, the loss associated with the 5th percentile of year 1 wealth is reported as an amount the user might lose over the short term, if markets perform poorly. Similarly, the long-term 95th, 50th, and 5th percentiles are reported as the long-term upside, median, and downside scenarios. Finally, the probability of achieving the long-term objective is reported using a graphical weather metaphor in addition to reporting the actual statistic. Irrespective of the implementation, it is important to recognize these types of challenges facing any outcomes-based approach to investing.

The second important challenge in implementing an outcomes-based model is the size of the computational requirements for the simulation approach. An advantage of Monte Carlo simulation is it yields approximate distributions even in cases where analytic distributions are unknown. But its disadvantage is that substantial simulation runs might be needed before the results are precise enough to form the basis for decision-making. As an example, we consider the problem of estimating the probability of achieving a particular wealth goal at retirement. Irrespective of the complexity of the stochastic process, the wealth associated with each scenario will either be deemed sufficient or falling short of the goal. In this sense, each scenario can be characterized as Bernoulli random variable that takes a value of 1 when the goal is met or exceeded and a value of zero otherwise. To express this statistically, we let:

$$X_i = \begin{cases} 1, & W_{T,i} > W^*, \\ 0, & \text{otherwise}, \end{cases}$$

where X_1 refers to the scenario i indicator variable ($=1$ if goal achieved); W_{Ti} *refers to scenario i* simulated wealth at investment horizon T; and W^* is the retirement wealth objective.

A natural estimator for the probability of achieving the wealth objective is to determine the fraction of scenarios that achieve the goal. Given the definition of X above, this estimator Y is simply expressed as follows:

$$Y = \frac{\sum_{i=1}^{N} X_i}{N},$$

where N = number of scenarios in the given simulation. For example, if there were 100 scenarios in the simulation ($N=100$), and 50 of these scenarios met or exceeded the wealth objective, then the estimate for the probability of achieving the wealth objective would be 50 percent (50/100).

Nevertheless the estimated probability of achieving one's wealth objective is a noisy estimate. In the example above, if another 100 scenarios were generated, only 40 might achieve the goal. In this case, the estimated chance of success is 40 percent even though the true chance of success is 50 percent. This dependency of the estimated chance of success on the particular sample of scenarios is called "sampling error." And as is well known, sampling error with only a few runs (e.g., 100 scenarios) can be so large as to invalidate decision making.

To determine the uncertainty associated with any particular estimate, the variance of the estimator must be calculated (Appendix). It turns out that the reasonable range of outcomes from a given Monte Carlo simulation is approximately $\pm 1/N^{1/2}$, where N is the number of scenarios simulated. For example, if N is 100, then the error bound is approximately $+/- \frac{1}{10}$ or 10 percent! Put another way, a 100-scenario Monte Carlo simulation would likely yield an estimated probability of achieving a particular goal of be-

TABLE 1. Potential Monte Carlo Results (Sample Size = 100) (percent)

Portfolio Risk Level	True Probability of Achieving Goal (P)	Likely Range for Monte Carlo Simulation	Potential Monte Carlo Results
1	46	36–56	36
2	48	38–58	58
3	50	40–60	40
4	52	42–62	62
5	54	44–64	44

Source: Author's calculations.

tween 40 and 60 percent, when the true underlying probability was 50 percent.

To put this result in context, consider an individual hoping to use Monte Carlo simulation to make outcomes-based investment decisions. Suppose this investor would like to evaluate five different portfolios, each generating a different probability of achieving his wealth objective. Table 1 illustrates the precision problem faced when relying on a small number of Monte Carlo scenarios (in this case, 100 runs). With so few scenarios, only a very coarse assessment can be devised. What is interesting is that even when the scenario count rises to 400, the uncertainty is still large ($\pm$ 5 percent).[5]

To distinguish consistently the possible portfolios described in Table 1, research has shown that the Monte Carlo model would require on the order of 10,000 runs ($\pm$ 1 percent error). Depending on the complexity of the simulation, this number of scenarios may not be computationally feasible. Fortunately, sampling techniques exist with the potential to decrease significantly the number of computations required to achieve a low-variance estimate. The best variance reduction technique depends on the particular problem. Based on our experiments, we find that stratification techniques seem to work well with the wealth accumulation problem. This refers to a technique for reducing the variance of a Monte Carlo simulation. The draws used for the simulation are not chosen completely at random. Rather, specific statistics of the sample are required to match their theoretical distributions exactly.

As an example of stratified sampling, consider a Monte Carlo experiment to find the average elevation of Massachusetts (hypothetically deemed to be a rectangle for our purposes). Suppose we can choose 12 points within the state, and at each of these points we measure the elevation, taking the mean of these measurements as an estimate of the average state elevation. The question arises as to how the 12 points should be selected. If we were to select 12 points at random, there is some chance that they might cluster about the low-lying Cape Cod seashore. A more scientific approach would be to divide Massachusetts into 12 equal areas and choose one point ran-

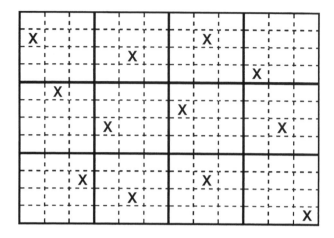

Figure 1. Two-dimensional stratification. Source: Author's calculations.

domly from each area (Figure 1). Theoretically, each of these areas should be sampled with equal frequency, and this stratification scheme enforces this result. This is an example of two-dimensional stratification.

Stratified sampling tends to reduce variance primarily because the stratified sampling avoids the potential clumping of samples. For example, Figure 2 illustrates a potential sample using standard Monte Carlo. This particular sample overweights the western portion of the state, and thus the result could deviate substantially from the true average elevation. Stratified sampling explicitly rules out this type of clustering, thus increasing the likelihood that an estimate closer to the true value is achieved.

Returning to the wealth accumulation problem, we posit that stratification could reduce the variance of the terminal wealth distribution and thus reduce the noise around a statistic derived from the wealth distribution. Suppose the objective was to create an estimate of the probability of achieving a particular goal that was precise to within ± 1 percent. As described above, a Monte Carlo simulation with 10,000 samples would ensure this level of precision. An interesting question is, how much improvement could stratification provide? To simplify the example, let us suppose that the wealth accumulation process is as follows (ignoring future contributions):

$$W_T = W_0 \prod_{j=1}^{T} (1 + R_j) \; .$$

In other words, ending wealth is simply starting wealth accumulated at the appropriate (stochastic) rate of return. Ideally, retirement wealth could

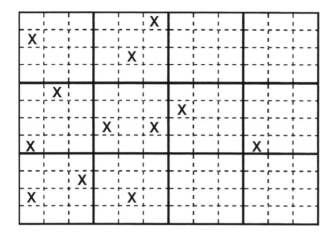

Figure 2. Potential Monte Carlo sample. Source: Author's calculations.

itself be stratified. In fact, if retirement wealth could be stratified, the resulting precision would be approximately $\pm\ 1/N$. In this case, our research shows that only 100 samples would yield the desired precision!

Unfortunately if retirement wealth could itself be stratified, this would imply knowledge of the analytic retirement wealth distribution. In this event, there would be no need to estimate the probability, since it could be calculated exactly. But since retirement wealth cannot be stratified, another alternative is to stratify the individual return random variables. The problem with stratifying the returns is that the dimensionality of the stratification becomes too high. Recalling the Massachusetts example, the stratification occurred along two dimensions: horizontal and vertical bands. This two-dimensional delineation required at least twelve observations (3*4) to appropriately sample the state. A full stratification of the returns would require a T-dimensional stratification (a dimension for each return random variable). Even if only two bands were considered per random variable, the resulting requirement for complete coverage would be at least 2^T scenarios. If returns were annual and the projection period was 50 years, the number of scenarios is clearly seen to be prohibitive.

One strategy might be to ignore some dimensions and simply stratify a few of the returns. Another desirable approach would be to stratify using some measure highly correlated with retirement wealth, if not wealth itself. The intuition is that if something highly correlated with retirement wealth is required to have minimal clustering, this should decrease the clustering properties of retirement wealth. In order to motivate a quantity correlated with retirement wealth consider the following approximation:

$$\ln(W_T) = \ln\left(W_0 \prod_{j=1}^{T} (1 + R_j)\right) ,$$

$$\ln(W_T) = \ln(W_0) + \sum_{j=1}^{T} \ln(1 + R_j) ,$$

$$\ln(W_T) \approx \ln(W_0) + \sum_{j=1}^{T} R_j ,$$

$$W_T = W_0 \exp\left(\sum_{j=1}^{T} R_j\right) .$$

This approximation indicates that retirement wealth should be highly correlated with the *sum* of the returns. If the returns in this problem were normal, then the sum of the returns is also normal. This fact can be exploited to stratify the sum of the individual returns.

The benefit of stratification in this simple case is clear from Table 2. For this simple problem, stratifying the sum of the returns decreases the number of scenarios required to achieve the objective precision by over an order of magnitude. In more complicated problems, the improvement tends to degrade because the correlation between the stratified quantity and the terminal wealth degrades. Even in this case where degradation occurs, we find that stratification can yield significant improvement over standard Monte Carlo simulations.

Conclusion

Improvement retirement planning requires better, more sophisticated, outcomes-based investing and Monte Carlo analysis. Simulation modeling can now permit evaluation of complex outcomes and better retirement decision-making. An outcomes-based approach has several benefits. One is the avoidance of the return/return trade-off problem, arising when riskier portfolios are perceived to be superior to less risky ones, solely due to their higher average expected return. Outcomes-based approaches also offer improved risk assessment by quantifying the risk of a particular plan in terms of the range of potential outcomes. This quantification allows trade-offs between short-term sensitivity to losses and long-term goal achievement. Outcomes-based approaches also can offer a single framework for interpreting new products and events.

We have also identified some solutions to many of the challenges faced by developers of outcomes-based models. Displaying key statistics in a way people can understand proves to be a nontrivial problem, which motivates the statistics shown by Financial Engines' outcomes-based approach. We also

TABLE 2. Stratification Results for Terminal Wealth Problem

Return Distribution Assumption	Simulation Technique	Samples Required to Ensure ± 1% Goal Probability Error
$R_j \sim \text{Normal}(0.1, 0.2)$	Simple Monte Carlo	10,000
$R_j \sim \text{Normal}(0.1, 0.2)$	Stratification	900

Source: Author's calculations.

show how to assess the probability that a particular retirement plan achieves a wealth objective, and the difficulty that arises with small numbers of simulations. We suggest that stratification is a method to reduce the variance of probability estimates.

Appendix

The variance for Bernoulli random variables is well-known, leading to the following result for our estimator, Y:

$$\text{Var}(Y) = \text{Var}\left(\frac{\sum_{i=1}^{N} X_i}{N}\right)$$

$$= \frac{\text{Var}\left(\sum_{i=1}^{N} X_i\right)}{N^2}$$

$$= \frac{\sum_{i=1}^{N} \text{Var}(X_i)}{N^2}$$

$$= \frac{N * P * (1 - P)}{N^2}$$

$$= \frac{P * (1 - P)}{N}.$$

In this derivation, P is the true probability of achieving the wealth objective and N is the number of scenarios created in the Monte Carlo simulation. The first equality above simply substitutes for Y. The second equality follows from a property of how scalars impact variances. The third equality recognizes that each Bernoulli random variable is independent, implying that the variance of the sum equals the sum of the variances. The fourth equality utilizes the fact that the variance of a Bernoulli random variable is $P * (1 - P)$, where P is the probability of the Bernoulli random variable taking a value of 1. In this case, P is the probability of achieving the wealth objective. Finally, the last equality is simply algebra.

In addition, as N becomes large, the estimator for the chance of reaching the goal becomes approximately normal. In other words, as N becomes large:[6]

$$Y \sim N(P, \text{Var}(Y)),$$

where P is the true probability of achieving the goal, and $\text{Var}(Y)$ is defined above. Assuming this normal approximation holds, then a reasonable confidence interval around Y would be $+/-$ two standard deviations. Using the variance above, two standard deviations is

$$2 * \text{STD}(Y) = 2 * \text{Var}(Y)^{1/2}$$

$$= 2 * \left(\frac{P * (1 - P)}{N} \right)^{1/2}$$

$$= \frac{1}{N^{1/2}}, \quad P = \frac{1}{2}.$$

The last equality occurs when the true goal probability, P, is 50 percent. Since this is the point that corresponds to maximum variance, it is useful to consider this as a worst-case approximation.

Notes

1. For example, an investor who receives a 50 percent return one year followed by a loss of 20 percent had a cumulative return of close to 10 percent. However, the average of the two returns is 15 percent.

2. This latter is sometimes referred to as "gap analysis."

3. This company offers a very sophisticated online adviser that "provides alternative portfolios based on four factors you are free to adjust: the year in which you choose to retire; how much income you expect in retirement; your savings rate; and the amount of risk you are willing to assume. To do 'what if' scenarios with one or more of these different variables, you simply adjust onscreen 'sliders' that resemble the bass and treble controls on a stereo. Adjust your retirement age, or your risk tolerance, for example, and the program quickly fashions an alternative portfolio" (Longman 2000). The program analyzes the user's portfolio using many different scenarios, and outputs probabilities of achieving retirement asset targets. For more information see www.financialengines.com.

4. As other analysis in this volume points out, earnings (and hence contribution) streams and investment horizons are also stochastic (Davis and Willen, this volume; Bernheim et al., this volume), as is life expectancy in retirement (Brown et al. this volume). However, as of this writing, the models employed by Financial Engines take contributions and investment horizon as exogenously determined by the investor.

5. This number of scenarios is consistent with the typical defined benefit asset/liability study, in our experience.

6. This argument is a bit loose, in that Y is actually degenerate as N becomes large. More formally, Y should be scaled up by the square root of N in order to approximate a normal distribution. The test offers a useful shorthand for the discussion; see Amemiya (1985) for additional detail.

References

Amemiya, Takeshi. 1985. *Advanced Econometrics*. Cambridge, Mass.: Harvard University Press.

Bernheim, B. Douglas, Lorenzo Forni, Jagadeesh Gokhale, and Laurence J. Kotlikoff. This volume. "An Economic Approach to Setting Retirement Saving Goals."

Bratley, Paul, Bennet L. Fox, and Linus E. Schrage. 1987. *A Guide to Simulation*. 2nd ed. New York: Springer-Verlag.

Brown, Jeffrey R., Olivia S. Mitchell, and James M. Poterba. This volume. "Mortality Risk, Inflation Risk, and Annuity Products."

Davis, Steven J. and Paul Willen. This volume. "Risky Labor Returns and Portfolio Choice."

Employee Benefit Research Institute (EBRI). 1999a. *Pension Investment Report, 4th Quarter 1998* (May): 9–10.

———. 1999b. *Retirement Confidence Survey: Summary of Findings*. 〈www.ebri.org/rcs/1999/rcssummary.pdf〉.

Leibowitz, Martin L., J. Benson Durham, P. Brett Hammond, and Michael Heller. This volume. "Retirement Planning and the Asset/Salary Ratio."

Longman, Phillip J. 2000. "Fiscal Therapy Online Is Right at Your Fingertips." *US News & World Report*, August 8. 〈www.usnews.com/usnews/issue/000807/nycu/calculator.htm〉.

Moore, James F. and Olivia S. Mitchell. 2000. "Projected Retirement Wealth and Saving Adequacy." In *Forecasting Retirement Needs and Retirement Wealth*, ed. Olivia S. Mitchell, P. Brett Hammond, and Anna M. Rappaport. Pension Research Council. Philadelphia: University of Pennsylvania Press. 68–94.

Profit Sharing/401(k) Council of America (PSCA). 1999. *Growth of Defined Contribution Plan Participation and Assets*. 〈www.psca.org/dcstats1.html〉.

Sharpe, William F. 1997. *Financial Planning in Fantasyland*. 〈www.stanford.edu/~wfsharpe/art/fantasy.htm〉.

Shefrin, Hersh. 2000. *Beyond Greed and Fear*. Boston: Harvard Business School Press.

Warshawsky, Mark J. and John Ameriks. 2000. "How Prepared Are Americans for Retirement?" In *Forecasting Retirement Needs and Retirement Wealth*, ed. Olivia S. Mitchell, P. Brett Hammond, and Anna M. Rappaport. Pension Research Council. Philadelphia: University of Pennsylvania Press. 33–67.

Part III
Innovations for Managing Retirement Wealth

Chapter 7
Taking the Subsidy Out of Early Retirement: Converting to Hybrid Pensions

Robert L. Clark and Sylvester J. Schieber

The fraction of the U.S. labor force covered by an employer-provided pension plan has remained stable during the past three decades. However, the outlines of the pension universe have been transformed significantly. Since the passage of the Employee Retirement Income Security Act (ERISA) in 1974, there has been a strong and ongoing trend away from the use of defined benefit plans as more and more firms have chosen to offer defined contribution plans, especially 401(k) plans (PBGC 1999). This movement toward greater utilization of defined contribution pensions has occurred primarily among smaller employers.[1]

In the past decade, another significant development has emerged, with the conversion of traditional final-pay defined benefit plans to cash balance and pension equity plans. This recent change is occurring mainly among larger employers, although a number of smaller employers have also made the shift. Among larger employers, the adoption of hybrid plans has been particularly prevalent in the financial services, utilities, and telecommunications industries. Among smaller or intermediate sized employers, the adoption of these new plans has often occurred in the health services industry. Each of these industrial sectors has undergone some restructuring in recent years, and hybrid plans may be a response to the dynamic business environment in which employers have found themselves.

The ongoing growth of defined contribution plans has been the focus of research studies for over a decade, as analysts have attempted to explain the reasons for the shift and its impact on workers and firms (Clark and McDermed 1990; Gustman and Steinmeier 1992; Ippolito 1997). By contrast, the conversion of traditional defined benefit plans to hybrid plans has only recently become the focus of scholarly research (Brown et al. 2000; Clark and Munzenmaier, 2000). The void in research has to some extent been filled by reporting in the popular press that has relied extensively on selected interviews with senior workers in large companies who have been adversely affected by the adoption of hybrid plans. The present analysis extends the debate by offering new evidence on the impact of plan conversions on workers who stay with their employers under hybrid plans. We examine the full extent of the conversion process including changes in supplementary defined contribution plans and the use of transition benefits to moderate the effect of the conversion on senior workers.

Three results from the shift to hybrid pension plan have been identified by Brown et al. (2000). First, they showed that the shift to hybrid pensions would benefit the vast majority of affected workers, if they were to quit their jobs under the new plans prior to the early retirement eligibility age. Second, they found that the conversion to the hybrid plans generally meant the elimination of early retirement subsidies characterizing the prior plan designs. Third, they demonstrated that the majority of benefit reductions that would occur in the shift to hybrid plans would be concentrated among portions of the covered populations that remained with their employers beyond retirement age eligibility. This prior study did not document the extent to which the elimination of early retirement subsidies was the reason for benefit reductions occurring in the shift to hybrid plans. The present analysis focuses on the elimination of these early retirement subsidies in the shift to hybrid plans, to measure whether this explains the benefit reductions that sometimes occur during plan redesign.

Our assessment of plan conversions is divided into three parts. We begin with a description of a unique sample of 77 plan sponsors that converted a traditional defined benefit plan to a hybrid plan after 1985. We evaluate whether the replacement of the traditional pension with a hybrid plan increased or decreased company retirement costs, whether changes were made in related retirement benefits, and whether transition benefits were provided to some or all existing workers at the time of the conversion. We then assess the characteristics of workers who can expect to have increased retirement benefits after the plan conversion and the characteristics of those workers who expect to be adversely affected by the change. Next, we disentangle the impact of plan conversions per se on retirement income, from changes that would have occurred if the traditional plan had been maintained but all early retirement incentives were eliminated. Finally, we close by placing our results in the context of evolving retirement policy and practice. Our conclusions support previous findings that younger workers with limited job experience gain disproportionately from plan conversions, because traditional pensions tend to benefit disproportionately workers toward the end of their careers. Younger workers are less likely to remain with their current employer until retirement, and so will typically get little benefit from traditional plans. Hybrid plans, on the other hand, usually provide larger benefit accruals to younger workers than the plans they replace.

Senior workers with considerable job tenure at the time of the conversion often receive lower benefit accruals under the new hybrid plans than they would have under their prior plans unless special transition rules are applied. We also conclude that most of the reduction in benefits for workers adversely affected by the shift to a hybrid plan is due to the elimination of subsidized early retirement benefits, not to the plan conversion itself.

Understanding Conversions to Cash Balance Plans

The effect of converting traditional defined benefit plans into cash balance or pension equity plans is examined using a sample of 77 employers who converted their pension plan between 1985 and 2000. The sponsors of all of these plans are clients of Watson Wyatt Worldwide, a major benefits consulting firm, and the sample is composed of all the plans for which Brown et al. (2000) were able to access sufficient plan information to compute retirement benefits under the prior traditional plan and the new hybrid plan.[2] Among the plan conversions considered are 46 employers who established cash balance plans and 31 firms that adopted pension equity plans. The number of active participants in these plans ranges from 100 to over 100,000. The distribution of plans by number of active participants is shown in Table 1. Although the sample includes plan conversions during a 15-year period, most of the changes have occurred since 1997; 31 of the plan conversions were made between 1985 and 1996, and 46 conversions were made between 1997 and 2000.

Benefits in the prior traditional DB plans were determined using an average earnings formula, with 87 percent of the plans employing some measure of final average earnings, and 13 percent using a career average formula. Among the final average plans, 70 percent based benefits on the final five years of earnings. Only 16 percent of these plans were not integrated with social security, with half of the sample using an excess integration formula and one-third using a benefit offset method. This sample of traditional plans that were converted to hybrid plans tended to have a higher percentage of plans using final average salary in the benefit formula and a higher percentage of firms integrated with social security than was true more generally.[3] The preretirement earnings replacement rate for workers hired at age 30, who remained in these plans until age 65, ranged between 25 and 50 percent for 88 percent of the plans in the sample. All but two of the prior plans included subsidized early retirement benefits.

After the conversion process, new formulas in both the cash balance and the pension equity plans provided specified credits to a benefit account for each worker. Less than half of the new cash balance plans (20 out of 46) provided for a uniform percentage of base pay to be credited to an employee's account, varying from 2 to 10 percent of pay each year. Slightly over half of the plans (26) varied the amount credited by age and/or years of

TABLE 1. Distribution of Sample Plans by Size and Type of Plan

Number of Active Plan Participants	Cash Balance Plans	Pension Equity Plans	Total Plans
100–499	4	3	7
500–999	10	3	13
1,000–2,499	6	10	16
2,500–4,999	10	6	16
5,000–9,999	8	1	9
10,000–19,999	3	6	9
20,000 and over	5	2	7
Total	46	31	77

Source: Authors' calculations; see text.

service. Thirteen of the plans increase the pension credit for earnings above a designated level that is a percentage of the social security wage base. Most of the plans credit an annual return on the account balance equal to the rate on some specified Treasury bill or bond ranging from three month to 30-year bonds, while seven plans specified some other rate or tied the annual return to the consumer price index. Among the 31 pension equity plans, 4 specified a fixed percentage of earnings to be credited annually to each individual's account ranging from 7 to 12 percent; 27 plans had differential annual credits to participants' accounts that varied by age and or years of service. In 18 plans, individuals received a higher pension credit above a designated level of earnings which was a specified percentage of the social security wage base or average social security covered compensation.

Benefit formulas in the traditional final pay DB plans produced a sharp increase in the value of retirement benefits with continued service at older ages. Subsidized early retirement provisions in those plans provided a sharp increase in present value of pension benefits once the worker had reached the age of early retirement. Together these characteristics of the traditional defined benefit plans provided greater benefits to long service workers who remained with the company until the age of eligibility for early retirement. Pension equity plans and cash balance plans more closely approximate career average defined benefit plans without early retirement options than do defined contribution plans. These plans provide for a more uniform increase in benefits with continued employment and do not have the significant spike in pension benefits that is embedded in final average pay plans with early retirement provisions.

Elimination of Early Retirement Subsidies

Economists have been studying the retirement incentives embedded in our retirement systems for over two decades (Quinn 1977; Burkhauser 1979;

Gordon and Blinder 1980; Fields and Mitchell, 1984; and Kotlikoff and Wise, 1985). One plan feature that has garnered substantial attention is the pattern of accruing benefits for workers who work beyond the normal retirement age in these plans (typically age 65). Often failure to retire and begin to take benefits by this age results in a negative accrual of benefits for additional years of work, primarily because plans may limit the number of years of covered service allowed and because there are no adjustments in the actuarial value of accrued benefits beyond normal retirement age.[4] Failure to take a benefit in this situation simply results in the ultimate monthly or annual annuity being paid over a shorter period of time, thus reducing the total lifetime benefit paid. This provides an economic incentive for workers to retire at the normal retirement age, and most empirical studies report a spike in the probability of retirement at this age.

A second plan feature that received considerable attention is the effect of early retirement subsidies on work and retirement decisions. To clarify how these subsidies affect lifetime benefits, consider the accrual pattern of benefits shown in Figure 1 for a worker hired at age 30 at a starting salary of $40,000 per year who is participating in one of the benefit plans in our sample. For example, the solid line in the figure shows that the present value of pension benefits for this worker grows in value from zero at the point of hire, to the equivalent of roughly one and a half years of annual pay at age 54.[5] By working from age 54 to 55, the value of the benefit for this worker suddenly jumps from one and a half times pay to slightly more than three times pay. This occurs because the plan provides an immediate benefit at age 55 with less than a full actuarial reduction relative to the benefit that would be provided at normal retirement. If the worker does not continue to work under the plan until reaching age 55, he or she would not qualify for this special subsidy and would receive benefits under the regular benefit formula.

The dashed line in Figure 1, which shows the pattern of accrued benefits that would be provided if early retirement were not subsidized, may be compared to the subsidy curve. The value of the subsidy is roughly one and a half years of pay at 55; it holds relatively steady until age 59, and then it declines steadily beyond that. At the normal retirement age of 65, the subsidy has been completely exhausted. The existence of the subsidy at age 55 provides a significant step up in pension wealth and thus increases the incentive to retire. The gradual "wearing away" of the subsidy acts as a significant disincentive to continued employment for workers subject to this benefit formula. In this case, it acts as a discount of one-third of a worker's pay for work between age 62 and 63 or 63 and 64, and as much as 40 percent of pay for work between age 64 and 65. This pattern evidently provides a significant economic incentive to retire after a worker has satisfied the requirements for early retirement, and it generates a substantial increase in the probability of retirement at the early retirement age. Thus, traditional

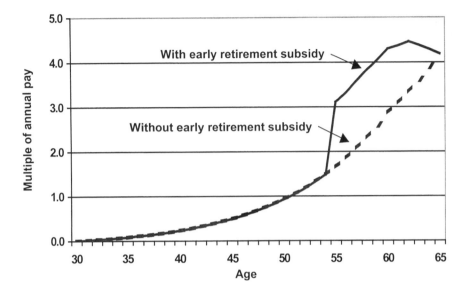

Figure 1. Value of accrued pension benefit (present value) as a multiple of annual pay: new hire at age 30 with a starting pay of $40,000. Source: Authors' calculations from data provided by Watson Wyatt Worldwide.

defined benefit plans encourage early retirement of workers many of whom are probably still in the productive portions of their working lives.

Table 2 arrays the plans in our sample according to the rate at which their early retirement subsidies wear away, computed as a percentage of pay by age of retiree. In this case, we are looking at a worker with 25 years of service at age 55. We assumed this worker's starting salary was $40,000 per year in current terms and that it would grow over time at the rate of average wages in the economy. Between age 55 and 60, 38 percent of plans reduced the value of workers' earnings by 0 to 20 percent per year through the erosion in the value of the early retirement subsidies. Between age 60 and 62, more plans reduce the value of early retirement and the size of the annual wear away is increased. Nearly three-quarters of the plans reduced their early retirement subsidies for workers in this age range. Between the age of 62 and 65, 96 percent of the plans reduced their early retirement subsidies and 39 percent did so at a rate that reduced the economic value of the wage earned for added years worked by at least 25 percent. One plan offset the wage earned by 50 percent per year from age 62 to 65. Some of these plans had very significant penalties for continued employment of workers with substantial service.

Figure 2 shows how the accrual pattern under the pension plan represented in Figure 1 changed when the traditional DB plan was converted to a

TABLE 2. Percent of Plans with Alternative Annual Wear Away Rates of Early
Retirement Subsidies

Wearaway Rate as % of Annual Earnings	(Percent of Plans)		
	55–60	60–62	62–65
0.0–4.9%	14.3	13.0	9.1
5.0–9.9	6.5	7.8	18.2
10.0–14.9	15.6	15.6	7.8
15.0–19.9	1.3	32.5	11.7
20.0–24.9	0.0	1.3	10.4
25.0–29.9	0.0	1.3	7.8
30.0–34.9	0.0	0.0	9.1
35.0–39.9	0.0	0.0	14.3
40.0–50.0	0.0	1.3	7.8

Source: Authors' calculations (see text), assuming worker has 25 years of service at age 55, starting salary of $40,000, and average nominal wage growth.

cash balance plan. The solid line in the figure shows the accrual pattern under the old plan, and the dashed line shows the accrual pattern under the new cash balance plan that replaced it. This particular worker would clearly be better off under the new plan if he or she terminated employment prior to age 55, since the early retirement subsidy in the old plan was eliminated in the shift to the new plan. Even at the normal retirement age of 65 the new plan's benefits are not as generous as the old plan's. Nevertheless, continued employment beyond the normal retirement age will ultimately make the new plan more valuable.

Very different incentives apply to workers who terminate their employment prior to immediate pension eligibility, as is evident from Figure 2. The hybrid plan provides a stronger incentive for workers to stay with their employer at earlier ages, while it also imposes less penalty if they leave prior to reaching early retirement eligibility. Very different incentives also apply for continued employment beyond both the early retirement age, and the normal retirement age for long-career workers. The new plan does not subsidize early retirement, nor does it penalize continued work.

A significant element of the story behind the shift from traditional defined benefit plans to a hybrid plan type is the elimination of early retirement subsidies that had existed in the former. Of the 77 cases under study here, 75 had early retirement subsidies in their traditional plans. We have estimated the magnitude of these subsidies by estimating what share of plan costs was attributable to the subsidies paid for early retirement benefits. In developing these cost estimates, we employ the projected unit credit cost method that the Financial Accounting Standards Board (FASB) requires private plan sponsors to use in developing accounting measures of their plans' expenses and liabilities.[6]

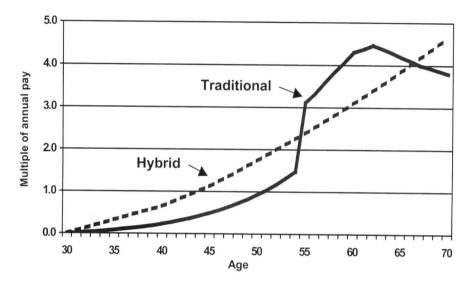

Figure 2. Value of accrued pension benefit (present value) as a multiple of annual pay: new hire at age 30 with a starting pay of $40,000 under a traditional and a hybrid pension plan. Source: Authors' calculations from data provided by Watson Wyatt Worldwide.

For purposes of comparison the cost analyses are based on a simulated workforce that we created and then applied to all firms, rather than on the characteristics of each individual firm's labor force.[7] We generated a synthetic workforce of 10,000 workers randomly selected from a combined pool of roughly 165,000 workers, taken from over a dozen of Watson Wyatt's larger clients. For each of the workers, we had information on date of birth, date of hire, and pay level. We used turnover assumptions consistent with those that would generally prevail in large firms offering a defined benefit plan. We did not employ plan-specific turnover experience, although higher turnover rates are applied to the health and hospital plans consistent with observed behaviors.[8]

For the plans under study, the distribution of early retirement subsidies as a percentage of total plan costs is shown in Figure 3. The plans are ranked by the estimated total cost of the original plan. Early retirement subsidies tended to be somewhat larger, on average, in plans with higher costs than in those with lower costs. For example, among the 20 plans with the lowest costs, the average share of the total costs attributable to the early retirement subsidies was 10 percent of the total plan costs, whereas among the highest cost 20 plans, the early retirement subsidy accounted for 19 percent of total plan cost. However, some of the low cost plans had early retirement sub-

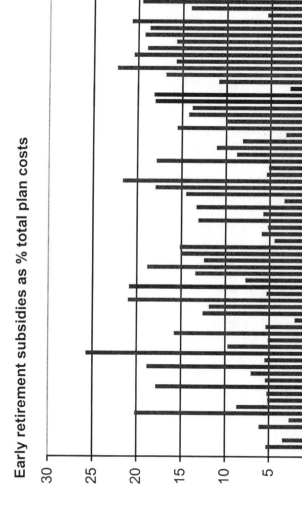

Figure 3. Ranking of projected unit pension costs attributable to early retirement subsidies. Source: Authors' calculations.

sidies as large as plans at the upper end of the cost distribution, and some of the highest cost plans had relatively minimal early retirement subsidies. To link back to the earlier discussion, the cost of the early retirement subsidies in the original pension plan described in Figures 1 and 2 was about 19 percent of the total plan costs in that case. Within our sample, that plan was among the more generous in subsidizing early retirement, but it was definitely not the most generous.

As the above discussion suggests, the elimination of early retirement subsidies offers a pension sponsor the opportunity to reduce the cost of the retirement plan without making any other changes. Technically, an employer can eliminate the early retirement subsidies in its pension plan with certain limited grandfather provisions. For example, assume that a plan with significant early retirement subsidies for a worker at age 55 with 30 years of service was amended on July 1, 2000 to require full actuarial reductions for retirements prior to the plan normal retirement age of 65. This full actuarial reduction could be implemented immediately, upon adoption of the amendment, for anyone who terminated employment after July 1, 2000, who had not reached age 55 lacked and lacked 30 years of service. For a participant had reached age 55 and completed 30 years of service prior to July 1, 2000, the benefit could not be reduced below the earned accrued benefit if the worker retired immediately before the plan amendment took effect.

If the participant in this case had not met the early retirement subsidy criterion prior to the effective date of the amendment, but subsequently did meet it, then the amount of the subsidy earned under the prior formula would be preserved. In this case, the worker's benefit would be the larger of the benefit earned up to the point of transition, including the early retirement subsidy, or the benefit under the plan as modified at the date of retirement. Thus, the worker's accrued benefit would not be reduced by the amendment, but he or she would not accrue additional benefits until subsequent service and pay raises led to an accrued benefit under the new formula that exceeded the grandfathered benefit under the old formula. Because this worker's accrued benefits already reflect the value of the early retirement subsidies, elimination of early retirement subsidies from the plan would not result in any significant employer cost savings. Virtually all the potential cost savings from eliminating early retirement subsidies reflected in Figure 3 would therefore drive from the elimination of subsidies for workers not yet eligible for early retirement at the point of transition.

The grandfather requirements for early retirement subsidies result in a "wearaway" situation for plan sponsors who eliminate such plan subsidies. This phenomenon has created a significant amount of adverse publicity in the conversion to hybrid plans, because some workers receiving a grandfathered portion of the early retirement subsidy in prior plans could go for several years without earning added benefits under the new plan. But as Table 2 and the discussion around it shows, there is a significant amount of wearaway *already* built into traditional defined benefit plans with early retirement subsidies. It is quite likely that some workers who believe they were adversely affected by the wearaway phenomenon in the transition to a hybrid plan are actually not suffering wearaway as rapidly under their new plan as they would have under their original one, had they stayed under it. Also, in the case reflected there, workers covered under the plan who terminate employment prior to age 55 would typically be better off under the new plan than the old one.

It is clear from Figure 2 that some of the cost savings resulting from the reduction in benefits to people reaching early retirement age are redistributed to workers who leave prior to that age. What is not clear is whether the added benefits provided to shorter term workers would be more or less costly than the benefit reductions resulting for people who would have attained early retirement age under the old plan. In this particular case, we estimate that the plan sponsor realized some added costs over and above reinvesting the early retirement subsidies back into the plan in the shift from a traditional plan to a hybrid plan. Of course the standardized workforce and turnover assumptions used in estimating these cost changes may not reflect the actual cost changes realized by any particular employer. In earlier work, Brown et al. (2000) reported that on average the projected unit credit service cost reduction in the shift from traditional hybrid plans was around 10 percent of the original plans' costs. When modifications to the 401(k) plans by these same sponsors were factored in, they estimated that the average service cost reduction employers realized in shifting to their new retirement plans dropped to around one percent.

Next we take a different look at plan cost changes by considering them against the base plans after eliminating their early retirement subsidies. The purpose of this exercise is to see if employers were reducing plan costs beyond the elimination of early retirement subsidies, or whether this was the extent of savings they were realizing and whether they actually put the early retirement subsidy reductions back into the plan. Considering the net change in plan costs due to eliminating early retirement subsidies, we find that 48 percent of the plan sponsors put at least the full value of the savings into their combined defined benefit and defined contribution package. Another 14 percent put some of the value realized back into the plan. Some 35 percent of plans reduced costs somewhat more than what they would have realized by simply eliminating early retirement subsidies, though, as reflected in Figure 3, many plans had relatively small early retirement subsidies. Nearly one-fifth of those sponsors that kept some portion of the savings realized from eliminating early retirement subsidies had total reductions in plan costs of 5 percent or less.

Cumulative Benefit Changes in the Shift to Hybrid Plans

One reason that the shift to hybrid plans has been so controversial is that some redistribution of benefits among plan participants accompanies the conversions. Even a plan conversion that increased pension costs may make some workers worse off under the hybrid plan than they would have been under the prior traditional plan. One way to show the effects of the transition is to calculate benefits for prototypical workers to show how their benefits compare under the old and new environments.

Comparative pension benefits for three hypothetical workers in the plans under analysis appear in Table 3. The first worker, in the top panel, is hired at age 30 with an annual salary of $40,000 per year in 1999. The second worker, represented in the middle panel of the table, is 40 years of age and 10 years into his career by 1999, earning a salary of $50,000 per year. The third worker is assumed to be age 50 and 20 years into a career by 1999, earning $60,000 per year. Higher or lower salaries will change the numbers slightly, but not enough to change the pattern of accruals in the alternative types of plans.[9]

A number of the plans analyzed here were converted from a traditional defined benefit structure to a hybrid plan structure several years ago, with one as long as 15 years ago. Some of the earliest hybrid plans have been modified since they were first adopted, and we did not have all the detail on the time path of these modifications. For purposes of these comparisons, we have estimated the benefits for our hypothetical workers under the defined benefit plan in operation at the time of the initial shift to a hybrid plan, and then we compare the initial benefit to the benefit provided by the current hybrid plan.[10] This means that when we consider the implications of the shift to a hybrid plan adopted 10 years ago for a worker who is 40 years of age with 10 years of service in 1999, we are comparing the accruals of a worker who has already been covered for 10 years under the new plan with one covered under the prior plan for that whole period. This has particular implications for older workers who might have been covered under transition provisions in the shift to a hybrid plan. Often plan sponsors will adopt transition provisions that may cover workers who will reach retirement eligibility in the first five to ten years after the transition to the new plan. For the oldest hybrid plans, the transition provisions are likely to have expired for the older, longer service workers we are considering here. Our choice of calculating comparison benefits in this case would result in smaller benefits under the hybrid transition arrangements than actually were provided for older workers in most cases. In that regard, our estimates of benefit reductions in the shift to hybrid plans for older workers are upper bounds of the likely effects on plan participants at the time of the conversions.

The row labels in Table 3 reflect the ratio of benefits from the hybrid plan relative to benefits that would have been provided to the same worker under

TABLE 3. Accumulated Benefit Provided by Hybrid Pension Plan Relative to Prior Plan Benefit (% of Plans)

Ratio of Hybrid Plan to Hybrid Plan Benefit	Age 40	Age 50	Age 55	Age 60	Age 62	Age 65
New hire at age 30, beginning pay of $40,000 in 1999						
<50	0.0	1.3	7.8	7.8		
50–99	3.9	10.4	50.7	61.0		
100–149	5.2	31.2	28.6	24.7		
150–199	13.0	26.0	6.5	2.6		
200–249	19.5	18.2	3.9	2.6		
250–299	26.0	5.2	1.3	0.0		
300–349	10.4	2.6	0.0	0.0		
350–399	10.4	3.9	0.0	0.0		
400+	11.7	1.3	1.3	1.3		
Worker at age 40 with 10 years service, pay of $50,000 in 1999						
<50		1.3	5.2	9.1		10.4
50–99		11.7	58.4	62.3		57.1
100–149		40.3	29.9	23.4		27.3
150–199		28.6	3.9	3.9		3.9
200+		18.2	2.6	1.3		1.3
Worker at age 50 with 20 years service, pay of $60,000 in 1999						
<0.50			1.3	5.2	13.0	9.1
050–099			9.1	44.2	50.7	50.7
100–149			55.8	48.1	35.1	39.0
150–199			19.5	1.3	1.3	0.0
200+			14.3	1.3	0.0	1.3

Source: Authors' calculations; see text.

the prior pension plan. For example, consider the row labeled 150–199 for the worker hired at age 30 in the top panel of the table. It indicates that 13 percent of the hybrid plans would provide this worker a benefit at age 40 that was 150 to 199 percent of the benefit that would have been provided by the prior plan. The next line shows that 19.5 percent of the hybrid plans would provide a benefit at age 40 that was 200 to 249 percent of the benefit that would have been provided by the prior plan. The evidence indicates overall that the shift to hybrid plans increased benefits for workers who terminate employment at younger ages. Nearly 90 percent of the hybrid plans provide higher benefits for workers leaving prior to age 55 than did the prior plan. Beyond age 55, however, most of the new plans provide smaller benefits than the prior plans would have. It is these benefit reductions for long-career workers reaching the prevalent retirement eligibility ages under traditional pension plans that has created some negative publicity about the shift to hybrid plans.

TABLE 4. Future Pension Accruals as a Percentage of Pay for Workers Shifted into a Hybrid Plan with the Same Cost as the Prior Plan, by Age and Service at Date of Shift

Tenure at Time of Conversion (years)	Age at Time of Conversion to a Hybrid Plan					
	20–29.9	30–39.9	40–49.9	50–54.9	50–59.9	60–65
Future pension accrual rate as % of pay for those winning or held harmless						
0–4.9	1.98	3.26	4.80	6.42	6.43	6.60
5–9.9	2.17	3.24	4.75	6.19	7.02	7.41
10–14.9	2.57	3.37	4.52	5.81	6.70	7.74
15–19.9		3.49	4.51	6.16	6.48	7.75
20–24.9		4.13	4.62	6.01	6.98	7.32
25–29.9			4.95	6.26	5.78	7.61
30+			5.51	5.84	6.29	6.55
Future pension accrual rate as % of pay for losers						
0–4.9	4.27	5.31	6.30	7.76	8.36	9.01
5–9.9	4.80	5.29	6.25	7.71	8.43	9.08
10–14.9		5.33	6.25	7.71	8.47	9.13
15–19.9		5.40	6.24	7.59	8.50	9.14
20–24.9		5.39	6.30	7.60	8.53	9.13
25–29.9			6.68	7.62	8.53	9.14
30+			7.12	7.69	8.54	9.13

Source: Brown et al. (2000).

We acknowledge that the impact of plan conversions is more complex than simply one of cutting retirement benefits. Brown et al, (2000) simulated a "synthetic" workforce of 30,000 workers through the remainder of their careers with three employers who had shifted from a traditional pension to a hybrid plan. These workers were randomly drawn from the same workforces of 15 of Watson Wyatt's larger actuarial clients, as described earlier. By simulating these workers through the remainder of their careers, the authors compared estimated benefits under the prior and replacement plans. They conclude that replacing a traditional plan with an essentially equivalent projected unit credit cost left about 80 percent of workers at least as well off under the new plan, and many would be better off. Among workers who would be worse off under the new plan, benefits would be reduced on average between 15 and 20 percent relative to their prior plans.

That analysis also found that tagging those who would be worse off under the new plan as "losers" did not adequately reflect how they would continue to benefit under the new plan relative to their counterparts who might be characterized as "winners." This point is illustrated in Table 4, which shows future pension accruals as a percentage of pay for workers classified as winners and losers in that case study of an actual employer's shift to a cash balance plan.[11] The top panel reflects accrual rates for workers who would be better off under the cash balance plan than they would be under the prior plan, while the bottom portion represent those who would be worse off. It is interesting to note that for every age and service category, the "losers" accrued pension value at a higher rate than did the "winners." So some participants were made worse off by the transition, but they will gain more from delayed retirement. In other words the shift resulted in a more equitable allocation of pension accruals and benefits across workers who leave prior to retirement eligibility and those who stay longer. For the most part, these younger workers who end up being losers in the pension shift are the ones who work under the new hybrid plan until they reach the age of early retirement eligibility under the prior traditional pension plan. For these workers, it is the elimination of early retirement subsidies that accounts for much of the benefit reduction in the shift to hybrid plans.

Cutting Benefits Through Curtailment of Early Retirement Subsidies

Are companies changing their plans as a means of reducing retirement benefits to save employment costs, or are they instead implementing a new human resource model that retains older workers in the twenty-first century? Understanding what is motivating the shift to hybrid plans depends in part on whether the plan conversion lowers annual pension benefits and how much of any benefit changes is attributable to the elimination of early retirement subsidies. Therefore we next analyze the overall benefit changes that workers eligible for early retirement subsidies incur in the move to hybrid plans. These changes in benefits are divided into two components: the first is the extent to which the elimination of the early retirement subsidy by itself affects benefits, and the second is the extent to which benefits are adjusted beyond the elimination of the early retirement subsidy.[12]

Suppose that in a traditional pension plan, the worker could expect to accumulate a benefit at age 58 that had a value of three times his pay, at point A in Figure 4. Suppose further that the early retirement subsidy made up one third of the value of that accumulated benefit at that age. If the employer simply eliminated the early retirement subsidy, the benefit at age 55 would only be worth twice the worker's pay, point B in Figure 4. Instead, however, this employer might adopt a new hybrid plan that eliminated the early retirement subsidy in the traditional plan, and also adopted further benefit modifications such that this worker's accrued benefit at age 58 is only one and a half times his pay (point C). In this case, the worker would incur a 33.3 percent benefit reduction in moving from the traditional to the hybrid plan, due to the elimination of the early retirement subsidy. She would incur an additional 16.7 percent reduction from further modifications to the prior accrual pattern of the pension. Stated alternatively, two-

Accrued benefit as a multiple of annual pay

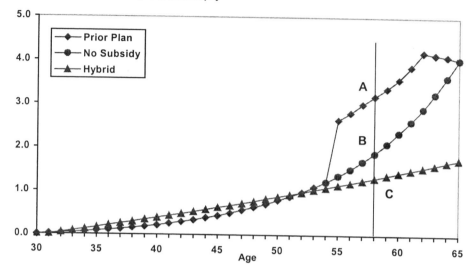

Figure 4. Relative role of the elimination of early retirement subsidies in the total reduction in benefits in the shift to a hybrid pension, scenario 1. Source: Authors' calculations.

thirds of the total benefit reduction in this case would be attributable to the elimination of early retirement subsidies in the transition from the traditional to the hybrid plan. The extent to which benefits were reduced by more than simply the elimination of early retirement subsidies is summarized in Table 5. The three panels summarize the results for the same prototypical workers as appeared in Table 3. Row labels show the percentage benefit reduction due to the shift from traditional to hybrid plan attributable to the elimination of the early retirement subsidy. For example, the top panel in the first column focuses on a worker who retires at age 55 with 25 years of service: in 2.6 percent of all the plans, the elimination of the early retirement subsidy represented between 0.0 and 24.9 percent of the total reduction in benefits for such a worker. For the 30-year-old new-hire at the point of transition to the new plan, only 15.6 percent of all hybrid plans would provide a benefit at age 55 that reduced benefits by more than simply eliminating the early retirement subsidies in the prior plan. In eight of nine cases in Table 5, fewer than half of the new plans cut benefits by more than if plan sponsors had simply eliminated early retirement subsidies, but left the remainder of the benefit formula intact. Even when benefits were cut by more than the early retirement subsidy, the subsidy elimination accounted for most of the benefit reduction.

Some employers did reduce benefits for many early retirees in the shift

TABLE 5. Benefit Reductions Attributable to the Elimination of Early Retirement Subsidies in the Shift to Hybrid Plans: Cases Where Benefits Were Reduced by More Than the Value of the Subsidy

Total Benefit Reduction from Elimination of Early Retirement Subsidy (%)	Percent of plans at age		
	55	60	62
New hire at age 30, beginning salary of $40,000			
0.0–24.9	2.6	7.8	13.0
25.0–49.9	1.3	7.8	10.4
50.0–74.9	7.8	11.7	15.6
75.0–99.9	3.9	14.3	9.1
Plans where benefit cut exceeds early retirement subsidies (%)	15.6	41.6	48.1
Worker at age 40 with 10 years of service, earning $50,000 at transition to new plan			
0.0–24.9	2.6	7.8	13.0
25.0–49.9	3.9	9.1	11.7
50.0–74.9	3.9	13.0	16.9
75.0–99.9	6.5	13.0	9.1
Plans where benefit cut exceeds early retirement subsidies (%)	16.9	42.9	50.7
Worker at age 50 with 20 years of service, earning $60,000 at transition to new plan			
0.0–24.9	2.6	9.1	11.7
25.0–49.9	3.9	6.5	10.4
50.0–74.9	2.6	11.7	14.3
75.0–99.9	13.0	9.1	9.1
Plans where benefit cut exceeds early retirement subsidies (%)	22.1	36.4	45.5

Source: Authors' calculations; see text.

from a traditional plan to the hybrid, but by less than the reduction that would have been imposed by only eliminating the early retirement subsidies in the original plan. Scenario 2 is depicted in Figure 5, where we focus on a worker at age 57. Under the traditional plan, this worker would have earned a benefit worth three and a half years of pay, point *A* in Figure 5. If the plan sponsor had simply eliminated the early retirement subsidy in the plan, the accrued benefit would be worth only two years of pay, point *B* in the figure. But under the new hybrid plan, the benefit was actually worth two and a half years of pay, point *C*. In this case, the value of the early retirement subsidy was one and a half year's pay but the reduction in benefits in the shift to the new plans was only one year's pay. In other words, the elimination of the early retirement subsidy in this case represented 150 percent of the total reduction realized in the shift to the new plan.

The prevalence of this scenario where total benefits were reduced but by

Accrued benefit as a multiple of annual pay

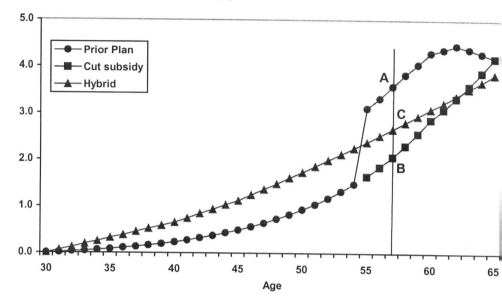

Figure 5. Relative role of the elimination/ of early retirement subsidies in the total reduction in benefits in the shift to a hybrid pension, scenario 2. Source: Authors' calculations from data provided by Watson Wyatt Worldwide.

less than the elimination of early retirement subsidies is summarized in Table 6. Our sample plan sponsors put some of the reduction in benefits realized from eliminating early retirement subsidies in their prior plans back into the new hybrid plan. Thus between 20 and 44 percent of the plans fell into this category, depending on age and service of workers at various early retirement ages. Workers retiring at younger ages appear to be more likely to fall into this category, where some portion of the early retirement subsidy was put back into the new benefit, than those retiring at older ages. In the cases where elimination of the early retirement subsidy was a very large percentage of the total benefit reduction, it is an indication that most of the early subsidy reduction was put back into the plan. For example, when the early retirement subsidy elimination represents 400 percent of the total benefit reduction in the shift to the hybrid plan, it implies that more than three-fourths of the subsidy in the old plan was reinstated in the new plan benefit. The workers represented in Table 6 all would end up getting a smaller benefit under their new plan than under the prior one, but many of the benefit reductions are relatively small, especially in comparison to the early retirement subsidies in the original plans.

In a third scenario, employers eliminated the early retirement incentives

TABLE 6. Benefit Reductions Attributable to the Elimination of Early Retirement Subsidies in the Shift to Hybrid Plans: Cases Where Total Benefits Were Reduced by Less Than the Value of the Subsidy

Total benefit reduction realized from elimination of the early retirement subsidy (%)	Percent of Plans at Age		
	55	60	62
New hire at age 30, beginning salary of $40,000			
100.0–124.9	7.8	7.8	7.8
125.0–149.9	6.5	2.6	1.3
150.0–199.9	6.5	6.5	2.6
200.0–399.9	11.7	5.2	6.5
400.0+	10.4	2.6	1.3
	42.9	24.7	19.5
Worker at age 40 with 10 years of service, earning $50,000 at transition to new plan			
100.0–124.9	7.8	9.1	7.8
125.0–149.9	7.8	6.5	2.6
150.0–199.9	9.1	3.9	3.9
200.0–399.9	9.1	3.9	3.9
400.0+	10.4	3.9	2.6
	44.2	27.3	20.8
Worker at age 50 with 20 years of service, earning $60,000 at transition to new plan			
100.0–124.9	5.2	5.2	3.9
125.0–149.9	2.6	6.5	0.0
150.0–199.9	6.5	0.0	5.2
200.0–399.9	5.2	9.1	5.2
400.0+	6.5	5.2	5.2
	26.0	26.0	19.5

Source: Authors' calculations; see text.

that had been embedded in their prior plans as they set up the replacement hybrid plans, but in the aggregate they ended up increasing benefits. This scenario is reflected in Figure 6. In this case we will focus on a worker at age 61. Under the traditional plan, this worker would have earned a benefit worth two times pay as reflected in the figure. If the sponsor in this case had simply eliminated the early retirement subsidy in the prior plan, the worker's benefit would have dropped to the equivalent of one and a half year's pay as reflected by point *B* in the figure. But under the new hybrid plan, the benefit was actually worth two and a half year's of pay as reflected by point *C*. Despite losing his early retirement subsidy at age 55, this worker would actually be better off under the new plan than under the prior one. In shifting to the new plan in this case, the sponsor put back into the plan the full value of the early retirement subsidy that was eliminated in the shift to the new plan plus even more for the hypothetical worker.

Accrued benefit as a multiple of annual pay

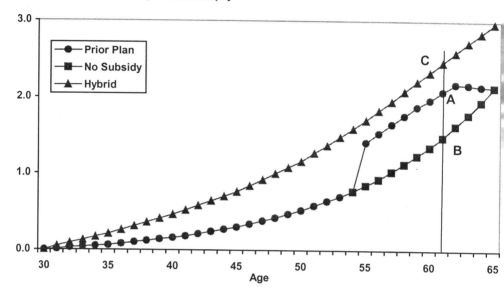

Figure 6. Relative role of the elimination of early retirement subsidies in the total reduction in benefits in the shift to a hybrid pension, scenario 3. Source: Authors' calculations from data provided by Watson Wyatt Worldwide.

The prevalence of this scenario appears in Table 7.[13] In most of the cases, the majority of the new hybrid plans would end up reducing benefits for the prototypical workers by less than the amount of the reduction that would occur if employers had simply eliminated their early retirement subsidies. For cases where the worker is assumed to retire at age 55, fewer than one-quarter of the plans would reduce benefits by more than the elimination of the early retirement subsidies. For these workers 40 to 50 percent of the plans would actually enhance benefits relative to the old plan, even though they had eliminated the subsidies related to early retirement. The only case in the table where most plans would end up reducing benefits by more than the value of the early retirement subsidy is when the worker was hired at 30, was converted to a hybrid plan at 40, and worked until age 62. In that case, just over half of the plans would pay a benefit reduced by more than the amount of the early retirement subsidy.

The Role of Pensions and National Retirement Policy

Retirement became an important segment of the lives of most Americans in the 20th century, attributable to rising real incomes and shifts in the struc-

TABLE 7. Shares of Benefit Reductions Attributable to the Elimination of Early Retirement Subsidies in the Shift from Traditional Pensions to Hybrid Plans

	Percent of Plans at Age		
	55	60	62
New hire at age 30 at a beginning salary of $40,000			
Benefit cut exceeds subsidy	15.6	41.6	48.1
Benefit cut less than subsidy	42.9	24.7	19.5
Benefit not cut or increased	41.6	33.8	32.5
Worker at age 40 with 10 years of service earning $50,000 at transition to new plan			
Benefit cut exceeds subsidy	16.9	42.9	50.7
Benefit cut less than subsidy	44.2	27.3	20.8
Benefit not cut or increased	39.0	29.9	28.6
Worker at age 50 with 20 years of service earning $60,000 at transition to new plan			
Benefit cut exceeds subsidy	22.1	36.4	45.5
Benefit cut less than subsidy	26.0	26.0	19.5
Benefit not cut or increased	52.0	37.7	35.1

Source: Authors' calculations; see text.

ture of the national economy that altered older persons' employment prospects. Retirement has evolved because of the conscious development of national retirement policies that have undergone substantial change since the establishment of social security. Initially, those policies sought to provide adequate retirement income to a segment of the elderly population facing low income and difficulty finding employment. In addition, retirement was sometimes encouraged to create job opportunities for younger workers. social security was designed to provide retirement income and required "retirement" as a condition of eligibility. Medicare offered national health care for those aged 65 and older. Preferential tax treatment was granted to employer pensions that met certain regulatory standards, and for many years national policy permitted mandatory retirement at age 65.

These policies have come under scrutiny in the last quarter century, with this reconsideration producing the elimination of mandatory retirement, the raising of the normal retirement age under social security, and the elimination of the earnings test for persons older than the normal retirement age. From a societal perspective, we have switched from subsidizing early retirement to encouraging delayed retirement, partly due to a changing perception about what is "fair." For instance, mandatory retirement provisions were eliminated because policymakers decided it was unfair to force productive people out of their jobs simply because of age. Social security's retirement age was raised because policymakers decided the cost of sustaining the original age would be unfair to workers in the face of growing dependency levels significantly driven by increases in life expectancy of retirees.

Retirement policies have also changed because of the changing dynamics of the labor market. Social security's earnings test was criticized because it discouraged people eligible for benefits from working. In the 1930s, when unemployment was rampant and policymakers thought that an older worker's retirement would create a job opening for a young worker, this policy appeared to make sense. In today's economy, where labor force growth rates are the lowest they have been in a half century and where they are expected to fall even lower in the coming decades, such policies are less persuasive.

Employers today operate in exactly the same environment as that dictating changes to social security policies. In an era of unprecedented tight labor markets, bribing workers to retire more than a decade before they will be eligible for full social security benefits is probably undesirable for many employers. This is a partial explanation for the strong and continued trend toward greater use of defined contribution pensions over time, plans that rarely have subsidized early retirement options. This transition is the result of various regulatory and economic factors, including the higher cost of complying with federal regulation, especially for small firms, along with changes in worker and firm preferences concerning deferred compensation. As a result, many employers terminated their defined benefit plans and established defined contribution plans, while emerging companies were much more likely to select defined contribution plans. Many large companies that have retained their defined benefit plans have also been concerned about the economic incentives in these plans. Key points include the attraction to young workers who have a relatively low probability of remaining with the company until retirement and the inability to retain older workers due to the significant early retirement incentives imbedded in their traditional plans. A growing number of these companies have converted their traditional plans to a type of hybrid plan that provides an individual account balance that appeals to younger workers, and also eliminates the early retirement incentives discouraging continued employment of workers still in their productive prime.[14]

Conclusions and Discussion

Interestingly, the almost three decade long shift to defined contribution plans has received relatively little adverse publicity, while the more recent shift to hybrid plans has been the target of considerable hostile reaction by Congress, the press, and labor organizations. It is ironic that the effects of the two types of plan changes are actually quite similar. In both cases, early retirement incentives are eliminated, individual accounts are established, younger short-tenured workers almost always gain, and older more senior workers who anticipated the early retirement subsidy lose retirement income relative to what they had expected.

Is the move to hybrid pension plans desirable? The answer to this question is in the eye of the beholder. Individuals who expect to remain with a single employer throughout their career and retire from this company typically will prefer a traditional defined benefit plan. In contrast, workers who anticipate that they will change employers several times will prefer retirement plans that include portable individual accounts such as defined contribution plans and cash balance plans. Workers who want to manage their own retirement funds and are willing to bear the investment risk associated with financial decisions will prefer defined contribution plans, while those seeking to avoid this type of risk will want to be covered by a defined benefit or cash balance plan.

The primary advantages of cash balance plans for employees are universal coverage, portability of benefits, and little investment risk. These plans allow employers to appeal to mobile workers and offer guaranteed benefits that do not include subsidized early retirement. Employers who wish to continue to use their pension plans to encourage lower turnover or to provide strong retirement incentives at particular ages will maintain traditional defined benefit plans. Companies seeking to attract younger, more mobile workers along with those seeking to discourage early retirement will tend to offer defined contribution and cash balance plans.

We believe that the shift to hybrid plans is consistent with a number of other elements of national retirement policy described above, and in particular it will bring employer pensions in greater alignment with evolving social security policy. Proponents of social security have often suggested its superiority to employer pensions because of its greater portability. Hybrid plans provide significantly more portability than traditional defined benefit plans. Critics of hybrid plans suggest that such plans are unfair because they do not provide the accelerated growth in benefits late in workers' careers that traditional defined benefit plans provided. However, hybrid plans provide more level accruals over workers' whole careers and provide much higher accruals late in workers' careers than does social security. As policymakers struggle to encourage workers to extend their careers to make entitlement programs more sustainable, it would be expected that they would be simultaneously interested in encouraging employers to adopt pension plans that supportive of that policy goal.

Notes

We thank Gordon Goodfellow, Tomeka Hill, and Lex Miller for their help with statistical analysis. we also thank Kyle Brown, Dick Joss, Eric Lofgren, Richard Luss, and Janemarie Mulvey for helpful comments. Opinions and conclusions are solely the authors'. Robert Clark's research was supported by the American Compensation Association and the Shannon J. Schieber Retirement Policy Institute of the Association of Private Pension and Welfare Plans.

1. The PBGC (1999) reports that the proportion of the labor force covered by a defined benefit plan declined from 38 percent in 1980 to 23 percent in 1995. As a result, the proportion of pension participants with primary coverage in a defined benefit plan declined from 83 percent to 50 percent. The number of defined benefit plans with fewer than 1,000 workers dropped from 92,000 in 1980 to 38,000 in 1998, while there was a slight increase in the number of plans with over 1,000 employees. The number of active participants in defined benefit plans of all sizes less than 10,000 participants declined sharply during this period.

2. While the plans studied here are all sponsored by Watson Wyatt clients, Watson Wyatt consultants were not involved in the design of the new plans in all cases. The choice of particular consulting firms by companies seeking to develop hybrid plans may have some influence on the plan characteristics ultimately adopted by the plan sponsor. This conjecture is based on the observation that the benefit consulting firms have different positions concerning the philosophy of retirement plan design that may motivate clients with different plan goals to select one consulting firm over another when they are redesigning their pension plans.

3. This conclusion is based on a comparison with roughly 350 defined benefit pension plans in the Watson Wyatt Comparison™ database for 1999.

4. By law, wage increases for those who continue to work after the normal retirement age must be reflected in higher future benefits. However, companies are allowed to cap years of service and they are not required to provide actuarial adjustments associated with declining life expectancy at older ages (see McGill et al. 1996).

5. Throughout this example, earnings are assumed to grow at 4.0 percent per year. The discount and benefit conversion rates used throughout are 7.0 percent per year. We used the GAM83 mortality rates for males with a 3-year setback.

6. This methodology is outlined in paragraph 40, FASB (1985).

7. As a result our estimates will not precisely replicate actual plan costs or change in costs that these plan sponsors would have incurred and reported on their financial statements, if they had eliminated early retirement subsidies while retaining all other aspects of their prior plans.

8. If these assumptions understate turnover patterns, our estimate of the projected unit credit cost for the traditional pension may be too high, since traditional plan costs fall with high turnover. However, if we understate turnover, estimated cost of hybrid plans might also be too high. In this case the issue is primarily related to the portion of workers that can be expected to vest in the new plan. In the traditional plan, the benefits earned in the early part of the career tend to be so negligible, that understating vesting rates for new hires will have little effect on plan costs. In the hybrid plan, on the other hand, benefits at the date of vesting are typically substantial. Understating vesting in this case could have a significant effect on the cost estimate. We do not have access the actual turnover experience for the individual plans being studied, but we have no reason to believe that our methodology biases the analysis or results.

9. This would occur because of the variations in benefit formulas across pay levels in the plans both before and after the transition to the hybrid plans.

10. In assessing the implications of the shift to hybrid plans we were faced with a choice of moving the transition date across time so all plans were treated as having changed at the same time, or taking them at their current state of evolution from the prior to current system. For purposes of this analysis, we use the plan's actual transition date.

11. To derive this, the authors calculated the present value of benefits that would be paid at termination for each worker whose career we were simulating and compared it to the present value of their accrued benefit at the point the employer shifted to the cash balance plan. The difference between the two is the additional amount that each worker would earn between the point of transition and their actual departure from the company. The authors divided this difference by the present value of future earnings while still with the employer. The result is what actuaries refer to as the aggregate normal cost, reflecting the accrual of future benefits as a constant percentage of pay over the remainder of workers' careers with the employer.

12. In the second case, there are three possibilities. The first is that benefits are cut further than the elimination of the early retirement subsidy. The second is that some portion of the reduction in benefits from eliminating early retirement subsidies is put back into the new benefit formula effecting workers reaching early retirement ages but it is not enough to completely offset the elimination of the subsidy. The third is that benefits are sufficiently enhanced in the new formula that the reduction in early retirement subsidies is completely offset. In this last case, workers reaching early retirement ages will end up getting larger benefits under the new planes even though the incentives encouraging early retirement have been eliminated in the process. We estimate the extent to which all three cases arise.

13. These results are shown in the third row of each panel in the table. The first two rows in each panel are the subtotal results from the prior two tables summarizing the prior two scenarios. In one of the prototypical examples shown there, the majority of new plans would fall into this scenario. In most of the cases, roughly one-third of the plans would fall into this category.

14. Another interesting parallel between changes in national retirement policy and pension plan conversions involves the transitional effects on current workers associated with significant changes in plan type or in plan benefit formulas. Conversions of pensions from defined benefit to cash balance or defined contribution plans tend to have an adverse effect on older workers nearing retirement. As we have discussed, companies can moderate this impact through the use of special transition benefits for these workers. Congress faced the same problem in 1977 when the benefit formula for social security benefits was altered. The change in the social security benefit formula meant that workers faced substantially lower annual benefits under the new rules. In this case, individuals born prior to 1917 were allowed to remain under the old benefit formula, persons born from 1917 to 1921 faced a declining benefit formula, and everyone born after 1921 would receive retirement benefits under the new formula. This change meant that similar workers were treated differently based on their birth year. The transition policy adopted by Congress is similar to that used by many employers in pension conversions and it also produced considerable reaction from the so-called "notch babies." One can only imagine the reaction if the Social Security Administration had been sending out benefits statements in 1977 as it is now required to do.

References

Brown, Kyle N., Gordon P. Goodfellow, Tomeka Hill, Richard R. Joss, Richard Luss, Lex Miller, and Sylvester J. Schieber. 2000. *The Unfolding of a Predictable Surprise: A Comprehensive Analysis of the Shift from Traditional Pensions to Hybrid Plans.* Bethesda, Md.: Watson Wyatt Worldwide.

Burkhauser, Richard V. 1979. "The Pension Acceptance Decision of Older Workers," *Journal of Human Resources* 14, 1: 63–75.

Clark, Robert L. and Anna A. McDermed. 1990. *The Choice of Pension Plans in a Changing Regulatory Environment.* Washington, D.C.: American Enterprise Institute.

Clark, Robert L. and Fred W. Munzenmaier. 2000. "Impact of Replacing a Defined Benefit Plan with a Defined Contribution or a Cash Balance Plan." Paper presented to Retirement 2000 Conference sponsored by the Society of Actuaries, Washington, D.C., February 23–24.

Fields, Gary and Olivia S. Mitchell. 1984. *Retirement, Pensions and Social Security.* Cambridge, Mass.: MIT Press.

Financial Accounting Standards Board (FASB). 1985. *Employers Accounting for Pensions.* Statement of Financial Accounting Standards 87. Stamford, Conn.: FASB.

Gordon, Roger H. and Alan S. Blinder. 1980. "Market Wages, Reservation Wages, and Retirement Decisions." *Journal of Public Economics* 14 (October): 277–308.

Gustman, Alan L. and Thomas L. Steinmeier. 1992. "The Stampede Towards Defined Contribution Plans." *Industrial Relations* 31: 361–69.

Ippolito, Richard A. 1997. *Pension Plans and Employee Performance.* Chicago: University of Chicago Press.

Kotlikoff, Laurence J. and David A. Wise. 1985. "Labor Compensation and the Structure of Private Pension Plans: Evidence for Contractual Versus Spot Labor Markets." In *Pensions, Labor, and Individual Choice,* ed. David A. Wise. Chicago: University of Chicago Press. 55–85.

McGill, Dan M., Kyle N. Brown, John J. Haley, and Sylvester J. Schieber, eds. 1996. *Fundamentals of Private Pensions.* Pension Research Council. Philadelphia: University of Pennsylvania Press.

Pension Benefit Guaranty Corporation (PBGC). 1998. *Pension Insurance Data Book 1998.* Washington, D.C.: PBGC.

Quinn, Joseph E. 1977. "Microeconomic Determinants of Early Retirement: A Cross-Sectional View of White Married Men." *Journal of Human Resources* 12 (Summer): 329–46.

Chapter 8
Mortality Risk, Inflation Risk, and Annuity Products

Jeffrey R. Brown, Olivia S. Mitchell, and James M. Poterba

> "Buy an annuity cheap, and make your life interesting to yourself and everybody else that watches the speculation." (Jonas Chuzzlewit to his father, in *Martin Chuzzlewit* by Charles Dickens)

Future retirees are likely to shoulder an increasing share of the burden of managing their wealth after they leave the labor force. This is primarily the result of the rapid growth of self-directed retirement accounts. Poterba, Venti, and Wise (1999) project that the average retiree balance in 401(k) accounts will rise tenfold between 2000 and 2030. The popularity of self-managed retirement resources is further supported by U.S. corporate pension plans permitting, and in some cases even encouraging, lump sum distributions when participants retire. Interest in retiree responsibility for asset decumulation has also emerged in policy discussions of "individual account" programs that could supplement or replace government-provided social security. As the leading edge of the baby boom approaches retirement, more attention is likely to be directed toward the development of financial products such as annuities that provide households with a structure way to draw down the assets that they have accumulated during their working lives.

Annuities feature prominently in theoretical discussions of asset decumulation in life cycle models, so it has been disappointing to economists that, in practice, the market for privately purchased annuities in the United States is very small. Most elderly households in the U.S. receive government-provided social security benefits that provide an inflation-indexed lifetime annuity. Many also receive a nominal annuity from a defined benefit company pension plan. But few elderly households in the U.S. convert their financial assets accumulated outside a defined benefit pension plan into an annuity providing a lifetime retirement income. The Life Insurance Marketing Research Association (LIMRA, 1999) reported that in 1998 there were only 1.56 million individual annuity policies in "payout" phase, meaning that the policy owners were currently receiving benefits. These policies covered a total of 2.35 million lives, since many of the policies were joint and survivor annuities paying benefits to both members of a married couple.

A number of previous studies have investigated the demand for annuity products and evaluated various aspects of annuity pricing (cf. Friedman and Warshawsky 1990, and Mitchell, Poterba, Warshawsky, and Brown 1999; hereafter MPWB). In the current study, we present new evidence on the pricing of annuity products in the United States and several other countries. We focus on three issues. First, we offer new computations on the "money's worth" of nominal annuities, the present value of annuity payouts relative to their purchase price, in the United States during the late 1990s. Our findings broadly confirm previous results that suggest money's worth values between 80 and 90 cents per premium dollar for randomly selected individuals in the population, but values between 90 cents and one dollar for the average annuitant. Second, we assess the U.S. market for real annuities, annuities that offer a payout stream indexed to the price level. There is effectively no market for inflation-protected annuities in the United States, but there are active markets in other nations, notably the United Kingdom. Third, we summarize available evidence on annuity pricing in other nations. We describe some of the shortcomings of studies that have analyzed prices in annuity markets outside the United States and the United Kingdom, and we note the difficulties associated with obtaining key data inputs for these studies.

The Market for Annuities in the United States

Annuities may be purchased either by members of a group or by individuals. In this analysis we focus on individual policies. These are most directly relevant for older people who might wish to use the annuity market to spread their accumulated assets over a remaining lifetime of uncertain length. By contrast, a group annuity contract is typically obtained via an employer-provided defined benefit pension plan. In some cases, group annuities may also be obtained via a defined contribution pension plan. The key distinction between an annuity purchased as an individual and one obtained through a group is that individuals purchasing annuities on their own are more likely to be self-selected to live longer than average. As in other insurance contexts, group purchases of annuities reduce the risk of adverse selection. In the present paper, we focus on individual annuities as a means to manager retirement assets outside pension plans.

The U.S. individual annuity market is one component of the broader market for life insurance products. The American Council on Life Insurance (ACLI 1999) reports that premiums paid for *immediate individual* annuities, which are our main focus, totaled $7.9 billion in 1998. By comparison, premiums for *immediate group* annuities totaled $16.3 billion, and premiums for *group deferred* annuities, typically representing contributions to defined benefit pension accounts, were $117.7 billion. Further, the $7.9 billion figure for individual annuity premiums overstates the importance of annuity products in retirement, since about half of all newly purchased individual annuities represent "structured settlements" (typically resulting from legal cases) and hence do not represent income flows to retirees. Moreover, of the remaining "annuities," half are "period certain" policies. These policies promise a fixed nominal payout stream for a specified time period without a mortality contingency; they are effectively bonds issued by insurance companies. Thus, premium flows for annuity products providing lifetime income from an initial asset stock are currently only about $2 billion per year.

Premium volume for individual *immediate* annuities is dwarfed by that for individual *deferred* annuities. Deferred products attracted $87.5 billion in premiums in 1998, mostly for purchases of variable annuities during the preretirement period. It is not clear whether the assets that accumulate in these financial instruments will ultimately be used to finance the purchase of traditional immediate annuities. Survey results presented by the Gallup Organization (1999) suggest that many purchasers of variable annuities regard the accumulating principal in these products as a source of emergency resources for health care or other needs, not as a source of stable retirement income.

Although the U.S. individual annuity market is currently small, it is likely to grow substantially in the future. Many current retirement saving vehicles permit individuals to exert substantial discretion over how they draw down their accumulated assets. These vehicles include 401(k) plans, 403(b) plans, and Individual Retirement Accounts (IRAs). Potential draw-down options from these include lump-sum distributions, periodic partial distributions, and annuitization. Brown (1999) reports that data for individuals aged 51–61 from the Health and Retirement Survey suggest that 48 percent of households with a defined contribution pension plan permitting a phased withdraw or annuity option intend to annuitize at least a portion of their account. When coupled with the rapid prospective growth in the number of retirees who will have participated in a defined contribution plan during their working lifetime, this should yield significant future growth in the annuity market.

While the *number* of future retirees who will have resources that could be annuitized is likely to increase in the future, it is possible that the *percentage* of retirees with such accounts who choose to annuitize will decline, at least if current stock market valuation levels persist. Individuals reaching retirement age with large accumulations in retirement accounts may feel less need for annuity-type products to product them against outliving their resources than would less wealthy retirees. The increase in share values in recent years, and the associated rise in the value of retirement account assets, has apparently affected the demand for annuity products. At one major retirement annuity provider, TIAA-CREF, King (1996) reports that retirees who control their assets have been gradually shifting away from annuity distributions and toward lump sum options. A different study at the same firm by Ameriks (1999) reports that participants with larger account balances tend to choose the lump sum route for distributing plan assets. Even if the *fraction* of defined contribution plan participants selecting annuities declines somewhat in the future, the fact that the retiree population with self-directed accounts is growing rapidly still suggests prospective growth in the annuity market.

Valuing U.S. Annuity Products

We now consider the set of nominal annuity products currently available to annuity buyers in the United States. We also develop a framework for evaluating the payouts from annuity products by calculating the ratio of the expected present discounted value of such payouts to the purchase cost (initial premium) of these products. In the next section we report empirical results based on this framework.

Currently Available Annuity Products in the United States

Virtually all the annuity products marketed to individual annuity buyers in the United States are nominal annuities. They pay benefits that are not inflation-indexed. Two forms are common: (a) level-payout annuities that provide a fixed payment, typically monthly, for as long as the annuitant is alive; and (b) graded annuities paying benefits that increase over time at a prespecified rate (e.g. at 3 or 5 percent per year). The payout streams associated with these two types of policies differ, with the real value of payouts from a level-payout nominal policy declining faster than that from a graded annuity. A graded annuity does not offer inflation protection, however, since the stream of benefits provided is not affected by the inflation rate over the contract's lifetime.

An annuity may be purchased as either an individual policy or a joint and survivor policy. In the former case, in the absence of a period-certain clause, benefit payments continue as long as the insured person is alive. In the latter case, benefits are paid for as long as either of *two* individuals is alive. Brown and Poterba (2001) explain that joint and survivor products vary in the ratio of the payout that second to die annuitant receives relative to the payout when both annuitants are alive. There are three common types of joint and survivor products, and several variants. One, a "100 percent survivor policy," provides the same benefit when both members of a couple are alive as when only one survives. A related policy, a "50 percent survivor policy," provides the survivor with half of the benefit that was paid when both annuitants were alive. The third common policy is a "50 percent contingent beneficiary policy." In this case, one of the annuitants is defined as the primary and the other as the contingent beneficiary. The full amount of the annuity payout continues for as long as the primary beneficiary is alive. If the primary beneficiary predeceases the contingent beneficiary, the contingent beneficiary receives a payout equal to half of the primary beneficiary's payout.

A final factor affecting annuity products is their tax status, which has to do with the source of the funds used to purchase the annuity. In the U.S., contributions to employer-provided pension programs are not included in taxable income provided that the plan meets regulatory standards. In this paper, we focus on annuities purchased using nonqualified funds.[1]

Table 1 reports the average annuity payouts available to 65-year-old annuity buyers in the United States over the period 1995–99. For comparability purposes, the table reports only on annuities with a premium of $100,000; the data represent single premium, nonparticipating, annuities. Premiums are reported gross of state premium taxes. By restricting the sample to nonparticipating annuities, we exclude annuity products for which the payout to the annuitant depends on either the investment returns or the mortality experience of the insurance company writing the policy. TIAA-CREF is an example of a firm that sells participating annuities, and that is therefore excluded from our sample.

Data for the period 1995–98 are drawn from the Life/Health edition of *Best's Review.* For many years this major publisher of insurance market information conducted an annual survey of single premium immediate annuity policies, but it ceased doing so in 1998. The Best's survey generally included around 100 firms with consistent representation from the larger national insurers, along with many small companies with a strong regional presence. Table 1 also reports information from 1998 and 1999 from the *Annuity Shopper,* which is a print and electronic publication providing annuity price quotes to prospective buyers. The *Annuity Shopper* has collected information on annuity prices since the early 1980s. This publication does not offer a representative sample of insurers; rather, listing with the *Annuity Shopper* is at the discretion of the insurer. In 1998 there were 99 firms in the *Best's* database, compared with 35 firms in the *Annuity Shopper* database. It is interesting that for the overlap year of 1998, average monthly annuity payouts agree quite closely across the two sources.

The evidence in Table 1 suggests that annuity payouts have declined in the United States between 1995 and 1999. For instance, a 65-year-old man purchasing a $100,000 single premium annuity in 1995 would expect to receive a monthly payment of $794 on average ($9,528 per year). By 1998, the nominal payout would have dropped by 8 percent to $733 ($8,796 per year).

TABLE 1. Average Monthly Payouts from Single Premium Immediate Annuities Offered to 65-Year-Olds, United States, 1995–99

	Best's Survey				Annuity Shopper	
	1995	1996	1997	1998	1998	1999
Male Annuitant	$794.12	761.79	772.22	732.74	731.94	734.77
Female Annuitant	716.98	685.62	699.67	661.62	659.29	667.36

Source: Authors' tabulations from *Best's Review* (various issues) and *Annuity Shopper* of payouts for nonqualified individual annuity purchases. Monthly payouts are based on a $100,000 initial premium.

Women live longer than men on average, so the 65-year-old female paying the same $100,000 premium in 1995 would have anticipated receiving about 10 percent less than her male counterpart, $717 per month ($8,604 per year). By 1998, her nominal benefit would also have fallen by 8 percent or to $662 per month ($7,944).

Table 1 does not present information on joint and survivor annuities, but we have also examined data on those products to place them in perspective. In 1999, for instance, a couple consisting of a 65-year-old male and a 62-year-old female buying a joint and full survivor annuity would receive $587 monthly, about 20 percent less than a single male.

The *Annuity Shopper* and *Best's* data appear to compare reasonably well in 1998, the year for which we present summary measures from both data sets. If we extend the time series of annuity payouts for 65-year-old men to 1999 using the *Annuity Shopper* data, the average monthly payout for the 65-year-old annuity purchaser falls by around 8 percent over the 1995–99 period. It is likely that this fall in monthly payouts is partly attributable to the decline in nominal long-term interest rates of over 100 basis points that occurred between 1995 and 1999.

The information on mean monthly annuity payouts shown in Table 1 does not reflect the substantial variation across insurance companies in the montly payouts offered. MPWB (1999) report that different insurance companies can vary widely in their annuity payouts, and that these payout differences do not appear to be systematically related to factors such as insurance company ratings. This implies that some annuity purchasers may receive payouts substantially different from the average values shown in Table 1.

Valuing Annuity Payouts: The "Money's Worth" Calculation

Annuity products provide a stream of payouts lasting many years. The exact value of this payout stream is uncertain because it is conditional on an individual annuity buyer's longevity. In order to evaluate how the future annuity stream compares with the current price of an annuity product, we must therefore undertake an expected present discounted value calculation to account for the future payment stream and annuity buyer's mortality risk. The "money's worth" valuation approach we undertake here builds on prior research including Warshawsky (1988), Friedman and Warshawsky (1990), Mitchell, Poterba, Warshawsky, and Brown (1999), and Brown, Mitchell, and Poterba (2001). Specifically, the formula used to calculate the expected present discounted valued (EPDV) of a nominal annuity with an annual payout A_n, purchased by an individual of age b is:

$$(1) \qquad V_b(A_n) = \sum_{j=1}^{115-b} \frac{A_n * P_j}{\Pi_{k=1}^{j} (1 + i_k)} .$$

We assume that no annuity buyer lives beyond age 115. P_j denotes the probability that an individual of age b years at the time of the annuity purchase survives for at least j years after buying the annuity. The variable i_k denotes the one-year nominal interest rate k years after the annuity purchase. We value annuities without regard to the tax consequences of receiving annuity income, in part for comparability with previous literature, and in part because calculations in MPWB (1999) suggest that there is little difference in the money's worth ratio calculated before and after taxes.

In the U.S. market, virtually all annuities sold offer only nominal payout streams, but in other countries, real annuities that provide inflation-indexed payout streams are also available. To compute the EPDV for such products, equation (1) must be modified to recognize that the amount of the payout is time-varying in nominal terms but fixed in real terms. The easiest way to handle this is to allow A_r to denote the real annual payout, and to replace the nominal interest rates in the denominator of (1) with corresponding real interest rates. We use r_k to denote the annual real interest rate k years after the annuity purchase. While historically it was difficult to measure real interest rates without some assumptions about the future course of inflation rates, it may be possible to use data on the interest rates on inflation-indexed bonds in the United States and the United Kingdom to obtain direct estimates of these rates. The expression that we evaluate to compute the EPDV of a real annuity is

$$(2) \qquad V_b(A_r) = \sum_{j=1}^{115-b} \frac{A_r * P_j}{\Pi_{k=1}^{j} (1 + r_k)} .$$

The "money's worth" of an annuity is defined as the ratio of the expected present value of the annuity's payouts and its purchase price. For a nominal annuity that costs \$100,000, for example, the money's worth is $V_b(A_n)/100,000$. Our discussion focuses on money's worth ratios because they provide a scale-free metric for comparing annuities over time or across countries.

Money's Worth Calculations for Nominal Annuities

The framework developed above can be used to calculate the money's worth for a variety of different nominal annuity products. To calculate expected present discounted values based on equations (1) and (2), we require three types of data input. The first is the payout rate on the annuities being valued, which was reported in Table 1. The second is a set of mortality rates that can be used to calculate the probability that an annuitant will be alive in future years. The third is a set of discount rates. We describe our choices for these assumptions and then present our empirical EPDV calculations.

Mortality Assumptions for Annuity Valuation

Equations (1) and (2) are evaluated using mortality tables drawn either for the population as a whole, or for a subset of annuitants. The first set of results uses survival probabilities for the population at large, and for this we rely on birth cohort mortality rates taken from the Social Security Administration's 1999 Trustees' Report (1999). It is not sufficient to use current period mortality tables, since over time populations generally experience mortality improvements. Annuity valuation requires mortality projections that model the *prospective* survival experience of today's retirees. When estimating the money's worth of an annuity for a 65-year-old in 1995, we therefore use the projected mortality experience of the 1930 birth cohort, since this is the group that would have been 65 years old in 1995. Similarly, we use the 1931 through 1934 birth cohort mortality rates for the 1996 through 1999 money's worth calculations.

The second set of results acknowledges that annuity purchasers tend to have a mortality experience that differs from that of the general population. Whether this is the result of those who have information that they are likely to be long-lived purchasing annuities, or simply a function of different (and potentially observable) characteristics of annuitants and nonannuitants, is not clear. In any case, because annuitants have longer life expectancies than the broader population, insurance companies have developed a second set of mortality rates. This *annuitant* mortality table describes the mortality experience of those who actually purchase annuities. MPWB (1999) develop an algorithm that combines information from the Annuity 2000 mortality table described in Johansen (1996), the 1983 Individual Annuitant Mortality table, and the projected rate of mortality improvement implicit in the difference between the Social Security Administration's cohort and period mortality tables for the population. Our algorithm generates projected mortality rates for the set of annuitants purchasing annuity contracts in a given year. Our calculations use an updated version of that algorithm that incorporates the most recent social security data.

The population and annuitant mortality tables differ substantially. Figure 1 shows the projected mortality rates in 1999 for 65-year old male annuity buyers and 65-year-old men in the population at large. Between the ages of 65 and 75, the mortality rate for annuitants is roughly half of that for the general population. The mortality differential is somewhat smaller at older ages. Because cash flows in the first few years after annuity purchase contribute importantly to determining the expected present discounted value (EPDV) of the annuity payout, the large mortality differential between 65 and 75 generates significant differences in EPDVs when we switch from one mortality table to another.

Discount Rate Assumptions for Annuity Valuation

In equation (1) above, the term i_k denotes the one-year interest rate k years after the annuity purchase. In our baseline calculations, we measure these interest rates using the term structure of yields for zero-coupon U.S. Treasury "strips." We estimate the pattern of interest rates that are implied by these yields. The data on the U.S. Treasury strips yield curve were collected from *Bloomberg Financial Markets* for the same dates on which the *Best's Review* and *Annuity Shopper* data were collected. These are riskless interest rates, and using them to discount future annuity payouts implicitly assumes that there is no default risk associated with these payouts. The argument for using such discount rates is that insurance regulation makes the default risk for annuity providers very low. In most states, annuity buyers are protected against insurance company defaults through state insolvency funds. While these funds do not make all annuity purchases riskless, they do further reduce the chance that an annuity buyer will not receive the promised payouts.

One can argue, however, that riskless interest rates generate discount rates that are too low, particularly from the standpoint of the insurance companies that offer annuities. Life insurance firms generally invest their portfolios in risky bonds, so the return at which the insurers may discount their liabilities may exceed the riskless rate. To explore the sensitivity of our findings with respect to alternative interest rate assumptions, we also calculate discount rates from the term structure for BAA corporate bonds. These rates were also taken from *Bloomberg* on the same dates as the annuity price quotes, and correspond to a Bloomberg bond rating of BBB-2. The risk premium associated with these bonds varies with maturity, and over the five years of our sample period. However, the typical yields of these corporate securities at a 30-year horizon are approximately 90–140 basis points higher than comparable yields on riskless Treasury bonds of the same maturity. The yield spread at shorter maturities is in the 70–100 basis point range.

Using a market-based term structure for interest rates on risky bonds represents a methodological advance relative to previous work on annuity valuation. Early studies of the value of annuity payouts used a single dis-

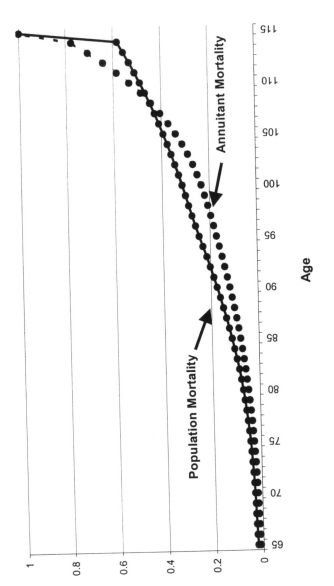

Figure 1. U.S. annuitant and population mortality. Source: Mitchell, Poterba, Warshawsky and Brown (1999), with updates as described in the text.

TABLE 2. Money's Worth of Single Premium Immediate Annuities Offered to 65-
Year-Olds, United States, 1995–99

Mortality Table	Term Structure	Best's Survey				Annuity Shopper	
		1995	1996	1997	1998	1998	1999
Men							
Population	Treasury	0.830	0.821	0.837	0.855	0.844	0.852
Population	Corporate	0.790	0.783	0.800	0.808	0.798	0.783
Annuitant	Treasury	0.937	0.929	0.938	0.974	0.960	0.970
Annuitant	Corporate	0.885	0.879	0.891	0.913	0.900	0.881
Women							
Population	Treasury	0.840	0.829	0.849	0.872	0.857	0.872
Population	Corporate	0.793	0.784	0.806	0.818	0.804	0.792
Annuitant	Treasury	0.909	0.899	0.921	0.953	0.936	0.952
Annuitant	Corporate	0.854	0.846	0.870	0.888	0.872	0.858

Source: Authors' tabulations as described in the text.

count rate, typically the interest rate on a ten-year government or corporate bond, to discount annuity payouts. MPWB (1999) used a market-based term structure for riskless bonds, but constructed a synthetic term structure for risky bonds by adding a constant risk premium to the riskless interest rates. There is currently some variation in the yield spread between corporate and government bonds at different maturities, so the most accurate approach is one that exploits the actual term structure of corporate and government interest rates.

New Results on the Money's Worth of Nominal Annuities in the United States

Table 2 presents our central findings regarding the money's worth of nominal annuities in the U.S. market. The table presents results for both men and women purchasing annuities at age 65, and the table shows money's worth calculations using (a) both the Treasury yield curve and the corporate bond yield curve, and (b) both population and annuitant mortality tables. To illustrate how to interpret the finings, consider the 1999 *Annuity Shopper* results. For a 65-year-old man purchasing a $100,000 annuity using funds accumulated outside a qualified retirement account, our results suggest that annuity payouts have an expected value of $85,200 using the Treasury yield curve for discounting, and $78,300 with the BAA corporate yield curve. These values translate into money's worth ratios of 0.852 and 0.783 respectively; these are the values shown in the table. These calculations are based on the population mortality table. If the annuity purchaser faced mortality rates corresponding to the typical annuity buyer, then the EPDV of payouts rises to $97,000 (with the Treasury yield curve) or $88,100 (with the corporate yield curve). Corresponding money's worth ratios for women are 0.872 or 0.792 with the population mortality rates, and 0.952 and 0.858, respectively, with annuitant tables.

Table 2 shows that there has been a small rise in money's worth of individual annuities over the 1995–99 period when we compute EPDV using the Treasury yield curve. There is virtually no change in the money's worth ratio, however, when we use the corporate yield curve for valuation. This reflects a slight widening of the yield spread between Tresury and corporate bonds over the period in question, particularly from 1998 to 1999. These findings are consistent with insurance companies pricing annuity products using risky interest rates.

Real Annuity Offerings in the United States: What Are the Options?

Our discussion of annuity products thus far has focused on nominal annuities. One disadvantage of this type of annuity is that it exposes buyers to the risk of unexpected inflation, which can cut the real value of their benefits and leave them late in retirement with a substantially lower than expected standard of living. In other nations, notably the United Kingdom, there is a well developed market for annuities that offer inflation-indexed payout. In the United States, even though inflation-indexed Treasury bonds have been available since 1997, there is still virtually no market for inflation-indexed annuities. We now summarize the types of inflation-indexed annuity products that are available in the United States, drawing on Brown, Mitchell, and Poterba (2000).

To date we have identified only two annuity products in the U.S. that offer substantial inflation protection to retirees. The first is the "Freedom CPI Indexed Income Annuity," offered by the Irish Life Company of North America (ILONA), and the second is the "Inflation Linked Bond Account" annuity, offered by TIAA-CREF. It is possible that other inflation-indexed products will become available in the future, as insurers adapt to the availability of inflation-indexed Treasury bonds. If inflation should become a more substantial concern with consumers, that could also stimulate the development of inflation-indexed products.

The ILONA Real Annuity

Index-linked annuities in the United States are offered by Irish Life PLC, an international insurance firm headquartered in Dublin, Ireland, through the Interstate Assurance Company. Interstate Assurance is a division of Irish

TABLE 3. Monthly Payout and Money's Worth of Nominal and Inflation Indexed
Annuities Offered by Irish Life of North America to 65-Year-Olds

	Monthly Annuity Payment	Money's Worth	
		Population Mortality	Annuitant Mortality
Men			
Nominal	$781.79	0.892	1.013
Inflation Indexed	548.42	0.749	0.871
Women			
Nominal	708.57	0.904	0.989
Inflation Indexed	475.21	0.741	0.824

Source: Authors' tabulations as described in the text. Payouts are for a $100,000 initial
premium.

Life of North America ((ILONA), a well-rated insurance company. ILONA's
real annuity product is the "Freedom CPI Indexed Income Annuity." The
annuity payout for this product rises annually in step with the increase in
the prior year's CPI. Annuity benefits from the Freedom CPI Indexed Income Annuity cannot decline in nominal terms, even if the CPI were to fall
from year to year. The minimum (maximum) purchase requirement for the
ILONA annuity product is $10,000 ($1 million). The ILONA real annuity
can be purchased as a simple life annuity, as well as with a "years certain"
provision, and it can be purchased by an individual or as a joint and survivor
product. Though the "Freedom CPI Indexed Income Annuity" has been
offered by ILONA for two years, as of this writing there have been no buyers
for this product. We are not sure what accounts for the lack of market
interest in this product, or more generally for the apparent lack of interest
on the part of retired households in purchasing assets that offer inflation
protection.

In Table 3 we report the monthly payout and the money's worth values for
both nominal annuities and inflation-indexed annuities offered by ILONA
in April 2000. The payouts on the ILONA inflation-linked annuity are 30
(33) percent below those on nominal annuities for men (women). In valu-
ing inflation-indexed annuities, we used data on the term structure of yields
on Treasury Inflation Protection Securities to discount future cash flows. As
in the calculations reported above, we focus on pretax EPDV calculations.

For the *nominal* annuities offered by ILONA, we found money's worth
values of approximately 0.89 for men, and 0.90 for women. These calculations use the population mortality table for individuals turning 65 in 2000.
Using the annuitant mortality table for nominal ILONA annuities yields a
larger value, approximately 1.01 for men and 0.99 for women. For inflation-

linked ILONA annuities, however, we found much smaller values. For example, with population mortality tables, the value was 0.75 for men and 0.74 for women. One way to interpret these results is to say that purchasing inflation protection adds more than 15 percent to the cost of an annuity policy. The low demand for the ILONA real annuity may reflect the substantial charge that the insurer levies for providing inflation protection.

Annuities Linked to the CREF Index-Linked Bond Account

In May of 1997, the College Equities Retirement Fund (CREF) launched a new investment account, the CREF Inflation-Linked Bond Account (ILBA). This new fund was intended to appeal to those saving for retirement as well as to retirees in the retirement decumulation phase. The fund holds a portfolio that consists primarily of inflation-indexed bonds, although it may also hold other inflation-indexed securities. Foreign inflation-indexed bonds cannot account for more than 25 percent of the portfolio. Expenses total 31 basis points annually, lower than many mutual and pension fund expense levels but comparable to other, more actively managed CREF accounts. The ILBA has no sales, surrender, or premium charges. The ILBA has grown slowly since its inception, and it is currently the smallest of the retirement funds offered by TIAA-CREF. Active participants, rather than retirees, apparently account for most of the funds in the ILBA. This means that the fund is not used primarily to provide inflation-protected retirement annuities, at least at present.

Annuitants intending to use the ILBA to provide an inflation-indexed annuity would purchase a variable annuity, with the payout variation linked to the performance of the ILBA. Although this financial product offers some inflation protection, its protection is incomplete. This is because the ILBA is marked to market daily, meaning that asset values fluctuate and the account could lose money. This might occur if real interest rates rose, or if there were changes in the definition of the Consumer Price Index. The mark-to-market feature means that the payouts on a variable annuity that is linked to the ILBA *do not* offer a guaranteed real payout stream to prospective annuitants. Another factor that may result in incomplete inflation protection arises from the way mortality experience of the annuitant pool affects subsequent payouts. TIAA-CREF annuities place mortality risk for the annuity pool on the set of participants in the pool, so if there were a substantial and unforecast change in the mortality experience of the annuitant pool, this would affect payouts.

Fundamental design features of CREF variable annuities backed by the ILBA raise the possibility that purchasers of such annuities might fail to keep pace with inflation. Any variable annuity is defined by an initial payout amount, which we shall denote A(O), and an "updating rule" that relates the annuity payout in future periods to the previous payout and the intervening returns on the portfolio that backs the variable annuity. To determine A(O), the initial nominal payout per dollar of annuity purchase on a single-life variable annuity without any guarantee period, the insurance company solves an equation like

(3)
$$1 = \sum_{j=1}^{T} \frac{A(0) * P_j}{(1 + R)^j},$$

where R is the variable annuity's assumed interest rate (AIR) and T is the maximum potential lifespan of the annuitant. To determine annuity payouts in subsequent periods, the insurer applies an updating rule related to the return on the return on the assets that back the annuity (z_t). This updating rule is

(4)
$$A(t + 1) = A(t) * \frac{1 + z_t}{1 + R}.$$

The AIR is a key design parameter for a variable annuity. Assuming a high value enables an insurance company to offer a large initial premium, but, for any underlying portfolio, the stream of future payouts will be more likely to decline as the assumed value rises. Equation (4) clearly indicates that an individual who purchases a variable annuity will receive payouts that fluctuate with the nominal value of the underlying portfolio.

All CREF variable annuities use an AIR of 4 percent. Thus when the unit value of the investment account underlying the variable annuity rises by less than 4 percent, the nominal payout on the variable annuity declines. When the nominal return on the underlying assets exceeds this rate, the variable annuity payout rises. The assumption of a 4 percent AIR makes it possible for the *nominal* payout on the CREF ILBA variable annuity to decline over time. Consider the experience of 1998, when the total return (after expenses) on the ILBA account was 3.48 percent. Given the AIR of 4 percent, annuities backed by this portfolio had to reduce their nominal payout by 0.52 percent. This reduction in nominal payout took place at a time when the price level was rising, so the CREF ILBA variable annuity did not deliver a constant real payout stream.

In order to avoid the situation that occurred in 1998, it would be necessary for the returns on Treasury Inflation Protection Securities to exceed 4 percent. The CREF variable payout annuity linked to the ILBA would be more likely to deliver a future real payout stream if the Air on this annuity were set equal to the real interest rate on long-term TIPS at the time when the annuity is purchased. In this case, the return on the bond portfolio would typically equal the AIR plus the annual inflation rate, leaving aside some of the other risks of holding indexed bonds.

Equity-Linked Annuity Products

One recent development in the U.S. annuity market is the rise of products known as "equity linked annuities." These products make use of stock-index options to expand the menu of risk/return choices open to investors. As explained by Bodie (1999), index options make it possible to combine downside protection with some upside gain potential tied to the performance of an underlying index portfolio, essentially providing a guaranteed income "floor." In practice, U.S. equity-linked annuities typically invest most of the annuity premium in a traditional fixed nominal annuity and the remainder in a portfolio of options on stock market indices. A common division is to place 90 percent of the assets in a fixed annuity, and to invest 10 percent in call options on the S&P 500 index. By splitting the investment this way, an annuity buyer will never receive less than the payouts from a fixed annuity that he could have purchased with 90 percent of the initial premium. If the equity market rises enough that the index exceeds the exercise price on the option, then the call option is "in the money," and thus provides additional resources to increase future annuity payments.

Bodie (1999) offers a useful illustration of this approach for an individual with $1 million who is assumed to live another 20 years. With a risk-free interest rate of 3.5 percent, the individual could purchase a real annuity that pays $67,216 per year. If, instead, the individual invested only 90 percent in a real annuity and the other 10 percent in a series of 20 index options of increasing maturity, the minimum amount received would be $60,494. Assuming that the exercise price on the options are set equal to the value of the index at the time the annuity is purchased, and assuming an annualized volatility of the stock index of 0.2, this individual would receive an additional $13,188 for every percentage increase in the index. By increasing the fraction of wealth invested in the call options, one reduces the guaranteed income floor but increases the rate at which the individual participates in the upside potential of the index.

Equity-linked annuities were introduced in 1995. The marketing materials for these products suggest that they provide purchasers with some degree of inflation protection, because their payouts are partly related to stock market returns. (A similar argument could be made for investing in traditional variable annuities with the underlying assets invested in a broad-based portfolio of common stocks.) Whether an equity portfolio really offers an inflation hedge depends on investor's planning horizon. Brown, Mitchell, and Poterba (2001) present evidence showing that the U.S. stock market has historically not provided a good inflation hedge at short horizons. In the long run, however, Boudoukh and Richardson (1993) and others have argued that equities may offer some degree of inflation protection. This debate notwithstanding, it is clear that equity-linked annuity products do not offer potential annuitants a payout stream guaranteed to retain a constant purchasing power in all future years.

International Evidence on Annuity Products

Our analysis so far has focused on annuity products available in the United States. But there are also annuity markets in other countries, and in some cases these markets are substantially larger than those in the United States. This is particularly true with regard to markets for inflation-protected annuities. In this section we offer a brief overview of recent cross-national evidence on the money's worth of both nominal and inflation-indexed single premium immediate annuities.

Comparisons of annuity market operations across countries pose several challenges. One is that annuity pricing data are often difficult to obtain, though an important effort in this direction was recently undertaken for a World Bank project summarized by James and Vittas (1999). Another problem is that insurers in other countries often lack country-specific mortality tables, and hence they must rely on some adaptation of the U.S. or UK mortality tables. Which they choose will matter, as a glance at Figure 2 confirms. When mortality patterns are not well known, insurers may build in additional reserves to cover eventualities. McCarthy and Mitchell (2001) argue that these additional reserves have the effect of making the annuity streams less valuable to purchasers, because they reduce the money's worth of annuity products.

Finally, computing the money's worth of annuities requires obtaining either a government Treasury yield curve or the relevant corporate yield curve, either of which can be difficult to obtain, particularly in developing economies. It is also not clear whether insurance companies selling annuity products in emerging nations are actually investing a substantial fraction of the assets that back these annuities in the domestic bond market. These operational difficulties in annuity valuation underscore the need for further data collection and refinement in the annuity valuation process.

International Comparisons of the Money's Worth of Nominal Annuities

James and Vittas (1999) present evidence on the money's worth of nominal annuities in five countries. Table 4 reproduces their central results. The table refers to single premium immediate nominal annuities for 65-year old men or women; James and Vittas (1999) provide information for other potential annuitants as well.[2]

The results in Table 4 suggest that money's worth ratios for nominal annuities in the countries surveyed are rather high. All the money's worth values are at least 0.85. Nevertheless, the values frequently exceed 0.90 and

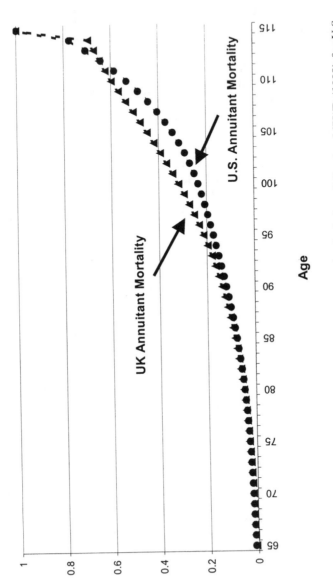

Figure 2. U.S. and UK annuitant mortality. Source: Authors' calculations following MPWB (1999) for U.S. and Finkelstein and Poterba (1999) for UK.

TABLE 4. International Comparisons of Money's Worth Values for Single Premium Nominal Life Annuities Offered to 65-Year-Olds

Annuitant Sex	Mortality Table	Term Structure	UK	Australia	Canada	Switzerland	Singapore
Male	Population	Treasury	0.897	0.914	0.925	0.965	NA
Male	Population	Corporate	0.854	0.846	0.869	0.922	NA
Male	Annuitant	Treasury	0.966	0.986	1.014	1.117	1.256
Male	Annuitant	Corporate	0.916	0.906	0.947	1.11	1.073
Female	Population	Treasury	0.910	0.914	0.937	1.029	NA
Female	Population	Corporate	0.860	0.846	0.874	0.974	NA
Female	Annuitant	Treasury	0.957	0.970	1.015	1.115	NA
Female	Annuitant	Corporate	0.901	0.906	0.941	1.083	1.058

Source: James and Vittas (1999).

sometimes are greater than 1.0 for computations involving annuitant mortality tables (particularly with the lower Treasury discount rates). This latter finding is surprising since it implies that purchasers receive more, in an expected value sense, than the premium they pay for the product. We are skeptical of results that suggest money's worth values of more than unity, and we suspect that insurers offering these annuities do not price using Treasury rates, or that the annuitant mortality tables that are used to calculate the EPDV of annuity payouts are not the ones used by insurance companies selling these products. While further work is clearly needed, the key findings also indicate that annuity offerings elsewhere are not inferior to offerings in the United States, at least when measured by money's worth ratios.

International Comparisons of Inflation-Indexed Annuity Products

Inflation-indexed annuity products are offered in several countries, including the United Kingdom, Australia, Israel, Mexico, and Chile. Information about these annuities is even more difficult to obtain, however, than data on nominal annuities. Table 5 summarizes the available information for the UK, Chile, and Israel, focusing on inflation-indexed products for 65-year old men and women.

Overall, the money's worth values for the real annuity products appear lower than for the nominal products, a pattern consistent with our findings for the United States and with the results in Finkelstein and Poterba (1999) and Murthi, Orszag, and Orszag (1999) for the United Kingdom. However the gap between real and nominal annuities is smaller in countries other than the United States. This is particularly evident in the U.K., where real annuities have been sold for many years. The difference in money's worth values for real and nominal annuities in this case is only on the order of 5

TABLE 5. International Comparisons of Money's Worth Values for Single Premium Inflation-Indexed Life Annuities Offered to 65-Year-Olds

Annuitant Sex	Mortality Table	Term Structure	UK	Chile	Israel
Male	Population	Treasury	0.801	0.868	0.799
Male	Population	Corporate	0.756	0.802	0.742
Male	Annuitant	Treasury	0.878	0.939	0.921
Male	Annuitant	Corporate	0.823	0.863	0.847
Female	Population	Treasury	0.798	0.866	0.760
Female	Population	Corporate	0.745	0.788	0.703
Female	Annuitant	Treasury	0.850	0.947	0.911
Female	Annuitant	Corporate	0.791	0.859	0.83

Source: James and Vittas (1999).

percent. Why there is such limited demand for real annuities in the United States, and why the available inflation-linked products are priced so unfavorably relative to nominal products, remains an open issue for further study.

Conclusions and Discussion

Our analysis of annuity markets in the United States and our review of evidence on annuity markets in other nations suggests several broad conclusions. First, the present discounted value of annuity payouts typically falls below the cost of these products by between 10 and 20 percent for a randomly selected person in the population. For typical annuity buyers, however, the expected present value of the payouts is much closer to the purchase price of the annuity. Differences in prospective mortality experience between typical annuity buyers and individuals in the population at large, what we call "adverse selection," therefore may explain a substantial share of the effective cost of an annuity for a randomly selected individual.

Second, the money's worth of nominal annuities exceeds the money's worth of inflation-indexed annuities both in the United States, where only one "inflation-indexed" annuity product has been brought to market thus far, and in other countries, where there are more active markets for real annuities. This is true even though insurance companies may have access to bond markets in which they can purchase inflation-indexed government securities. The gap in money's worth values is smaller in the more established markets.

Third, the operation of annuity markets in the United States does not appear to differ in significant ways from the operation of annuity markets in other nations, at least given current evidence. Money's worth values for nominal annuities offered in a range of different nations are remarkably similar. This conclusion must be qualified, however, by the recognition that past studies have made strong assumptions to obtain the necessary mortality data and interest rate data for annuity valuation in countries other than the United States and the United Kingdom.

The research presented here raises a number of issues for further study. One is why consumers do not place greater value on inflation-indexed annuity products, and why the demand for these products is not greater than it currently appears to be, particularly in the United States. It is possible that investors do not understand the meaning of, and the substantial value of, inflation protection. Another possibility is that inflation-protected securities, bonds as well as annuities, are still novel products, and it will take time for these products to attract a substantial following among the investing public.

A second issue requiring further study concerns the relationship between planned and actual annuitization on the part of households with significant retirement resources. Surveys of households that are still several years away from retirement suggest that many people plan to annuitize a part of their financial portfolio at retirement. Whether these households' plans are borne out remains to be seen, and this will play a critical role in affecting the future size of the annuity market. If there are fixed costs of operating an annuity market, then it is possible that the effective cost of annuities for prospective buyers will decline as the size of the potential market expands.

A third important issue concerns group annuities. Limits on data availability led us to concentrate on individually purchased annuities for this research, yet little is currently known about the market for group annuities. It may be that in the future, employers will negotiate arrangements with annuity providers that will permit their employees to annuitize their retirement resources in a group setting. This may reduce the evident disparities between the mortality experience of the annuitant pool and of the population at large.

Notes

The authors are grateful to Amy Finkelstein and Mark Warshawsky for helpful discussions, to Soojin Yim and David McCarthy for research assistance, and to Joseph Bellerson for kindly providing data. We thank the National Institute on Aging (Brown and Poterba), the Pension Research Council at the Wharton School (Mitchell), and the National Science Foundation (Poterba) for research support. Opinions are solely those of the authors.

1. McGill et al. (1996) summarize the regulations that govern qualified plans. Brown, Mitchell, Poterba, and Warshawsky (1999) analyze the tax treatment of distributions from qualified and nonqualified plans.

2. There are important institutional details that affect the analysis of each country's annuity market. For example, in the United Kingdom, the information in Table

4 refers only to the "voluntary" annuity market. As Finkelstein and Poterba (1999) explain, there is also an active "compulsory" annuity market in the UK, where individuals who have accumulated assets in a set of tax-favored self-directed retirement plans are required to annuitize a share of their assets.

References

American Council on Life Insurance. 1999. *Life Insurance Factbook 1999*. Washington, D.C.: ACLI.

Annuity Shopper Magazine. Summer 1998 and 1999 issues. United States Annuities.

Best's Review. A.M. Best Review, Oldwick, N.J.

Blake, David. 1999. "Annuity Markets: Problem and Solutions." Discussion Paper PI-9907. Pension Institute, Birkbeck College, London.

Bodie, Zvi. 1999. "Financial Engineering and Social Security Reform." In *Risk Aspects of Social Security Reform*, ed. John Campbell and Martin Feldstein. Chicago: University of Chicago Press.

Bodie, Zvi. 1990. "Inflation Insurance." *Journal of Risk and Insurance* 57, 4: 634–45.

———. 2001. "Financial Engineering and Social Security Reform." In *Risk Aspects of Investment-Based Social Security Reform*, ed. John Campbell and Martin S. Feldstein. Chicago: University of Chicago Press. 291–311.

Bodie, Zvi and James Pesando. 1983. "Retirement Annuity Design in an Inflationary Climate." In *Financial Aspects of the United States Pension System*, ed. Zvi Bodie and John B. Shoven. Chicago: University of Chicago Press, 291–316.

Boudoukh, Jacob and Matthew Richardson. 1993. "Stock Returns and Inflation: A Long-Horizon Perspective." *American Economic Review* 83 (December): 1346–55.

Brown, Jeffrey R. 1999. "Private Pensions, Mortality Risk, and the Decision to Annuitize." NBER Working Paper 7191.

Brown, Jeffrey R., Olivia S. Mitchell, and James M. Poterba. 2001. "The Role of Real Annuities and Indexed Bonds in an Individual Accounts Retirement Program." In *Risk Aspects of Investment-Based Social Security Reform*, ed. John Campbell and Martin S. Feldstein. Chicago: University of Chicago Press. 321–69.

Brown, Jeffrey, Olivia S. Mitchell, James M. Poterba, and Mark J. Warshawsky. 1999. "Taxing Retirement Income: Nonqualified Annuities and Distributions from Qualified Accounts." *National Tax Journal* 52 (September): 563–92.

Brown, Jeffrey R. and James M. Poterba. 2001. "Joint Life Annuities and Annuity Demand by Married Couples." *Journal of Risk and Insurance* (forthcoming).

Finkelstein, Amy and James M. Poterba. 1999. "The Market for Annuity Products in the United Kingdom." NBER Working Paper 7168.

Friedman, Benjamin and Mark J. Warshawsky. 1990. "The Cost of Annuities: Implications for Saving Behavior and Bequests." *Quarterly Journal of Economics* 105, 1 (February): 135–54.

Gallup Organization. 1999. "Committee of Annuity Insurers: 1999 Survey of Owners of Non-Qualified Annuity Contracts." Princeton, N.J.: Gallup Organization.

James, Estelle and Dimitri Vittas. 1999. "Annuities Markets in Comparative Perspective." Presented at the World Bank Conference on New Ideas About Old Age Security, Washington, D.C.

Johansen, R. 1996. "Review of Adequacy of 1983 Individual Annuity Morality Table." *Transactions of the Society of Actuaries* 47: 101–23.

King, Francis P. 1995. "The TIAA Graded Payment Method and the CPI." *TIAA-CREF Research Dialogues* 46. New York: TIAA-CREF.

McCarthy, David and Olivia S. Mitchell. 2001. "Estimating International Adverse

Selection in Annuities." Pension Research Council Working Paper. Wharton School, University of Pennsylvania.

McGill, Dan, Kyle Brown, John Haley, and Sylvester J. Schieber. 1996. *Fundamentals of Private Pensions.* 7th ed. Pension Research Council. Philadelphia: University of Pennsylvania Press.

Mitchell, Olivia S., James M. Poterba, Mark J. Warshawsky, and Jeffrey R. Brown. 1999. "New Evidence on the Money's Worth of Individual Annuities." *American Economic Review* 89 (December): 1299–1318.

Moore, James F. and Olivia S. Mitchell. 1999. "Projected Retirement Wealth and Saving Adequacy." In *Forecasting Retirement Needs and Retirement Wealth,* ed. Olivia S. Mitchell, P. Brett Hammond, and Anna M. Rappaport. Pension Research Council. Philadelphia: University of Pennsylvania Press.

Murthi, Mamta, J. Michael Orszag, and Peter R. Orszag. 1999. "The Value for Money of Annuities in the U.K.: Theory, Experience, and Policy." Mimeo, Birkbeck College, London.

Poterba, James M., Steven F. Venti, and David A. Wise. 1999. "Implications of Rising Personal Retirement Savings." NBER Working Paper 6295.

Poterba, James M. and Mark J. Warshawsky. Forthcoming. "The Costs of Annuitizing Retirement Payouts from Individual Accounts." In *Administrative Costs and Social Security Privatization,* ed. John B. Shoven. Chicago: University of Chicago Press.

National Academy of Social Insurance (NASI). 1998. *Evaluating Issues in Privatizing Social Security.* Washington, D.C.: National Academy of Social Insurance.

Social Security Administration. 1999. *Trustees Report: United States Life Table Functions and Actuarial Functions based on the Alternative 2 Mortality Probabilities.* Washington, D.C.: U.S. Government Printing Office.

Warshawsky, Mark J. 1988. "Private Annuity Markets in the United States." *Journal of Risk and Insurance* 55, 3 (September): 518–28.

Chapter 9
Integrating Life Annuities and Long-Term Care Insurance: Theory, Evidence, Practice, and Policy

Mark J. Warshawsky, Brenda C. Spillman, and Christopher M. Murtaugh

The aging of the baby boom generation, the lengthening of life spans, and the political shift away from government and employer solutions to retirement issues toward individual responsibility have all combined to heighten concerns about how future retirees will manage and assure their financial security in old age. This chapter explores two separate financial and insurance instruments—life annuities and long-term care insurance—that we suggest could address the need for income security and the potential need for age- and disability-related long-term care. We evaluate reasons why these currently available products are not widely used and explore limits on current markets for both products. It appears that a combination of the two products has the potential to make them available to a broader range of the population, with minimal underwriting and at lower cost. We also explore tax and design issues that may affect the ability to introduce this and other innovative products.

In what follows, we first examine the current market for life annuities and long-term care insurance. Next we contrast the economic and conventional wisdom concerning the optimal use of life annuities, review current trends in annuitization, and note possible reasons for market failure, particularly adverse selection. We then describe how an individual's risk of needing costly long-term care services represents a substantial threat to his or her economic wellbeing, explain the current financing of long-term care services, and review the literature on why coverage through private long-term care insurance remains relatively low. In particular we discuss the impact of medical underwriting on access to long-term care insurance.

The Market for Life Annuities

A life annuity is an insurance product that pays out a periodic amount for the life of an individual or the lives of a couple in exchange for a premium charge. Annuity payments may be either guaranteed (fixed or increasing) or variable, depending on the contract structure and underlying investments. Life annuities frequently offer a guaranteed period over which benefits will be paid even if the annuitant does not survive. A life annuity can be offered through an employer-sponsored retirement plan or as an individual product, funded either on a pre-tax or after-tax basis. It is also the form of payment from the U.S. social security system.

Economic and Conventional Wisdom Contrasted

According to the economic theory of life cycle savings, a straight life annuity should be the cornerstone of financial planning and practice in retirement. In this context the chief principle governing household saving behavior is the desire to smooth consumption patterns over an uncertain lifetime, within the constraints imposed by limited lifetime resources; here life annuities should be used widely (Friedman and Warshawsky, 1990). Without access to life annuities, elderly individuals would need to conserve wealth to self-insure against the risk of having to reduce consumption in later years, should their life span turn out to be unexpectedly long. As a result of husbanding wealth, the consumption path that these individuals can safely pursue is lower than one afforded by a fairly priced annuity.

The amount of wealth an individual would be prepared to give up in order to gain access to a life annuity, so as to avoid the constrained self annuitization strategy, has been calculated by Mitchell, Poterba, Warshawsky, and Brown (hereafter MPWB 1999). They employ an expected utility/ dynamic stochastic optimization framework and use reasonable estimates for market (interest and mortality rates) and preference (risk aversion and time discount) parameters in their simulations. The results show that individuals would forgo 20–30 percent of discretionary wealth (that is, wealth exclusive of the present value of social security benefits) to obtain a life annuity.

A mystery, then, is why life annuities are not widely recommended by the financial planning community. Indeed, almost all financial planning software programs and websites ignore mortality uncertainty and hence the possible beneficial use of life annuities. Instead, planners recommend that households should expect to finance retirement expenditures over a static life expectancy (or to be conservative, life expectancy plus 10 years; see Warshawsky and Ameriks, 2000). Professional financial advisors rarely recommend life annuities to their retiree clients but instead suggest a combination of withdrawal rates and investment strategies for asset portfolios to try to assure adequate income in retirement (Rekenthaler 2000; Jarrett and Stringfellow 2000).

Current Annuitization Trends

Almost 43 percent of the income flow of the average retired worker age 65 and older in the U.S. currently comes from social security (EBRI 1997). These benefits are provided in the form of a joint and survivor inflation-indexed straight life annuity, that is, an annuity whose benefits cease with the death of the last surviving member of the elderly household. Already, the social security annuity payout is being delayed as the normal retirement age under the system is gradually raised. Moreover, the system's actuarial imbalance may necessitate some fairly fundamental changes in the future, changes that could include benefit cuts or privatization (see Mitchell, Myers, and Young 1999). These changes would be likely to produce lower automatic annuity payments at the same time that life expectancies of the population are projected to rise, thus increasing risk exposure from lifetime uncertainty.

There have also been significant changes in the employer-sponsored pension plan environment. Defined benefit plans traditionally provided a life annuity as the only payment form, but these have been giving way to defined contribution plans that are much less likely to even offer a life annuity as a payment option, let alone mandate it as one (Gordon et al. 1997). Even defined benefit plans and their cash balance progeny are now increasingly offering plan participants the choice between a life annuity and other payment methods such as systematic and lump sum withdrawals.[1]

These trends imply that there will be an increased need for the private market to offer attractive life annuity products in the future. Currently, however, the market for single premium immediate annuities (SPIAs) is small and annuitization rates from deferred annuities are quite low. Premium payments for individual immediate annuities were just under $8 billion in 1998 with reserves of $69.4 billion and 2.3 million covered persons (ACLI 1999). Just over 112,000 new contracts were issued in 1998, and there were 1.5 million contracts in force. Marketing statistics show that, in 1995, the average single premium immediate annuity sold in 1995 cost $79,600 (MPWB 1999); most (55 percent) SPIAs were sold to men, and most (74 percent) were not part of a tax qualified retirement plan such as an IRA. As of 1996, just over one percent of individual variable deferred annuities were making periodic payments, presumably in life annuity form; total annualized income to annuitants, $381 million, also represented just one percent of premiums (ACLI 1997). These low annuitization rates could represent a growing and still immature market, or they might represent more fundamental aversion to the annuity payment form.

Current Failures in the Private Voluntary Market

Adverse selection figures prominently as a possible explanation for the lack of popularity of individual life annuities (Friedman and Warshawsky, 1990; MPWB, 1999). A recent study (MPWB 1999) found that the expected present discounted value of annuity payments per dollar of SPIA premium averages between 80 and 85 cents for an individual with the mortality prospects of the general population, and between 90 and 94 cents for an individual with mortality prospects of annuitants. Stated another way, the cost of adverse selection is about 10 cents on the dollar. In addition, there are transactions costs unique to insurance products, covering marketing and sales commissions to agents, at about seven cents on the dollar. Together these costs could discourage purchase of individual life annuities.

Several other factors also may contribute to restraining the market for individual annuities. One is that the life annuity purchase is irreversible and irrevocable, so it can be construed as an illiquid investment, resulting in loss of control for the annuitant. Yet some individuals highly value liquidity and control, particularly those facing possible long-term care expenses. A second issue is that a life annuity does not help finance a bequest motive. Although the economic literature debates how significant bequest motives are, for at least some middle and upper income households, they may be a factor deterring their purchase of a life annuity. A third explanation may be institutional considerations, including unimaginative marketing by the insurance industry, sales incentives that discourage selling immediate annuities, and negative recommendations from financial advisors that may confuse investors, who are ignorant of the longevity insurance provided by life annuities. Finally, excluding annuities available through social security and a few pension systems, life annuities in the United States do not adjust for inflation.[2] Elderly households are therefore exposed to the risk of uncertain inflation that they might be able to hedge better through other means, such as asset allocation strategies. All of these reasons may explain why the U.S. marketplace for annuities remains thin despite what would seem to be a rise in factors prompting the demand for life annuities.

Current Methods for Financing Long-term Care Services[3]

The term long-term care (LTC) represents a broad range of services and assistance for people with chronic illnesses or disabilities who are unable to care for themselves over a relatively long period of time. The need for long-term care services is particularly high among the elderly, especially the "old-old" (85 or above), and this is a segment of the population projected to grow rapidly as the baby boom generation ages. LTC services are expensive, and their cost is increasing more rapidly than that of other goods and services in the economy, including other health care services.

In the U.S., federal and state governments currently provide substantial resources to support households that cannot finance their own long-term care needs. Some would argue that the existence of this social safety net has impinged on the growth of private insurance coverage. Nevertheless some individuals and families do use long-term care insurance policies to finance their own future needs. Current market mechanisms, however, have certain drawbacks and there seems to be some resistance to, and a lack of understanding among the public about, the need for insurance coverage for long-term care needs.

Costs of Long-Term Care Services

LTC services include skilled nursing care as well as supportive services such as assistance with activities of daily living; these can be provided in a person's home or in a residential care facility. More than 40 percent of people aged 65+ are expected to spend some time in a nursing home, and almost one in 10 will spend five or more years there before death (Kemper and Murtaugh 1991). A larger proportion will need some long-term care, including home care, in their remaining lifetimes. About 17 percent of those age 65+ had a disability requiring some type of human help, yet only 29 percent of these were in nursing homes in 1994 (Spector et al. n.d.). The likelihood of spending some time in a nursing home at some point during the remainder of life increases with age, from 39 percent at age 65, to 56 percent at age 85 (Murtaugh et al. 1995). Similarly, the probability of needing help with the "Activities of Daily Living" (or ADLs, including bathing, dressing, feeding, toileting, and transferring) increases with age. People tend to lose their ADL functions in the opposite order in which they acquired them when young. For example, only 3.5 percent will need help bathing between ages 65 and 74, but more than 20 percent will need such assistance at age 85 or older.

The average stay in a nursing home among users of all ages is 2.4 years (Murtaugh et al. 1999). The expected stay for most is less than one year; but for 16 percent of users, it is more than five years. Women, whites, those widowed or never married, and midwesterners are more likely to experience a stay in a nursing home and have relatively longer expected stays. The mean number of years of nursin home residence among users declines with age at first admission, from 2.8 years in the 65 to 74 age group, to 1.9 years in the 85+ age groups. The average lifetime home health care use is just over 200 visits. About half of those expected to use home health care will use fewer than 90 visits during their lifetimes, while 12 percent can expect to use more than 730 visits (HIAA 1997).

The cost of long-term care service represents a substantial expenditure for older individuals and their families. The nature of the care received, whether at home or in a facility, will clearly influence costs, as will the intensity of medical care referred. Individuals who are more dependent, or who need more skilled care that can normally only be rendered by a medical professional, will realize greater costs than someone who requires limited assistance in bathing or dressing. The average annual cost in 1995 for a stay in a nursing home was about $40,000; assisted living facilities charge about $26,000 per year; and home care visits cost $50–$100, depending on the skill level of services provided (Warshawsky, Granza, and Madamba 2000).

Figure 1 compares cost trends for nursing homes, health services, and all goods and services over the period 1995–99, drawing on data from the USBLS (various years). Nursing home services costs have consistently risen faster than health services and all goods and services, even as the overall inflation rate in the economy has declined. In particular, nursing home cost increases exceeded general inflation in the economy by three percentage points in the latter half of the 1990s. At that rate, the real cost of nursing home care will double over the next 23 years. The rate of cost inflation for nursing home services does not appear to be influenced by the same factors that influence the broader category of health services. This may reflect the importance of HMO penetration and other innovations in health care production and financing over this period, that have not yet affected nursing homes. It may also reflect a change in the population served by nursing homes from a predominantly long-term population to more of a post-acute care population.

The cost of a stay in a nursing home varies widely by the area of the country. As one might expect, urban areas are usually costlier than suburban or rural areas. In 1998, a nursing home in New York City, for example, could cost more than $250 a day, for an annual cost of more than $91,000. In Oklahoma, on the other hand, the cost was closer to $70 a day. The cost of nursing facilities also depends on the level of sophistication and breadth of the amenities offered. Those with private insurance or substantial assets appear to purchase more costly long-term care services, as private-pay nursing home stays are about 25 percent more expensive than stays paid by Medicaid (Warshawsky, Granza, and Madamba 2000).

A related issue is that life expectancies of American adults have increased significantly in the last century and are projected to increase further. Longer life expectancy has meant that increasing numbers of individuals will survive into what has been called "old-old" age (age 85 or above). In fact, individuals in this age group will be the fastest growing segment of the population by the year 2030. This population aging will also contribute to higher LTC costs in the future. Of course it is not completely clear whether longer life expectancies are the result of an increase in the age at which certain diseases present themselves, or the outcome of lower age-specific death rates among the infirm (Crimmins et al. 1997). Some researchers now believe that the older population is healthier than ever, and that the simultaneous rate of decline in mortality and disability will continue because these

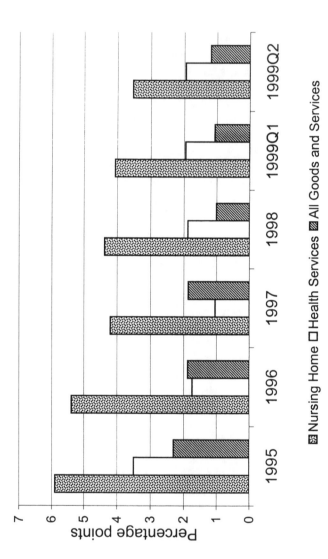

Figure 1. Medical care cost inflation, 1995–99. Source: Warshawsky, Granza, and Madamba (2000).

TABLE 1. Sources of Funding for Long-term Care Expenses (1997)

Funding Source	Nursing Home (%)	Home Health Care (%)
Out-of-Pocket	31.10	21.67
Private Insurance	4.90	11.46
Other Private	1.90	12.07
Medicare	12.30	39.63
Medicaid	47.60	14.55
Other Government	2.30	0.31

Source: Braden et al. (1998).

rates are lower in younger cohorts (Manton, Stallard, and Corder 1997a, b). Nevertheless, those who survive to "old-old" age are much more likely to need long-term care than those in their 60s, so the growth in the number of such individuals will continue to inspire demand for TCL services in the future.

Americans spent almost $83 billion on nursing home services and more than $32 billion on home health care in 1997.[4] Table 1 shows the sources of funding for these expenditures in percentage terms. Clearly, government support is significant, but there are several constraints on that support.

One issue is that Medicare is designed to pay for acute and post-acute care needs. That program covers care in a skilled nursing facility for up to 100 days (with a substantial copayment applied after the twentieth day), following a hospital stay of at least three days. In aggregate, Medicare pays for about 12 percent of nursing home expenses. That program also provides home health care benefits on a part-time or intermittent basis; this entitlement has grown rapidly over time and now pays for 40 percent of aggregate home health care expenses. Medicare benefits, however, must be medically oriented; once care is no longer rehabilitative and becomes custodial in nature, benefits may no longer be payable.[5] Moreover, in 1997, Medicare instituted strict limits on payments to home health care agencies and vigorously began to pursue instances of fraud and abuse. A prospective payment system was recently introduced for skilled nursing facilities and home health care benefits under Medicare, in response to increases in cost and to fears that Medicare was becoming a long-term care benefit. Future funding for long-term care from Medicare is also likely to be limited due to fiscal trends. The Hospital Insurance Trust Fund is projected to be depleted by 2015, and payroll taxes are projected to cover only one-half of its cost 75 years from now (Social Security Administration, 1999).

Medicaid is a joint federal/state health care program for those with low income and few assets (or those who deplete their assets paying for long-term care) that currently pays for almost 50 percent of aggregate nursing home expenses and almost 15 percent of home health care expenses.[6] For most middle and high income households, however, Medicaid is either unavailable or undesirable. Few resources are exempt from the eligibility guidelines, asset transfers are strictly controlled during a look-back period, spousal protection is somewhat limited, and only participating providers can be used, which in practice often limits choice.[7] Neither Medicaid nor Medicare pays for the room and board segments of expenses incurred in assisted living facilities. Future funding for long-term care from Medicaid may come under some pressure due to fiscal trends. Assuming current law and reasonable demographic and economic projections, growth in Medicaid spending will likely outpace growth in tax revenues traditionally devoted to Medicaid over the next 30 years (Mulvey and Stucki 1998).

It is clear from Table 1 that private insurance currently pays for a small but important portion of long-term care expenses in the United States. Private-insurance-paid expenses that are medical in nature are covered by health insurance (including Medigap); the remainder are covered by private long-term care insurance, whether purchased individually or through a group plan.[8] Surveys of insurance companies selling LTC coverage find that the market is growing and evolving rapidly, but it is still relatively small. Between 1972, when the product was first introduced, and the end of 1996, 120 insurance companies had sold almost 5 million policies; approximately 80 percent of these policies were purchased individually. A different survey found that terminations were occurring at 5.4 percent annual rate, so that the number of LTC policies outstanding (2.8 million in 1998) was lower than the number of policies sold (ACLI 1999). The average annual premium on an individual LTC insurance policy with inflation protection issued to a 65-year-old was $1,829 in 1996 (Coronel 1998).

This number of outstanding policies translates into a coverage rate for overall American population of only about 1 percent. This definition understates effective coverage through the private market, however, since the risk of needing care arises substantially in middle and old age, and most individual LTC policies are purchased by older people — the average age of buyers in 1996 was 67 (Coronel 1998). If the coverage rate is limited to people age 65 and older, then about 8 percent of older individuals are covered by private long-term care insurance. This coverage rate also differs substantially by state: north and midwestern states with sparse and relatively old populations, like Montana, North and South Dakota, and Iowa, have much higher private LTC insurance penetration than some southern and northeastern states (Coronel 1998). Alabama, where income is low, and New York, where Medicaid benefits are relatively generous, have low private LTC insurance penetration.

Private LTC coverage rates can also be computed from national surveys — including the Asset and Health Dynamics of the Oldest Old Study (AHEAD) and the Health and Retirement Study (HRS) (Sloan and Norton, 1997). In 1993 the AHEAD interviewed a national sample of community-based individuals aged 70 and over and their spouses of any age, whereas the 1992 HRS surveyed a national cohort of individuals aged 51 to 61. In the AHEAD and HRS respectively, 2.2 and 1.6 percent of persons had private LTC insurance. Clearly, these coverage rates are much lower than those reported from insurance company sources; the difference may be due to the growth of the private market over time, or to reporting errors.

Thus far, most LTC policies have been sold to individuals, but of late there is growing interest and activity in sales through employer-sponsored group plans. According to the U.S. Bureau of Labor Statistics (1998), almost 3 million workers (7 percent of the relevant workforce) were eligible to participate in group LTC plans sponsored by medium and large private establishments in 1997; only 2.1 million workers in medium and large firms had been eligible as of 1995. As of 1996, almost 600 thousand workers (1.5 percent of the relevant workforce) were eligible to participate in group LTC plans sponsored by small private establishments; only 200 thousand workers in small firms were eligible as of 1994. A survey of employers with between 1,000 and 5,000 employees accounted for the largest percentage of firms sponsoring this benefit (40 percent); the majority of sponsoring employers offered a voluntary, employee-pay-all LTC insurance benefit (80 percent) (McSweeney and Aarhus 1999). In addition to private sponsors, many state and local governments sponsor group LTC plans for their public workers. In particular, California and Alaska have very successful, carefully designed, and strongly promoted programs; the Alaska plan is totally integrated with retirement planning and is available to employees at retirement without underwriting (Pincus 2000). It should be noted that eligibility numbers for group plans mask much lower participation rates. Nearly three-quarters of employers sponsoring group LTC insurance had participation rates under 10 percent, with the majority of those having participation rates under 5 percent (McSweeney and Aarhus 1999). The average age of a purchaser of LTC insurance through a group plan is 43 (Coronel 1998).

The advantages of group LTC plans include lower administrative costs for large employers, convenience to employees, and guaranteed issuance, yet there are business considerations and risks that may also discourage employers from establishing such plans. One reason is that young employees may not appreciate such a program in the absence of a strong educational effort by the employer. Given that one of the main business reasons for sponsoring employee benefit programs is their attractiveness to workers, especially prospective ones, most employers will tend to devote their attention to benefits areas better appreciated, such as health insurance and child care benefits. Another reason for reluctance is that employers avoid creating a new employee entitlement program, especially one involving long range health care costs that could add unknown costs and liabilities in the distant future. Finally, employers tend to avoid sponsoring programs that, in the future, may be burdened by government regulations that could increase costs or limit flexibility.

Could increased ownership of long-term care insurance by the general population help to finance future long-term care expenditures? A recent study by Mulvey and Stucki (1998) uses a large-scale simulation model and concludes that increased ownership could cut future Medicaid nursing home expenditures by 21 percent and reduce out-of-pocket expenditures for nursing home care by 40 percent. The key assumptions of this model are that everyone age 35 and older in the year 2000 who can afford to purchase a long-term care policy will do so, and that three-fourths of the purchasers will retain their policy until old age. Realization of these assumptions would evidently require a major change in behavior among consumers; as mentioned above, at most eight percent of the current elderly have private LTC, and even fewer younger individuals have coverage. There would also need to be great public trust placed in the long-term financial capability of insurers, and a strong belief that government and social insurance programs will not be forthcoming in the future to cover long-term care needs. The main advantages to the purchase of LTC at younger ages are lower annual premiums and fewer underwriting problems; about three-quarters of the individuals age 35 to 44 could afford a policy if they spent 2 percent or less of their income on private insurance, and if a policy were available to nearly all individuals in that age grouping. It is unclear whether younger individuals would be willing to incur such a significant expenditure to insure against a risk that is so abstract and distant at that age.

Possible Reasons for the Small Market for Private LTC Insurance

Marketing and policy analysts tend to explain the relatively small penetration of private long-term care insurance (small as compared to other types of insurance and employee benefits) by appealing to consumer irrationality and ignorance. In particular, "behavioral" arguments are invoked to explain peoples' tendency to ignore low probability, high-loss events that may occur in the distant future. Some note that people are confused about whether Medicare covers nursing home expenses, while others point to factors traditionally used in explaining lack of demand for, or supply of, insurance, that is, moral hazard and adverse selection. The economic literature, by contrast, attempts to explain the small penetration of long-term care insurance among the population by examining fundamental preference and incentive issues. Pauly's (1990) analysis launched this literature by setting up a rational framework of expected utility maximization for a risk-averse individual with no bequest motive. This consumer is seen as having a pool of assets to finance consumption and to cover a large but uncertain and random cost of chronic illness, over a future of unknown length and health. If perfect insurance markets were available, Pauly shows that the consumer would use his entire wealth to purchase a life annuity that financed an optimal stream of consumption when well, and paid for the cost of chronic illness when sick. This plan of action is precisely what would be provided with an integrated life annuity and long-term care insurance policy. If such an annuity were not available, an older American could still be assured that the U.S. Medicaid program would provide him with care after nursing home expenses exhausted his wealth. Hence, he would not buy fairly priced long-term care insurance.[9]

While this model offers one rationale for the absence of a correctly designed annuity with a LTC insurance component, others have noted instead the limitations in currently available LTC insurance policies (Cutler 1993; Cohen 1998). That is, LTC insurance tends to adopt the classic indemnity approach, covering only eligible expenses for specified services. This means that even currently well designed policies can become outdated quickly. For this reason, a disability approach might be preferred: income benefits are paid on clear diagnosis of a disability, regardless of the exact nature and amount of the expenses incurred and services selected. Another reasonable explanation for the thin private LTC insurance market is people's desire for control, flexibility, and liquidity. Older households are often concerned about family emergencies, personal contingencies, and other uninsurable and unhedgeable events that might require access to a pool of liquid assets. However LTC purchase is irrevocable and also carries a load for marketing, administrative, and underwriting expenses. Hence, for many households, LTC insurance might not be desired.[10]

Another explanation for lack of LTC coverage among the elderly population arises when medical underwriting indicates that the individual has an elevated risk of needing care and refuses to sell the policy. This phenomenon may explain a significant part of the lack of private coverage, given current purchase patterns. Given underwriting criteria typically used by insurance companies, between 12 and 23 percent of the elderly population would probably be rejected for private LTC insurance for health reasons if everyone applied at age 65 (Murtaugh et al. 1995). According to these same criteria, between 20 and 31 percent would likely be rejected by age 75. Although some insurers are now offering risk-rated premiums, underwriting remains a substantial impediment to the expansion of private LTC insurance coverage with an average decline rate of 20 percent (Collett et al. 1999).

Additional reasons for the lack of LTC coverage might include ignorance, discomfort, and dissonance. Recent surveys suggest that older Americans believe obtaining long-term care poses a significant risk to their standard of living in retirement, and most believe that they could not afford to stay in a nursing home for a substantial length of time. It may be that a massive educational effort on this subject is required to increase consumer knowledge and understanding.[11]

Integrating a Life Annuity and Long-Term Care Insurance Coverage

A product not yet on the market is an integrated life annuity and long-term care insurance coverage, yet integration has the potential to remedy many of the problems just described in the life annuity and long-term care insurance markets. Moreover, encouragement of private life annuities and long-term care insurance may reduce the demand for long-term care financed out-of-pocket or via public programs.

The Theoretical Issues

On theoretical grounds, a fairly priced life annuity with extra benefits payable following the onset of disability would be consistent with the preferences of many households (Pauly 1990). On practical grounds, the integration of the two components would appear to be reinforcing. The life annuity would no longer be seen as quite so illiquid because a major source of uncertainty, long-term care expenses, could be covered with the integrated product. The argument that the life annuity is unresponsive to a bequest motive would also be mitigated, because the long-term care insurance component would hedge parents' nonannuitized assets against the risk of long-term care expenses borne by the estate to be inherited by children. Further, postponing decisions about long-term care insurance until retirement, when households are better able and more willing to consider the options available to them, could solve the reluctance problem. Finally, aversion to long-term care insurance would be counterbalanced by tying it to the purchase of a life annuity, whose payoff, in contrast to a long-term care insurance, would be largest when the annuitant lived a long (and often healthy) life.

Empirical Evidence on an Integrated Product

Murtaugh et al. (2000) evaluate an integrated product using data from the 1986 National Mortality Followback Survey (NMFS) projected to represent hypothetical purchasing pools at age 65 and 75 in 1995. They simulate the number of people eligible to purchase a combined product with minimal medical underwriting for the disability benefit, and also the number of people eligible to purchase LTC insurance and most likely to purchase a life annuity, sold as stand-alone products. Premiums are completed for the combined product and for stand-alone products. "Minimal" underwriting is defined as allowing all individuals to purchase the combined product except those who would be immediately able to make a claim, that is, those already significantly disabled.

The first integrated product modeled is a fixed life annuity with payments that increase on the determination of a chronic disability. More specifically, the basic product is a life annuity that pays $1,000 a month for life with a guaranteed 10-year minimum payout, combined with a disability annuity that pays an additional $2,000 a month if the purchaser becomes chronically disabled in at least two activities of daily living (ADLs) or cognitively impaired; and an additional $1,000 a month if the purchaser becomes disabled in four ADLs. Premiums are also estimated for a product having annually increasing benefits: three percent for the life annuity segment and five percent for the LTC insurance segment. Small loads are added to cover administrative (but not marketing) costs; the assumed discount rate used in pricing is six percent. Benefit amounts are chosen to be such that, combined with social security, they would cover both basic consumption needs and the cost of nursing home care in most geographic regions, for those with the greatest level of disability. Charges for both the life annuity and LTC disability insurance are estimated as a single premium paid at purchase. Premiums for LTC insurance currently are typically level premiums paid monthly or quarterly. This practice makes the timing of eligibility for LTC benefits of prospective purchasers more important, since it affects the amount of prefunding through premium accumulations. For comparability in this analysis, all premiums were modeled as lump sums paid at purchase.

Access and prospective purchasers. The evidence shows that minimal underwriting dramatically increases the pool of eligible purchasers from 77 percent under current underwriting practice to 98 percent of persons at age 65. This expansion has relatively modest impacts on mean risk and expected duration of disability in the prospective purchaser pool under minimal underwriting, but it reduces average survival by 1.5 years. The relatively small difference in risk and duration of disability between the purchaser pools is consistent with the positive relationship between age and disability, and with previous research showing that expected nursing home use among those who would be accepted for LTC insurance at age 65 was higher than for most groups excluded by underwriting (Murtaugh et al. 1995). The key to the higher annual LTC insurance premiums for the excluded groups was the lack of adequate prefunding of benefit costs, because their service use was more likely to happen in the near term. This pattern also applies to the onset of disability, with prospective purchasers of LTC insurance under current strict underwriting who ultimately become eligible for benefits doing so 17 years in the future, compared with generally 10 years or less for the excluded groups.

Nonpurchasers under current underwriting practice are found to differ from eligible purchasers primarily in mean survival time, which is just under 12 years, compared with 19.5 years for currently eligible purchasers. Risk and expected duration of disability are similar to that of currently eligible purchasers. In contrast, minimal underwriting excludes persons whose sur-

TABLE 2. Long-Term Care Premiums at Age 65 for Income Annuity with Disability Benefits, Current Underwriting Versus Minimal Underwriting

	$1,000 mo. Life Annuity only	$2,000 mo. 2+ ADL Disability Benefit	$1,000 mo. 4+ ADL Disability Benefit	Combined Premium
Without inflation protection				
All Persons	$139,098	$ 15,950	$ 3,155	$158,203
Prospective purchasers				
Current LTC Underwriting	$145,041	$ 13,900	$ 2,843	$161,784
Minimal Underwriting Only	$139,827	$ 13,723	$ 2,777	$156,326
Nonpurchasers				
Current LTC Underwriting	$119,051	$ 22,866	$ 4,207	$146,124
Minimal Underwriting Only	$104,147	$122,764	$ 21,293	$248,203
*With inflation protection**				
All Persons	$177,238	$ 35,649	$ 7,630	$220,517
Prospective purchasers				
Current LTC Underwriting	$187,102	$ 35,258	$ 7,791	$230,151
Minimal Underwriting Only	$178,426	$ 33,122	$ 7,220	$218,768
Nonpurchasers				
Current LTC Underwriting	$143,963	$ 36,969	$ 7,086	$188,018
Minimal Underwriting only	$120,268	$156,864	$ 27,295	$304,427

Source: Murtaugh, Spillman, and Warshawsky (2000).
Note: Base income annuity policy is $1,000 per month for life with a minimum 10-year benefit.
* Income annuity inflates at 3 percent per year compounded, and disability benefits inflate at 5 percent per year compounded, consistent with long term care insurance industry standard for inflation protection.

vival is only six years on average and whose expected duration of disability is about four times that of prospective purchasers.

Premium estimates. Table 2 shows individual premium estimates for three levels of benefit and a combined premium for the "at risk" populations just described. Estimates in the top panel assume no annual increase in benefits, while those in the lower panel include annual increases meant to provide protection against likely future rates of inflation. The life annuity premium of $139,827 for the expanded purchaser pool under minimal underwriting is 3.6 percent lower than that for likely purchasers under current practice, because of the expanded pool's lower average survival.[12] The premium for disability benefits, like risk and duration of disability, are similar for the two purchase groups. This is because minimal underwriting excludes two percent of persons representing the worst disability cost risks, and the remaining "poor risks" actually have lower disability costs than those currently accepted for LTC insurance; the inclusion of these risks reduces the average premium for the expanded pool. Combined with the lower annuity costs of prospective purchasers under minimal underwriting, the premium for the combined product is $156,326, about 3.4 percent lower than that for stand-alone life annuity and equivalent long term care insurance products under current underwriting practice.

This pattern is similar when inflation protection is added, in the lower panel of Table 2, but differences are larger because of the greater impact of the inflation protection on both life annuity and long-term care benefits received farther in the future by prospective purchasers under current underwriting practice. In particular, this can be seen in the premium for insurance coverage with minimal underwriting, against two-ADL disability, which is $33,122, or six percent lower than under current practice. With inflation protection, the premium for the combined benefits for the expanded pool is about five percent below the premium for the standalone products under current underwriting practice.

A key question is whether the combined product would be attractive to those groups currently excluded from purchasing LTC insurance and unlikely to buy a life annuity. Combining LTC insurance coverage with the life annuity improves the ratio of expected benefits to premium costs for all "at-risk" groups in the population, in some cases significantly so. Including a minimum annuity benefit, or guaranteed period, contributes to this result, as would allowance for some "ADL creep" in the presentation of reported disability among those insured, and flexibility in the offered mix of life annuity and LTC insurance benefits. Nevertheless, the ratio of expected benefits to premium costs is below one for most groups and hence some perceived insurance value will be needed to elicit purchases.

Potential Markets

Life annuities and long-term care insurance are potentially relevant for most retirement age persons. It must be recognized, however, that a combined long-term care insurance/life annuity may not appeal to two socio-economic groups: the poor and the wealthy. Those with the lowest income and assets are likely to qualify for medical assistance through Medicaid if they need long-term care, particularly nursing home care, and they are unlikely to have income from pensions or accumulated assets with which to purchase private long-term care insurance or annuities. By contrast, and almost by definition, wealthy persons have more than sufficient assets to cover almost all length of life and disability contingencies. Excluding these two groups, however, most retired persons face a risk of outliving their assets, and nursing home and home care costs represent major threats to financial security. For the most part, these persons have incentives to avoid Medicaid eligibility because nonhousing assets must be exhausted, the choice of LTC providers often is limited, and there is greater risk of poor quality of care; for some individuals, their income may be too high to qualify for Medicaid eligibility in some states.

There are several potential markets where a combined product could be offered. The most obvious and largest is the retirement product market, which includes both employer-sponsored pension plans (defined benefit and defined contribution) and individual retirement accounts. The combined product could also be made available as a distribution option for another huge market, after-tax annuities (deferred and immediate, fixed and variable).

Current Product Developments

Several insurance companies in the United States and the United Kingdom have begun marketing products combining an annuity with a long-term care rider. All these products have the feature that LTC underwriting is eliminated or substantially reduced; most employ after-tax deferred variable annuities as the base product. The combined products vary considerably, however, in the waiting periods imposed to become eligible for LTC benefits. Only one company has a product where benefits are triggered by disability as opposed to incurred expenses, and whose LTC insurance is connected with an immediate life annuity as opposed to an accumulating (that is, deferred) annuity. Hence the integrated product we are examining is unique and not yet available in the marketplace.

Public Policy and Product Design Issues

Although it might be possible to introduce an integrated long-term care insurance policy and life annuity in the current environment, there are legal and product design issues that would have to be dealt with before the product could be offered in its most desirable form.

Tax Environment

The recent enactment in 1996 of the Health Insurance Portability and Accountability Act (HIPAA) clarified the tax treatment of long-term care benefits and premiums, providing that LTC expenses and insurance premiums can be treated like medical expenses with respect to the individual income tax. Accordingly, LTC expenses are now deductible from federal income taxes, provided that the expenses exceed 7.5 percent of adjusted gross income. HIPAA also allows individuals to deduct long-term care insurance premiums up to certain limits based on age, again provided that medical expenses and premiums exceed 7.5 percent of income; single-premium LTC policies, however, are not deductible.[13] It also stipulates that benefits payable under a tax qualified LTC policy will not be treated as taxable income, provided that the policy needs certain benefit trigger and other design conditions stated in the law. In addition, HIPAA provides employers with a tax incentive if they elect to pay some or all of the LTC insurance premiums for employees. Employees also benefit from this provision, as their employer's contribution is not included in the taxable income of the employee.

One possible logical approach to taxing the integrated product would break the combined long-term care annuity into its competent life annuity and single-premium long-term care insurance policy. The purchase of the insurance policy would presumbly represent a taxable distribution from the qualified retirement plant. The single premium for that policy would not be deductible from the taxable income of the plan participant, but the benefits paid under the policy would not be taxable. The life annuity component would be gradually taxable when periodic payments are made from the retirement plan.

An alternative environment for the integrated product. A more favorable environment would be one where the "purchase" of long-term care insurance was not considered a taxable distribution and the long-term care benefits paid from the plan, like accident and sickness benefits paid from an insurance policy, would be excluded from taxable income. This could be rationalized by analogy with section 401(h) of the Internal Revenue Code permitting tax qualified status for health plans for retired employees, Employer contributions to pay faor such benefits are not taxable income to the employee, and the benefits, when received, are also not included in retiree taxable income. Long-term care benefits can probably be considered health benefits for the purpose of 401(h). There are strict conditions imposed on benefits provided through 401(h), including the necessity to establish a separate account where the employer's contributions are collected; 401(h) was added to the Code in 1964 in response to conditions in certain defined benefit plans. It is unlikely that the long-term care annuity we are envisioning here could meet these conditions, but the precedent of the 401(h) law could allow legislators to craft new provisions that would fit the long-term care annuity option.[14]

Indemnity Versus Cash Disability Approach

Most of the administrative considerations pertinent to the integrated LTC annuity are not unique to the integrated product, but rather affect its component parts, that is, the life annuity or the long-term care benefits. Indeed, our choice of focusing on a disability rather than an indemnity approach to long-term care insurance benefits presents some special administrative issues, both positive and negative.

In an indemnity approach to long-term care insurance, the claims procedure is often quite complicated for the insurer to administer. Insured expenses must be carefully defined in the policy, and claims for reimbursement must be examined in some detail. Furthermore, the insured must establish a process of dispute adjudication as well as a system for tracking limits or maximums. There is also a tendency for insurance companies to get involved in case management, which can be quite complex and sensitive. Because an indemnity approach must specify covered benefits, it is not dynamically flexible, that is, as new treatment methods and modalities arise, the indemnity policy becomes outdated and must be modified either by rider or by replacement. In contrast, the disability approach has a much simpler claims process to administer and it is dynamically flexible. Because benefits are paid as long as the insured is disabled, regardless of the specific expenses incurred, if any, the only determination necessary is whether and when the disabled insured meets certain specified criteria. Finally, the disability approach is much less prescriptive; it allows, indeed encourages, the insured to consider carefully how best to use the policy benefits being paid to meet his needs.

In both the indemnity and the disability approaches to LTC insurance, disability must be assessed before benefits can be paid and periodically after payments thereafter, but in the disability approach this determination is more critical. There will be an incentive for some insured individuals to claim that they have a disability in order to collect the benefits. It would therefore seem to be preferable for the disability assessments to be done by a trusted third-party organization, evaluating for the presence of a combination of highly objective and well-understood criteria. Criteria for determining whether individuals meet disability thresholds have been successfully developed in both private and public sectors, and they are being administered by nurses, social workers, and other professionals. A few insurance companies sell disability-based long-term care insurance policies. State government agencies administer benefit programs for the elderly providing services solely based on the determination of disability.[15]

The disability approach might be more open to abuse by the insureds and their relatives or guardians, though it is unknown how extensive this problem is or would be. Any insurance policy can lead to greater utilization of (that is, induced demand for) the policy benefit, but in the indemnity approach cost-sharing features are typically introduced to minimize the problem. Perhaps an inability to include cost-sharing features explains the higher premium charged by the few companies utilizing the disability approach for essentially the same level of benefits as those companies using the indemnity approach. Even in the disability approach, of course, it may be possible to include benefit maximums and other design features that give policyholders incentives to consume their benefits appropriately.

Conclusion and Discussion

This chapter describes current life annuity and long-term care insurance markets and explores why these products are not widely used. To solve many of the problems identified, we suggest integrating the life annuity and long-term care insurance and review how this would operate. The tax treatment of this combination could be improved, and product design issues must be considered carefully. Furthermore, additional research is required to look at more recent data and different permutations of the product as well as more refined analysis of the population groups who might utilize it. A favorable public policy environment, including tax and insurance regulation, is needed to encourage this innovation, and insurance companies must be creative in exploring the possibility of improving the financial security of current and future retirees.

Notes

The authors thank Lee Granza for sharing her knowledge on the long-term care insurance market, and John Ameriks, Wayne Gates, Stuart Gillan, Michael Gordon, and Olivia Mitchell for helpful comments. Opinions expressed are solely those of the authors.

1. A cash balance plan is a defined benefit plan that stimulates a defined contribution plan; account balances are created for each worker and are credited with a fixed rate of return. See Rappaport et al. (1997).

2. Inflation-indexed annuities do, however, exist in the United Kingdom and a few other countries; see Brown et al. (this volume; 2001).

3. This section draws on Warshawsky, Granza, and Madamba (2000).

4. These statistics exclude LTC provided by hospital-affiliated facilities and agencies, which amounted to over $17 billion in 1996.

5. Medicare also pays for long-term care for the terminally ill through hospice care.

6. Based on data from 1985, 44 percent of persons who use nursing homes after age 65 start and end as private payers, 27 percent start and end as recipients of Medicaid benefits, and 14 percent spend down assets to become eligible for Medicaid benefits (Spillman and Kemper 1995). A 1995 projection found that 17 percent of those turning 65 in 1995 would enter a nursing home and remain private payers throughout, 6.3 percent would enter as private payers but become Medicaid eligible by exhausting their assets, and 10.7 percent (three in five of those ending up in a nursing home on Medicaid) would already be Medicaid eligible on entry.

7. Some have claimed that there is wide scope for evading the rules requiring the use of assets to pay for nursing home care before the utilization of Medicaid, although there is no formal evidence supporting or denying this assertion.

8. For a description of the benefits typically offered in long-term care insurance policies, see Granza, Madamba, and Warshawsky (1998).

9. Pauly also notes that when Medicaid spending is low but the desired level of care is an increasing function of wealth, there may be some scope for LTC insurance to cover the difference between the desired and fixed levels of care. But under current law Medicaid pays nothing if an individual has LTC insurance, so insurance would be purchased only if the individual highly valued additional quality of care; presumably this would be more likely when the individual is starting retirement with a relatively high standard of living.

10. The Pauly analysis also implies the desirability of LTC insurance with high deductibles or insurance purchased at relatively advanced ages. This is moderated in the presence of a spouse and children. For example, if the death of the spouse did

not affect income and LTC costs are less than the present value of the future consumption had the person survived (which is likely, given the positive correlation of LTC disability and mortality), then LTC insurance for both lives might not be worthwhile. If, further, children are able to provide care to their disabled parents, and if parents prefer care from their children over care from others, children might encourage the early admission or treatment of their parent.

11. Of course there is significant intertemporal uncertainty about future cost of a nursing home, that may be uninsurable in private markets (Cutler 1993). Private insurers can pool cross-section risk, but not aggregate risk (especially if the serial correlation over time of LTC cost increases). In this environment insurance companies may not be able to pool across cohorts as they do in the catastrophe insurance line of business. In practice, LTC insurance policies sold in the marketplace tend to pay a fixed dollar amount for care, use nominal rules to update payments over time, and reserve the right to increase rates in response to adverse cost shocks. These limitations, combined with benefit maximums found in many policies, reduce the risk-sharing features of LTC insurance, and hence curtail the demand for it. Combined with commissions and other marketing expenses, these features may imply that consumers simply view LTC insurance as providing an expected value less than the actual cost of the policy; see also Sloan and Norton (1997).

12. This reduction in the cost of adverse selection is below the 10 percent estimate of the cost of adverse selection cited earlier in the current annuity market. The difference is in part due to the 10-year minimum benefit in these estimates, which increases life annuity benefits disproportionately among groups excluded from the prospective purchaser pool under current practice because of their shorter survival. The straight life annuities on which the 10 percent estimate of the cost of adverse selection was based did not include a minimum benefit. For more direct comparison, Murtaugh, Spillman, and Warshawsky (2000) indicate that the cost of adverse selection in their life income annuity with no minimum benefit would be about six percent. Moreover, the NMFS database is meant to be representative of the entire U.S. population, whereas purchasers of life annuities and LTC insurance are more likely to come from population of higher socioeconomic status, who have higher life expectancies than average.

13. The Long-Term Care and Retirement Security Act of 2000, a bill introduced in March 2000 by Senators Grassley and Graham, would give individuals an above-the-line tax deduction for the cost of their qualified LTC insurance policy, subject to the age-based deduction levels that currently exist. The bill would also allow employers to include the deduction provision in cafeteria plans and flexible spending accounts.

14. Another tax issue is the relatively unfavorable treatment of long-term care reserves within the life insurance company as compared to qualified retirement plan reserves. Previously qualified plan reserves held by life insurance companies were not afforded favorable treatment, but when employers began to establish trusts for their pension plans, putting life insurance companies at a competitive disadvantage, Congress changed the tax treatment. It is possible that the establishment by employers of 401(h) accounts to fund long-term care benefits would result in similar pressure on Congress to change the tax treatment of long-term care reserves. Pauly (1989) argues that there is a basis for public policy encouragement of private long-term care insurance, where the optimal subsidy would be higher for low wealth people. He also argues that a subsidy should be extended as far up the income distribution as there is positive expected value of Medicaid payments; such a subsidy will induce the purchase of insurance.

15. Nyman (1999) speculates that the widespread existence of health insurance contracts using the indemnity approach may be explained by a smaller welfare loss

realized from the purchased-price effect than the welfare loss realized from the expected fraud and fraud avoidance measures or from writing complex contracts when the cash disability approach is used. The choice among approaches in any particular situation is ultimately based on experience, empirical evidence, and intuition regarding the relative magnitudes of these welfare losses.

References

American Council of Life Insurance. 1999. *Life Insurance Fact Book*. Washington, D.C.: ACLI.

Braden, Bradley et al. 1998. "National Health Expenditures, 1997." *Health Care Financing Review* 20, 1 (Fall): 83–126.

Brown, Jeffrey R., Olivia S. Mitchell, and James M. Poterba. 2001. "The Role of Real Annuities and Indexed Bonds in an Individual Accounts Retirement Program." In *Risk Aspects of Investment-Based Social Security Reform*, ed. John Y. Campbell and Martin S. Feldstein. Chicago: University of Chicago Press. 321–60.

——. This volume. "Mortality Risk, Inflation Risk, and Annuity Products."

Cohen, Marc A. 1998. "Emerging Trends in the Finance and Delivery of Long-Term Care: Public and Private Opportunities and Challenges." *Gerontologist* 38, 1: 80–89.

Collett, Douglas A., Carl L. Austin, and John W. White. 1999. "Long-Term Care Insurance: A Rapidly Growing, Little Understood Product." *BestWeek Special Report*, October 25.

Coronel, Susan. 1998. *Long-Term Care Insurance in 1996*. Health Insurance Association of America monograph. Washington, D.C.: HIAA. September.

Crimmins, Eileen M., Sandra L. Reynolds, and Yasuhiko Saito. 1997. "Summary of Research Grant: 'Trends and Differences in Health and Ability to Work.' " *Social Security Bulletin* 30, 3: 50–52.

Cutler, David. 1993. "Why Doesn't the Market Fully Insure Long-Term Care?" NBER Working Paper 4301. March.

Employee Benefit Research Institute (EBRI). 1997. *EBRI Databook on Employee Benefits*. 4th ed. Washington, D.C.: EBRI.

Friedman, Benjamin M. and Mark J. Warshawsky. 1990. "The Cost of Annuities: Implications for Saving Behavior and Bequests." *Quarterly Journal of Economics* 104 (February): 135–54.

Gordon, Michael S., Olivia S. Mitchell, and Marc M. Twinney, eds. 1997. *Positioning Pensions for the Twenty-First Century*. Pension Research Council. Philadelphia: University of Pennsylvania Press.

Granza, Lee, Anna Madamba, and Mark J. Warshawsky. 1998. "Financing Long-Term Care: Employee Needs and Attitudes, and the Employer's Role," *Benefits Quarterly* 14, 4 (Fourth Quarter): 60–72.

Health Insurance Association of American (HIAA). 1997. *Long-Term Care: Knowing the Risk, Paying the Price*. Washington, D.C.: HIAA.

Jarrett, Jaye C. and Tom Stringfellow. 2000 "Optimum Withdrawals from an Asset Pool." *Journal of Financial Planning* 13, 1 (January): 80–93.

Kemper, Peter and Christopher M. Murtaugh. 1991. "Lifetime Use of Nursing Home Care." *New England Journal of Medicine* 324: 595–600.

Manton, Kenneth G., Larry Corder, and Eric Stallard. 1997. "Chronic Disability Trends in Elderly United States Populations: 1982–1994." *Proceedings of the National Academy of Sciences* 94 (March): 2593–98.

Manton, Kenneth G., Eric Stallard, and Larry Corder. 1997. "Changes in the Age

Dependence of Mortality and Disability: Cohort and Other Determinants," *Demography* 34, 1 (February): 135–57.

McSweeney, Mary Helen and Larry V. Aarhus, Jr. 1999. "Employer-Sponsored Group Long-Term Care Insurance: Did HIPAA Matter?" International Foundation of Employee Benefit Plans monograph. Milwaukee: IFEBP. June.

Mitchell, Olivia S., Robert J. Myers, and Howard Young, eds. 1999. *Prospects for Social Security Reform*. Pension Research Council. Philadelphia: University of Pennsylvania Press.

Mitchell, Olivia S., James M. Poterba, Mark J. Warshawsky and Jeffrey R. Brown. 1999. "New Evidence on the Money's Worth of Individual Annuities." *American Economic Review* 89, 5 (December): 1299–1318.

Mulvey, Janemarie and Barbara Stucki. 1998. "Who Will Pay for the Baby Boomers' Long-Term Care Needs? Expanding the Role of Private Long-Term Care Insurance." American Council of Life Insurance monograph, April. New York: ACLI.

Murtaugh, Christopher M., Peter Kemper, and Brenda C. Spillman. 1995. "Risky Business: Long-Term Care Insurance Underwriting." *Inquiry* 32 (Fall): 271–84.

Murtaugh, Christopher M., Peter Kemper, Brenda C. Spillman, and Barbara Lepidus Carlson. 1999. "The Amount, Distribution, and Timing of Lifetime Nursing Home Use." *Medical Care* 35, 3: 204–18.

Murtaugh, Christopher M., Brenda C. Spillman, and Mark J. Warshawsky. 2000. "In Sickness and in Health: An Annuity Approach to Financing Long-term Care and Retirement Income." TIAA-CREF Institute Working Paper. February.

National Council on Aging and John Hancock Life Insurance Company, "1999 Long-Term Care Survey Highlights." Viewed March 3, 2000, ⟨www.jhancock.com/company/newsroom/ncoa/highlights99.html⟩.

Nyman, John A. 1999. "The Economics of Moral Hazard Revisited." *Journal of Health Economics* 18 (1999): 811–24.

Pauly, Mark V. 1989. "Optimal Public Subsidies of Nursing Home Insurance in the United States," *Geneva Papers on Risk and Insurance: Essays in Insurance Economics* 14, 50 (January): 3–10.

———. 1990. "The Rational Nonpurchase of Long-Term-Care Insurance." *Journal of Political Economy* 98, 1: 153–68.

Pincus, Jeremy. 2000. "Employer-Sponsored Long-Term Care Insurance: Best Practices for Increasing Employer Sponsorship and Employee Participation." Employee Benefit Research Institute Issue Brief. Washington, D.C.: EBRI.

Rappaport, Anna M., Michael L. Young, Christopher A. Levell, and Brad A. Blalock. 1997. "Cash Balance Pension Plans." In *Positioning Pensions for the Twenty-First Century*, ed. Michael S. Gordon, Olivia S. Mitchell, and Marc M. Twinney. Pension Research Council. Philadelphia: University of Pennsylvania Press. 29–44.

Rekenthaler, John. 2000. "A Different Twist on Asset Allocation." *Journal of Financial Planning*, January 13, 1: 40–43.

Richter, W. 1993. "Bequeathing like a Principal." Discussion Papers in Economics 93–01. University of Dortmund, Germany.

Sloan, Frank A. and Edward C. Norton. 1997. "Adverse Selection, Bequests, Crowding Out, and Private Demand for Insurance: Evidence from the Long-Term Care Insurance Market." *Journal of Risk and Uncertainty* 15: 201–19.

Social Security Administration Board of Trustees. 1999. Report of the Federal Hospital Insurance and Supplemental Medical Insurance Trust Funds. Social Security Administration. ⟨www.ssa.gov⟩.

Spector, William, John A. Fleishman, Liliana E. Pezzin, and Brenda C. Spillman. No date. "The Characteristics of Long-Term Care Users." Paper commissioned by the

Institute of Medicine, Committee on Improving Quality in Long-Term Care. Washington, D.C.

Spillman, Brenda C. and Peter Kemper. 1995. "Lifetime Patterns of Payment for Nursing Home Care." *Medical Care* 33, 3: 280–96.

U.S. Bureau of Labor Statistics. 1996. *Employee Benefits in Small Private Establishments, 1994.* Bulletin 2475. Washington, D.C.: USGPO. February.

———. 1998. *Employee Benefits in Medium and Large Private Establishments, 1995.* Bulletin 2496. Washington, D.C.: USGPO. April.

———. 1999a. *Employee Benefits in Medium and Large Private Establishments, 1997.* Bulletin 2517. Washington, D.C.: USGPO. September.

———. 1999b. *Employee Benefits in Small Private Establishments, 1996.* Bulletin 2507. Washington, D.C.: USGPO. April.

Warshawsky, Mark J. and John Ameriks. 2000. "How Prepared Are Americans for Retirement?" In *Forecasting Retirement Needs and Retirement Wealth,* ed. Olivia S. Mitchell, P. Brett Hammond, and Anna M. Rappaport. Pension Research Council. Philadelphia: University of Pennsylvania Press. 33–67.

Warshawsky, Mark J., Lee Granza, and Anna Madamba. 2000. "Financing Long-term Care: Needs, Attitudes, Current Insurance Products, and Policy Innovations." TIAA-CREF Institute Research Dialogue 63. March.

Chapter 10
Survivor Bonds and Compulsory Annuitization: Reducing the Costs of Pension Provision

David Blake, William Burrows, and J. Michael Orszag

Governments throughout the world are examining how their pension programs might be improved for those who are poorly served by existing systems. Most attention to date has focused on the *accumulation stage*, or the period of active membership in a pension scheme until retirement. Issues here include the advantages and disadvantages of funding versus pay-as-you-go (PAYG), defined benefit versus defined contribution, and active versus passive fund management.[1] What has received much less attention is pension performance at the *retirement stage*. This lack of focus on retirement issues is not surprising, since when a new system is established, the retirement phase is typically 40 years or more ahead. Furthermore, for members of defined benefit schemes (whether public or private sector, funded or unfunded), someone other than the scheme member is guaranteeing or at least promising to deliver a particular level of pension in retirement. However, this is not the case with defined contribution plans, and most new pensions being established throughout the world are DC schemes.

With many DC schemes, there is no guaranteed pension at retirement. Rather, the retiree must live on whatever fund value has been accumulated at the time of retirement. In addition, because of uncertain life expectancy, individuals also face the risk of outliving their resources. They can insure against the risk of living too long by buying a life annuity from an insurance company, although the purchase of an annuity is not compulsory in many countries (e.g., the United States, Australia, and Germany). But two problems may arise with this arrangement:

1) Mortality risk. Mortality has improved substantially over the last century, but it is very difficult to forecast improvements in mortality accurately. This is what is meant by *mortality risk*. Under a state-run unfounded system, the government bears this mortality risk directly. While governments or large occupational schemes may have the ability to adjust contribution rates to bear such a risk, it is quite another thing for insurance companies to take this on. Of special concern is the role of new insurers being established in a country with no previous history of annuity provision. Because lifetimes are uncertain, insurers must construct hedged investment portfolios consisting of many types of long-term bonds; however, such portfolios may be costly to manage and, in any case, often provide imperfect hedges against mortality risk.

2) Adverse selection. Those who expect to live the longest will tend to have the highest demand for annuities. In such circumstances, if people are given choice about whether or when to purchase an annuity asset yields will have to be lower than actuarially fair for the population as a whole to compensate for the fact that the buyers of annuities are likely to experience lighter mortality (Brown et al., this volume). In other words, there is *adverse selection* in the demand for annuities and, to compensate, the providers of annuities need to lower the annuity yields they offer (the amount by which the annuity yield falls is known as the *adverse selection bias*). With defined benefit schemes in the UK, this choice is limited or even nonexistent. However, DC arrangements in the UK permit a wide range of choice over both the amount and timing of the annuity purchase. The pension can currently be provided in one of four ways: a life annuity purchased from a life assurance company, a life annuity provided by the scheme itself in the case of occupational DC schemes, a phased life annuity, or an income drawdown facility.[2] Members of personal pension and group personal pension schemes[3] are required to purchase annuities from life companies before they reach the age of 75, but they are currently not obliged to buy annuities on the date they retire (which can be from age 50 upwards).

This analysis investigates how these two problems can be minimized. We believe that only compulsory pension annuities from a mandatory funded pension system can help resolve the problem of adverse selection. Further, the age of purchase must coincide with the retirement date. But such annuities only cope with the second problem while they do nothing about the first. To address the first problem, we propose that the government help current and future retirees by providing insurance against aggregate or cohort mortality risk. To do so, we show how a government can issue a new type of bond, a *survivor* (or *indexed life*), *bond,* one that allows its holders to hedge aggregate mortality risk and so reduce the management charges associated with constructing a hedged investment portfolio. We expect that there would be a strong demand for the new bond from insurance companies, mature pension funds, and occupational money purchase or 401(k)-type schemes.

Mortality Risk

Consider an individual who will live for exactly T additional years. This individual could use a lump sum to purchase an annuity from an insurance company, or to buy an annuity bond (which pays coupons only and has no principal repayment) directly from the financial markets. Both products will yield a constant income stream for T years. In the absence of arbitrage, both investments will cost the same. The market price of a T-year annuity bond is (Blake, 2000):[4]

$$(1) \qquad P = \frac{d}{r} \left[1 - (1 + r)^{-T} \right],$$

where d is the annual coupon and r is the relevant discount rate (as a proportion). If someone purchased this bond at price P and then lived exactly T years, this would be equivalent to someone purchasing a T-year annuity for an amount P which paid d per year in arrears.

In reality, neither individuals nor insurance companies know exactly how long any individual annuitant will live. In the case of an annuity bond which continues to pay out coupons for as long as the individual is alive, its price depends on the whole probability distribution of death rates for this individual. In other words, T is a random variable, and not a fixed parameter. As a consequence, the market price of such annuity bonds depends on expectations about the random variable T as follows:

$$(2) \qquad P = E \left[\frac{d}{r} \left[1 - (1 + r)^{-T} \right] \right],$$

where E is the expectations operator.

Annuity bonds with random maturities are currently not available on financial markets, but insurance companies do provide life annuities with uncertain T. Each insurance company would be expected to attempt to minimize its exposure to mortality risk by holding a portfolio of fixed-term bonds that matched the anticipated mortality profile of its annuitants, and by building up a large enough pool of annuitants to minimize the risk of lighter than expected mortality. Nevertheless, an insurance company cannot predict mortality perfectly. To consider the effects of errors in forecasting mortality improvements, we denote the probability of dying at age x having survived to age $x - 1$ by q_x. Suppose that the insurance company forecasts mortality improvements by adjusting data from an actuarial table q_x^0 by multiplying by an exponential factor $f^{x - x_0}$, where x_0 is the current age of the annuitant and f is a scalar (which is less than unity if mortality improves over time and equal to unity in the case of no mortality improvement). This is one way in which the United Kingdom Institute of Actuaries Continuous Mortality Investigation Bureau (CMIB) makes mortality adjustments. In terms of the q_x, the unconditional probability of dying after $T > 0$ periods (conditional on having lived to age x_0) is

$$q_{T+x_0} \prod_{x=x_0}^{x_0+T-1} (1 - q_x) ,$$

where q_x is the conditional probability of dying at age x having survived to age $x-1$. This unconditional probability is used in computing the expected value in equations (2), so (2) is equivalent to (if we also take into account the improvement factors):[5]

$$(3) \quad P = \sum_{T=1}^{\infty} \left[\frac{d}{r} \left[1 - (1 + r)^{-T} \right] \right] q_{T+x_0}^0 f^T \prod_{x=x_0}^{x_0+T-1} (1 - q_x^0 f^{x-x_0}) .$$

Errors in the adjustment factor f can have a large impact on equation (3). Historical evidence on mortality forecasts in the UK suggest that forecast errors of 15–20 percent in f for intervals of 10 or more years ahead are not uncommon (MacDonald 1996). Another indicator of the difficulty in forecasting mortality improvements is that historical values of these improvement factors are not constants: they differ considerably for men and women, different ages, and different types of pensioners. For instance, the historical improvement rate for men aged 70 between 1967–70 and 1979–82 was 0.74 for life office pensioners and 0.91 for immediate annuitants, i.e., those who purchase annuities voluntarily (MacDonald, 1996). The impact of such forecast errors on survival probabilities is significant. For example, assume a 20-year improvement factor of 0.80 for a 65-year old man and forecast errors for mortality rates of up to 10 percent over a 10-year period. Using the PMA80 mortality tables (constructed to reflect the mortality experiences of males who purchase pension annuities), the forecast probability of a 65-year old man living to 85 ranges between 33.7 and 43.8 per cent, while that of him living to 95 ranges between 5.3 and 15.3 per cent.[6]

To determine the effects of these forecast errors on annuity yields, we use Eq. (2) to solve for the annuity yield d/P:

$$(4) \quad \frac{d}{P} = \frac{1}{E\left[(1 - (1 + r)^{-T})/r \right]} .$$

To compute the actuarially fair yield (i.e., one with a zero cost loading), we substitute in survival probabilities determined from standard actuarial tables into Eq. (4). For a male aged 65, using a discount rate r of 7 percent, and a 20-year improvement factor f of 0.80, the PMA80 tables lead to an actuarially fair annuity yield of 10.6 percent, but forecast errors suggest it lies between 10.3 and 10.9 percent. Thus the percentage difference in yields is about 5 percent.[7] For a woman, the PFA80 tables lead to an actuarially fair yield of 9.5 percent in the absence of mortality risk, but forecast errors suggest it lies between 9.2 and 9.7 percent, again a percentage difference of about 5 percent.

The effects of mortality forecast errors are more serious for escalating annuities, because payments in the future will be higher than with flat annuities. For escalating annuities, Eq. (4) becomes:

$$(5) \qquad \frac{d}{P} = 1 \bigg/ E\left[(1 + \pi)\left(\frac{1 + \left((1 + \pi)/(1 + r)\right)^T}{r - \pi}\right)\right].$$

where π is the uprating factor. For example, with an annuity escalating at 4 percent per annum, the percentage difference between upper and lower forecast bounds[8] rises considerably, to 9.5 percent for women and to 8.9 percent for men.

Given the significance of mortality forecasts for insurance company profitability, it is not surprising that cost loadings to cover mortality risk are built into prices. Further, some insurers may simply offer uncompetitive annuity rates, thereby effectively staying out of the market. Insurance companies cannot at present reduce these loadings without taking on unreasonable risks; indeed, anecdotal evidence for the UK indicates that the failure of some insurance companies accurately to predict improvements in mortality has led to serious problems among suppliers of deferred annuities, which are even more susceptible to mortality risk than immediate annuities.[9] Similar calculations for a 20-year deferred annuity escalating at 4 percent per annum to be received by a woman when she reaches the age of 65 suggest a range of about 22 percent in annuity yields under different mortality forecasts. These business considerations may explain why the market for deferred annuities in the United Kingdom is relatively thin.[10] Deferred annuities are particularly important in the case where a defined benefit scheme is wound up, say, as a result of the insolvency of the sponsoring company and also, potentially, for early leavers.

Because the private sector may be less able to absorb the aggregate risks associated with mortality forecast errors than the government, we next evaluate what a government might do to help alleviate this problem and reduce costs to annuitants. First, however, we review another factor which can reduce the value of DC pensions.

Adverse Selection

A second problem which contributes to the cost of annuities is adverse selection: people who purchase annuities tend to live longer than the population as a whole. This issue may be illustrated in the UK context by comparing annuities priced using the English Life Tables (ELT14), which reflects the mortality experiences of the population as a whole, with those priced using PMA80 and PFA80, which reflect the mortality experiences of, respectively, male and female pension annuitants.[11] No life insurance company would be prepared to offer an annuity yield based on ELT14. People who want to purchase annuities have private information (say, from their own family history and health experience) that they will likely have higher than average life expectancies. The insurers are thus subject to an adverse selection problem in that demanders of annuities do not reflect the statistical experience of the population as a whole.

How much does adverse selection contribute to the cost loadings for annuities in the U.K.? Using equation (4) with r set at 8 percent and no future mortality improvements, the PMA80/PFA80 tables (downrated two years)[12] suggest annuity yields (annual in arrears) of 11.2 percent for a 65-year-old man, and 10.2 percent for a 65-year-old woman. ELT14 (downrated two years) suggests much higher annuity yields: 12.9 percent for a 65-year-old man, and 11.2 percent for a 65-year-old woman. This adverse selection bias increases with age: ELT14 suggests that a 75-year-old man purchasing an annuity should receive an actuarially fair rate of 17.5 percent, whereas PMA80 suggests a rate of just 14.6 percent.

Consider the case of two identical 65-year-old males: one retires with a state PAYG pension of £20 per week, and the second retires with a DC pension and purchases an annuity from an insurance company. Suppose for simplicity that all insurance companies are nonprofit organizations and that there is no mortality risk, so that actual experience corresponds exactly with PMA80 (downrated two years). If the second retiree were typical of the population as a whole (i.e., ELT14), he should receive an annuity with a 12.9 percent yield. Suppose this also results in a pension of £20 per week. But the insurance company will only offer an annuity yield of 11.2 percent or £17.36 per week, a reduction of close to 15 percent. Administrative cost loadings and adjustments to cover mortality risk will result in an even lower pension.[13]

The second 65-year-old may even be worse off than indicated, because state PAYG schemes usually provide indexed or inflation linked pensions. For escalating annuities, the adverse selection problem is more severe because there is a greater gain from living longer. PMA80 suggests that a 4 percent escalating annuity should offer a yield of 8.24 percent, whereas ELT14 suggests 9.93 percent, which implies a pension reduction of nearly 20 percent.

Unlike the costs analyzed in the previous section associated with mortality risk, adverse selection costs depend on the choices exercised by purchasers of insurance. The introduction of a lump sum option (known in the U.K. as an income drawdown), while increasing choice, also leads to yet larger adverse selection problems and thus higher costs for annuities for those who might need them most.

A Possible Solution: Survivor Bonds and Compulsory Annuitization

When insurance companies write annuities, they often use premiums collected to buy *matching assets*, that is, assets whose cash payments match as closely as possible the anticipated pattern of payouts on the liabilities that they face. In the case of level annuities, insurers invest principally in fixed-income bonds. In the case of index-linked annuities, insurers may hold index-linked bonds: insurers would not be prepared to write index-linked annuities if they could not lay off the resulting inflation risk through the purchase of an index-linked bond (issued by the government or a utility). However, insurance companies face two risks for which there are no existing matching assets: mortality risk and adverse selection, as already discussed.

A potential simple solution to the problem of mortality risk would be for the government to issue *survivor* (or *life-indexed*) *bonds*. These would be bonds whose future coupon payments depend on the percentage of the population of retirement age (say 65) at the date of issue still alive at future coupon payment dates. For a bond issued in 2000, for example, the coupon in 2020 will be proportional to the fraction of 65-year-olds in the population who have lived to age 85. The coupon is therefore directly proportional to the amount an insurance company needs to pay out as an annuity to the average individual with an average pension. Large employer or occupational schemes that also bear aggregate mortality risk could similarly be purchasers of such bonds.

Survivor bonds aim to lower the costs of retirement provision for the average pensioner, because they help to hedge *aggregate* mortality risk. However, they cannot hedge *specific* mortality risks. There are two key specific risks to take into account: (1) pensioner annuitants are a select group who are likely to live longer than the average of the population of the same age, and (2) given that an insurance company is underwriting a finite sample of lives, the characteristics of any particular insurance company's pool of annuitants may differ from that of the pensioner annuitant population as a whole. For example, women and wealthy pensioner annuitants with large lump sums to annuitize tend to live longer than the average pensioner annuitant. The bonds we describe here can only eliminate the risk associated with aggregate mortality improvements for the entire population, but they do not eliminate idiosyncratic risks such as those associated with wealth or other select effects.

In short, by minimizing aggregate risk, insurance companies would have the proper incentives to develop wide mortality pools and do what they do best: provide insurance against idiosyncratic risks. For instance, if the mortality of the rich improved more than that of the poor and the insurance company chose an equally weighted pool of rich and poor, the payouts by the insurance company would decline less rapidly than the coupon payments from the survivor bonds. The rate at which this happens depends on the differences between terms in

$$q^0_{T+x_0} f^T \prod_{x=x_0}^{x_0+T-1} (1 - q^0_x f^{x-x_0})$$

for the insurance company's own annuitant pool, versus those for the population as a whole. The q's and f's will be lower for the insurance company's annuitant pool and the forecast errors higher than for the population as a whole. The implication of this is that insurance companies that have mortality pools different from the population at large continue to bear specific mortality risk. Of course this is a commercial decision, and insurance companies should be expected to charge a residual load based on these differences to cover them.

An important point to recognize is that there are no obvious matching assets for the select mortality risks assumed by annuity providers, once they hold survivor bonds to hedge aggregate mortality risk. The provider will hedge these select risks by offering *lower* annuity rates to *all* annuitants. This disadvantages the average annuitants who are not members of the select groups. One way of dealing with this problem is to reduce the select mortality risks to zero by making pension plans and pension annuities mandatory for all members of society.[14]

The issue price of survivor bonds would be determined by a central body such as the Government Actuary in the UK. We do not envisage any major problems with determining the issue price: the government could publish its underlying assumptions concerning mortality. It is likely that the risk of underestimating mortality improvements is a smaller risk than that of underestimating future inflation, and there appears to be no problem with determining the issue price of retail price index-linked bonds in the UK or the U.S. Thereafter, the government would have to produce a monthly mortality index just as it produces a monthly retail price index. These bonds could be traded on the open market and could be resold with the secondary market prices indicating the market's expectations concerning future mortality.

Why should governments (and ultimately taxpayers) issue survivor bonds and absorb the risks associated with mortality fluctuations? A possible justification can be found in the Arrow-Lind Theorem (1970) on social risk-bearing, which shows that by dispersing an aggregate risk across the population (of taxpayers) as a whole, the associated risk premium can be reduced to zero. A government might then issue survivor bonds at a lower yield (namely, the risk-free rate) than could any private corporation. A private company would have much fewer shareholders than there are taxpayers, and some of the shareholders might hold large blocks of shares which would constitute a significant proportion of their net worth. These shareholders would demand a risk premium, whereas the government can act as a risk-neutral player. Another potential justification lies in the government's own public health campaigns, which are aimed directly at reducing mortality in the entire population; this has important implications for annuity provision by the private sector. Similarly, the reform of Social Security and the transfer of pension provision from the public to the private sector would be greatly eased by the existence of survivor bonds.[15]

By issuing survivor bonds, a government could help to complete markets. But why has the private sector not issued survivor bonds? One apparent natural class of issuer is insurance companies themselves, since they are in a position to hedge mortality risk with their other products: greater longevity raises the payouts on annuities but lowers them on endowment or life insurance policies. But in practice, endowment or life insurance policies provide a poor hedge for annuities, since mortality improvements are not spread evenly across ages, but rather are concentrated at older ages. To illustrate, the percentage improvement in mortality between the PMA80 and PA90M tables (based on mortality experience for United Kingdom male annuitants in 1980 and 1990 respectively) was 12 percent at age 35, 9 percent at age 55, 23 percent at age 75 and 20 percent at age 95. The family itself also provides an informal mechanism for the issuing survivor bonds between different generations of the same family, as implied by Kotlikoff and Spivak (1981), but the breakdown of the family in many countries makes this an increasingly unreliable mechanism. So we may be left with the state as the only realistic issuer of survivor bonds.

Conclusion

Some governments have helped pension funds insure against inflation by issuing index-linked bonds in the UK and more recently in the United States. We contend that the issuance of survivor bonds would help mature pension funds insure against the uncertainties involving an increasingly aging population. The reduction in cost loadings on annuities could be significant, and might be further reduced by eliminating the select effects associated with the voluntary purchase of annuities and requiring the mandatory annuitization of pension funds on retirement.

Appendix: A Brief Overview of the UK Annuities Market

Although annuities have been available in the United Kingdom for several centuries, the market for annuities did not develop until after the adoption of self-employed pensions (the precursor to personal pensions) in the 1950s. These policies, known as Section 226 retirement annuities, stipulated that at retirement a tax-free cash sum could be paid and the remaining balance had to be used to purchase an annuity from an authorized insurance company. The legislation provided for an open market option which allowed the policyholder to purchase an annuity from another insurance company. This was the beginning of the competitive market in UK annuities.

The calculation of annuity yields is based primarily on: (1) mortality tables, (2) prevailing long term interest rates, (3) the insurance company's balance sheet and capital requirements, (4) the insurance company's tax position, and (5) the insurance company's corporate strategy. For example, one major insurer (Legal & General) has recently repriced its annuities, favoring smaller annuities; such a strategy helps develop a wide pool of annuitants and minimizes the adverse selection problems discussed above. In general, large annuities are offered at more favorable rates, which benefits the wealthier investor at the expense of those who have smaller pension policies. The reason for this is the relatively high cost associated with administering each new policy.

Annuity yields have been falling since 1990 in the UK; by 2000, they had fallen by over 30 percent. This trend is set to continue as longer term interest rates fall and companies readjust their mortality tables to take into account longer life expectancy. The government responded to the reduction in annuity yields by introducing income drawdown with the Finance Act of 1995. Income drawdown allows individuals with personal pensions to defer annuity purchase until age 75 and in the meantime invest in higher yielding assets. Income drawdown plans typically have reasonably high charges and hence are only economical for the relatively well-off.

The difference between the best and worst annuity yields can be as much as 50 percent over all the companies offering annuities; even across the top 10 providers, the difference can be substantial. These price differentials between suppliers are quite surprising, given there is almost no variation in the type of policy offered. There is a distinct absence of competition outside the few companies which compete at the very top of the annuity yield tables. Most companies make an active decision to offer unattractive annuity yields, thereby effectively staying out of the market. This leaves only a handful of companies in the UK now prepared to write new annuity business. Although companies wanting to attract new business will want to offer the best annuity yields, there must invariably come a point when some of these companies will either have written their quota or make a commercial decision to concentrate on other types of business which are subject to smaller long-term risks.

There was very little innovation in the standard annuity policy at first and, although companies such as Commercial Union, M&G, and the then Provident Mutual offered investment-linked annuities, these were restricted to their own policyholders. It was not until 1987 that Equitable Life launched a range of with-profit annuities and unit-linked annuities that were available to all retiring pensioners through the open market option. The other important recent developments in the annuity market included the introduction of inflation-linked annuities and impaired life annuities (see also Finkelstein and Poterba 1999).

Notes

We thank Angus MacDonald, Olivia S. Mitchell, Tim Sheldon, Guy Thomas, and Steve Zeldes for very useful insights and comments. Opinions are solely those of the authors.

1. For a review of issues involved in the debate in the United Kingdom see Blake and Orszag (1997, 1998), and Finkelstein and Poterba (1999).

2. Income drawdown is also known as income withdrawal, pension fund withdrawal, or drawdown, cash withdrawal or capital withdrawal. For more details, see the Appendix.

3. These are broadly comparable with individual retirement accounts and 401(k) plans in the United States, respectively.

4. We assume for simplicity a flat yield curve.

5. An alternative way of writing Eq. (3) is:

$$P = \sum_{T=1}^{\infty} \left[d(1+r)^{-T} \right] \sum_{x=x_0}^{x_0+T-1} (1 - q_x^0 f^{x-x_0}) \ .$$

6. The quoted improvement factors are in units of 20 years and need to be converted to one-year factors. This is done in our case as follows. For a 20-year improvement factor of 0.8, the one-year improvement factor is $0.8^{1/20}$. The lower bound on the improvement factor is the one-year improvement factor times $0.90^{1/10}$, while the upper bound is the one-year improvement factor times $1.10^{1/10}$; this converts a 10 percent forecast error either way over 10 years to the appropriate one-year forecast error.

7. Computed as $(10.9 - 10.3) / 10.6$.

8. We use the term "bound" to represent outcomes with typical historical forecast errors.

9. Currently, life companies are having to make annuity payments for two years longer than originally anticipated, according to UK industry information.

10. Only £10 million in single premium deferred annuities were issued in 1996, about one-eighteenth of the level of single premium immediate annuities sold that year (Association of British Insurers 1997).

11. PMA80/PFA80 reflects the mortality experiences of pension annuitants subject to some degree of compulsion on annuity purchase. Adverse selection arises here as a result of: (1) commutation into lump sums, (2) choice of retirement date, (3) fund size at retirement, and (4) income drawdown election, all of which depend on individuals' private information. The IM80/IF80 tables, in contrast, reflect the mortality experiences of immediate annuitants who willingly purchase annuities; we have chosen instead to focus on the problem as experienced by typical pensioners.

12. This reflects mortality improvements since the PMA80 tables were constructed.

13. The United Kingdom Government Actuary's Department allows for a cost loading of 2 percent for the annuity purchase in its calculations for DC occupational schemes contracting out of the second state pension (SERPS).

14. There is an alternative way of dealing with the problem, namely for the government to select the population of pensioner annuitants as "the population" for which

it issues survivor bonds, but it is highly unlikely that any government would agree to do this, on the grounds that it may represent a substantial subsidy to the better-off members of society.

15. The risk associated with unexpected cohort longevity will likely be correlated with the tax burden of paying off this now more-costly survivor bond, and if older persons shoulder some of this risk, the Arrow-Lind theorem would be violated.

References

Arrow, Kenneth and R. Lind. 1970. "Uncertainty and the Evaluation of Public Investment Decisions," *American Economic Review* 60: 364–78.

Association of British Insurers. 1997. *Insurance Statistics Yearbook, 1986–1996.* London: Association of British Insurers.

Blake, David. 2000. *Financial Market Analysis.* Chichester: Wiley.

Blake, David and J. Michael Orszag. 1997. "Toward a Universal Funded Second Pension: A Submission for the 1997 Pensions Review Focusing on the Financial Aspects of the Provision of a Second Tier Funded Pension." Working Paper. Pensions Institute, London.

———. 1998. "Stakeholder Pensions: Exploiting Scale Economies." Working Paper. Pensions Institute, London.

Brown, Jeffrey R., Olivia S. Mitchell and James M. Poterba. This volume. "Mortality Risk, Inflation Risk, and Annuity Products."

Finkelstein, Amy and James M. Poterba. 1999. "Selection Effects in the Market for Individual Annuities: New Evidence from the United Kingdom." NBER Working Paper W7168.

Kotlikoff, Laurence, J. and Avia Spivak. 1981. "The Family as an Incomplete Annuities Market." *Journal of Political Economy* 89: 372–91.

MacDonald, Angus. 1996. "United Kingdom." In Angus MacDonald (editor) *The Second Actuarial Study of Mortality in Europe,* ed. Angus MacDonald. Brussels: Groupe Consultatif des Associations d'Actuaires des Pays des Communautés Européennes.

Chapter 11
Turning Assets into Cash: Problems and Prospects in the Reverse Mortgage Market

Andrew Caplin

Academic writers have long expressed enthusiasm regarding the potential of the reverse mortgage market to help the elderly turn housing equity into cash. Yet this market is tiny in the United States, and virtually nonexistent in other developed nations. This chapter explores some of the economic forces that may help to explain the gap between the current market and its theoretical potential, including transactions costs, moral hazard, and consumer uncertainty about future preferences. In addition we evaluate psychological forces that may help explain lack of enthusiasm among homeowners for these products. We also focus attention on impediments to market development attributable to the legal, regulatory, and tax systems. It is likely that similar inertial forces may constrain the supply of a far broader class of innovative financial contracts. These include equity insurance products proposed by Case et al. (1993) and equity participation products proposed by Caplin et al. (1997). These are all examples of schemes in which there is some shifting of risk and return from the homeowner to the broader financial community. We outline some of the policy measures that may be required if policymakers wish to encourage development of any or all of these markets.

The Current Status of the Reverse Annuity Market

In the United States, reverse mortgages are the most important product in the market for home equity conversion. Reverse mortgages have advantages over more standard home equity loans, since many elderly households would fail to qualify for the latter due to low income. The reverse mortgage never requires a homeowner to make interest payments, and only becomes due when the owner moves out of the house or dies.

The most important and long-lived reverse mortgage currently on the market is the Home Equity Conversion Mortgage (HECM) offered by the Department of Housing and Urban Development (HUD). This has been available since 1989, when Congress authorized a HUD pilot program with 2,500 reverse mortgages. Authorization was increased to 25,000 in the early 1990s, and it was increased again in 1996.

Federal involvement goes far beyond authorizing the program, since it includes an intricate set of cross-subsidies. The Federal National Mortgage Association (Fannie Mae) agreed at the outset to purchase HECM loans originated by approved lenders, subject to some minor conditions. In addition, HUD has offered a wide array of insurance guarantees on HECM loans at a hard-to-beat price. Given the potential costs of these guarantees, HUD retains strong controls on the various lenders who have been approved to originate these mortgages. In addition, HUD insists that counseling be provided to borrowers who apply for HECM loans.

In addition to the HECM, a second important type of reverse mortgage is the HomeKeeper, offered by Fannie Mae since 1995. While this product is still primarily a creature of federal policy, there have been private companies offering reverse mortgages. The Financial Freedom Senior Funding Corporation not only offers its own proprietary reverse mortgage, but has also successfully issued the first secondary market product in the history of the reverse mortgage market. In 1999, Lehman Brothers issued $317 million in bonds against Financial Freedom's portfolio of reverse mortgages. Not surprisingly, these private sector products are designed to appeal to higher wealth home owners who are not well catered to in the federal programs.

The various reverse mortgage products have similar structural features. When a homeowner meets the appropriate criteria, the financial institution offers a loan that can be taken as a lump sum, as an income stream, or as a line of credit, with various degrees of flexibility permitted between methods of borrowing. The income stream can be taken either for a fixed term or as an annuity. There are various costs involved in taking out the loans, which can be financed in part from loan proceeds. The amount of money that can be borrowed depends on the age of the borrower, the value of the house, and some interest rate variables. We describe the HECM in greater detail to clarify the fundamental economic forces at work.

In order to qualify for a HECM loan, a household head must be age 62 or older, and either own his home free and clear, or at least be able to pay off all remaining debt with the proceeds of the loan. There are additional requirements that relate to the condition of the property at the time of purchase, and also to the need to undergo some counseling on the nature of the product. Once the household qualifies, an initial "principal limit factor" is set, determining the maximum loan available to the borrower. As time passes, the limit factor grows according to a formula based on interest rates and certain ongoing insurance costs.

The principal limit factor on a new loan is determined by a fixed function that depends only on the age of the youngest borrower, and two additional numbers that are themselves determined by reasonably simple algorithms. The first number is the "adjusted property value" or maximum claim amount, which is the minimum of the appraised value of the house and the maximum loan in the FHA 203(b) program. The second number is the "expected average mortgage interest rate," which historically has been between 1.5 and 1.7 percent above the one-year Treasury bond rate. More generally, interest charges for HECM borrowers are somewhat intricate. The interest costs on outstanding balances follow a variable rate pattern, with limits both on the rate at which the interest costs can change within a year and over the life of the product. The expected average mortgage interest rate used in the calculation of the initial principal limit factor is generally higher than the contemporaneous adjustable rate of interest, in an effort to take account of the long term of the loan. A final complication is that the term of the loan itself may be impacted by future interest rates, since it may be advantageous to refinance a HECM should the rate of interest drop significantly.

The single most important determinant of the principal limit factor is the age of the youngest borrower.[1] For a house with an appraised value of $150,000 and with expected interest rate of 8 percent per annum, the initial principal limit factor increases from roughly $50,000 at age 65, to $70,000 at age 75, to $105,000 at age 90 (Scholen 1996). At an interest rate of 9 percent per annum, the corresponding numbers are $40,000 at age 65, $60,000 at age 75, and $100,000 at age 90. As the loan ages, the principal limit factor grows at a rate that exceeds the expected interest rate by 0.5 percent. The additional 0.5 percent reflects a monthly insurance fee that is charged on HECM loan balances. This monthly fee is in addition to an up-front insurance fee amounting to two percent of the adjusted property value.

This premium serves in part to provide a guarantee to the borrower against lender default, but in fact this risk is negligible in the current market, since Fannie Mae owns most of the loans. The more serious risk that HUD bears concerns the growth in the principal limit factor over time. There is "crossover risk," which is realized when the principal limit factor exceeds around 90 percent of the house value. When one bears in mind transactions costs, the homeowner is left with no equity in the house. From this point on, it is clear that the lender might be unable to recover the full amount owed. To prevent this risk from discouraging lenders, HUD allows them to assign a mortgage to the FHA when the balance has risen to 98 percent of the maximum claim amount. Following assignment, the leader files an insurance claim for an amount equal to the mortgage balance and has no further obligations. The Department continues to make payments that are owed the borrower, and it accepts full responsibility in case of loss.

In addition to insurance costs, there are a wide variety of other tax and transaction costs involved in taking out a HECM. In its report to Congress evaluating the HECM insurance program HUD found that actual transactions costs had averaged roughly $4,500 per loan, excluding insurance costs. These numbers are very high when counted against the median adjusted property value of $97,000, and even more so against the median initial principal limits of $47,000. If we include the two percent up front insurance fee, the average cost of taking out a reverse mortgage amounted to some $6,500, or almost 14 percent of the initial loan.

In addition to characterizing the various transactions costs, the 1995 HUD report also detailed the basic economic characteristics of a large random sample of the early users of the product. The findings are as one would expect in most respects. The median age of HECM borrowers at closing was 76, well above the average age of all eligible households. The median property value was $102,000, as opposed to $70,418 for all elderly homeowners. Yet median income was 44 percent below than the median of all elderly homeowners, and HECM borrowers got more than 78 percent of their total income from Social Security payments, as opposed to 38 percent for the broader pool of older homeowners. Finally HECM borrowers generally had few children, with more than 75 percent reporting no children at all.

The Reverse Mortgage Market: Estimating Market Potential

Five years into the pilot program in July 1994, HUD had issued only 7,994 HECM loans, despite being authorized for up to 25,000 (USHUD 1995). The numbers have recently increased more rapidly, but in 1998 total issuance was still short of 25,000. While precise numbers are hard to find, it seems safe to say that when one adds up all reverse mortgages of all types issued in the United States to date, a reasonable "guesstimate" would be in the order of 50,000.

These small numbers stand in strong contrast to most estimates of market potential. Of course an important preliminary step in analyzing the market is to identify any powerful reasons that elderly households might have to eschew home equity conversion. Two of the strongest reasons for avoiding the market altogether may be a desire to move from the current home, and a powerful bequest motive.

For an elderly household planning to move in the near future, a reverse mortgage would seem to be a very bad idea, since the transactions cost alone would take a huge bite out of the housing equity. However, for a household planning to stay put, the calculus is very different. One may gain some insights on market potential simply by studying the actual and anticipated patterns of mobility for older homeowners. The most striking finding in this respect is the profound desire of elderly homeowners not to move (Venti and Wise, this volume). Roughly 80 percent of households with the head of household aged 65 or higher own their own homes, and the vast majority have lived in the home long enough to pay off their mortgage fully. Having lived in their current homes for a very long time, such households respond to survey questions on the subject by stating a strong preference for staying put for the rest of their lives.

A second possible motivation for avoiding the reverse mortgage market is a strong bequest motive. Yet there is evidence that for households not among the super rich, the bequest motive is far from powerful. Sheiner and Weil (1992) find that savings respond little to increases in the value of housing equity, as they would if this equity was intended to satisfy a bequest motive. They estimate that 42 percent of households will leave behind a house when the last member dies. For most of these the house will be owned free and clear, and there will be few if any additional assets left in a bequest. What a miracle it would be if the value of this house (which is at any rate very hard to estimate ex ante) was precisely the optimal value of the bequest! No wonder such bequests are typically referred to as "involuntary."

For households who intend to stay in their current home for life, yet do not have an overwhelmingly strong bequest motive, the reverse mortgage seems like a potentially important product. Even if one limited attention to the most obvious category of potential borrowers, elderly homeowners who are house rich, cash poor, and have no children, the numbers run well into the millions. Unless they take out a reverse mortgage, these households will die leaving their homes as an essentially unintended bequest. When one adds back in the other elderly households for whom the product may also be desirable, market possibilities seem robust.

The first serious attempt to clarify market potential was offered by Venti and Wise (1991) using SIPP data. They provided detailed summaries of the wealth composition of the elderly and confirmed that many elderly households live primarily on pension income. Then also found that housing equity is the only asset available to potentially increase their consumption. To estimate the quantitative significance of housing equity, they annuitized the entire net housing wealth with an actuarially fair life tenure reverse mortgage, and estimated the extent to which this could increase the household's annual income (or consumption). They estimated the median increase in annual income from such an annuity at around 10 percent.

Though these authors concluded that a 10 percent income increase is surprisingly low, their numbers are a long way from suggesting that the market has no potential. Indeed Rasmussen et al. (1995) use essentially the same procedure to show that even when attention is restricted to households 69 or older with income less than $30,000, there are 3 million who would gain at least 25 percent from the reverse annuity mortgage. The potential for the reverse mortgage to raise consumption at the lower end of the income spectrum is noteworthy. Housing equity is distributed in a far more equitable manner across households than are the more liquid forms of financial wealth. Using data from the Health and Retirement Study, Mitchell and Moore (1998) show that the median net financial wealth of the highest income quintile is 55 times as high as that of the lowest quintile, while the equivalent ratio for housing wealth is 7.4. The importance of housing equity for minority households is also proportionately far greater than it is for white households.

In a second study, Venti and Wise (1990) posit that if there were a large frustrated desire to reduce housing equity, then we should expect to see a large number of older households moving to smaller homes. Empirically, however, they find that the actual number of movers is relatively low, and among those who do move, as many increase housing equity as decrease it. While this is an intriguing finding, it is not clear to me that it suggests little interest in home equity conversion products. After all, some elderly households who buy more valuable houses are likely to be doing so to increase housing consumption rather than housing equity. Furthermore, Sheiner and Weil (1992) note that when one looks at the "older" old, there is indeed a relatively quick decline in housing equity at the end of life. They also provide evidence that much of the housing equity released in a house sale gets used almost immediately for consumption purposes; see also Megbolugbe et al. (1997) and Venti and Wise, this volume. This observation led Skinner (1996) to hypothesize that the most important use of reverse mortgages may be to help release funds for emergency purposes, for instance if there is a health problem. Housing equity maybe a potentially important form of precautionary saving, but tends to be tapped when bad contingencies arise.

There is a second reason to downplay the significance of the early Venti and Wise (1990) findings for the home equity conversion market. Those who move to more valuable houses late in life may not be typical elderly households. Either they were wealthy enough to buy their house free and clear, or they had incomes high enough to qualify for a mortgage. It is plausible that such households would not be interested in reverse mortgages. On the other side, anyone without heirs, who dies without a will, and who leaves a house owned free and clear to be sold at probate would seem to have suffered unnecessarily low consumption, unless housing equity is enjoyed in and of itself.

Some Market Imperfections

Other explanations for why the market for home equity conversion is so small pertain to high transactions costs and severe moral hazard problems. Another set of impediments may arise from household uncertainty about future medical expenses, and the connection between medical expenses and the desire to move to a new home. Finally, we consider the potential impact of psychological issues, such as the possibility that older households are simply unwilling to take on debt of any kind except in the case of dire emergencies. Institutional barriers to market development are explored next.

Transactions Costs and Moral Hazard

The most obvious impediment to market development is the high level of transactions costs. In the U.S. market, a 75-year-old could end up paying roughly $6,500 in fees to borrow a net amount of no more than $41,000 up front on a home worth $100,000. This is rather a disappointing payoff, and certainly the mere act of taking out this loan produces a significant reduction in net worth. Given these high costs, it may not be surprising that many households would leave what might otherwise be termed involuntary bequests. If the ideal bequest were somewhere in the $50,000 to $75,000 range, the household may be better off not taking out a reverse mortgage, consuming somewhat less than they would otherwise desire, and leaving a somewhat excessive bequest, rather than paying the costs of entering this market.

A second economic problem with even greater significance may be moral hazard in home maintenance and in home sale. Those who apply for HECM loans are generally very old, poor, and living in homes that are more valuable than they can afford to maintain, at least according to standard loan qualification criteria. They may also anticipate significant health problems during the life of the loan. These households would seem to be prime candidates to let their homes fall into serious disrepair. Unfortunately, in the reverse mortgage market, an initial failure to maintain the home properly can feed on itself, creating ever worse incentives for maintenance and a growing problem for the lender. Deterioration in the property value combined with the inevitable increase in the size of the outstanding loan balance soon leave the homeowner with no financial stake in the house. The loan quickly hits a crossover point, and 100 percent of any incremental damage or depreciation to the house is borne by HUD. In practice, the contracts contain a provision that declares that failure to maintain the house constitutes a default on the loan. But will HUD try to enforce this clause? Even if HUD should be so bold as to try to enforce the contract, would the courts let them? As Rosenbaum et al. argue:

> The contract provisions by which a reverse mortgage lender seeks to bind seniors to home maintenance liability fly in the face of reality. Enforcing such covenants may ultimately be more bitter and expensive than they are worth, and in the circumstances, there is no assurance that they can be enforced. . . . Will a court find that a ninety year old widow, who years ago borrowed the last of her home equity, must install a new twenty-year roof? . . . The responsibility of property-management and maintenance cannot be displaced upon home owners as if they were ordinary borrowers in the prime of life, with good incomes and growing equity. . . . They are increasingly frail, needing financial assistance and spending down that home-equity that would otherwise be their incentive to maintain the property. (1995: 22–23)

Moral hazard problems extend well beyond the maintenance phase, as Rosembaum et al. (1995) point out. It is predictable that in cases in which the crossover point is passed before the homeowner dies, the sale will wind up being handled either by relatives who have no stake in the sale price, or by the probate court. It is well known that probate sales bring lower prices than common home sale transactions, because of various problems and restrictions such as sealed bids, statements of financial qualification, as-is terms, court appearances, and delays. In addition, the court is exempt from statutory disclosures required of other sellers, such as reporting known defects, the history of improvements, and pending events or conditions. Sale by a relative could be even worse than a probate sale, due to a combination of laziness and corruption (e.g. asking for some reciprocal economic gain when selling the house at a bargain-basement price). If the reverse mortgage lender sought to gain control of the sale process, the first step would be a costly and lengthy foreclosure proceeding.

Confirmation that these problems are beginning to rear their heads may be found in a memorandum of July 24, 1998, submitted to HUD from the Santa Ana Homeownership Center ⟨www.hud.gov:80/hoc/sna/snathc02 .html⟩:

> The purpose of this memorandum is to keep you abreast of a counseling issue concerning the Home Equity Conversion Mortgage. Currently we are experiencing an increase in the number of elderly home owners with a Home Equity Conversion Mortgage that are unable to pay their taxes and insurance or maintain the condition of their property. Failure to meet these requirements is a default under the terms of the mortgage agreement. The HUD lender is required to notify HUD of this default. We must make the home owner aware that they may consult with a HUD-Approved Counselor. During this consultation, the counselor may assist the home owner in submitting information to HUD or the lender that may assist all parties in reaching a resolution.

The memorandum goes on to provide five suggestions on counseling the homeowner on how to recover good standing. Aggressive enforcement of the default clause does not appear to be in the picture. HUD's upbeat assessment to Congress on the sufficiency of the HECM insurance premium was written a mere six years after the program was initiated, and it seems premature.

Healthcare, Mobility, and Precautionary Savings

One danger for the borrower in taking out a reverse mortgage is that it may interact very badly with a later health problem. There are several aspects to this interaction. The first is that having spent down equity at an earlier stage, the household will enter the period of sickness in a somewhat worse net asset position.

A second and more significant issue concerns the interaction between health status and living arrangements. When an elderly person develops a significant health problem, it may be necessary to leave the home for some time for treatment and convalescence. At such points, there is also an incentive to reconsider the optimal living arrangement (Feinstein 1996). For many who are sick, it may be a good idea to move into more appropriate transitional housing. If some of their housing equity has been depleted, however, it may prove impossible to raise enough capital from selling the existing home to make such a move possible.

Things may be even worse for elderly who develop major health problems but nevertheless have a preference for staying in their current homes. Technically, such households are very likely to default on the terms of the reverse mortgage, either by being kept in convalescence out of the home for too long, or by falling behind on taxes or house repairs. At this point, the lender has the right to force sale of the house. The risk of being evicted from the home after an unfortunate medical stay may rationally deter many households from considering a reverse mortgage.

The Complex Psychology of Reverse Mortgages

It is often suggested that many elderly households are simply reluctant to take on debt, having spent so much of their lives trying to pay off their initial mortgage. Whatever the psychological origins of this discomfort, it turns out to have a basis in reality in the case of the reverse mortgage. After all, the reverse mortgage does involve a commitment to live in the house, and any prolonged period in convalescence would place the household at genuine risk of losing the right to live in the house. The mere hint of this aversive future possibility may be sufficiently anxiety inducing to discourage all but the most desperate.

Other possible dangers of the reverse mortgage market for elderly households have recently been highlighted not only by such consumer advocates as the Consumers Union of the United States (Wong and Paz-Garcia 1999) and the AARP, but also by HUD itself. There are cases of elderly households being contacted by "home repair" companies offering to fix up problems with no cash down, if only the owner will sign the following small document. The document turns out to be a reverse mortgage, in which the contractor charges exorbitant fees.

Even more serious is the possibility that fear of being "suckered" into a bad deal, or even fear of being evicted from one's home after sickness, influence the desire to avoid thinking about a reverse mortgage. As such, it may be part of a broader pattern in which psychological factors play a role in limiting the demand for reverse mortgages. Indeed there is evidence of inertia in many decisions that are important to the quality of life in later years. Lusardi (1999) shows that many households save very little for retirement and report not having given retirement much thought. To back up their claims, many of them report being unaware even of the level of their social security benefits.

O'Donoghue and Rabin (1999) characterize this form of "avoidant" behavior as following from a more general tendency to excessive procrastination when actions involve current costs and future benefits. Starting from very different theoretical viewpoints, the work of Becker and Mulligan (1997) and Caplin and Leahy (1997) also suggests that households may be especially unwilling to spend current resources to prepare for possible future unpleasant events. This means that aversive future events could be highly discounted from the current perspective. At the most extreme level, a low level of consumption in a house owned free and clear may be preferable to a somewhat higher level in a house on which there is debt, with the corresponding increase in insecurity.

Finally, we note that the counseling programs, while intended to provide reassurance, may themselves be enough to discourage many households. After all, the mere presence of the counseling program makes potential applicants aware that there are complexities to the product that may possibly come back to haunt them at a later date. In the thin market that currently exists, most households may not know anyone who has a reverse mortgage, so that there is no background of personal knowledge to help allay worries about being evicted by an angry creditor. If someone known to them took out the product for strong reasons of direct motivation, and if their use appears successful, then neighbors may imitate. In this way, one may get a form of gradual takeoff in consumption, in just the same manner that one does in stories of technological diffusion. There may be a great deal of social learning and imitation required for the market to grow.

Combining these various mechanisms produces a vision in which many may be disinterested in reverse mortgages, at least until they appear to be the answer to a pressing current problem. In this sense, the various psychological theories may provide further backing for the hypothesis that reverse mortgages may be most important in providing funding for emergencies, rather than for funding day-to-day consumption.

A Question of Supply

Powerful as they may seem, it is unlikely that the economic and psychological forces outlined above are sufficient to explain the low level of use of home equity conversion products in the U.S. market. The most straightforward supply-side factor that contributes to the low level of use of reverse mortgage is the relatively low fee paid by HUD to institutions that issue HECMs. These fees are insufficiently high to make aggressive marketing of the HECM a worthwhile activity for most banks, helping to keep the program small.

Beyond this, the various market impediments outlined above such as transactions costs are largely endogenous. In a thick market, transactions would be lower. Also, a significant portion of these costs takes the form of taxes, and these might be reduced if there was political pressure in this direction coming from either side of the market. With respect to issues of moral hazard, these may be far less significant in a world with contracts in which the lender had the incentive to carry out important tasks of maintenance. Similarly, healthcare concerns at the end of life could in principle be handled by richer insurance contracts.

A larger point is that in a mature market, contracts would contain clauses that could reduce most of the incentive problems and many of the psychological problems to manageable proportions. Combining this with the strong incentives for some initial homeowners to use the products at time of crisis, and the general spread of comfort that this history could induce, one can imagine the market operating far closer to its theoretical potential than is currently the case. In the end, there is simply an inefficiency involved in so many individuals dying with assets in excess of their desired bequests. The apparent lack of private sector interest in supplying products to exploit this efficiency will remain mysterious, at least until we have explored the institutional environment.

The Fiscal, Legal, and Regulatory Environments

In addition to the economic and psychological forces that may impede the development of the market, there are institutional impediments. The home equity conversion market sits at the intersection of many different, confusing, incomplete regulatory systems. The incompleteness of these systems impacts both the demand and the supply side of the markets, as is outlined next.

A Few Lessons from History

Economists are not the only ones to have spotted the great potential of reverse mortgage markets. In the U.S., much of the credit for the development of the market belongs to one individual, Ken Scholen. He founded the National Center for Home Equity Conversion in Apple Valley, Minnesota, in 1978, well before there were any reverse mortgages on the market. He has continued to be a major figure inspiring public and private sector involvement on the supply side in this market. However, he did not take his idea and make millions from it, as some might have in other sectors of the economy. Instead, he recognized that the process of introducing these markets would involve politics.

The pitfalls on the road to building the market are illustrated by the significant number of commercial enterprises that have tried to start these markets, without success. American Homestead was the first U.S. company to offer reverse mortgages, starting in the mid-1980s. This firm funded 1500 mortgages and then ran short of capital. Other private efforts to launch the market were those of Providential and Capital Holdings. Capital Holdings originated about 2000 reverse mortgages, but then it withdrew from the marketplace when the housing market turned down in 1993. Providential issued several hundred mortgages before running out of mortgage capital in 1991. At this stage, Providential stopped making new loans, but continued to pay off existing loans and took applications for more. In 1992, armed with qualified applicants and properties, Providential raised $65 million in an oversubscribed public offering. All seemed to be going well for Providential, and indeed its stock was appreciating. However at this point the Securities and Exchange Commission announced an investigation into the company's accounting practices. In July 1992, it ruled that the company should not assume any future changes in property value when projecting cash flows. More opinions led the SEC to revise its ruling in September 1992, allowing the use of Monte Carlo techniques using a reasonable projection of expected mean rate of return, as well as variation of individual around market returns. But Providential's shares never recovered after the initial investigation, and the company has since withdrawn from the marketplace.

The Regulatory Minefield

Why might an accounting challenge be sufficient to end Providential's participation in the reverse mortgage market? Because it is merely the tip of the iceberg in terms of the regulatory and institutional complexities surrounding reverse mortgages. Hammond (1997: 175) gives some hints as to the deeper complexities:

> The laws governing the creation, perfection, and enforcement of security interests in real estate are the mortgage laws of the state in which the real estate is situated. . . . On the other hand the rules governing the type of loans a lending institution is authorized to offer (including loans secured by real estate) are set by state and federal regulatory agencies. . . . When state mortgage law and the rules regulating a federal lending institution conflict or are inconsistent, generally the local, state law will be applicable unless the federal law preempts the state law. . . . The fact that a lending institution is authorized to make reverse mortgage loans does not mean the elderly citizen of such a state can take advantage of this device.

The problems for reverse mortgages caused by the vagaries of state law are profound. In its initial report to Congress, HUD was very concerned with legal issues at the state level. In its followup report (USHUD 1995: ES-2), it noted that some progress has been made:

> With respect to legal barriers at the state level, the Department finds improvements since the previous evaluation, although obstacles do remain. . . . Texas, with the homestead provision in its state constitution that prohibits mortgage lending except

for certain specific purposes, is the only state where it is clear that no class of lender may legally originate reverse mortgages.

To get to this happy state required a large scale lobbying effort to obtain appropriate legal changes in many states. Specific enabling legislation had to be passed in New York, Tennessee, and South Carolina. New York also eliminated recording taxes, and Tennessee had to eliminate a 20-year maximum for open-ended credit. Illinois went back and forth on whether or not to eliminate a restrictive law. On the negative side, Minnesota determined that mortgage bankers were not authorized to originate reverse mortgages, and Texas fought hard to retain the constitutional provision that prohibits lenders from making home mortgages for any reasons except to purchase a home, to pay taxes on a home, or to finance repairs to a home.

But there is a far bigger legal issue on the horizon, one that concerns the sale of property when the crossover point has been passed (USHUD 1995: 5–13):

The Department remains concerned about the uncertainty of state laws that may affect enforcement of HECM as a first mortgage. This is of particular interest to HUD because enforcement of lien priority against other creditors becomes an increasingly important issue over time as loan balances begin to exceed property values so that some secured creditors might not be able to have their loans satisfied from the sales proceeds. Most HECM loans will probably be assigned to HUD before this situation occurs so that HUD has legal concerns not necessarily shared to the same degree by originating lenders. . . . The laws in some states are not clear regarding the lien priority to be granted to loan advances made over an extended number of years under a mortgage that was recorded as a first mortgage. HUD has attempted to ensure that all HECM loan advances will be regarded under state law as mandatory or obligatory advances that, under the law prevailing in most states, would also have a first lien priority, but there remains some legal risk in some states.

Hammond (1997: 176) asserts more broadly:

a number of legal issues remain as a hurdle to reverse mortgages. These include priority of liens, mortgage-recordation taxes, restrictions on terms and rates of mortgages, limitations on use of proceeds, and mandatory counseling requirements.

This is far from the end of the regulatory problem. The Federal Reserve Board considers a reverse mortgage to be an "open end consumer credit plan under which extensions of credit are secured by a consumer's principal dwelling." Hence the Truth-in-Lending-Act applies, and the lender must state "loss of dwelling may occur in the event of default." Unfortunately, this is not accurate: the household only stands to lose the property if it fails to pay taxes, fail to keep the property in good repair, or otherwise endangers the lender's security interest in the property.

Legal uncertainty runs even deeper than this, since it is not clear what to do if a household declares bankruptcy. How will bankruptcy law be applied?

Further, what if there is a dispute concerning whether the household has maintained occupancy? What happens when the occupants die, and there is some wastage of the house in the meantime: is the family liable?

The Homeowner's Perspective: Taxes and Benefits

Uncertainty about the implications of the reverse mortgage is felt not only by suppliers, but also by homeowners. Indeed, while HECM requires borrower counseling by an agency approved by HUD, none of these agencies is a law firm. It will not reassure borrowers that they must sign a certificate disclosing that a HECM "may have tax consequences, affect eligibility for assistance under Federal and State programs, and have an impact on the estate and heirs of the borrower." What specific tax issues arise? One question concerns the potential taxability of the proceeds of the reverse mortgage. While the IRS does not consider loan advances to be income, annuity advances are in fact partially taxable. A second question concerns the possibility of a phantom gain that may occur when an elderly household sells the home for a handsome capital gain, but at a time when the loan has grown to be even larger than this. The end result may be a tax bill that the household is unable to pay.

Rosenbaum et al. (1995) content that the uncertainties about the IRS attitude to reverse mortgages run far deeper than this. They argue that a reverse mortgage is a sale rather than a loan as a matter of legal definition, given the high probability that the entire value of the house will ultimately accrue to the grantor of the mortgage. While IRS revenue procedure 91-3 states that the service will not rule whether a particular structure shall be construed as a loan or recast as a sale, there is a possibility that the IRS will ultimately rule that reverse mortgages are sales rather than loans. Such a ruling would have a disastrous impact on the financial positions of the supposed owners (Rosenbaum et al. 1995: 49n47):

The Revenue Reconciliation Act of 1993 introduces a new provision designed to reclassify from capital gains to ordinary income the proceeds of transactions which are, in effect, disguised sales marketed as loans. If applied to reverse mortgages, such a reclassification might minimize or eliminate the gains against which a senior's one-time $125,000 exclusion would otherwise be useful. Gain would be converted to fully taxable ordinary income, without exclusion.

The situation with respect to benefits is almost as confusing. Currently, it appears that social security and Medicare benefits are not affected by whether or not the household has taken a reverse mortgage (Scholen, 1996). But the situation with respect to the Supplemental Security Income (SSI) and Medicaid programs is far more complex, as described in Nauts (1997) and Hammond (1997). In the federal SSI program, a loan advance cannot affect one's SSI benefits if one spends the loan advance in the calendar month in which it is received. But if one's total liquid assets at the end of any month are above a very low limit, eligibility is lost. In addition, the money received from an annuity can reduce SSI benefits dollar for dollar, or make one ineligible for Medicaid. Even these current complexities pale in comparison with the possible scenarios regarding how these programs will change over time.

Inertia in the Large

The inertial forces outlined above can have a devastating impact on the incentive of private sector investors to develop all manner of new products. The inherent incompleteness of the surrounding regulatory environment makes it very hard to design products that provide a company with a competitive edge. The only way to reduce regulatory uncertainty to manageable proportions would appear to be through expanded public discussion of the products and an effort to capture the attention of the important legislators. Unfortunately this public discussion removes the incentive to innovate, since contract clauses are so easy to imitate. These problems could be greatly diminished if it were possible to purchase comprehensive insurance against regulatory and legal uncertainty prior to introduction of the products.

Difficulties in obtaining patents on contracts imply that a first mover can emerge only if the innovator can establish brand name and a central role as a market maker. But there is no reason to expect the first few efforts at product introduction to succeed. Even HUD is unsure as to the legal standing of reverse mortgages, despite sympathies among legislators and the American Bar Association. This means that the only real test of the regulatory system is some form of product introduction, resulting in inevitable challenges and problems, with the precise pitfalls varying from case to case, from agency to agency, and from state to state. The ultimate rulings in these cases will be public goods benefiting not only the innovator, but also any imitators who choose simply to wait and see. In terms of a private sector venture becoming a market maker, the presence of Fannie Mae and Freddie Mac, with their close access to politicians and cheap funding, will likely end any such fantasies.

Powerful as these institutionally determined incentive problems are, they do not fully explain the failure of the market to develop. Inertia on the demand side is also a factor. The clearest evidence of the independent importance of demand side inertia is the slow takeoff of the existing market despite all the implicit and explicit federal subsidies. But the deeper point is that institutions themselves are endogenous in the longer run. The presence of potentially huge gains from trade might be expected to produce pressure to correct and to clarify the appropriate branches of federal laws, state laws, and the tax code. Older households looking to increase consumption should encourage groups such as the AARP to seek changes in legal and regulatory barriers. So why isn't this happening in the case of reverse mortgages?

The psychological forces outlined above may be important if we are to understand the lack of demand side pressure for change. Of particular interest are forces that lessen the political involvement of those who may, at some future date, benefit from a thick market. These are the forces that make it uncomfortable even to contemplate going into debt except in an emergency. At any given time, the only people demanding such a product are those with a need for emergency funds, but they may have more pressing things on their mind than lobbying for the necessary regulatory clarifications.

Policies to Promote Innovation

The government has a long record as a promoter of innovation in the U.S. housing finance market. Indeed two of the key products in the current market, the 30-year mortgage and the mortgage-backed security, were developed by the public sector. It is this interest in promoting innovation that lies behind the policies promoting richer development of the reverse mortgage market. Yet our analysis suggests that the reverse mortgage is unlikely to be seen as a hugely successful innovation unless there is some change in federal strategy. What changes in policy might speed up the development of the reverse mortgage market and stimulate more rapid innovation in the stodgy field of housing finance?

The current method of federal intervention is to push agencies to create the reverse mortgage market themselves. This strategy has both pluses and minuses. On the plus side, by introducing a new product and following up on the various regulatory and legal problems, this approach exposes the hidden dangers that the regulatory and legal systems have in store for these contracts. On the minus side, there is no evidence to suggest that government agencies should maintain a monopoly on product design. We sketch a few possible variations on the reverse mortgage theme to illustrate the complexity of the various questions of optimal product design.

Alternative Products

Alternatives to the current reverse mortgage range all the way from such minor changes as adding richer insurance features to the existing contracts, through wholesale changes in the nature of the transaction, and from loan to sale.

Contract enhancements and insurance features. The most obvious problems in the current reverse mortgage concern moral hazard in home maintenance, and homeowner uncertainty about future health care costs and the possible desire to move to a new home. In principle, all of these could be better addressed with only minor changes to the market.

With respect to moral hazard, a first cut at the solution would be to include average maintenance expenditures directly in the reverse mortgage price, at least once the crossover point is approached. Rosenbaum et al. (1995) indicate how this could be done with relatively little expense. In fact, it may enable the lenders to increase the principal limit factors, since it removes the need to price in an efficiently low level of house maintenance expenditures. It may be objected that this clause would worry homeowners, since it would mean that they no longer have complete control over decisions on the physical maintenance of the home. Against this, they would no longer be in danger of default or eviction based on their nonfulfillment of the maintenance clause.

If a homeowner's uncertainty about future health status were important, then this too could be alleviated with the appropriate additional clauses. One could add an optional insurance feature, whereby a wide class of possible health problems would give rise to payments sufficient to enable the owner to move to transitional housing if so desired. Again, the richer the insurance coverage, the more the market may ultimately take off, as the worries about this dangerous new product get replaced by relief at having additional margins of safety in stressful and costly future contingencies.

Outright sale. There are two different legal formats that could be used to enable the owner to sell a home outright while retaining the right of abode. One is the sale-leaseback discussed by Hammond (1997), and other is the remainder sale proposed by Rosenbaum et al. (1995). The sale-leaseback arrangement is already in use in both England and France, although the scale of the market appears small. Rosenbaum et al. point out that sales of the remainder have an 800-year history in English law.

There are strong economic arguments in favor of such arrangements, since there is a once-and-for-all shift of responsibility for maintenance away from the elderly owner. These also maximize the amount that the elderly can earn from the house, since buyers always get the full value of the house, rather than the potentially lesser amount of the outstanding loan balance. A possible drawback of schemes based on a change of ownership is that these may not appeal to most owners unless psychological issues are handled carefully. There is a powerful belief that ownership *per se* is important, and this may indeed turn out to be true if one does not take care of clauses such as what to do when the resident falls sick. Moreover, the new owner has a monetary incentive to drive the residents out of their home. Of course, over time one could hope for standards to develop to prevent this, but there may not be many early takers of such a scheme.

Shared equity schemes. A hybrid proposal would involve partial sale of equity rather than only debt finance. One could imagine the use of shared appreciation mortgages, or some form of partnership contract along the lines outlined by Caplin et al. (1997). It is worth noting that the shared appreciation route is already being experimented with by Fannie Mae in its

HomeKeeper product (with apparently limited success). One objection from consumer groups is that the consumer may not understand what he is promising to give up (Wong and Paz-García 1999).

This class of product may have tremendous potential to change the entire landscape of housing finance, not just the last few years of life. The current evidence strongly suggests that many households end up leaving a bequest comprising the house and the house alone. Apparently many households are reluctant to take any act to change their housing equity in late life, and this may be expected to remain true even with better designed products on the market. If this is so, then the best time to change the end of life level of equity may be when the house is initially purchased. In a market dominated by inertia, prevention can be better than cure.

Consider what would happen in an institutional environment in which there were partnership markets, so that an individual never bought all of the equity in the current home. Suppose that the household purchased a $150,000 home for a total up-front cost of $120,000, and that correspondingly it owned a less-than-100-percent share in the final sale price of the home. Suppose further that the household was never going to move out of the house. Would the household feel that it was necessary to save an additional amount to compensate for the lower level of housing equity? Common sense backed by the evidence of Sheiner and Weil (1992) suggests that the answer is no. The most likely outcome is that the lower level of equity would feed directly into higher consumption during the lifetime, with a corresponding increase in welfare.

Conclusions and Policy Implications

Current U.S. policy involves federal agencies taking the role of monopoly product designer in the market for home equity conversion. However, given the vast array of possible products that would allow for home equity conversion, a more enlightened federal policy may involve taking a more aggressive role in sweeping the regulatory minefield, while at the same time ensuring the strongest possible competition on the supply side of the market.

In order to play the minesweeping role as effectively as possible, one important first step could be for some federal agency to open the door to innovative product designs, at least at the conceptual level. Well-thought-out proposals could be encouraged either by direct payment, or by some indirect method such as the offer of royalties should the proposed contract forms be adopted. When proposals were gathered, the next stage could involve getting all relevant regulators and representatives of various branches of the law together. They would be asked to identify the relevant aspects of existing codes that might impact the performance of these contracts, and to consider additions or changes that would clarify the standing of the proposed contracts. The end result would at least be announcements of regulatory intent, or, "private letter rulings" on controversial questions, or even direct changes in regulations.

The most ambitious policy would address the issue of home equity conversion for all households, not just for elderly households. As has been argued elsewhere (Caplin et al. 1997), increased use of equity finance may help alleviate many of the current problems in the housing finance market, including affordability problems for younger home buyers. Of course these richer markets in home equity conversion open far more subtle regulatory questions. Why does the IRS view sharing of losses on the home as stripping the owner of the right to take the mortgage interest deduction? What is the legal definition of home ownership, and is this an economically sensible definition? This is the uncharted territory that must be mapped out to encourage large-scale and beneficial innovations in the housing finance market.

Note

1. A complete discussion of the nature and motivations for the principal limit factor can be found in Szymanoski (1994).

References

Becker, Gary and Casey Mulligan. 1997. "The Endogenous Determination of Time Preference." *Quarterly Journal of Economics* 112: 729–57.

Caplin, Andrew and John Leahy. 1997. "Psychological Expected Utility Theory and Anticipatory Feelings." C. V. Starr Working Paper 97–37.

Caplin, Andrew, Sewin Chan, Charles Freeman, and Joseph Tracy. 1997. *Housing Partnerships.* Cambridge, Mass.: MIT Press.

Case, Karl, Robert Shiller, and Allan Weiss. 1993. "Index-based Futures and Options Markets." *Journal of Portfolio Management* 19: 83–92.

Feinstein, Jonathan. 1996. "Elderly Health, Housing, and Mobility." In *Advances in the Economics of Aging,* ed. David A. Wise. Chicago: University of Chicago Press.

Hammond, Cecilia. 1997. "Reverse Mortgages: A Financial Planning Device for the Elderly." In *Reverse Mortgages: A Lawyer's Guide to Housing and Income Alternatives,* ed. David A. Bridewell and Charles Nauts. New York: American Bar Association. 215–30.

Lusardi, Annamaria. 1999. "Information, Expectations, and Planning for Retirement." In *Behavioral Dimensions of Retirement Economics,* ed. Henry Aaron. Washington, D.C. Brookings Institution Press. 81–115.

Megbolugbe, Isaac, Jarjisu Sa-Aadu, and James Shilling. 1997. "Oh, Yes, the Elderly will Reduce Housing Equity Under the Right Circumstances." *Journal of Housing Research* 8, 1: 53–74.

Merrill, Sally R., Meryl Finkel, and Nandinee Kutty. 1994. "Potential Beneficiaries From Reverse Mortgage Products for Elderly Homeowners: An Analysis of American Housing Survey Data." *Journal of the American Real Estate and Urban Economics Association* 22: 257–99.

Mitchell, Olivia S. and James F. Moore. 1998. "Retirement Wealth Accumulation and

Decumulation: New Developments and Outstanding Opportunities." *Journal of Risk and Insurance* 65: 371–400.

Nauts, Charles. 1997. "Legal Counseling for Reverse Mortgages and Sale-Leasebacks." In *Reverse Mortgages: A Lawyer's Guide to Housing and Income Alternatives*, ed. David A. Bridewell and Charles Nauts. New York: American Bar Association. 105–15.

O'Donoghue, Ted and Matthew Rabin. 1999. "Procrastination in Planning for Retirement." In *Behavioral Dimensions of Retirement Economics*, ed. Henry Aaron. Washington, D.C.: Brookings Institution Press. 125–56.

Rasmussen, Dennis, Isaac Megbolugbe, and Barbara Morgan. 1995. "Using the 1990 Public Use Microdata Sample to Estimate Potential Demand for Reverse Mortgage Products." *Journal of Housing Research* 6, 1: 1–23.

Rosenbaum, David, Thomas Goren, and Laurence Jacobs. 1995. *Risk and Benefit: Structural Efficiency in Senior Home-Equity Conversion*. Walnut Creek, Calif.: Lifetime Security Plan.

Scholen, Kenneth. 1996. *Your New Retirement Nest Egg: A Consumer Guide to the New Reverse Mortgages*, Apple Valley, Minn.: NCHEC Press.

Sheiner, Louise and David N. Weil. 1992. "The Housing Wealth of the Aged." NBER Working Paper 4115.

Shiller, Robert and Allan Weiss. 1998. "Moral Hazard in Home Equity Conversion." Cowles Foundation Discussion Paper 1177. New Haven, Conn.: Yale University.

Skinner, Jonathan. 1996. "Is Housing Wealth a Sideshow?" In *Advances in the Economics of Aging*, Ed. D. Wise. Chicago: University of Chicago Press. 241–68.

Szymanoski, Edward. 1994. "Risk and the Home Equity Conversion." *Journal of the American Real Estate and Urban Economics Association* 22, 2: 347–66.

United States Department of Housing and Urban Development (USHUD). 1995. *Evaluation of the Home Equity Conversion Mortgage Insurance Demonstration*. Washington, D.C.: USGPO.

Venti, Steven F. and David A. Wise. 1990. "But They Don't Want to Reduce Housing Equity." In *Issues in the Economics of Aging*, ed. David Wise. Chicago: The University of Chicago Press, 13–29.

——. 1991. "Aging and the Income Value of Housing Wealth." *Journal of Public Economics* 44, 3: 371–97.

——. This volume. "Patterns of Housing Equity Use Among the Elderly."

Wong, Victor and Norma Paz-Garcia. 1999. *There's No Place Like Home: The Implications of Reverse Mortgages on Seniors in California*. Yonkers, N.Y.: Consumers Union.

Chapter 12
Aging and Housing Equity

Steven F. Venti and David A. Wise

Housing equity is the most important asset of many older Americans. In principle, these assets could be used to support consumption after retirement, but earlier studies have concluded that unless there is an alteration in family status, there is little if any reduction in housing equity as people age.[1] Indeed, our prior research concluded that even among movers, there was little change in home equity. We did find, however, that people with large home equity relative to other welath were more likely to reduce home equity when they moved, and those with low housing equity relative to other wealth were more likely to increase home equity when they moved. Large reductions in home equity were typically associated with the death of a spouse or with other precipitating shocks. Our earlier analyses relied on data from the Retirement History Survey (RHS) and covered persons age 58–73 interviewed over the 1970s. Merrill (1984) also analyzed RHS data and reached conclusions consistent with ours. Feinstein and McFadden (1989) base their analysis on information from the Panel Survey of Income Dynamics (PSID), a survey that includes households with heads over age 75. Their findings were also consistent with our earlier findings. In a somewhat later analysis, Venti and Wise (1991) used data from the Survey of Income and Program Participation (SIPP) and again obtained findings consistent with prior studies. Sheiner and Weil (1993) find some decline in home equity at older ages, associated with shocks to family status and health; their results appear to us to be consistent with the prior studies.

Despite the seeming unanimity of opinion, some alternative views have recently begun to emerge. Recently, Megbolugbe et al. (1997), using PSID data, found that:

1. Homeownership rates remain high until age 70, after which a noticeable decline begins.
2. Each year, 97 percent of homeowners remain owners, and 91 percent of renters remain renters. When they move, renters are more likely

than owners to switch tenure, but renters are more likely to move, so on net there is a trend to renting.

3. When they move, owners aged 55–64 are more likely to trade down, owners aged 65–74 are more likely to trade up, and those 75+ are as likely to trade up as down.

4. Liquidity constraints tend not to influence homeowning patterns. In fact, asset-rich but income-poor households tend to trade up, in contrast to earlier findings.

Another study bucking the mainstream view was by Hurd (1999), who examined two waves of the Asset and Health Dynamics Among the Oldest Old (AHEAD) survey. He concluded: "Downsizing of home owning is the norm, and prior contradictory findings were due to inadequate data."

In this chapter we once again examine patterns of change in home equity as peple age, using a new dataset. The key question we ask is whether housing wealth is typically used to support general consumption in old age. We examine particularly attention to older households, between the age of 70 and 90, using data from the AHEAD.

To the extent that housing equity is treated just like financial assets to support consumption after retirement, it might be considered as a substitute for financial wealth and perhaps treated interchangeably with financial wealth in considering the wellbeing of the elderly. On the other hand, if housing wealth is not drawn down with age, it may be more realistic to consider nonhousing consumption derived mainly from accumulated financial wealth, including social security and other annuities. Analysts considering how well households are prepared for retirement have treated home equity in different ways. Some analysts include housing wealth in the set of assets that can be used to finance retirement (Moore and Mitchell 2000; CBO 1993). Others exclude housing wealth in making a determination (Bernheim, 1992). Engen et al. (1999) and Gustman and Steinmeier (1999) bound their estimates at 0 and 100 percent of housing equity.

Empirical Approach: Tracing Home Equity over the Life Cycle

We consider first the relationship between age and housing equity over the life cycle, drawing on data from the Survey of Income and Program Participation (SIPP). We then turn to more detailed analysis for older households, using the AHEAD data. In particular we consider the effect of precipitating shocks. We have given considerable attention to the possibility of possible misreporting and errors in the AHEAD data, yet we are left with substantial noise in changes in housing wealth over time, particularly when persons move. Indeed, the reduction in housing wealth calculated from the difference between self-reported owner-occupied home value before sale and the reported sale value after moving may exaggerate to a considerable degree the actual reduction in housing equity. There is substantial evidence that respondents tend to overestimate the value of the house in which they are living.

Findings Using SIPP Evidence

The SIPP provides housing equity values obtained from home value and mortgage debt in seven years: 1984, 1985, 1987, 1988, 1991, 1993 and 1995.[2] From the random sample of cross-section surveys in each of these years we have created cohort data. For example, to trace the home equity of people age 26 in 1984, we begin with the average home equity of persons age 26 based on the random sample of persons age 26 in the 1984 survey. Next, we obtain the average equity of people age 27 from the 1985 survey, age 29 in the 1987 survey, and so forth. We identify cohorts by their age in the 1984 survey. We do this for 17 cohorts defined by the age of the cohort in the first year of the data. In fact, to obtain more precise estimates of housing equity, the data for a given cohort like age 26 is the average of data for a three-year age interval (25, 26, and 27). We do this for cohorts, age 26, 29, . . . , 71, 74. All cohorts are followed until age 80 in the SIPP.[3]

The fraction of two-person SIPP households who own a home, by cohort, appears in Figure 1. These patterns can be affected by differential mortality: for example, suppose that homeowners were less likely to die at any age than renters. Then the ownership rate rises with age simply because the owners lived and the renters died. To account for this possibility, we have made a mortality correction to the data (explained in the appendix), and report these mortality-corrected data for two-person households. To make the figure easier to read, only selected cohorts are reported. The lesson of the figure is that home ownership does not decline with age, at least through age 79. In addition, there appear to be no important cohort effects until about age 70. That is, there are no large jumps when the data for one cohort end and the data for another cohort begin. For the oldest ages, however, there do appear to be noticeable cohort effects. Home ownership is lower for the last two cohorts. Yet as with the other cohorts, there is no evident decline in ownership as these cohorts age.

Figure 2 reflects the result of "smoothing" SIPP data by regressing home ownership on age, age squared, and age cubed, together with cohort effects. The functional form is

$$\text{Own} = \alpha + \beta_1 A + \beta_2 A^2 + \beta_3 A^3 + \sum_{\text{cohort}} \delta_i C_i,$$

where i indexes cohorts and δ_i indicates the ith cohort effect. In this model, the sum of the δ_is is zero. In Figure 2, the "average" relationship between

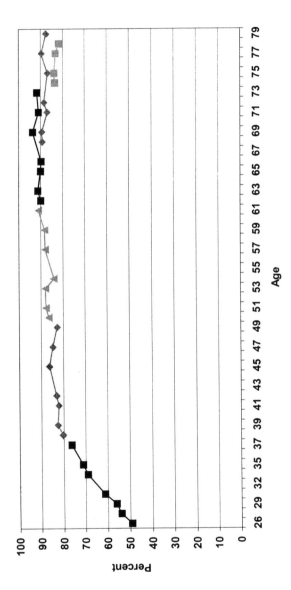

Figure 1. Percent owning homes among two-person households (mortality adjusted data from SIPP). Source: Authors' calculations from SIPP data.

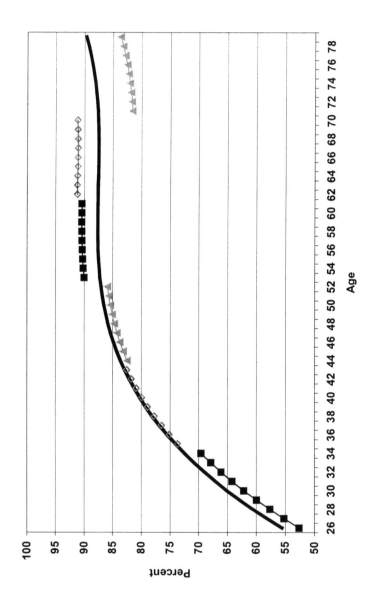

Figure 2. Percent owning homes among two-person households (mortality adjusted data from SIPP, smoothed). Source: Authors' calculations from SIPP data.

age and ownership, based on the age parameters in the above equation, is shown by the heavy solid line. The cohort effects are represented by the deviations of individual cohort lines from the overall average. These more formal estimates indicate that both the oldest and the youngest cohorts are less likely than the average to own, while the middle-aged cohorts are more likely to own.

Home ownership data for one-person SIPP households are shown in Figure 3. Again there is no apparent decline in ownership with age. Indeed, the data seem to show some increase in ownership at the oldest ages.

Home Equity

Home equity values reported by two-person families are shown in Figure 4. These are in current dollars and thus reflect the influence of rising home prices over the 1984 to 1995 period, nor are the data corrected for differential mortality. The same data, now in 1995 dollars and corrected for mortality, appear in Figure 5. Within a cohort, there is no decline in home equity as the cohort ages; there may even be some increase in equity within a cohort between age 65–80. There do appear to be some cohort effects in equity, as evidenced by the jumps when the data for one cohort ends and the data for another cohort begins.

To illustrate more clearly the cohort effects, we have fit the cohort data with a regression equation just like the one above, now replacing home ownership with home equity:

$$\text{Equity} = \alpha + \beta_1 A + \beta_2 A^2 + \beta_3 A^3 + \sum_{\text{cohort}} \delta_i C_i.$$

The results for selected cohorts are shown in Figure 6 and for all SIPP cohorts in Figure 7. It is clear that both older cohorts — those over age 70 in 1984 — and younger cohorts — those younger than 36 in 1984 — have lower home equity than the average, while the middle-aged cohorts have higher equity than the average. For example, consider cohorts who attained age 32 in successively later calendar years: The cohort that was age 32 in 1984 had more home equity than the cohort aged 32 in 1988, and the later cohort had more home equity than the cohort that attained age 32 in 1995. We have not analyzed the reason for the cohort effects in any systematic way, although differences in housing price changes over time may explain the cohort effects.[4]

Figure 8 shows the similar self-reported equity data for one-person households, and Figure 9 shows the data corrected for mortality and inflation. As with the two-person households, there seems to be no decline in equity through age 78.

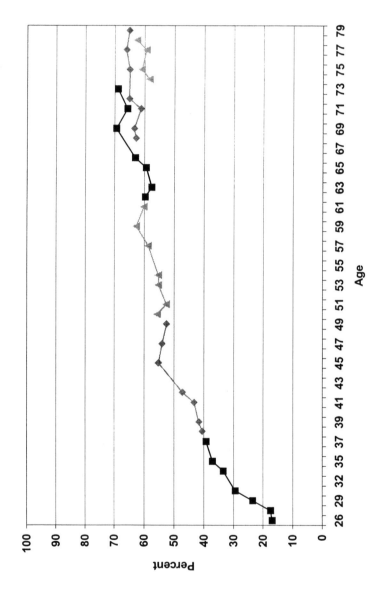

Figure 3. Percent owning homes among one-person households (mortality adjusted data from SIPP).
Source: Authors' calculations from SIPP data.

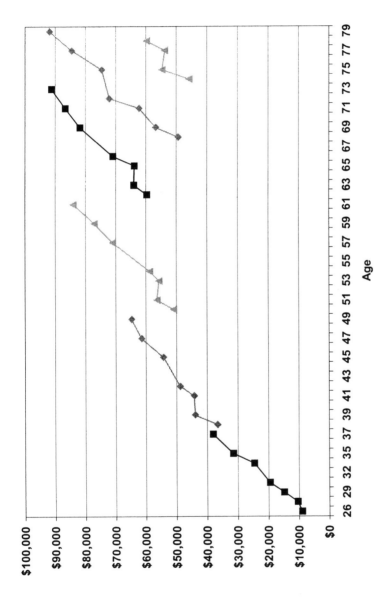

Figure 4. Home equity for two-person households (data from SIPP). Source: Authors' calculations from SIPP data.

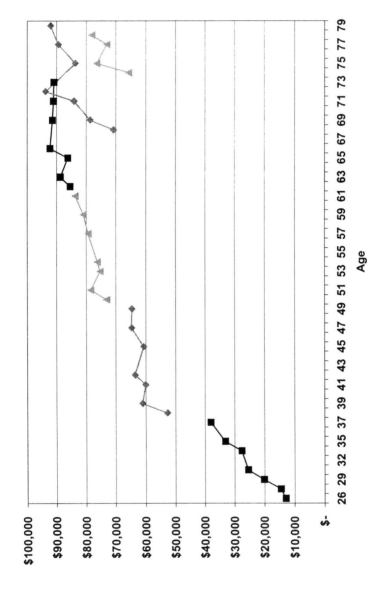

Figure 5. Home equity for two-person households (mortality and CPI-adjusted data from SIPP). Source: Authors' calculations from SIPP data.

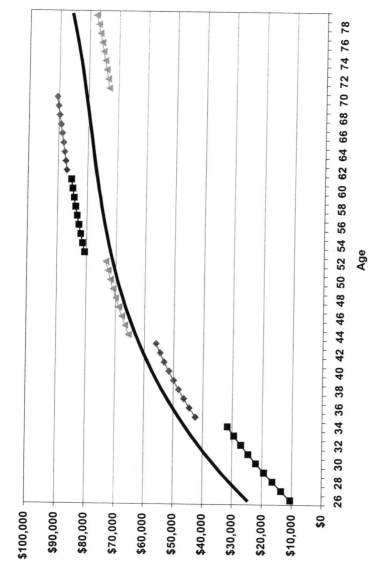

Figure 6. Home equity for two-person households (smoothed data from SIPP, selected cohorts). Source: Authors' calculations from SIPP data.

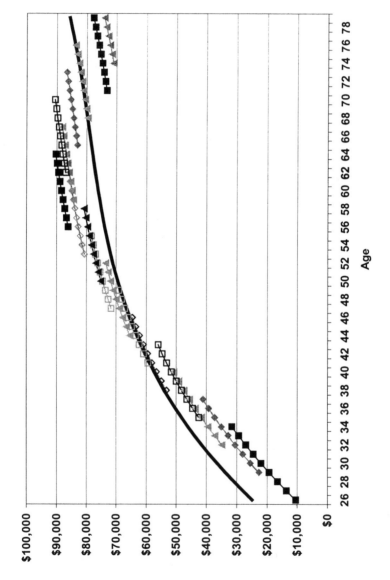

Figure 7. Home equity for two-person households (smoothed data from SIPP, all cohorts). Source: Authors' calculations from SIPP data.

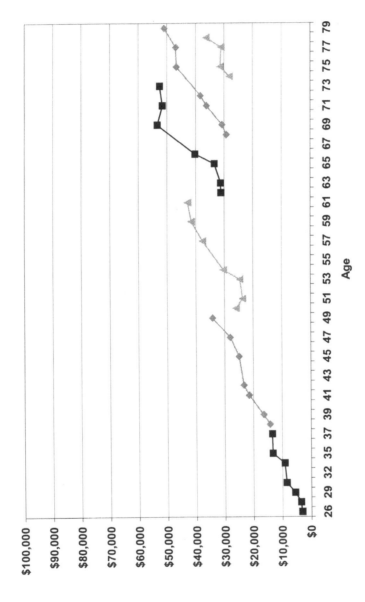

Figure 8. Home equity for one-person households (data from SIPP). Source: Authors' calculations from SIPP data.

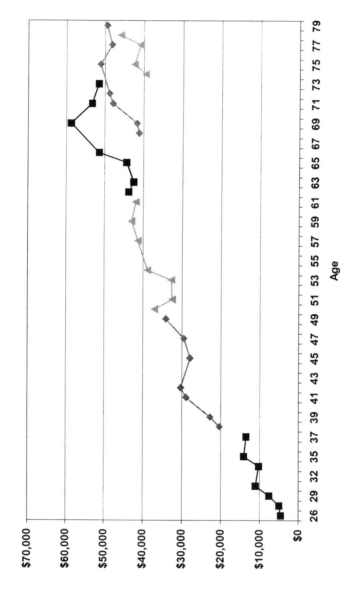

Figure 9. Home equity for one-person households (mortality and CPI-adjusted data from SIPP). Source: Authors' calculations from SIPP data.

Findings Using AHEAD Data

To understand trends in home equity at older ages, we turn to an examination of the AHEAD data. Once again we consider home ownership cohort data first and then home *equity* cohort data. Then we consider the effect of precipitating shocks strongly related to change in home equity at older ages.

Homeownership

AHEAD is a panel data file that follows the same families over time. We use data from wave 1 (1993) and wave 2 (1995) of this survey, along with a resurvey in 1998, wave 4 of the Health and Retirement Study [HRS]. Thus we have three data points spanning five years for each household. To obtain cohort data comparable to the SIPP, we construct cohorts data by grouping AHEAD households in two-year age intervals. These constructed cohorts are the basis for our cohort evidence shown next.

Homeownership cohort data for two-person families appear in Figure 10, which covers ages from 70 to 90. A comparison of these with the SIPP data in Figure 1 shows that the ownership percent for two-person families in their early 70s is about 90 percent in both sources, though the AHEAD results suggest a modest decline in ownership among persons in their 70s. Nevertheless, the within-cohort data do not show a decline in ownership at older ages, though there are cohort effects, with lower ownership among the oldest cohorts.

Analogous information for one-person households appear in Figure 11. For these households, the within-cohort data do suggest a decline in ownership as persons age. But they also suggest a positive cohort effect, with higher ownership among households in their 80s than among those in their late 70s.

Home Equity

CPI-adjusted home equity cohort information for two-person households is shown in Figure 12, and here there is a rather consistent decline with age in housing equity with no substantial cohort effects. (The anomalous age 82 cohort data are apparently the result of a small sample size.) Equity patterns for one-person households are shown in Figure 13 and also show consistent decline with age, and without noticeable cohort effects with the possible exception of the oldest cohort.

When we amalgamate the patterns observed in the SIPP and AHEAD surveys for two-person households (Figures 5 and 12), our tentative conclusion is that home equity seems to peak in the early 60s and remain more or less constant until the early 70s. Thereafter, there may be some modest decline in home equity. Among one-person households, the evidence

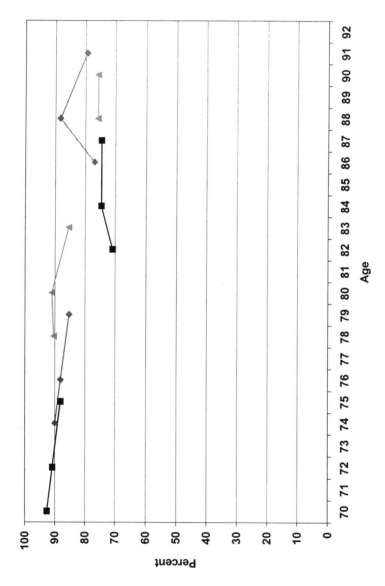

Figure 10. Percent owning homes for two-person households (data from AHEAD). Source: authors' calculations from SIPP data.

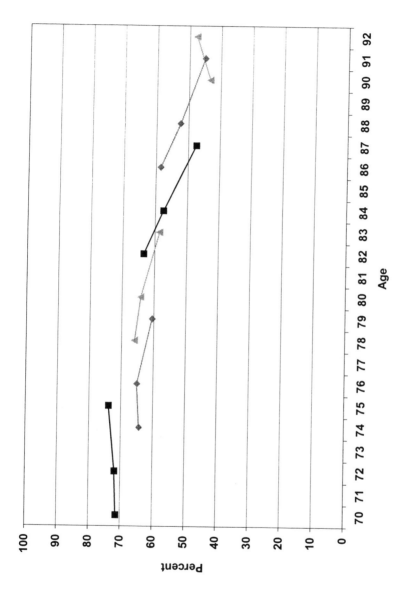

Figure 11. Percent owning homes for one-person households (data from AHEAD). Source: authors' calculations from SIPP data.

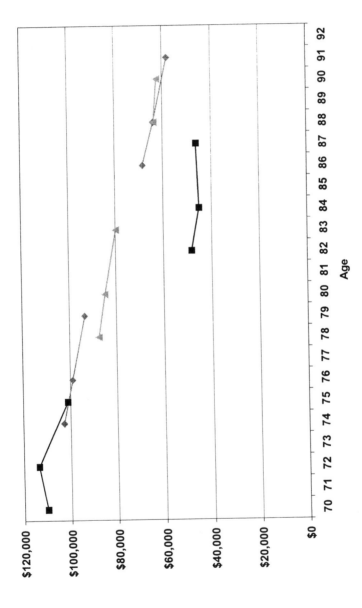

Figure 12. Home equity for two-person households (CPI-adjusted data from AHEAD). Source: Authors' calculations from SIPP data.

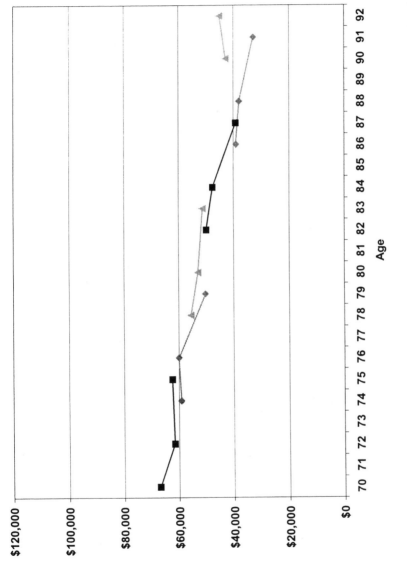

Figure 13. Home equity for one-person households (CPI-adjusted data from AHEAD). Source: Authors' calculations from SIPP data.

(Figures 9 and 13) is similar, although the decline in the mid 70s seems larger and perhaps more consistent.

How Changes in Family Status Influence Home Equity in the AHEAD Data

We begin by exploring change in home ownership, by initial ownership status and by change in family status, again considering two- and one-person households separately.

We focus on changes in ownership during the 1993–95 interval and the 1995–98 interval. Data from both periods are combined in the table (separate analyses for each of the two intervals revealed similar results). Table 1 pertains to two-person families who were homeowners at the beginning of the periods.[5] Of all two-person households at the beginning of the period, 87.8 percent initially owned a home. Of those initial owners, most (94.7 percent) still owned a home by the end of the period, 1.9 percent were renting by the end of the period, and 3.5 percent had some other living arrangement. The remainder of the panel shows transitions by family status change. For example, consider two-person households at both the beginning and the end of the period (2 to 2 households, representing 82.4 percent of initial owners): of these, 96.6 percent still owned at the end of the period. Of the 96.6 percent, 95.6 percent were still in the same home, while 4.4 percent had moved to a different house. A small portion of the continuing homeowner two-person households (1.5 percent) was renting at the end of the period. Of this group, 25 percent still lived in the same house (perhaps the home had been transferred or sold to children).

The remainder of the panel shows outcomes for households that experienced shocks to family status. The rows labeled "2 to 1" pertain to households that had two members in the initial period and one member in the subsequent period. The rows labeled "2 to NH" include all households with two members in the initial period and at least one member in a nursing home in the subsequent period. Households that changed from two- to one-person were more likely to change ownership: 89.6 percent still owned at the period end, but 3.2 percent were renting, and 7.2 percent had some other living arrangement. Most of these were living with children. The third family status change is from a two-person household to a nursing home for at least one member of the household at the end of the interval. Of these households, only 66.3 percent were still owners, 4.5 percent rented, and 29.2 percent had another living arrangement. The implication of our data is that most moves are associated with a precipitating shock — the death of a spouse or with entry to a nursing home.

Changes in home equity that parallel the observed changes in home ownership are shown in detail in Table 2 (all values are in 1995 dollars). The last column shows the mean initial housing equity for each of the transition

TABLE 1. Changes in Family Status and Homeownership: AHEAD, 1993–95, 1995–98, Two-Person Households at Beginning of Interval Only

Initial Family Status and Change	Subsequent Status			Initial Home Ownership and Family Status Change (%)
	Own (%)	Rent (%)	Other (%)	
Own	94.7	1.9	3.5	87.8
2 to 2	96.6	1.5	1.9	82.4
Stay	95.6	25	78	
Move	4.4	75	22	
	(100)	(100)	(100)	
2 to 1	89.6	3.2	7.2	14.8
Stay	92.4	13.3	41.2	
Move	7.6	86.7	58.8	
	(100)	(100)	(100)	
2 to NH	66.3	4.5	29.2	2.8
Stay	89.8	25	0	
Move	10.2	75	100	
	(100)	(100)	(100)	(100)

Source: Authors' calculations from AHEAD and HRS data; data for one-person households available on request.
Note: NH means at least one member in nursing home.

TABLE 2. Mean Change in Home Equity by Initial Homeownership and Family Status Change: 1993–95, 1995–98, Two-Person Households at Beginning of Interval Only

Initial Family Status and Change	Subsequent Status				Initial Home Equity
	Own	Rent	Other	All	
Own				$−3603	$110524
2 to 2	$2026	$−73011	$−78488	−553	110165
Stay	2516	−61231	−82869	936	109456
Move	−9179	−77303	−57989	−26093	122371
2 to 1	−10233	−68639	−108295	−18633	113755
Stay	−10113	−18616	−124546	−13668	112622
Move	−11598	−71795	−97261	−48138	120393
2 to NH	4834	−49118	−102827	−24545	119020
Stay	4678	−79207	—	4005	112816
Move	6253	−45441	−102827	−75104	92461

Source: Authors' calculations from AHEAD and HRS data; data for one-person households available on request.
Note: — means not calculated due to small sample sizes.

groups. The average for all initial homeowners was $110,534, and the average decline over the two intervals was $3,603, accounting for about 15 percent of the average income of these households or about 3.4 percent of non-housing wealth.

The upper left portion of the table pertains to two-person households that owned a home at both the beginning and the end of the interval. On average, their housing equity increased by about $2,000. This was due to non-movers, since movers reduced their home equity by $9,179, or about 7.5 percent of their average initial home value. It must be recalled that the typical elderly household only moves once, so the reduction will likely be a one-time reduction. In evaluating the change in home values of movers, one might therefore use the change for "stayers" as a control, suggesting that in this case movers actually reduce home equity by $11,695. Nevertheless the reduction in home equity when people move may be exaggerated, as discussed below.

It is clear from this table that moves associated with changes in household structure do produce large changes in home equity. The data also show a reduction in the home equity of *stayers* who changed from a two- to a one-person household. It is possible that this change represents random misreporting, perhaps because the more knowledgeable respondent is no longer in the household. To reduce errors in data reporting, we therefore report medians in Table 3. (In addition of course, the medians may be different from the means simply because of the shape of the distributions of accurately reported data.) In some cases there are large differences between the medians and the means. For example, the median reduction for continuing owners who move is now $5,294, instead of almost twice that level ($9,179). The overall reduction for continuing two-person households who moved is $12,805, instead of $26,093. The reduction for all initial owners is $2,540, instead of $3,603.

Supporting the view that reporting errors may yield exaggerated reductions in housing equity when homeowners move, we cite previous studies that conclude that homeowners do tend to overestimate the value of their homes (cf Kiel and Zabel 1999). Hence the realized sale price of a home is typically more accurate but lower than the prior estimated home value, which would create a bias in our estimate of the *change* in housing equity among movers. We believe that both the AHEAD and HRS data show this tendency. In AHEAD2 (1995) and HRS4 (1998), widows were asked if they sold their homes since the last interview. If so, they were asked for the selling price. If the recent sale price was accurately reported as we expect, then the difference in the pre-sale estimated value and the post-sale price would be a measure of how much people "overestimate" housing values. The estimated home values and the reported sale prices for these widows suggest that home values are overstated by about 10 percent.[6] If this were more generally

TABLE 3. AHEAD, Median Change in Home Equity by Initial Homeownership and Family Status Change, 1993–95 and 1995–98, Two-Person Households at Beginning of Interval

Initial Family Status and Change	Subsequent Status				Initial Home Equity
	Own	Rent	Other	All	
Own				$-2540	$84488
2 to 2	$-1488	$-60000	$-58085	-2165	84488
Stay	-1402	-66534	-63366	-1963	84488
Move	-5294	-60000	-57029	-12805	100000
2 to 1	-490	-52805	-79207	-3984	80000
Stay	83	-12000	-68646	-841	80000
Move	-24589	-52805	-85000	-47212	85000
2 to NH	-7012	-47524	-84488	-12573	73297
Stay	-7012	-79207		-7012	75000
Move	4623	-47524	-84488	-50693	68646

Source: Authors' calculations from AHEAD and HRS data.
*This is the first panel from Appendix Table 3a.

true, our estimates of the reduction in home equity when a home is sold could be overestimated by as much as $10,000 to $12,000. Indeed, the reported reduction in mean housing equity when continuing two-person households move from one home to another ($-$9,179) might fully attributable to exaggeration of the initial home value.

More Formal Estimates of Home Equity Change

We return to an examination of the change in home equity of movers and stayers, now considering movers as the "treatment" group and stayers as the "control" group. In this case, the home equity of stayers and movers at the beginning and at the end of the interval can be represented by a two-by-two matrix as follows:

	Beginning	End
Stayers	α	$\alpha + t$
Movers	α	$\alpha + t + m$

In this case, a difference-in-difference estimate $((\alpha + t + m - \alpha) - (\alpha + t - \alpha) = m)$, yields the "treatment" effect m. We can estimate m for all households combined, or for any subgroup, by

$$\Delta E = t + mM,$$

where t is a constant term and represents a time (inflation) effect and m is the additional effect for movers, with M a dummy variable identifying movers. The same equation can be estimated for any subgroup using the specification

$$\Delta E_k = (t_k + m_k M) * D_k,$$

where the dummy variables D represent different changes in family status and home ownership.

Estimates obtained in this way are shown in Table 4, which presents estimates only for people who were homeowners at the beginning of the interval. Data are presented by the subsequent (at the end of the interval) status of the initial homeowners. Ordinary least squares (OLS) estimates are shown in the left portion of the table, and the right portion shows median regression estimates. The latter estimates are not as sensitive as OLS estimates to reporting errors or other data outliers. In either case, the change in equity of movers is likely to be overestimated because of the inflated assessment of home values, as explained above.

For all two-person homeowner stayers, the change in home equity was not significantly different from zero based on the OLS estimates, but the median regression estimates suggest that home values fell somewhat during the intervals. For continuing homeowners, the OLS estimates show no statistically significant reduction in home equity, even for movers (with the exception of the anomaly for stayer households whose family status changed from two to one). The median results show some statistically significant, but smaller, declines. Accounting for the tendency to overestimate the value of owner-occupied housing, it is likely that continuing owners—even movers—had no decline in housing value, and they may have even increased housing equity. Recall that the results for widows above suggest that the method used here may exaggerate the decline in equity by $10,000–$12,000.

Important declines in home equity do occur among the 1.9 percent of two-person families who switch from owning to renting, and the 3.5 percent who switch from owning to some other living arrangement. First, none of the "mover" effects for those who switch from owning to renting or other are significantly different from zero. This suggests that there is no difference in the reduction of housing equity between movers and stayers. In the AHEAD data, of the nearly 25 percent of those reported to switch from owning to renting who have not moved from their initial home. Further, the housing equity of all the new renters who are "stayers" is reduced by around $60,000, as estimated by both OLS and median regression.

Given this apparent anomaly, we put little faith in the "control" method results reported here, but we do tentatively conclude that those who switch

TABLE 4. Estimates of Mover Equity Effect Using Stayers as "Control" Group, for Initial Homeowners, Two-Person Households, by Estimation Method

Subsequent ownership and family status change	OLS estimates				Median regression estimates			
	Stayers		Movers		Stayers		Movers	
	coef	t-stat	coef	t-stat	coef	t-stat	coef	t-stat
All	−807	0.2	−37217	2.8	−2012	4.6	−26832	17.5
Own at end of interval								
All	1020	0.3	−10085	0.6	−1534	3.3	−5710	2.8
2 to 2	2516	0.6	−11696	0.5	−1402	2.9	−3892	1.7
2 to 1	−10113	2.1	−1485	0.1	82.7	0.1	−24672	4.4
2 to N	4678	0.4	1574	0.1	−7012	2.7	11635	1.7
Rent at end of interval								
All	−58935	3.9	−14424	0.9	−66534	3.8	7534	0.4
2 to 2	−61231	3.6	−16072	0.8	−66534	3.5	6534	0.3
2 to 1	−18616	0.3	−53179	0.9	−12000	0.6	−40805	1.8
2 to N	−79207	1.8	33766	0.7				
Other at end of interval								
All	−92279	6.9	−536	0.0	−63366	8.2	−11634	1.1
2 to 2	−82869	5.7	24880	0.7	−6366	4.9	6337	0.2
2 to 1	−124546	3.8	27285	0.6	−68646	3.2	−16354	0.6
2 to N	−102827	5.9			−84488	5.5		

Source: Authors' calculations from AHEAD and HRS data. Data for 1-person households available on request.

from owning to renting release home equity worth about $60,000. In future analysis, we will seek to determine whether this change in home equity for "stayers" or "movers" shows up as an increase in other assets. Similar anomalies show up in the data for those who switch from owning a home to some other living arrangement. We therefore tentatively conclude that housing equity is reduced by somewhere between $60,000 and $100,000 for this group.

Comparable estimates for single persons not reported in detail here indicate that the housing equity of stayers was reduced by $2,000 to $4,000. Contrary to national data on home values, these estimates imply that home values declined over the survey intervals. On average, the 11 percent of one-person households who moved reduced housing equity by approximately $40,000 to $50,000. After accounting for the overestimation in the self-reported value of owner-occupied housing, these reductions would be less. Like two-person households, one-person households do not typically reduce home equity if they continue to own. Indeed, for continuing owners, none of the move effects are significantly different from zero. As with two-person households there appear to be many anomalies in the data for those who report switching from homeowners to renting or to "other."

Conclusion and Discussion

In examining the change in home equity as families age, we find that, barring changes in household structure, elderly families are unlikely to discontinue home ownership: only about 5.4 percent of older two-person households owning a home change status over a 2½ year period. Even among movers who continue to own, we argue that there is essentially no reduction in mean home equity, allowing for what appears to be some exaggeration in self-reported home value Liquidation of home equity is more likely in the face of precipitating shocks, experienced by about 18 percent of older two-person families over 2½ year period. When a spouse dies, about 10 percent of these households discontinue home ownership; about 35 percent discontinue home ownership when a spouse enters a nursing home. The reduction in home equity among families that discontinue ownership is between $60,000 to $70,000. Mean home equity among all families that experience these shocks is over $110,000. Thus we conclude that home equity is typically not liquidated to support *general* nonhousing consumption needs. While the results presented here are based in large part on the home equity of families aged 70 and older, the results are much like those reported in earlier work based mainly on families under age 75.

These results suggest to us that when assessing whether families have saved enough to maintain their preretirement standard of living after retirement, housing equity should not be counted on to support general nonhousing consumption. Families apparently do not intend to save for retirement through investment in housing, as they might through a 401(k) plan or through some other financial form of saving. Rather our findings indicate that families purchase homes to provide an environment in which to live, even as they age through retirement years. It may be appropriate, nevertheless, to think of housing as a reserve or buffer that can be used in catastrophic circumstances that result in a change in household structure.

These conclusions correspond closely to the findings of a recent survey of older households (age 45+) sponsored by the AARP. Respondents were asked, "Do you agree with the statement: 'What I'd really like to do is stay in my current residence as long as possible.' " Over 75 percent of the 45–54-year-olds indicated that they "strongly agree" or "somewhat agree" with the statement, while 95 percent of those 75+ concurred. In addition, nearly 75 percent of the respondents age 55+ thought that their current residence is where they would always live. When asked what they would prefer to do if they eventually needed help caring for themselves, they responded overwhelmingly that they preferred to remain in their current home, with assistance. As with our findings, the AARP survey also implies that most older households do not intend to liquidate housing equity to support retirement consumption.

Even in the face of precipitating shocks, when home equity is sometimes liquidated, we have yet to determine how the funds from the sale of a home are used. Do funds show up as an increase in financial assets? Are the assets transferred to children? How much is used to support general consumption? How much goes to nursing home expenses or costs associated with the death of a spouse? We will return to these issues in future research.

Appendix: Mortality Correction

Our analysis using the SIPP data is based on cohorts constructed from cross-section surveys. For example, the home ownership (or home equity) profile for a cohort is constructed by combining data for all households age A in the first survey year with data for households age $A + T$ from a survey T years later. If the likelihood of survival from A to $A+T$ is related to wealth, then these cohort profiles can be affected by differential mortality. We correct for this problem by reweighting the sample. Households are assigned an adjusted weight that is inversely related to the probability of survival from age A to age $A+T$.

Baseline estimates of these survival probabilities for one- and two-person households are obtained from waves 1 and 2 of AHEAD. A one-person household "survives" if that person is present in both waves 1 and 2. A two-person household "survives" if both members are present in the second wave. Survival probabilities are estimated from the AHEAD for five year age intervals and for housing equity quartiles. Older households and households with lower levels of housing wealth are less likely to survive. Since the AHEAD only includes households age 70 and over, published survival rates by age (from the NCHS) were used to extrapolate the AHEAD survival probabilities back to age 50.

The final step is to reweight the data. For each household observation of age A and housing equity quartile Q, the SIPP frequentcy weight is multiplied by the inverse of the cumulative survival probability. The survival probabilities are assumed to be one for households less than age 50. Thus households that are unlikely to survive are given higher weights. For each observation the probability of surviving to age A given equity quartile Q is where $s(a,a+1;Q)$ is the one-year survival rate for a household in equity quartile Q. For each household in each year the SIPP frequency weight is multiplied by the inverse of $S(A,Q)$:

$$S(A,Q) = \prod_{a=50}^{A} s(a,a + 1:Q) \ .$$

Notes

The authors thank Todd Sinai, Olivia Mitchell, and Alan Gustman for their comments, and thank the National Institute on Aging for financial support. Our analysis uses data from preliminary releases of AHEAD wave 2 and HRS wave 4. These data have not been cleaned and may contain errors that will later be corrected in the final public release.

1. See Venti and Wise (1989a, b, 1990), Merrill (1984), and Feinstein and McFadden (1989).

2. The survey panels and wave that provide the data are as follows:

Panel	Wave	Dates in Field	Panel	Wave	Dates in Field
1984	4	Sept–Dec 1984	1987	4	Feb–May 1988
1984	7	Sept–Dec 1985	1990	4	Feb–May 1991
1985	3	Sept–Dec 1985	1991	7	Feb–May 1993
1985	7	Jan–Apr 1987	1992	4	Feb–May 1993
1986	4	Jan–Apr 1987	1993	7	Feb–May 1995
1986	7	Jan–Apr 1988			

3. Data for households over age 80 are not used because age is top-coded at 80.

4. For example, referring to Figure 5, assume that homes are bought at age 35 on average, and consider the cohort that was age 50 in 1984 compared to the cohort that was age 38 in 1984. The older cohort bought homes in 1969 on average and would have gained from large home price increases in the 1970s. On the other hand, the younger cohort would have bought homes in 1981 on average and would have seen much lower increases in home equity during the 1980s and 1990s.

5. We have not made a correction for the different lengths of the periods. If people who own at the beginning of a period are equally likely to move in any of the next few years, then more people would have moved during the 2-year than during the 2-year period. Thus on average these are move rates over a 2½-year period.

6. A comparison of estimated home values and sale prices shows:

Survey Interval and Sample Size	Mean Estimate of Home Value in Initial Survey Year	Mean Reported Sale Price in Next Survey Year	Difference
1993–95 N = 152	90,512	80,816	−9,696
1995–98 N = 178	123,672	111,043	−12,630

References

AARP. 2000. *Fixing to Stay: A National Survey of Housing and Home Modification Issues.* Washington, D.C.: AARP.

Congressional Budget Office (CBO). 1993. *Baby Boomers in Retirement: An Early Perspective.* September. Washington, D.C.: USGPO.

Bernheim, B. Douglas. 1992. "Is the Baby Boom Generation Preparing Adequately for Retirement?" Technical Report. Princeton, N.J.: Merrill-Lynch.

Engen, Eric M., William G. Gale, and Cori E. Uccello. 1999. "The Adequacy of Retirement Saving." Brookings Papers on Economic Activity 2. 65–165.

Feinstein, Jonathan and Daniel McFadden. 1989. "The Dynamics of Housing Demand by the Elderly: Wealth, Cash Flow, and Demographic Effects," in *The Economics of Aging*, ed. David A. Wise. Chicago: University of Chicago Press.

Gustman, Alan L. and Thomas L. Steinmeier. 1999. "Effects of Pensions on Savings: Analysis with Data from the Health and Retirement Study." Carnegie-Rochester Conference Series on Public Policy 50. NBER Working Paper 6681. June.

Hurd, Michael D. 1999. "Portfolio Holdings by the Elderly." Mimeograph. December 1999.

Kiel, Katherine and Jeffrey Zabel. 1999. "The Accuracy of Owner-Provided House Values: The 1978–91 American Housing Survey." *Real Estate Economics* 27, 2: 263–98.

Megbolugbe, Isaac, Jarjisu Sa-Aadu, and James Shilling. 1997. "Oh, Yes, the Elderly Will Reduce Housing Equity Under the Right Circumstances." *Journal of Housing Research* 8, 1: 53–74.

Merrill, Sally R. 1984. "Home Equity and the Elderly." In *Retirement and Economic Behavior*, ed. Henry J. Aaron and Gary T. Burtless. Washington, D.C.: Brookings Institution. 197–225.

Moore, James F. and Olivia S. Mitchell. 2000. "Projected Retirement Wealth and Savings Adequacy in the Health and Retirement Study." In *Forecasting Retirement Needs and Retirement Wealth*, ed. Olivia S. Mitchell, P. Brett Hammond, and Anna M. Rappaport. Pension Research Council. Philadelphia: University of Pennsylvania Press. 68–94.

Sheiner, Louise and David N. Weil. 1993. "The Housing Wealth of the Aged." NBER Working Paper 4115.

Venti, Steven F. and David A. Wise. 1989a. "Aging, Moving, and Housing Wealth." In *The Economics of Aging*, ed. David A. Wise. Chicago: University of Chicago Press. 9–48.

———. 1898b. "But They Don't Want to Reduce Housing Equity." In *Issues in the Economics of Aging*, ed. David A. Wise. Chicago: University of Chicago Press. 13–29.

———. 1991. "Aging and the Income Value of Housing Wealth." *Journal of Public Economics* 44: 371–97.

Chapter 13
Risk Management Through International Diversification: The Case of Latin American Pension Funds

P. S. Srinivas and Juan Yermo

> There are some investors who have a rooted prejudice against all foreign investment. This attitude is highly patriotic, no doubt, but like every other fancy, it has to be paid for. (*The Investment Registry*, London, 1904)

Much of this volume focuses on retirement issues in developed nations, particularly the United States. In contrast, the present chapter offers a different international dimension by focusing on retirement issues in Latin American old-age systems. This topic is of keen interest because many Latin American countries have instituted privatized mandatory funded defined contribution systems in the last two decades, and in the process they are seeking better ways to manage investment risk. Finance theory argues for international diversification of pension assets as a useful risk management tool, an argument particularly relevant in the context of emerging markets with a limited set of domestic investment opportunities. Nevertheless, with the exception of Chile, few pension funds in Latin America invest in foreign assets. Our goal in this chapter is to offer empricial evidence of the potential for improvement in risk-adjusted returns for Latin American pension funds, achievable through international investment. We show that restricting international investments imposes costs on pension stakeholders in terms of lost returns and higher levels of risk per unit of realized return.

Our discussion begins with a brief overview of the international pension reform context. Next we describe the main arguments for and against international diversification, followed by an overview of the private pension systems in Latin America and the regulatory environment under which they operate. Subsequent to a description of the data and methodology used for the analysis, we evaluate the gains from international diversification from the perspectives of investors in both developed and developing countries. Last we focus on pension fund performance under alternate investment strategies. We employ a standard mean-variance framework, market data from 1976–99, and risk adjusted returns as the measure of benefits. These indicate that pension funds in three Latin American countries with the longest history of private pension funds — Argentina, Chile, and Peru — would have benefited from diversifying into international markets. We conclude that, in these countries, pension funds could have achieved higher risk adjusted returns than they actually did by investing in international assets. Relaxing international investment restrictions would provide avenues for better risk management. In countries that do allow such investments, pension funds should look more actively into international diversification.

The International Pension Reform Context

It is well known that old-age systems in virtually every country are under stress, as they face the dual pressures of rapidly aging populations living longer in retirement, and declining birth rates reducing the pool of active workers. In a majority of countries, public pensions (or the income component of social security systems) were traditionally based on a mandatory defined benefit (DB) model where current workers pay social security taxes that finance current retirees' pension payments (pay-as-you-go; PAYG). Few public pension systems built up reserves of assets, and today most are underfunded to one degree or another.

As a natural consequence of population aging, the PAYGO DB model today confronts policymakers in many countries with highly unpalatable choices: raising tax rates, cutting benefits, or offering an entirely new framework for retirement income provision. Various countries have adopted different strategies to avert their old age crises, ranging from denial, to marginal changes, to large-scale revamping. Many Latin American and Eastern European nations, especially those where the old schemes were most under stress, have tended to adopt the third approach. This entails transforming their social security systems, generally moving from the traditional DB model to a privately managed, individual account based, defined contribution (DC) model.[1]

Latin America has been the leader in reforming old, dysfunctional social security systems, and the wide range of new DC models adopted in the region serve to spur debate in many developed economies, including those considering "privatizing" as in the United States.[2] The Latin American pension reforms have not been without their critics: for instance, Diamond (1998) eloquently argues that DB systems are the first-best design for social security systems, in light of their ability to transfer risk intergenerationally. He and others contend that a DC system is often a response to the poor implementation records of DB systems, so that their limitations should be recognized. In a separate paper, Orszag and Stiglitz (1999) highlight several problems with the Latin American reform models, and more recently Holzmann (2000a) shows that public DB systems can provide significant risk management benefits when there is low correlation between wage growth and financial asset returns. In this chapter we take the new pension models as a given and address certain aspects of a key implementation issue, namely how to manage assets in these reformed systems.

With the change in design of the pension system from a PAYG (unfunded) to a funded one, Latin American pension funds have begun accumulating substantial amounts of assets. At the end of 1999, mandatory private pension systems in Latin America had about $70 billion in assets under management (8 percent of combined GDP). Brazil, which has a voluntary and largely employer-based pension system, had over $80 billion in assets (10 percent of GDP). Salomon Smith Barney, the investment bank, projects that Latin pension fund assets will grow to about $850 billion by 2015. Despite these optimistic forecasts, Latin American private pension funds face many challenges operating within the context of relatively less developed financial markets and weaker institutional structures (compared to those in the developed economies). Specifically, as assets under management have grown and prior experience with asset management is limited, one major area of concern has been how these funds should be invested and how risks in the process should be managed. In particular, we focus on the debate that has accompanied the issue of Latin pension funds investing (at least a part of) their assets abroad, in the developed markets.

Given that emerging markets have traditionally been looked on as investment opportunities for investors in developed countries, rather than as investors in their own right, there is little empirical work that has taken the perspective of the emerging market investor looking outwards. In theory, the issues are identical, irrespective of the domicile of the investor. In practice, as we show below, emerging market investors considering diversifying into developed markets for risk management or return enhancement see the world somewhat differently. Developed country financial markets often offer better return per unit of risk characteristics, lower transactions costs, more favorable return distributions, and beneficial correlation characteristics. For this reason, constraining emerging market pension portfolios by restricting investments to less developed financial markets will therefore be likely to expose pension plan stakeholders to higher risks. Better risk management would argue for greater international diversification.

Invest at Home or Abroad: The International Diversification Debate

In a fully integrated and efficient financial market, modern finance theory has established that the world market portfolio is the optimal risky asset to hold.[3] Hence, at first glance, a debate over the appropriateness of international asset diversification might seem strange. Theory would argue that an investor exposed only to domestic investments should perceive that international diversification reduces risk per unit of return, achieved by investing in asset classes that are not perfectly correlated with his existing portfolio.

In line with this theory, initial empirical research indicated that there was a low correlation between U.S. and other developed market assets, as well as between U.S. and emerging market assets.[4] This research impelled U.S. pension funds to diversify into other developed country markets and, later, into emerging markets. More recently, however, new research is casting doubt on the value of international diversification, at least for U.S. investors. In bond markets, U.S. investors apparently face highly integrated international fixed-income securities markets; this integration reduces the benefits from U.S. diversification into foreign bonds. In equity markets, capital market integration has also led to an increase in the correlation between U.S. and other developed equity markets (Adrangi and Shank 1998). Furthermore, over the last three-quarters of a century, the U.S. equity market had the highest mean return of all equity markets in the world, and this return appears to be substantially higher than that of most other countries even after adjusting for volatility (Goetzmann and Jorion 1999). Other researchers have shown that U.S. investors can achieve the benefits of international diversification by investing in portfolios of domestic securities, so that gains beyond those attainable through homemade diversification have become statistically and economically insignificant (Errunza, Hogen, and Hung 1999). Correlation and covariance patterns between equity returns of the major industrialized countries are also unstable over time, and it appears that correlations tend to rise in periods of high volatility, thereby reducing the benefits of diversification (Longin and Solnik 1995). Focusing on U.S. investors diversifying into emerging markets, Blommenstein (1998) argues that the dollar returns in emerging markets over the past 20 years have not been significantly higher than those on the U.S. stock markets, but they have been much more volatile. As a result, gains are low to U.S. investors in terms of risk-adjusted returns from emerging market investments.

Turning to emerging markets, Bekaert et al. (1998) find that returns in several emerging markets exhibit skewness and kurtosis characteristics that deviate substantially from those that would be observed if the underlying return distribution were normal, and hence conclude that benefits of international diversification presented through mean-variance analyses may be biased. That analysis also provides evidence that the higher moments of emerging market return distributions change through time, making the ex ante investment decision and its ex post evaluation more difficult. Finally, some observers propose that, as with changing patterns of correlations between industrialized countries, developed and emerging market correlations also change over time, thereby reducing the appeal of investing in emerging markets. Correlations appear highest during downturns in developed markets, but this is just when investors most need low correlations. This arises because emerging market economies often follow in the wake of developed markets, especially that of the U.S. Indeed, U.S.-emerging market correlations are much more unstable than correlations between the U.S. and other developed markets. Financial models based on historical market data may also not fully take into account the event volatility associated with macroeconomic and political uncertainty, and the less transparent regulatory and legislative frameworks of developing countries.[5] Partly in reaction to a growing number of such findings, there is a suggestion that U.S. pension funds have recently begun rethinking their international investment strategies.[6]

For other OECD countries, however, portfolio diversification into emerging country assets still appears to provide significant gains (Fischer and Reisen, 1994). Moreover, some observers have found evidence that international diversification can be most beneficial when one takes into account the whole portfolio of retirement assets, including nontraded assets such as human capital and assets in public defined benefit pension plans. In particular, Baxter and King (2000) demonstrate important risk management benefits from holding international assets, even when the gains of international diversification by themselves are low, because human capital returns are more highly correlated with domestic financial returns than with international financial returns. Hence the optimal allocation to international securities may well be higher when one considers the full set of traded and nontraded assets, than when one only considers traded financial assets.

From an emerging market perspective, objections to international portfolio investment tend to be grounded less in financial risk management theory than in macroeconomic and political economy considerations. At least in part, these arguments rely on the multiple objectives offered for social security privatization. That is, old-age pension reform in emerging economies is undertaken for many reasons, and optimization of contributor risk and return is only one (and often not the most important) of several competing objectives. In developing economies it is often argued that pension funds should be restricted from investing abroad to ensure the development of domestic capital markets, and to make sure that domestic capital resources are channeled toward domestic investments.[7] Also, research has argued that domestic market liquidity is a major link between financial development and growth (Levine and Zervos, 1998). This stance is contested by Reisen and Williamson (1997), among others, who show that there is little evidence that domestic market liquidity improves as a result of investment restrictions on foreign securities.

Another rationale for restricting pension investments to domestic markets is that many governments need to finance debt, particularly the so-called "transition debt" associated with social security reform (Corsetti and Schmidt-Hebbel 1995). In this context, private pension funds are often required to invest in government securities so as to avoid driving up interest rates that might worsen government finances and crowd out private investment. Of course this argument does not imply that private pension funds should be required to invest *all* of their assets in government bonds, and hence this argument is silent on the allocation of assets beyond that portion that is required to be invested in government bonds.

Other reasons offered to justify limiting international investments by pension funds include the existence and necessity of capital controls in emerging markets and the importance of maintaining exchange rate stability (Fontaine 1997). Capital controls are often imposed in emerging markets to prevent capital flight and thereby to protect the domestic tax base. Often countries have justified controls on capital inflows with arguments that such flows may destabilize or accentuate the instability of financial systems. Chile had controls on capital inflows for almost two decades before relaxing them subsequent to the 1997/98 crises in East Asia and Brazil. More recently, Malaysia imposed such controls during the 1997/98 East Asian crisis, although these are gradually being relaxed. It is also argued that volatile capital flows may put pressure on exchange rate stability, increasing fluctuations in both nominal and real exchange rates and consequently domestic price levels and export competitiveness. Since emerging markets are believed to be less able to withstand the impact of such shocks, preventing domestic institutional investors such as pension funds from adding to these pressures has been a priority. In turn this has implied imposing strict limits on their international investments.

Against this backdrop — mixed evidence on benefits of international diversification for U.S. investors and objections to international diversification by emerging market investors — are there good financial reasons why Latin American private pension funds should invest abroad? Is there any evidence that diversification from an emerging market portfolio into one including developed market assets is advantageous? Would investment risks facing pensions be better managed if the pension funds were allowed to invest more abroad? We address these issues next.

Privatized Latin American Pension Systems

As noted above, eight Latin American countries have implemented fundamental reforms of their social security systems to date, moving from publicly managed DB systems to privately managed DC plans; additional countries are currently moving in the same direction. These new pension funds are accumulating assets at a rapid rate and are expected to continue their growth in the medium term (see Table 1). Unlike mature systems in developed countries, where most of the asset growth occurs due to investment returns, the major source of asset growth in these much younger pension systems of the Latin countries is, and will continue to be, fresh contributions.

TABLE 1. Assets Managed by Private Pension Funds in Latin America

	Assets Under Management (US$ million)		Assets Under Management/GDP (%)	
	1998	*1999*	*1998*	*1999*
Argentina	11,526	16,787	3.9	5.9
Bolivia	333	592	4.0	7.0
Chile	31,146	34,501	43.9	53.3
Colombia	2,119	2,887	2.4	7.3
El Salvador	47	213	0.4	1.7
Mexico	5,730	11,430	1.4	2.3
Peru	1,713	2,406	2.7	4.1
Uruguay	374	591	1.9	2.8
Total/Average	52,988	69,407	7.6	10.6

Source: Authors' calculations using data from various pension fund, national bank, and investment house sources.
Note: Local currency equivalents are converted to US$ using year-end exchange rates. The overall average assets-to-GDP ratio is the arithmetic mean of the individual country figures.

While future asset growth in these systems is clearly on an upward trend, there is more uncertainty regarding the performance of this new pension fund industry. Past performance by Latin pension funds, averaged across all pension funds in a country, has been claimed to be good by many policymakers and practitioners because of high (relative to developed countries) real returns (see Table 2). But relative to market benchmarks, arguably a more relevant comparison, the performance of Latin private pension funds has been mixed, with relative pension fund performance being affected by choice of both benchmarks and time periods (Srinivas and Yermo, 1999).

In the three countries with the longest running private pension systems — Argentina, Chile, and Peru — private pension fund returns gross of management fees have been both lower and more volatile in recent years (see Figure 1 and Table 3). Chilean pension funds' nominal gross returns were about 24.5 percent (about 11.2 percent in real terms) during January 1982–December 1999. Further, dividing this sample period into two equal parts (January 1982–December 1990 and January 1991–December 1999) reveals that average annual returns were higher in the first period (31.3 percent) and lower in the second, more recent, period (17.6 percent). Recent returns were also more volatile, with a standard deviation of 7.33 percent as compared to the volatility in the earlier period of 4.95 percent. The null hypothesis of equality of mean returns can be rejected at the 1 percent confidence level. Similar results hold for Argentina and Peru, although the time frame during which these private systems have operated here is shorter than in Chile.

This pattern of pension fund performance can be explained, at least in

TABLE 2. Latin American Pension Fund Returns from Inception to Year-End 1999 (%)

Country	Year of Inception	Nominal Return Since Inception	Real Return Since Inception
Argentina	1994	12.97	12.46
Bolivia	1997	15.11	9.24
Colombia	1994	28.34	9.08
Chile	1981	27.40	11.20
El Salvador	1998	12.94	14.09
Mexico	1997	30.24	9.65
Peru	1993	16.80	7.28
Uruguay	1996	21.54	7.94

Source: Authors' calculations using data from various pension fund, national bank, and investment house sources.
Note: Colombian pension fund returns measured since 1996 only; El Salvador returns correspond to calendar year 1999. All historical returns correspond to the geometric mean over the sample period. Average industry nominal returns calculated by weighting each pension fund return by its assets under management at the end of the period. Real returns are obtained by deflating nominal returns by the national consumer price index or by related price indices (e.g., the "unidad de fomento" in Chile, the "unidad reajustable" in Uruguay). Returns are gross of fees, i.e., administrative costs of managing pension assets are not deducted from returns.

part, by the fact that in the early stages of the introduction of these new systems governments sought to ensure that these funds showed positive returns, in order to establish system credibility. Toward this end, pension fund regulations were tight and investments were largely in government bonds that paid extremely high interest rates with low price volatility. Over time, as pension systems became more established, investment regimes were gradually liberalized, allowing pension funds to invest in a broader range of assets. This exposed them to more sources of volatility. Concurrently, as these economies became more stable, interest rates on government bonds fell, which in turn affected pension fund returns as a result of their large allocation to these bonds (see Table 4). Most recently, many Latin American domestic financial markets have been quite volatile due to the East Asian and Brazilian crises; these too have been a proximate cause of the decline in pension asset performance. These trends in performance provide a good motivation for these pension funds to examine alternate avenues — such as international diversification — to enhance performance.[8] Indeed, in Chile, pension funds have increased their exposure to foreign securities (mainly U.S.) in recent years (see Table 5). By December 1999, Chilean pension funds held 13.4 percent of their aggregate portfolio in foreign assets, up from zero at the system's inception.[9]

These new Latin American DC pension systems expose pension assets to a number of risks, so governments in these countries have often strictly regulated the pension fund management industry's structure, performance,

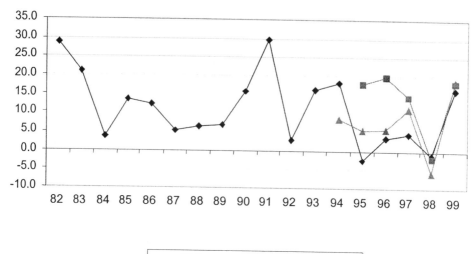

Figure 1. Realized annual pension fund return in Chile, Argentina, and Peru, percent per year from inception to year-end 1999. Source: Authors' calculations using data provided by Asociación Internacional de Organismos de Supervisión de Fondos e Pensiones (AIOS, the International Association of Pension Supervisors). Average industry nominal annual returns calculated by weighting each pension fund's annual return by its assets under management at the end of the year. Real returns are gross of fees; administrative costs of managing pension assets are not deducted from returns.

and asset allocation practices. Typically, industry structure is regulated through the establishment of fund management industries consisting of competing pension funds distinct from other financial institutions and new entrants into the financial system. This financial structure has been offered as the solution to the often poor record of performance and management in the preexisting financial services sector. Reflecting the fact that pension systems in Latin America are mandatory, countries have imposed strict performance criteria on the pension funds. The general structure of these requirements is that all pension funds are required to provide returns within a band around the ex post industry-average return. Penalties apply for underperformance, while "excess" returns are sequestered as a reserve against potential future underperformance. Finally, in a majority of countries, there are also restrictions on the type of investments that can be made and limits on allocations to asset classes.

Pension fund investment regulations in most countries have a prudential objective, namely, to ensure that they do not take excessive risks by overexposing their portfolios to specific securities and issuers. Latin American countries have established prudential regulations similar to those in devel-

TABLE 3. Latin American Pension Fund Mean Annual Returns and Standard Deviation

	Argentina	*Chile*	*Peru*
Time period of complete sample	Aug. '94–Dec. '99	Jan. '82–Dec. '99	Aug. '93–Dec. '99
Mean annual return	12.69	24.49	16.90
Standard deviation of returns	8.54	6.55	5.49
Time period of first sub-sample	Aug. '94–Mar. '97	Jan. '82–Dec. '90	Aug. '93–Oct. '96
(M1) Mean annual return	17.37	31.37	21.46
Standard deviation of returns	4.81	4.95	4.02
Time period of second sub-sample	Apr. '97–Dec. '99	Jan. '91–Dec. '99	Nov. '96–Dec. '99
(M2) Mean annual return	8.15	17.62	12.21
Standard deviation of returns	10.94	7.33	6.45
t-statistic for null	1.28	4.66	2.17
hypothesis of M1=M2	not significant	significant at 1%	significant at 5%

Source: Authors' calculations based on data supplied by Asociación Internacional de Organismos de Supervisión de Fondos de Pensiones (AIOS, the International Association of Pension Fund Supervisors).
Note: Data for Chile begin in January 1982, which was the first full year of operation. Panel A presents the performance of the pension funds since inception up to December 1999. For each country, the time since inception of the private pension funds up to year-end 1999 is divided into two equal halves to assess change in performance over time. Panel B presents the mean and standard deviation of pension fund returns in the initial period since inception and Panel C, the same data for the more recent period. Panel D presents the results of a t-test for equality of means of the two time periods, assuming different variances. The null hypothesis of equality of means can be rejected for Chile and Peru, but not for Argentina.

oped countries. These regulations cover single issuer and single security exposure limits and also require that fixed income investments be of a minimum risk rating. For example, in Chile, prudential regulation requires pension funds to limit their investments in a single issue of fixed income securities to seven percent of their portfolio and their investment in the equity of a single issuer to five percent of their portfolio. To avoid conflicts of interest, the limits are set lower for issuers that have financial interests in the pension fund management companies. The minimum acceptable risk category for fixed income securities is BBB or equivalent. There are similar prudential rules in other countries.

In addition to these prudential rules, all Latin American countries impose quantitative restrictions on portfolio allocation by asset type (see Table 6). In Argentina, for example, pension funds are not allowed to invest more than 50 percent of their assets in government securities, while Mexico does not permit any investment in equities. This contrasts with the situation in some developed countries such as Austria, Australia, Ireland, the Netherlands, New Zealand, the United Kingdom, and the United States which largely rely on "prudent-person" regulations.

TABLE 4. Latin American Pension Fund Portfolios (%, Year-End 1999)

	Government Securities	Financial Institutions	Corporate Bonds	Equities	Investment Funds	Foreign Securities	Others	Total
Argentina	52.3	15.5	2.1	20.5	6.3	0.4	2.9	100
Bolivia	67.2	32.4	0.4	0.0	0.0	0.0	0.0	100
Chile	34.6	33.2	3.8	12.4	2.6	13.4	0.0	100
Colombia	43.0	40.2	13.6	3.0	0.0	0.0	0.2	100
Costa Rica	90.3	8.8	0.0	0.0	0.9	0.0	0.0	100
El Salvador	64.6	31.7	0.0	3.7	0.0	0.0	0.0	100
Mexico	97.4	0.1	2.5	0.0	0.0	0.0	0.0	100
Peru	7.1	39.3	15.4	37.1	0.6	0.0	0.5	100
Uruguay	60.1	36.0	1.9	0.0	0.0	0.0	2.0	100

Source: Authors' calculations based on data supplied by the Asociación Internacional de Organismos de Supervisión de Fondos de Pensiones (AIOS, the International Association of Pension Fund Supervisors), Superintendencia Bancaria de Colombia (the Superintendent of Banks of Colombia), and Banco Central de Colombia (the Central Bank of Colombia).

Note: Government securities include all sovereign obligations including central bank and treasury paper. Corporate bonds are obligations of the non-financial private sector and includes certificates of deposit issued by such entities. Financial institutions include bonds and certificates of deposit issued by financial institutions, cash deposits of pension funds with the banking sector, and mortgage securities. Investment funds include investments by pension funds in mutual funds and other pooled investment vehicles that, in turn, manage those assets. Foreign securities include all foreign assets denominated in foreign currency. Investments in assets denominated in foreign currency but issued by domestic issuers are included in their respective categories and are not considered foreign assets. Others include loans by pension funds to sponsoring enterprises and contributors.

TABLE 5. Foreign Investment by Latin American Pension Funds

	Chile		Argentina	
Year	Amount (US$M)	Percent of Portfolio	Amount (US$M)	Percent of Portfolio
1991	0	0	—	—
1992	0	0.0	—	—
1993	95.7	0.6	—	—
1994	200.7	0.9	0.4	0.1
1995	50.3	0.2	18.2	0.7
1996	146.9	0.5	8.5	0.2
1997	368.7	1.1	32.9	0.4
1998	1,753.6	5.6	28.9	0.3
1999	4,623.1	13.4	67.2	0.4

Source: Authors' calculations using data from pension fund regulators.

Focusing on regulations governing foreign investments, only three Latin countries — Argentina, Chile, and Peru — permitted investment abroad by pension funds at the end of 1999, and even here at levels much lower than either those prevalent in developed countries or levels that would follow from the relative weight of these countries in a global portfolio.[10] In Chile, foreign investment was first allowed in 1992, at three percent of the portfolio. This limit was subsequently raised to nine percent in 1995, 12 percent in 1997, and 20 percent in 1999. Each time, the full allowance could be invested in foreign fixed income securities, but only half could be invested in foreign equities. Meanwhile, Argentina has restricted this level to 10 percent since the system's inception. Again, while the full allowance could be invested in foreign bonds, only a maximum of seven percent could be invested in foreign equity. In Peru, pension funds have recently been allowed to invest up to one percent of their portfolio abroad. In terms of actual investments, only Argentine and Chilean pension funds have invested in foreign assets (see Table 5). While Chilean pension funds began investing in foreign assets in 1993, their role in the overall portfolio was minimal until 1998 and became more substantial in 1999, with over 13 percent of assets being invested abroad. One reason for this large recent increase in Chilean pension funds' interest in international assets is the poor performance of domestic markets during the East Asian and Brazilian crises. Argentine pension funds still invest a very small fraction of assets overseas.

Other countries contemplate investment abroad in their pension legislation but, as was true in Peru until recently, the relevant central bank or other regulatory authority did not permit such investments. This is true in Colombia and Bolivia, where for instance in Colombia, the limit is set at 10 percent, while in Bolivia the law permits investment of between 10 and 30 percent of the portfolio in foreign securities. In fact, in neither of these countries have

TABLE 6. Maximum Portfolio Limits for Selected Latin American Pension Funds (Year-End 1999)

	Argentina	Chile	Peru	Colombia	Mexico	Uruguay	El Salvador
Government Securities	50	50	40	50	100	Min 50	100
Corporate Bonds	40	45	40	20	35	25	30
Financial Institutions/Deposits	28	50	40	50	10	30	40
Equities	35	37	35	30	0	25	5
Investment Mutual Funds	14	10	15	5	0	0	0
Foreign Securities	10	20	1	0	0	0	0
Hedging Instruments	2	9	5	5	0	0	0

Source: Authors' calculations based on data supplied by pension fund regulators.
Note: Columns do not need to sum to 100 percent as not all limits are simultaneously binding. Limits imposed by regulators and may differ from limits set by law. Government securities include all sovereign obligations including central bank and treasury paper. Corporate bonds are obligations of the non-financial private sector and includes certificates of deposit issued by such entities. Financial institutions includes bonds and certificates of deposit issued by financial institutions, cash deposits of pension funds with the banking sector, and mortgage securities. Equities are self-explanatory. Investment funds include investments by pension funds in mutual funds and other pooled investment vehicles that, in turn, manage those assets. Foreign securities include all foreign assets denominated in foreign currency. Investments in assets denominated in foreign currency but issued by domestic issuers are included in their respective categories and are not considered foreign assets. Hedging instruments are derivatives such as futures and forward contracts.

foreign assets actually been permitted in the pension funds. The other Latin countries with mandatory pension fund systems, Mexico, Uruguay, and El Salvador, do not contemplate foreign investment in their pension legislation.

While foreign investment has been controversial in some developed countries, for some of the same reasons as those currently being advanced in emerging markets, these limits have been liberalized over time. For example, in OECD countries that do have statutory limits on foreign investments, the ceiling is usually above 20 percent (see Table 7).

Modeling the Gains from Diversification

To explore further the potential gains from international portfolio diversification by Latin American pension funds, we first study the issue of diversification from domestic to international markets in general. Next we examine pension funds in the three countries that have the longest histories of operating national mandatory private pension funds in the region, namely Argentina, Chile, and Peru. We use stock market indices as a measure of overall stock market performance and construct different portfolios and

TABLE 7. Limits on International Investments by Pension Funds in OECD
Countries

Prudent person

Austria, Australia, Ireland, the Netherlands, New Zealand, UK, U.S.	(no limits)
Iceland	no foreign investments by public-sector funds
Japan	no limits for Employees Pension Funds
Spain	no limits in other OECD countries

Asset limits

Belgium	no investments in non-EU countries
Canada	30% limit
Czech Republic	no investments outside OECD countries
Denmark	20% limit.
Finland	20% in other EU states; maximum 5% in non-EU countries; there is also a minimum currency-matching requirement of 80%.
France	no foreign assets (insured funds)
Germany	maximum 20% in foreign assets overall; maximum 6% in non-EU equities, 6% in non-EU bonds; there is also a minimum currency-matching requirement of 80%.
Greece	maximum 20% in domestically based mutual funds, which in turn can invest abroad
Hungary	mandatory pension funds: 0% in 1999, increasing to 30% by Jan 1, 2002; voluntary pension funds: 20%; the ratio of investment in non-OECD countries shall not exceed 30% of all foreign investment.
Italy	50% limit on debt and equity securities of OECD countries traded in regulated markets; 5% limit on debt and equity securities of non-OECD countries traded in regulated markets; debt and equity securities of non-OECD countries traded in non-regulated market are prohibited.
Korea	10% limit
Luxembourg	10% in non-OECD countries
Mexico	no foreign investment
Norway	no limits
Portugal	20% limit
Poland	5% limit on foreign assets
Sweden	5–10% limit, depending on type of fund and assets concerned
Switzerland	30% global limit: 30% in foreign bonds, 25% in foreign equities, 5% in property

Source: Srinivas, Whitehouse, and Yermo (1999), Laboul (1998), OECD (1998).
Note: Investment by pension funds is not regulated in Turkey. Restrictions placed on international investments by pension funds in countries that are members of the Organization for Economic Cooperation and Development (OECD). The prevalent regulatory regimes in the countries are divided into two types. First, "Prudent person" regulation is similar to that in the United States, where there are few explicit limits on asset allocation. The second type of regulatory regime is one in which countries impose explicit asset allocation limits, usually in percentage terms, on pension fund investments.

assess their performance in a mean-variance framework. For individual countries, we use country indices from the Emerging Markets Database (2000 version) of the Standard & Poor's Corporation (S&P). These indices provide a good measure of the investment opportunities available to domestic investors in equity markets. For developed countries we use two measures: the Standard & Poor's 500 (S&P 500) index as a measure of U.S. equity market returns, and the Morgan Stanley Capital International Europe, Australia, and Far East (MSCI EAFE) index as a measure of developed-market equity returns (excluding the U.S.).[11] We also use the International Finance Corporation Latin America Investible (IFCI) returns index as a measure of investment opportunities available to U.S. investors when considering investments in the region. All data are given in terms of monthly total returns, except for the MSCI EAFE where only monthly price returns are available for the relevant time frame. We use data for each country since the inception of the respective series. For Argentina, the IFC index of monthly equity market returns is available from January 1979; for Brazil, Chile, and Mexico the corresponding starting date is January 1976 and for Peru it is January 1993. All data series end in December 1999. Corresponding to these dates, we use monthly data for the S&P 500 and the MSCI EAFE indices to construct portfolios.

Pension fund returns in Argentina, Chile, and Peru are obtained from annual reports of the pension funds and regulators in various countries, from their websites, and through personal communications. Monthly total return data are used for all countries, gross of pension fund administrative expenses.[12] Argentine pension fund return data are available from August 1994, Chilean data from January 1982, and Peruvian data from August 1993. Corresponding to these dates, we use monthly data for the S&P 500 and the MSCI EAFE indices to construct portfolios. All returns and standard deviations are calculated in the local currency of each country, since this is the relevant measure for a domestic investor. Throughout the analysis, we assume that investors are only interested in returns in their respective currencies and do not use instruments to hedge currency risk. Therefore, we abstract from currency hedging issues.[13] Since both the S&P 500 and MSCI EAFE returns are available in U.S. dollars, we convert these returns to local currency for each country using month-end exchange rates. From monthly returns, we obtain annual arithmetic returns by averaging across monthly returns and multiplying by twelve.

Emerging market financial data pose unique problems, and it is useful to keep these in mind while interpreting our results. While we have tried to use data for each country ever since these became available, some series are still too short to provide complete comfort in making inferences. The use of monthly data only partly mitigates this problem. Emerging stock markets are also very volatile and face frequent structural shocks, often as a result of shocks to the macroeconomy. While short data samples are unlikely to capture longer term trends, longer samples can put too much weight on old trends that may have been radically altered by structural shocks.

International Equity Investment: The Perspective of a U.S. Investor

To lay out our methodological approach, it is useful to first examine the case of a U.S. investor examining alternative diversification avenues for his equity portfolio. This analysis sheds light on the ongoing debate over the benefits of international diversification by U.S. investors that can then be compared with emerging market investors. To this end we construct alternate portfolios for a U.S. investor and examine the effect of diversification into emerging markets and other developed markets. The measure of benefits of diversification that we use is return per unit of risk or the *Sharpe ratio*. This measure is constructed as the arithmetic average of monthly returns divided by the standard deviation of monthly returns over the time period of interest. We examine portfolios that have incremental amounts of international assets: for example, we start with a U.S. investor investing his assets fully in the S&P 500 index with zero percent foreign assets, and then adjust from there. A first alternate portfolio has 90 percent allocation to the S&P 500 and 10 percent to the MSCI EAFE; the next has 20 percent invested in the MSCI EAFE, and so forth until the last portfolio constructed has 100 percent of its assets invested in the MSCI EAFE. For diversification into emerging markets, we consider a U.S. investor investing in Latin markets and measure returns and risk using the IFCI Latin America index.[14]

Looking first at diversification into other developed markets, we examine the argument as to whether benefits of diversification have declined as argued in recent literature. Table 8 shows that there is a clear trend of increasing returns per unit of risk to U.S. investors investing in other developed economies during 1976–89 (Panel A). International investments provided better risk-adjusted returns at all levels of foreign investment, as indicated by the monotonic increase in the Sharpe ratio. In practice, U.S. investors invested a relatively small fraction of their portfolio in international assets, but the trend of increasing returns per unit of risk is in line with the arguments presented in early literature that international diversification is beneficial.

The IFCI Latin America index was not available during this period, so no conclusion can be reached for diversification into emerging markets. However, Panel B indicates why the more recent evidence suggests that the benefits of international diversification are dropping for U.S. investors. During 1990–99, the flat or declining Sharpe ratios for all levels of diversification into both emerging markets and other developed countries implies that U.S. markets provided the highest levels of risk-adjusted returns during this period. Actual returns may have been higher in other markets, but they

TABLE 8. Impact of International Diversification on Risk Adjusted Returns

Percentage of Foreign Assets	United States		Argentina		Brazil		Chile		Mexico		Peru	
	IFCI	EAFE	S&P 500	EAFE	S&P 500	EAFE	S&P 500	EAFE	S&P 500	EAFE	S&P 500	EAFE
A.												
0	N/A	0.20	0.46	0.46	0.55	0.55	0.43	0.43	0.42	0.42	N/A	N/A
10	N/A	0.22	0.49	0.49	0.59	0.59	0.45	0.46	0.45	0.45	N/A	N/A
20	N/A	0.24	0.52	0.52	0.64	0.64	0.49	0.49	0.48	0.49	N/A	N/A
30	N/A	0.26	0.55	0.55	0.69	0.69	0.52	0.53	0.51	0.52	N/A	N/A
40	N/A	0.27	0.58	0.58	0.74	0.75	0.56	0.58	0.54	0.55	N/A	N/A
50	N/A	0.29	0.61	0.61	0.80	0.81	0.59	0.63	0.55	0.57	N/A	N/A
60	N/A	0.31	0.63	0.64	0.85	0.87	0.62	0.68	0.54	0.57	N/A	N/A
70	N/A	0.32	0.64	0.65	0.90	0.92	0.63	0.72	0.52	0.55	N/A	N/A
80	N/A	0.33	0.64	0.65	0.92	0.96	0.61	0.73	0.49	0.52	N/A	N/A
90	N/A	0.33	0.63	0.64	0.92	0.97	0.56	0.70	0.45	0.48	N/A	N/A
100	N/A	0.33	0.60	0.61	0.90	0.96	0.49	0.63	0.40	0.44	N/A	N/A

B.

0	0.33	0.33	0.18	0.18	0.62	0.62	0.31	0.31	0.32	0.32	0.24	0.24
10	0.33	0.31	0.19	0.18	0.65	0.64	0.33	0.32	0.34	0.33	0.27	0.26
20	0.32	0.30	0.19	0.18	0.68	0.67	0.35	0.33	0.38	0.35	0.30	0.29
30	0.31	0.28	0.19	0.18	0.71	0.69	0.38	0.34	0.41	0.37	0.34	0.31
40	0.29	0.26	0.19	0.18	0.74	0.72	0.40	0.34	0.44	0.38	0.39	0.34
50	0.27	0.23	0.19	0.18	0.77	0.74	0.43	0.34	0.47	0.38	0.44	0.37
60	0.25	0.21	0.19	0.17	0.79	0.76	0.45	0.33	0.48	0.38	0.50	0.40
70	0.24	0.18	0.19	0.17	0.81	0.78	0.47	0.31	0.48	0.36	0.57	0.44
80	0.22	0.15	0.19	0.16	0.83	0.78	0.46	0.28	0.46	0.33	0.62	0.46
90	0.21	0.13	0.19	0.16	0.83	0.78	0.45	0.24	0.43	0.30	0.64	0.48
100	0.20	0.11	0.19	0.15	0.82	0.77	0.42	0.20	0.39	0.26	0.62	0.48

Source: Authors' calculations based on data provided by Bloomberg and Standard & Poor's Emerging Market Database (2000 version), as well as personal communication with Morgan Stanley Capital International.

Note: Returns per unit of risk for investors in six countries for different percentages of foreign equities holdings. Panel A covers 1976–89 and Panel B, 1990–99. The first row in each panel is the return per unit of risk that an investor obtained holding a purely domestic equity portfolio (S&P 500 for United States investors and the respective country index of the International Finance Corporation (IFC) for other countries). Subsequent rows represent portfolios formed in increments of 10% of two foreign assets — the IFC Investable (IFCI) Latin America Index and the Europe, Far East and Australia (EAFE) index of Morgan Stanley Capital International for United States investors and the S&P 500 and EAFE for investors in other countries. Arithmetic average monthly returns and standard deviations are calculated in the local currency of each country, the ratio of which gives the return per unit of risk.

were accompanied by higher-than-proportionate levels of risk for which investors were not adequately compensated.

In a mean-variance framework, the first panel of Figure 2 shows the performance of various portfolios during 1990–99 from the perspective of a U.S. investor.[15] Beginning with a portfolio entirely invested in the S&P 500, the curve going from left to right tracks the risk and return of a combined portfolio of the S&P 500 and the IFCI Latin America index. Each subsequent point in the curve represents an increase of 10 percentage points in the share of the IFCI index in the portfolio. As the weight of the IFCI index is increased, both the average return and the volatility of the portfolio rise. The last data point, on the extreme right, is the risk and return of a portfolio invested fully in Latin American equities; it is easy to see that the risk increases proportionately much more than the return. From top to bottom, the curve tracks the performance of a portfolio of the S&P 500 and the MSCI EAFE. This portfolio has quite different characteristics from the one just discussed. As the weight of the MSCI EAFE rises in the portfolio (i.e. going down the curve), both average return and volatility fall. The minimum volatility portfolio is obtained at about 40 percent of investment in developed markets outside the U.S. However, as shown in Table 8 above, return per unit of risk is highest for the 100 percent S&P 500 portfolio, in line with the performance of the U.S. equity markets over this period.

Similar analysis has been used by researchers to justify why diversification into foreign securities offers limited benefits, from a U.S. investor's perspective. Investment in emerging markets during the 1990s would have led to only slightly higher returns than could be obtained at home, and at a very high cost in terms of portfolio volatility. Meanwhile, investment in the more developed markets of the world could have reduced volatility, but similar risk reductions could have also been achieved via investment in the United States domestic bond markets without necessarily having to invest abroad.[16]

International Equity Investment: The Latin American Perspective

We now turn the case of Latin American investors, so as to evaluate the performance of equity portfolios of Latin investors as the share of foreign assets held in their portfolio is increased. We focus on investors in five countries: Argentina, Brazil, Chile, Mexico, and Peru. These countries are selected for two reasons. First, these are the only countries with reasonably long time series of equity market data. Second, all have private pension funds; in the next section, we shall explore the performance of the funds in the first three countries.

We consider diversification by investors in these countries into U.S. markets (measured by the S&P 500 index) and into developed markets outside the U.S. (measured by the MSCI EAFE index). These are selected because

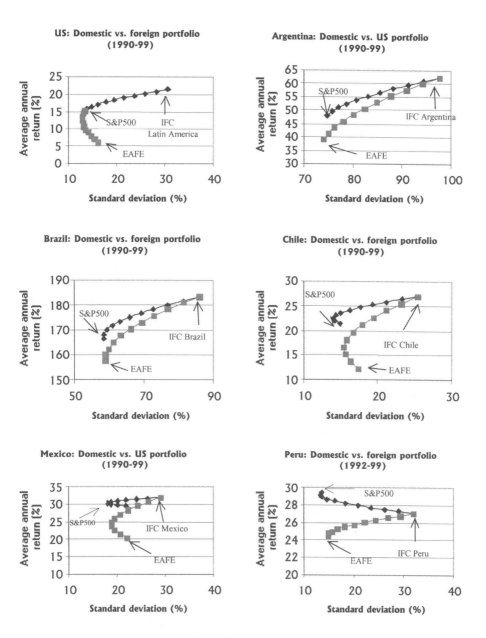

Figure 2. Impact of international diversification on risk and return: equity average return and risk. Source: Authors' calculations using data provided by Standard & Poor's Emerging Market Database (2000) version, Bloomberg, Morgan Stanley Capital International, and pension fund regulators. Note: Investors in each country begin by holding a portfolio consisting entirely of domestic assets and diversify into two foreign portfolios as indicated. All returns and standard deviations are in the domestic currency of the investor and calculated monthly and reported annually.

investments in developed countries are likely to be of primary interest to investors in emerging markets, especially when they are in the early stages of international diversification. In addition, the U.S. has the largest single equity market in the world, and hence it is a natural first choice for many emerging market investors. Data are used for the longest time period for which they are available: 1976–99 for Brazil, Chile, and Mexico, 1976–99 for Argentina, and 1993–99 for Peru. The analysis is undertaken in both a risk-adjusted returns (Sharpe ratios) format and a mean-variance framework, as in the case of the U.S. investor, above.

Table 8 displays results for the risk-adjusted returns that could have been obtained by investors in these countries. Similar to the U.S. case, two time periods are considered: pre-1990, and 1990–99. Portfolio returns and standard deviations are measured in the domestic currency of the respective country. Panel A of Table 8 indicates that during the pre-1990 period, investors in all countries (except Peru, where pre-1990 data were not available) would have benefited in terms of higher risk-adjusted returns by diversifying either into the S&P 500 or the MSCI EAFE index. The Sharpe ratio for portfolios containing international assets goes up for all countries. Argentine and Brazilian investors would have obtained much higher returns per unit of risk taken by investing their entire portfolios abroad. Brazilian investors obtained a return of 0.55 percent per year per unit of risk taken (standard deviation) by investing entirely in the portfolio of Brazilian equities represented by the IFC Brazilian index. By investing half of their portfolio in the S&P 500 and the other half in Brazilian assets, they would have obtained 0.8 percent per annum per unit of risk taken. For Chilean and Mexican investors, the Sharpe ratio increases up to some level of investment in foreign assets and then declines, indicating that while they would also have benefited from international diversification, they should have held some part of their portfolios in domestic equities. The evidence is broadly similar for the 1990–99 period (Panel B of Table 8), although the evidence is weak for Argentine investors. During the 1990s, Peruvian investors would have obtained higher returns per unit of risk by investing their entire portfolios abroad.

The last five panels of Figure 2 show the effect that international diversification would have had for investors in the five countries during 1990–99, using a mean-variance framework.[17] The construction methodology of the curves in the panels is the same as that described above. It is clear that for all countries except Peru, the highest returns were available only in the domestic equity markets, but these high returns came at the cost of high return volatility. The latter could have been reduced by investing internationally. Examining the fifth panel of Figure 2, for example, we find that investors holding their entire portfolio in Mexican equities during the period would have obtained a return of about 32 percent per year with a standard deviation of returns of about 29 percent. But by investing about 30 percent of their assets in the S&P 500 and holding the balance in domestic equities, returns in local currency would have been about 31 percent, with much lower standard deviation of returns of about 21 percent. In terms of returns per unit of risk, therefore, investors would have benefited from international diversification. Even more striking is the case of Peru, where over the period 1993–99, domestic investors would have obtained a "free lunch" by investing in the S&P 500 index with higher average return and lower standard deviation.

An important issue to be kept in mind here is that investors in emerging markets face risk of devaluation of their home currency. In this context long term foreign currency denominated assets can provide a natural hedge against the risk of devaluation. While the breakdown of overall foreign asset returns into those due to currency and those due to the performance of the underlying assets is beyond the scope of this chapter, there is no doubt that an analysis along these lines would yield greater insights into different sources of portfolio risk and enable investors to develop appropriate management tools for these risks.

The International Investment Behavior of Latin American Pension Funds

The financial evidence makes a case for international diversification of equity portfolios by Latin American investors; next we ask how pension fund returns in three Latin American countries would have changed had they invested abroad. Similar to our previous analyses, we examine diversification of pension funds into the U.S. equity market with returns measured by the S&P 500 index and other non-U.S. developed markets with returns measured by the MSCI EAFE index.

We start with the realized mean and standard deviation of returns of industry-wide pension fund portfolios in the three countries — Chile, Argentina, and Peru — since inception to year-end 1999. Srinivas and Yermo (1999) show that for each of the three countries of interest, individual pension fund portfolios and returns are not significantly different from the industry-wide average and therefore the latter portfolio is representative of individual pension fund portfolios. Monthly mean returns of industry-wide pension fund portfolios for each country are obtained by weighting the returns of each pension fund with the assets under its management. For Chile, where the longest data series is available (1982–99), we break up the series into pre-1990 and 1990–99 in order to examine differences in performance across these time periods.

We then ask how these pension funds would have been affected under alternate assumptions regarding investments in international equities. We construct alternate hypothetical portfolios for pension funds by combining their existing portfolios with different proportions of foreign investments, keeping the domestic asset allocation constant in proportional terms. This construction assumes that pension funds had an "optimal" asset allocation to domestic assets and therefore would make changes only at the margin if international assets were made available to them. Therefore, the results should be interpreted as those generated by a "marginal" change analysis. This construction allows us to focus on the issue of impact of international diversification as a risk management tool by pension funds, and to abstract from conjectures regarding what domestic asset allocation pension funds would have selected, if they also considered investing in international assets. In practice, of course, allocations to both domestic and international assets would be jointly determined using some form of an asset allocation model.

The patterns of returns per unit of risk under alternative assumptions regarding foreign investment appear in Table 9. One result is that during Chile's pension system's early days (pre-1990), higher risk-adjusted returns could not have been obtained by pension funds by investing abroad. The Chilean plans obtained extremely high risk-adjusted returns in comparison to all other markets (Table 8). This tends to support the view that the Chilean government worked to ensure that pension funds would obtain high returns at a low level of risk. In order to achieve this, the government provided the pension funds with access to government bonds that produced high rates of return. Stringent asset-allocation restrictions ensured that government bonds were often the largest asset class in which pension funds invested. This behavior on policymakers' parts is sometimes justified on the grounds that it is necessary to build the credibility of privatized social security systems. Over time, as the Chilean private pension system established itself, returns on domestic government bonds fell, and the pension funds were allowed to take on more risks and invest in a broader range of assets. During this process, opportunities for risk management by investing abroad increased. As a result, Chilean pensions would have obtained higher returns per unit of risk by investing a portion of their assets abroad during 1990–99, as indicated by the increase in ratios for investment up to almost about 40 percent of the portfolio in the S&P 500 and 10 percent for the EAFE index. The impact of the S&P 500 is much higher largely due to the stellar performance of the US equity market in the 1990s.

Similar results hold for Argentina and Peru. We reiterate that this analysis represents the impact of marginal changes rather than one where an asset allocation model is used to arrive at an optimal portfolio. Hence we do not suggest that any particular level of investment in foreign assets would be justified using this analysis. We do, nevertheless, find strong indication that pension fund risks could be better managed if the entire universe of investment opportunities were considered, including foreign assets.

Figure 3 shows the impact of increasing levels of international equity holdings on pension fund portfolios during the 1990s in a mean-variance framework, using construction methodology similar to that described above. Here

TABLE 9. Impact of International Diversification on Risk-Adjusted Returns of Pension Funds

Percentage of foreign assets in portfolio	Chile				Argentina		Peru	
	S&P 500 1982–89	EAFE 1982–89	S&P 500 1990–99	EAFE 1990–99	S&P 500 1994–99	EAFE 1994–99	S&P 500 1993–99	EAFE 1993–99
0	1.84	1.84	0.77	0.77	0.43	0.43	0.89	0.89
10	1.68	1.81	0.85	0.79	0.48	0.43	1.03	0.92
20	1.38	1.59	0.89	0.75	0.53	0.42	1.09	0.90
30	1.12	1.34	0.87	0.67	0.55	0.41	1.05	0.82
40	0.94	1.15	0.81	0.57	0.57	0.39	0.97	0.74
50	0.81	1.00	0.73	0.48	0.56	0.36	0.88	0.65
60	0.71	0.89	0.64	0.40	0.55	0.34	0.79	0.58
70	0.64	0.81	0.57	0.33	0.53	0.32	0.72	0.52
80	0.58	0.74	0.51	0.28	0.51	0.29	0.67	0.48
90	0.53	0.69	0.46	0.24	0.49	0.27	0.62	0.44
100	0.50	0.65	0.42	0.20	0.47	0.25	0.58	0.40

Source: Authors' calculations based on data provided by Bloomberg and Standard & Poor's Emerging Market Database (2000 version), as well as personal communication with Morgan Stanley Capital International.

Note: Returns per unit of risk for pension fund portfolios in three Latin American countries with the oldest private pension fund industries, for different percentages of foreign equity holdings. As Chile has the longest data series, two sub-sets of data are examined — 1982–1989 and 1990–99. Monthly returns across all pension funds in each country, obtained by weighting the return of each pension fund with the assets under management are used. The first row in each panel is the return per unit of risk that the pension funds in the country actually obtained. Subsequent rows represent portfolios formed in increments of 10% of two foreign assets — the Standard and Poor's 500 index (S&P 500) and the Europe, Far East and Australia (EAFE) index of Morgan Stanley Capital International. While investing in these foreign assets, pension funds are assumed to be investing the rest of their assets according to the same asset allocation that they actually had. Arithmetic average monthly returns and standard deviations of each portfolio is calculated in the local currency of each country, the ratio of which gives the return per unit of risk.

Peru: (1993-99)

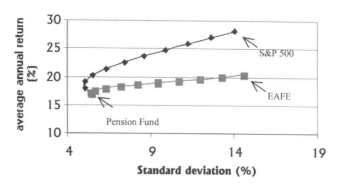

Argentina: (1994-99)

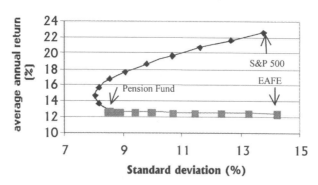

Chile: (1990-99)

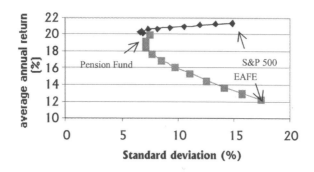

it is clear that pension funds in all countries took relatively low levels of risk. It is particularly revealing to compare the location of the risk and return point of the pension fund portfolios with the corresponding performance of the domestic equity market (Figure 2). Pension fund portfolios in all countries achieved substantially lower levels of risk than the domestic equity markets and proportionately higher levels of return. But Figure 3 also shows that Latin American pension funds would have benefited by investing internationally. Not surprisingly, the analysis shows that pension funds in all three countries could have benefited by investing in the S&P 500 during the 1990s. Peruvian pension funds would have benefited by investing in the other developed markets also as measured by the MSCI EAFE, while non-U.S. markets were not as attractive to Argentine and Chilean pension funds.

These results, together with earlier evidence, indicate that Latin pension funds would gain from investing abroad in terms of higher returns per unit of risk. Consequently, international investment would be a sound risk management strategy. Although these analyses focus on pension systems in Argentina, Chile, and Peru because of data limitations, it is likely that other countries such as Bolivia, El Salvador, Mexico, and Uruguay would also have large gains from diversification into developed markets. By not undertaking such investments, these pension funds have implicitly imposed costs on their stakeholders in terms of lost returns and higher risks.

Given these benefits, Latin pension funds would be expected to exploit these benefits. But in Chile and Argentina, the two countries permitting such investments during the second half of the 1990s, pension funds largely shunned foreign markets until recently. Restrictions on foreign investment regulations in both countries were not binding up to the end of 1999, as the actual investments were far below the permitted levels. Why was this the case?

One possible explanation for low levels of foreign investments could simply be a case of "home bias" for Latin American pension funds, a bias that might gradually erode over time. Pension funds in some OECD countries have been shown to have much lower levels of foreign investments than would be optimal in a mean-variance framework, and home bias has been

---

Figure 3. Impact of international investments on pension fund returns. Source: Authors' calculations using data provided by Standard & Poor's Emerging Market Database (2000) version), Bloomberg, Morgan Stanley Capital International, and pension fund regulators. Note: The figure shows the impact of international equity investment on portfolio returns of pension funds in three Latin American countries. Funds in each country begin by holding the same portfolio they actually did, indicated by the point marked "Pension Fund." Funds are then allowed to hold increasing percentages of two foreign portfolios, indicated by the S&P and EAFE curves. All returns and standard deviations are in domestic currency and calculated monthly and reported annually.

documented to be a major reason as to why pension funds prefer to stay at home among developed countries (Davis, 1991; OECD 1998). Chilean pension funds do seem to be overcoming this home bias in recent years, as they boost their international asset exposure. It is more difficult to explain the lack of interest in international investments shown by Argentine pension funds, given the large gains that could have been obtained during the late 1990s.

Home bias might be exacerbated in these countries by regulations that constrain the ability of individual investors to choose pension funds that offer them the most suitable combination of risk and return (Srinivas and Yermo 1999). In the three Latin countries examined here, each pension fund manager is required to offer only one fund.[18] Furthermore, returns to the funds are subject to strict profitability rules.[19] As a result, pension asset portfolios tend to be quite similar across pension funds and contributors are constrained from selecting diversified portfolios. In particular, relative rate of return rules may create inertia in investment management strategies and make international diversification more costly for any given fund. Even if some funds in the industry were to obtain significantly better returns by investing abroad, they are still required to deposit part of the gains (the return above the maximum of a band around the industry average) into a "reserve fund" that can be drawn down in case of future poor performance. This implies that neither pension funds nor contributors benefit fully in the short run from higher returns. And pension fund managers are immediately penalized in the event of poor performance: they are required to make up shortfalls either from the "reserve fund" or from its capital, if performance is below the minimum of the band. Latin pension funds therefore have strong incentives to "follow the leader" and ensure that their investments generate the industry average return. If one of the large pension funds does not invest abroad for any reason, it is very likely that the industry equilibrium is one where the whole industry does not do so either.

Conclusion and Discussion

International diversification of investment portfolios has been recommended for pension funds in developed country markets, and it has also been shown here to benefit Latin American investors. Contributors to pension funds could have obtained higher risk adjusted returns had pension funds invested abroad. When these benefits are not taken advantage of, costs are imposed on pension fund stakeholders, be they workers, retirees, or taxpayers. International diversification is especially important for countries with a limited supply of liquid domestic financial instruments, and for those with unstable macroeconomic conditions. The presence of the latter without the former may significantly reduce the attractiveness of domestic pension fund returns.

The lesson of this research for policymakers and pension fund managers is that costs are imposed on contributors, in terms of higher risks per unit of return, when foreign investments by national defined contribution pension plans are restricted. Furthermore, those countries that currently do permit international investment need to take a closer look at all features of their regulatory framework to identify constraints imposed on the ability of pension fund managers to invest abroad and to explore ways to relax these constraints. Prudential management of pension assets via diversification of pension fund portfolios must take into account contributors' interests in bearing an optimal mix of risk and return.

Notes

The authors thank Robert Holzmann, Sudhir Krishnamurthi, David McCarthy, Olivia Mitchell, Arun Muralidhar, and T. V. Somanathan for valuable comments. Opinions expressed are solely those of the authors and not those of any institution with which they may be affiliated.

1. New funded pension systems were launched in several Latin American countries over the last two decades, including Chile (1981), Peru (1993), Argentina (1994), Colombia (1994), Uruguay (1995), Bolivia (1997), Mexico (1998), and El Salvador (1998). Some transition economies in Europe and Central Asia have also reformed their pension systems along similar lines, including Hungary (1997), Kazakhstan (1997), Poland (1999), Croatia (1999), and Latvia (2000).

2. Feldstein (1974) shows that privatization of social security would reduce distortions that payroll taxes impose on household saving and labor supply decisions. More recently, Feldstein (1998) has argued for investment of at least a portion of social security taxes through individual accounts in the capital markets. Kotlikoff (1996), among several others, supports Feldstein's conclusions. However, Geanakoplos et al. (1998 and 1999) show that the claim made by advocates of U.S. social security privatization that rates of return under a defined contribution individual account system would be much higher than under the current U.S. social security system is inaccurate.

3. See Markowitz (1959), Sharpe (1964), Lessard (1973, 1974), Adler and Dumas (1975), Dumas (1993), Solnik (1991), and Claessens (1994) for discussions of various aspects of portfolio theory and applications to international diversification.

4. Agmon (1972), Grubel (1968), Grauer and Hakansson (1987), and Levy and Sarnat (1970), among others, find that international diversification is beneficial for developed countries in terms of reducing portfolio risk and/or enhancing portfolio return. This literature tends to rely mainly on a low measured correlation between returns on international equity markets. Solnik (1974) shows that the variance of returns of a portfolio of randomly selected U.S. stocks is higher than that of a portfolio of U.S. and international stocks.

5. An example is the inability of financial models to anticipate the impact of events such as the Mexican devaluation in 1994/95 or that of the East Asian crisis in 1997/98.

6. Personal communication with some large U.S. pension funds.

7. Discussions in the legislatures of El Salvador, Chile, Mexico, and Uruguay along these lines ensured that the privatized pension funds would not invest abroad. Chile has since relaxed the rules, but international investments are still not allowed in the other countries.

8. Investment in domestic stocks is another venue for diversification. However, this may be difficult in several countries in the region due to the relatively small size of equity markets and the large size of pension funds as compared to the market capitalization. Stock and bond returns have also been shown to be highly correlated in most emerging markets, reducing the gains from diversification.

9. A similar behavior has been observed among pension funds in Singapore (Holzmann, 2000b).

10. In September 1999, Latin America as a whole formed just 28.29 percent of the International Finance Corporation (IFC)'s Global Emerging Market Index. Individual country weights for the large countries were Argentina (2.71 percent), Brazil (8.17 percent), Chile (4.70 percent), and Mexico (10.85 percent). In a global portfolio including the developed countries, the weights of these countries would, of course, be substantially lower. This implies that in order to hold a truly "world portfolio," much more than the allowed level of investments would have to be made abroad by investors in these countries.

11. Data on the S&P 500 and MSCI EAFE were provided to the authors by Bloomberg and MSCI, for which we are grateful.

12. To subtract administrative costs, we would need to develop a full actuarial and economic model combining demographic and market return assumptions, an exercise beyond the scope of the present paper. For more on administrative cost estimates see Mitchell (1999).

13. It is clear that both the mean and variance of currency return play an important role in international diversification. To the extent that hedging instruments are available for currency risk management, it may be the case that investors would benefit from hedging their currency exposure. In many emerging markets, including those being examined here, long term hedging instruments either do not exist, or they have come into existence very recently. Hence our focus on unhedged returns is reasonable.

14. Allowing the U.S. investor to diversify into a portfolio of all emerging market stocks, as opposed to just Latin America, does not materially affect our results.

15. Similar figures for earlier time periods are available from the authors.

16. Analysis of this issue is not reported here but is available from the authors.

17. Figures for the earlier period are available from the authors.

18. Chile introduced new legislation at the end of 1999 that allows the establishment of a new fund, invested exclusively in fixed income securities. In countries like Mexico, Bolivia, and El Salvador, where pension assets are invested exclusively in government bonds, an equivalent reform would be to introduce an internationally diversified fund.

19. Similar regulations exist in other Latin American countries; only Mexico and Bolivia do not impose rate of return regulations.

References

Adler, Michael and Bernard Dumas. 1975. "Optimal International Acquisitions." *Journal of Finance* 30, 1: 1–20.
Adrangi, Bahram and Todd M. Shank. 1998. "Co-movement, Causality, and Diversification Benefits in International Equity Markets." *Journal of Foreign Exchange and International Finance* 12, 4: 297–312.
Agmon, Tamir. 1972. "The Relationship Among Equity Markets: A Study of Share Price Co-movements in the United States, United Kingdom, Germany, and Japan." *Journal of Finance* 27, 4: 839–55.

Baxter, Marianne and Robert G. King. 2001. "The Role of International Investment in a Privatized Social Security System." In *Risk Aspects of Investment-Based Social Security Reform,* ed. John Y. Campbell and Martin S. Feldstein. Chicago: University of Chicago Press.

Bekaert, Gert, Claude B. Erb, Campbell R. Harvey, and Tadas E. Viskanata. 1998. "Distributional Characteristics of Emerging Market Returns and Asset Allocation." *Journal of Portfolio Management* 24 (Winter): 102–16.

Blommenstein, Hans J. 1998. "Aging-Induced Capital Flows to Emerging Markets Do Not Solve OECD's Basic Pension Problem." In *Institutional Investors in the New Financial Landscape,* ed. Hans J. Blommenstein and Norbert Funke. Paris: OECD. 349–62.

Claessens, Constantijn. 1994. "Assessing Investment Potential and Security Design." In *Investing in Emerging Markets,* ed. Michael J. Howell. London: Euromoney Publications PLC. 104–15.

Corsetti, Giancarlo and Klaus Schmidt-Hebbel. 1995. "Pension Reform and Growth." Policy Research Paper 1471. Washington, DC: World Bank.

Davis, E. Philip. 1991. "International Diversification of Institutional Investors." Bank of England Technical Series of Discussion Papers. London: Bank of England.

Diamond, Peter A. 1998. "The Economics of Social Security Reform." NBER Working Paper 6719.

Dumas, Bernard. 1993. "Partial-Equilibrium Versus General-Equilibrium Models of International Capital Market Equilibrium." NBER Working Paper 4446.

Errunza, Vihang, Ked Hogan, and Mao-Wei Hung, 1999. "Can the Gain from International Diversification Be Achieved Without Trading Abroad?" *Journal of Finance* 54, 6: 2075–2107.

Feldstein, Martin S. 1974. "Social Security, Induced Retirement, and Aggregate Capital Accumulation." *Journal of Political Economy* 82, 5: 905–26.

———, ed. 1998. *Privatizing Social Security.* Chicago: University of Chicago Press.

Fischer, Bernard and Helmut Reisen. 1994. *Pension Fund Investment from Aging to Emerging Markets.* OECD Development Centre Policy Brief 9. Paris: OECD.

Fontaine, Juan Andres. 1997. "Are There (Good) Macroeconomic Reasons for Limiting External Investments by Pension Funds? The Chilean Experience." In *The Economics of Pensions: Principles, Policies and International Experience,* ed. Salvador Valdés-Prieto. Cambridge: Cambridge University Press. 251–74.

Geanakoplos, John, Olivia S. Mitchell, and Stephen P. Zeldes. 1998. "Would a Privatized Social Security System Really Pay a Higher Rate of Return?" In *Framing the Social Security Debate: Values, Politics, and Economics,* ed. R. Douglas Arnold, Michael J. Graetz, and Alicia H. Munnell. Washington, D.C.: Brookings Institution Press. 137–56.

———. 1999. "Social Security Money's Worth." In *Prospects for Social Security Reform,* ed. Olivia S. Mitchell, Robert J. Myers, and Howard Young. Pension Research Council. Philadelphia: University of Pennsylvania Press. 79–151.

Goetzmann, William N. and Phillippe Jorion. 1999. "Global Stock Markets in the Twentieth Century." *Journal of Finance* 54: 953–80.

Grauer, Robert and Nils Hakansson. 1987. "Gains from International Diversification: 1968–1985. Returns of Portfolios of Stocks and Bonds." *Journal of Finance* 42, 3: 721–39.

Grubel, Herbert G. 1968. "Internationally Diversified Portfolios: Welfare Gains and Capital Flows." *American Economic Review* 58, 5: 1299–1314.

Holzmann, Robert. 2000a. "The World Bank Approach to Pensions Reform." *International Social Security Review* 53, 1: 11–34.

———. 2000b. "Can Investments in Emerging Markets Help to Solve the Aging Problem?" World Bank Social Policy Discussion Paper 10.

Investment Registry and Stock Exchange. 1904. "How to Protect Capital Invested in Stocks and Shares." London: Investment Registry and Stock Exchange.

Kotlikoff, Laurence J. 1996. "Privatization of Social Security: How It Works and Why It Matters." NBER Working Paper 5330. October.

Laboul, Andre. 1998. "Private Pension Systems: Regulatory Policies." Aging Working Paper 2.2. Paris: OECD.

Lessard, Donald. 1973. "International Portfolio Diversification: A Multivariate Analysis for a Group of Latin American Countries." *Journal of Finance* 28, 3: 619–33.

———. 1974. "World, National and Industry Factors in Equity Returns." *Journal of Finance* 29, 2: 379–91.

Levine, Ross and Sara Zervos. 1998. "Capital Control Liberalization and Stock Market Development: *American Economic Review* 88, 3: 537–58.

Levy, Haim and Marshall Sarnat. 1970. "International Diversification of Investment Portfolios." *American Economic Review* 60, 4: 668–75.

Longin, Francois and Bruno Solnik. 1995. "Is the Correlation in International Equity Returns Constant: 1960–1990?" *Journal of International Money and Finance* 14, 1: 3–26.

Markowitz, Harry. 1959. *Portfolio Choice: Efficient Diversification of Investments.* New York: John Wiley.

Mitchell, Olivia S. 1998. "Administrative Costs of Public and Private Pension Plans." In *Privatizing Social Security*, ed. Martin S. Feldstein. NBER. Chicago: University of Chicago Press. 403–56.

Organization for Economic Co-operation and Development (OECD). 1998. *Maintaining Prosperity in an Aging Society.* Paris: OECD.

Orszag, Peter R. and Joseph E. Stiglitz. 1999. "Rethinking Pension Reform: Ten Myths About Social Security Systems." Paper presented at a World Bank Conference on New Ideas About Old-Age Security, Washington, D.C., November.

Reisen, Helmut and John Williamson. 1997. "Pension Funds, Capital Controls, and Macroeconomic Stability." In *The Economics of Pensions: Principles, Policies and International Experience,* ed. Salvador Valdés-Prieto. Cambridge: Cambridge University Press. 227–50.

Sharpe, William F. 1964. "Capital Asset Prices: A Theory of Market Equilibrium Under Conditions of Risk." *Journal of Finance* 19, 3: 425–42.

Solnik, Bruno. 1974. "The International Pricing of Risk: An Empirical Examination of World Capital Market Structure." *Journal of Finance* 29, 2: 365–78.

———. 1991. *International Investments.* Reading, Mass.: Addison-Wesley.

Srinivas, P. S. and Juan Yermo. 1999. "Do Investment Regulations Compromise Pension Fund Performance? Evidence from Latin America." *Revista de Análisis Económico* 14, 1: 67–120.

Srinivas, P. S., Edward Whitehouse, and Juan Yermo. 1999. "Regulating Private Pension Funds' Structure, Performance and Investments: Cross-Country Evidence." Pension Primer Series. World Bank: ⟨www.worldbank.org⟩.

Contributors

B. Douglas Bernheim is Lewis and Virginia Eaton Professor of Economics at Stanford University and a Research Associate of the NBER. His research examines taxation and fiscal policy, the determinants of saving, insurance issues, and topics in mathematical economics. He received the PhD in economics from MIT.

David Blake is Professor of Financial Economics and Director of the Pensions Institute at Birkbeck College in the University of London and Chairman of Square Mile Consultants. His research interests include the modeling of asset demand and financial innovations, pension fund investment behavior and performance, and pension plan design. He received the PhD at the London School of Economics.

Zvi Bodie is Professor of Finance at Boston University School of Management; he also serves on the Pension Research Council Advisory Board and is a member of the Financial Accounting Standards Board Task Force on Interest Methods. Previously he visited Harvard's School of Business Administration and served on the finance faculty at MIT's Sloan School of Management. His research interests include investment, portfolio choice, and finance. He received the PhD in economics from the Massachusetts Institute of Technology.

Jeffrey R. Brown is Assistant Professor of Public Policy at Harvard's Kennedy School of Government, and a Faculty Research Fellow at the NBER. His research examines the role of insurance, including public and private pensions, annuities, and life insurance products, in helping secure retirement income. He received the PhD in economics from MIT.

William Burrows is Director of Business Development at Prudential Annuities in London.

Andrew Caplin is Professor of Economics at New York University. He previously taught at Columbia University. His research focuses on macroeconomic and microeconomic theory and residential real estate markets. He received the PhD in economics from Yale University.

Robert L. Clark is Professor of Economics and Business at North Carolina State University. Previously he was a Visiting Professor at the Fuqua School of Business, Duke University. His research focuses on retirement and pension policies, economic responses to population aging, wellbeing of the elderly, and international pension issues. He received the PhD degree in economics from Duke University.

Steven Davis is Professor of Economics at the University of Chicago, a Research Associate with the NBER, and a Principal at Chicago Partners. His research interests include labor markets, risk7-sharing, consumption behavior, and business cycles. He previously held positions at MIT, the University of Maryland, the Hoover Institution at Stanford, and the Chicago Federal Reserve Bank. He received the PhD in economics from Brown University.

J. Benson Durham is a Research Officer in the Finance and Trade Policy Research Centre at the University of Oxford. His research examine stock market anomalies, the macroeconomic effects of international capital flows, and economic growth. Previously Dr. Durham worked at TIAA-CREF. He received the PhD from Columbia University .

Lorenzo Forni is an economist in the Research Department of the Bank of Italy in Rome. His research interests include the determinants of household financial security. He is completing his PhD in economics at Boston University.

Jagadeesh Gokhale is an economist at the Federal Reserve Bank of Cleveland. His research focuses on the impact of U.S. fiscal policy on the economy, particularly on social security and medicare, saving and intergenerational transfers, and wealth inequality. He received the PhD in economics from Boston University.

P. Brett Hammond is Manager of Corporate Projects at TIAA-CREF, and he also serves on the Pension Research Council Advisory Board. His research focuses on higher education and pensions, science and technology, finance and health policy. Dr. Hammond previously worked at the National Academy of Science. He received the PhD in public policy from MIT.

Michael Heller is Vice President of the Actuarial Pension Services division of TIAA-CREF, where he focuses on retirement plan design and funding issues. He is a Fellow of the Society of Actuaries and is an Enrolled Actuary. He received the BS in mathematics from the City College of New York.

Laurence J. Kotlikoff is Professor of Economics at Boston University, Research Associate at the NBER, and President of Economic Security Planning, Inc. His research interests include generational accounting and saving, macroeconomics and tax issues, and insurance. He previously taught at UCLA and Yale University. He received the PhD in economics from Harvard University.

Martin L. Leibowitz is Vice Chairman and Chief Investment Officer of

TIAA-CREF, and serves on the Boards of Trustees for the Institute for Advanced Study at Princeton, Carnegie Corporation, University of Chicago, and AIMR (Association for Investment Management Research). Previously he worked with Salomon Brothers, Inc. as the Managing Director in charge of both domestic and international fixed income and equity research. He received the MS in mathematics from the University of Chicago and the PhD in mathematics from the Courant Institute of New York University.

Philip B. Levine is Associate Professor of Economics at Wellesley College. His research interests focus on policy-relevant topics including unemployment insurance, welfare policy, and the effects of demographic change in labor markets. He is a faculty research fellow at the National Bureau of Economic Research. He has served as a senior economist at the White House Council of Economic Advisers on issues relating to the labor market, education, and welfare policy. He received the BS from Cornell University and the PhD from Princeton University.

Olivia S. Mitchell is International Foundation of Employee Benefits Professor of Insurance and Risk Management, and Executive Director of the Pension Research Council at the Wharton School of the University of Pennsylvania. She is also a Research Associate at the NBER and she serves on the Steering Committee for the Health and Retirement Survey for the University of Michigan. Her research focuses on private and social insurance, employee benefits, and pension reform in the U.S. and overseas. She previously taught at Cornell University, and she has visited Harvard University and the University of New South Wales in Sydney, Australia. She received the PhD in economics from the University of Wisconsin-Madison.

Christopher M. Murtagh is Associate Director of the Center for Home Care Policy and Research at the Visiting Nurse Service of New York. His research interests include state financing and delivery systems for home and community based services, and transitions between post-acute and long-term-care settings. Previously he worked with the AHCPR where he studied lifetime nursing home use and private long-term-care insurance underwriting. He received the PhD in chronic disease epidemiology from Yale University.

J. Michael Orszag is a Lecturer in Economics at Birkbeck College in the University of London. His research interests include pension asset-liability modeling, life insurance, and e-commerce. He received the PhD in economics from the University of Michigan.

John W. R. Phillips is an economist at the Social Security Administration. Previously he was a Postdoctoral Fellow at the Population Studies Center, University of Pennsylvania and taught at Syracuse University. His research interests include labor economics and public finance. He received the BA and PhD in economics from Syracuse University.

James Poterba is Mitsui Professor of Economics at MIT and Director of the Public Economics Program at the NBER. His research interests focus on public economics and particularly tax policy. He received the PhD in economics from Oxford University.

Sylvester J. Schieber is Director of Watson Wyatt Worldwide's Research and Information Center where he specializes in the analysis of public and private retirement policy and health policy issues; he also sits on the Social Security Advisory Board and the Advisory Board of the Pension Research Council. Previously he served as Research Director of the Employee Benefit Research Institute, Deputy Director of the Office of Policy Analysis at the Social Security Administration, and Deputy Research Director for the Universal Social Security Coverage Study at the Department of Health and Human Services. He received the PhD in economics from the University of Notre Dame.

Jason Scott is Director of Financial Research at Financial Engines Inc. where he model mutual fund and stock returns. His interests in pension economics include 401(k) tax benefits, the determinants of defined contribution employee participation, and the impact of pension plan lump sum distribution options on retirement income. Previously he worked as a litigation consultant on securities and valuation cases at Cornerstone Research. He received the PhD in economics from Stanford University.

Brenda C. Spillman is a Senior Research Associate at the Urban Institute. Her research interests include disability and long-term care use and financing, including nursing home and home care use, informal caregiving, and Medicare cost projections. Previously she was a researcher at the AHCPR. She received the PhD at Syracuse University's Maxwell School.

P.S. Srinivas is a Financial Economist in the Latin America & Caribbean Region of the World Bank in Washington, D.C. He works in the areas of capital markets, pensions, corporate finance, and investments. Previously he worked at the Asian Development Bank in Manila, Philippines in the areas of capital markets and project finance. He received the PhD in economics from Cornell University.

Steven F. Venti is Professor of Economics at Dartmouth College and a Faculty Research Associate at the NBER. His research examines the links between tax policy and saving, the effectiveness of saving incentives, housing policy, and the process of wealth accumulation. He received the PhD in economics from Harvard University.

Mark Warshawsky is Director of Research at the TIAA-CREF Institute where he directs work on investment and retirement behavior, and policy on pensions, insurance, investment products, corporate governance, and the financing of higher education. His research interests include pension and retiree health plans, annuities, corporate finance, and securities markets. Previously he worked at the IRS and the Federal Reserve Board. He received the PhD in economics from Harvard University.

Paul Willen is Assistant Professor of Economics at the University of Chicago Graduate School of Business. His research examines investments, market completeness, and financial innovation. He received the PhD in economics from Yale University.

David Wise is John F. Stambaugh Professor of Political Economy at Harvard's Kennedy School. He is also the Director of the NBER Program on Aging. His research examines social security and retirement patterns around the world, 401 (k) plans and retirement wealth accumulation, and population aging. He received the PhD in economics at the University of California, Berkeley.

Juan Yermo works at the Financial Affairs Division of the Organization for Economic Cooperation and Development (OECD). His research focuses on contractual savings and pension fund management. Previously Mr. Yermo was a consultant for the World Bank where he participated in numerous global pension reform projects. He received the MA in economics from Cambridge University and the MPhil in economics from Oxford University.

Stephen P. Zeldes is Benjamin Rosen Professor of Economics and Finance at Columbia University's Graduate School of Business; he is also a Research Associate with the National Bureau of Economic Research, and an Advisory Board Member of the Pension Research Council. In his research Professor Zeldes examines applied macroeconomic topics including social security reform, the determinants of household saving and portfolio choice, the effects of government budget deficits, and the relationship between consumer spending and the stock market. Previously he taught finance at the Wharton School of the University of Pennsylvania; he also served on the Technical Panel on Trends and Issues in Retirement Saving for the 1994–96 Advisory Council on Social Security and the National Academy of Social Insurance Panel on Social Security Privatization. He received the PhD in economics from MIT.

Index

The Pension Research Council

The Pension Research Council of the Wharton School at the University of Pennsylvania is an organization committed to generating debate on key policy issues affecting pensions and other employee benefits. The Council sponsors interdisciplinary research on the entire range of private and social retirement security and related benefit plans in the United States and around the world. It seeks to broaden understanding of these complex arrangements through basic research into their economic, social, legal, actuarial, and financial foundations. Members of the Advisory Board of the Council, appointed by the Dean of the Wharton School, are leaders in the employee benefits field, and they recognize the essential role of social security and other public sector income maintenance programs while sharing a desire to strengthen private sector approaches to economic security.

Executive Director

Olivia S. Mitchell, *International Foundation of Employee Benefit Plans Professor,* Department of Insurance and Risk Management, The Wharton School, University of Pennsylvania, Philadelphia.

Senior Partners

AARP
Actuarial Sciences Associates, Inc.
CIGNA Corporation
Fidelity Investments
Goldman Sachs
Morgan Stanley Dean Witter & Co.
Mutual of America Life Insurance Co.
PricewaterhouseCoopers
SEI Investments, Inc.

328   The Pension Research Council

State Street Corporation
The Vanguard Group
Watson Wyatt Worldwide
William M. Mercer Companies, Inc.

Institutional Members

Ford Motor Company
Hay Group
India Life Pension Services Limited
Investment Company Institute
Loomis, Sayles & Company, L.P.
Merck & Co., Inc.
MetLife
The Principal Financial Group
The Segal Company
TIAA-CREF
ULLICO
VALIC

Advisory Board

Gary W. Anderson, Executive Director, Texas Municipal Retirement System, Austin, Texas

David S. Blitzstein, *Director,* United Food & Commercial Workers International Union, Washington, D.C.

Marshall Blume, *Howard Butcher Professor of Finance and Director, Rodney L. White Center for Financial Research,* The Wharton School, Philadelphia, Pennsylvania

Zvi Bodie, *Professor of Finance,* Boston University, Boston, Massachusetts

Robert L. Clark, *Professor of Economics,* North Carolina State University, Raleigh, North Carolina

Michael S. Gordon, Esq., Law Offices of Michael S. Gordon, Washington, D.C.

P. Brett Hammond, *Manager of Corporate Projects,* TIAA-CREF, New York, N.Y.

Judith F. Mazo, *Senior Vice President and Director of Research,* The Segal Company, Washington, D.C.

Alicia H. Munnell, *Peter F. Drucker Chair in Management Sciences,* School of Management, Boston College, Boston, Massachusetts

Robert J. Myers, F.S.A., *International Consultant on Social Security,* Silver Spring, Maryland

Martha Priddy Patterson, *Director,* Deloitte and Touche LLP Washington, D.C.

Richard Prosten, *Director,* Washington Office, Amalgamated Life Insurance / Amalgamated Bank of New York, Washington, D.C.

Anna M. Rappaport, F.S.A., *Managing Director,* William M. Mercer, Inc., Chicago, Illinois

Jerry S. Rosenbloom, *Frederick H. Ecker Professor of Insurance and Risk Management,* The Wharton School, Philadelphia, Pennsylvania

Sylvester J. Schieber, *Vice President and Director of Research and Information Center,* The Wyatt Company, Washington, D.C.

Richard B. Stanger, *National Director*, Employee Benefits Services, Price Waterhouse LLP, New York, New York

Marc M. Twinney, Jr., F.S.A., *Consultant*, Bloomfield Hills, Michigan

Michael Useem, *Professor of Management and Sociology*, The Wharton School, Philadelphia, Pennsylvania

Jack L. VanDerhei, *Associate Professor of Risk and Insurance*, Temple University, Philadelphia, Pennsylvania

Paul H. Wenz, F.S.A., *Second Vice President and Actuary*, The Principal Financial Group, Des Moines, Iowa

Stephen P. Zeldes, *Benjamin Rosen Professor of Economics and Finance*, Columbia University, New York, New York

Pension Research Council Publications

Demography and Retirement: The Twenty-First Century. Anna M. Rappaport and Sylvester J. Schieber, eds. 1993.

An Economic Appraisal of Pension Tax Policy in the United States. Richard A. Ippolito. 1991.

The Economics of Pension Insurance. Richard A. Ippolito. 1991.

Forecasting Retirement Needs and Retirement Wealth. Olivia S. Mitchell, P. Brett Hammond and Anna M. Rappaport, eds. 2000.

Fundamentals of Private Pensions. Dan M. McGill, Kyle N. Brown, John J. Haley, and Sylvester Schieber. Seventh edition. 1996.

The Future of Pensions in the United States. Ray Schmitt, ed. 1993.

Inflation and Pensions. Susan M. Wachter. 1991.

Living with Defined Contribution Pensions. Olivia S. Mitchell and Sylvester J. Schieber, eds. 1998.

Pension Mathematics with Numerical Illustrations. Howard E. Winklevoss. Second edition. 1993.

Pensions and the Economy: Sources, Uses, and Limitations of Data. Zvi Bodie and Alicia H. Munnell, eds. 1992.

Pensions, Economics and Public Policy. Richard A. Ippolito. 1991.

Pensions in the Public Sector. Olivia S. Mitchell and Edwin Hustead, eds. 2001.

Positioning Pensions for the Twenty-First Century. Michael S. Gordon, Olivia S. Mitchell, and Marc M. Twinney, eds. 1997.

Prospects for Social Security Reform. Olivia S. Mitchell, Robert J. Myers, and Howard Young, eds. 1999.

Providing Health Care Benefits in Retirement. Judith F. Mazo, Anna M. Rappaport and Sylvester J. Schieber, eds. 1994.

Retirement Systems in Japan. Robert L. Clark. 1991.

Securing Employer-Based Pensions: An International Perspective. Zvi Bodie, Olivia S. Mitchell, and John A. Turner. 1996.

Social Security. Robert J. Myers. Fourth edition. 1993.

To Retire or Not? Retirement Policy in Higher Education. Robert L. Clark and P. Brett Hammond. 2001.

Available from the University of Pennsylvania Press, telephone: 800/445-9880, fax: 410-516-6998. More information about the Pension Research Council is available at the web site: http://prc.wharton.upenn.edu/prc/prc.html

QM LIBRARY
(MILE END)